Rdb

A Comprehensive Guide

Second Edition

Rdb
A Comprehensive Guide

Second Edition

Lilian Hobbs and Ken England

Digital Press
Boston • Oxford • Melbourne • Singapore • Toronto • Munich • New Delhi • Tokyo

Library of Congress Catalog Card Number: 95-76239

ISBN: 1-55558-124-2

The publisher offers discounts on bulk orders of this book.
For information, please write:

Manager of Special Sales, Digital Press
Butterworth–Heinemann
313 Washington Street
Newton, MA 02158–1626

Order number: EY–S450E–DP

10 9 8 7 6 5 4 3 2 1

Composition: P.K.McBride, Southampton, UK
Printed in the United States of America

In memory of Lilian's father
and her brother, Reggie

Lilian

To Margaret, Michael and Katy
for all their support and patience

Ken

To Steve Hagan,
for making the dream come true

Lilian & Ken

Foreword

Lilian Hobbs and Ken England have written the seminal book describing the Rdb product family. Today, Rdb is the fastest and most economical database system on the market – bar none (as measured by the Transaction Processing Performance Council TPC-A metric). Rdb is also one of the most sophisticated SQL database systems, including most SQL92 features, many SQL3 features, support for multimedia data, and support for object-oriented extensions.

The product family includes RdbExpert that automates database design and tuning, DEC Database Integrator that integrates multiple Rdb, DB2, Oracle, SYBASE, DBMS, RMS and other databases, to create the image of a single distributed database, and DEC DataDistributor that replicates data among Rdb and foreign databases. These products work on the VMS and UNIX (OSF/1) operating systems and are being ported to NT. Client software based on the Open Database Connectivity standard (ODBC) allow desktop tools like VisualBasic complete access to Rdb databases running on servers.

Hobbs and England have done an excellent job explaining how to use the Rdb product family and how each element of the family works. Along the way, they teach you how to use the SQL database language, complete with sophisticated techniques like referential integrity, stored procedures, triggers, outer joins, and many more. The presentation is extremely readable and informative – punctuated with examples and hints. It covers the core Rdb product, covers the related tools for system administration, performance tuning, data integration, data replication, and desktop data access.

This book is an essential reference to those who design, administer, program, or use Rdb databases. It also provides an excellent reference to those interested in advanced database techniques, or who are interested in comparing Rdb to other database systems.

Dr. Jim Gray,

Former Technical Director of Digital's Production Systems Group.

Contents

Preface

This book is based on Version 6.0 of Rdb, which was released in April 1994 and contains many of the features to be found in V6.1. This version provides a technically sophisticated and fully functional database management system for the OpenVMS and OSF/1 operating systems made by Digital Equipment Corporation. At the time of writing, Digital is in the process of selling its Rdb product to the Oracle Corporation.

Digital announced Rdb in 1984 as a relational database for its proprietary VAX/VMS operating system. The early versions of the Rdb system enjoyed mixed success. With Version 3.0, however, Rdb emerged as a relational database management system that could be used in high-performance transaction-processing systems running on Digital's popular VMSclusters. Since Version 3.0 the system's functionality has continued to be extended dramatically and at Version 6.0, with the addition of stored procedures and external functions, Rdb is one of the most functionality rich products in the marketplace today.

Ten years after its initial release, Rdb finds itself on a new operating system platform – OSF/1. With a Microsoft Windows NT version waiting in the wings, the proprietary nature of the product has started to diminish and its portability has started to increase.

The growing popularity of Rdb among customers, software development companies, and consultant firms has prompted us to write this book. It is intended to be a comprehensive introduction to the extensive capabilities offered by Rdb and a text in which we can impart some of our experience.

All the examples in this book use the OpenVMS version of Rdb and refer to the functionality available in that version. The OSF/1 version is almost identical to the OpenVMS version; therefore generally everything written in this text applies to this version. Specific differences can be found in Chapter 19.

The chapters are written to follow one another in a logical fashion, building on some of the topics introduced in previous chapters. The structure of the chapters is as follows:

- Chapter 1 introduces the components of Rdb, such as the architecture, management utility, and precompilers. The licensing strategy is also introduced.

- Chapter 2 presents the data definition features, such as how to create a database and a table as well as introducing multischema databases.

- Chapter 3 introduces the data manipulation features, including how to retrieve and store data, multistatement procedures, stored procedures and external functions.

- Chapter 4 discusses the storage structures that can comprise a database, such as multifile database features and the format of a database page.

- Chapter 5 describes indexed access, both sorted and hashed and buffering.

- Chapter 6 briefly describes the function of the optimizer as well as techniques to observe and influence its strategy, such as query outlines.

- Chapter 7 describes transaction management, especially locking techniques and strategies as well as transaction isolation levels.

- Chapter 8 discusses security, in terms of techniques to make data private.

- Chapter 9 describes maintaining the integrity of the data in the database in terms of referential integrity and failure management. Rdb backup, restore and recovery techniques using the after image journal are discussed.

- Chapter 10 explores various restructuring techniques available to the database administrator, and explains how a database can be changed.

- Chapter 11 explores the tuning and optimization of Rdb databases and introduces the RMU/SHOW STATISTICS utility.

- Chapter 12 discusses distributing databases around a network and introduces DEC Data Distributor, distributed transactions and DEC Database Integrator.

- Chapter 13 introduces the interoperability products, such as SQL/Services, Microsoft ODBC and the DEC Db Integrator Gateway family.

- Chapter 14 discusses the Repository, CDD/Repository, and its use.

- Chapter 15 describes how Digital's transaction processing architecture, DECdta, and ACMS TP monitor can enhance a Rdb environment.

- Chapter 16 introduces the tools available for DEC Rdb, such as DECtrace, RdbExpert as well as introducing some popular third party tools for Rdb such as the FrEnd family of tools, Forest & Trees and Microsoft Access.

- Chapter 17 discusses writing Rdb programs and introduces SQL Module Language.

- Chapter 18 introduces the multimedia capabilities of Rdb.

- Chapter 19 discusses the differences between Rdb implementations on the new operating system platforms, OSF/1.

- Chapter 20 speculates on the future direction of Rdb.

A reader unfamiliar with Rdb may wish to skip chapters 4, 5, and 7 because they are quite detailed. Other chapters can be read with little or no prior knowledge of relational systems.

Acknowledgments

Most of all, we would like to thank Margaret England and Mrs. Lilian Hobbs for their long suffering while we were writing this text. It quickly became apparent to us that writing and being sociable were sometimes mutually exclusive! We also would like to thank them for the great favor they did us in proofreading. Michael and Katy England are too young to understand databases but they were very patient while their dad kept disappearing in front of a PC for protracted periods of time!

As well as the friends and colleagues who helped with the first edition of the book, we would like to give an extra special thanks to the following people.

A very special thank you to Steve Hagan for not only giving us full access to the Rdb development team, but for also being one the best managers we have ever had the pleasure of working with.

We were extremely grateful to the Rdb engineers who helped review some of the materials. Writing a chapter on the optimizer is certain to fill any author with trepidation. Therefore we are very grateful to Gennady Antoshenkov, one of the consulting engineers responsible for the optimizer who very kindly reviewed this chapter.

A big thank you to Rick Anderson for reviewing the chapter on after image journaling, backup and restore and all that good stuff.

Ian Smith, who many customers from down-under will remember, before he left his warm climate for the warm and snow of New England to further his career with Rdb Engineering, reviewed the huge SQL chapter.

When it comes to CDD/Repository, no one knows the product's integration with Rdb better than Carol Dillingham. Thanks for reviewing and guidance with the new features.

Larry Carpenter in Munich is one of the Rdb engineers located in Europe and thanks for your assistance and support during the compilation of this book.

There are so many people involved with the development of Rdb that we could fill this whole page with their names, but here are just a few of the people who have guided and helped us, not just during the writing of this book but throughout our involvement with Rdb: Peter Spiro and Russ Holden, Jay Feenan database system Technical Directors; Jim Gray, Andy Schneider, Susan Hillson, Zia Mohammed, Ranga, Ashok, Abe Mathew, Steve Horn, Ramu Sunkara, Dave Campbell, Chuck Friewald, Chris Davis, Tom Tobin, Fred Vona and Kate Brown.

We would like to express our deep gratitude and thanks to Mike Cash from Butterworth–Heinemann (UK) and Mac Bride our typesetter. Thanks to all their efforts and the use of desktop publishing tools we were able to release this book at the same time as Rdb 6.1 instead of months later.

Finally, a thank you to Steve Hiscock and Rob Higman in the UK CSC for all their help while this book was being written.

Many thanks to our other friends in Rdb engineering, without whose skill and hard work Rdb would not be the superb product it is today.

Lilian Hobbs
Ken England
Basingstoke, U.K.
October 1994

1 Components

1.1 THE DIGITAL INFORMATION MANAGEMENT FAMILY

Rdb is a relational database system developed by Digital Equipment Corporation and, at the time of writing, is about to be sold to the Oracle Corporation. For ten years it was only available for computers using the OpenVMS operating system. 1994 saw that change with the first release on another platform, OSF/1. The plans do not intend to stop there and Rdb will be implemented on other platforms like Windows NT.

Rdb is one of a number of information management products that work together in an environment, designed so that information can be easily shared throughout an enterprise. The products that comprise the Information Network family, illustrated in Figure 1.1, are designed to function in isolation or together with the other tools in the family. If any of these tools are unsuitable, then some may be substituted for non-Digital tools, of which there are a wide number to choose from. Using this approach, systems can be created and tailored to match an organization's information management needs.

Information management products have been selected to provide the following:

- Common storage

- Data management

- Data access

- Distributed processing

- Decision support

- Application management

- Terminal management

Figure 1.1 The Information Network

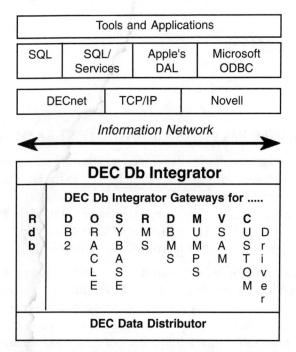

The products from Digital that comprise the information management family are shown in Table 1.1. A complete system cannot be created without them, or a non-Digital tool equivalent, since Rdb is only a relational database management system.

1.2   COMPONENTS OF RDB

1.2.1   Overview

Originally Rdb only ran on the VAX range of computers and was perceived as a database system that could only exist on this hardware platform. The introduction of Alpha machines and the implementation on the OSF/1 platform should convince any sceptics that Rdb is capable of running on other platforms. During its lifetime a wide range of features have been incorporated into the product, making it a very sophisticated relational database system. Today there are so many features and tuning options that one might

Table 1.1 Digital Information Management Products

Product	Description
ACMS	Digital's TP Monitor for VMS
ACMSxp	Digital's TP Monitor for OSF/1
CDD/Repository	Distributed, data dictionary that permits the storage of data definitions accessed by many of the products in the information management family, including Rdb. Enables relational databases, RMS files, application programs, and form management systems to be built using the same data definitions
DEC Data Distributor	An optional, layered product of Rdb that provides an automatic extraction or replication transfer from and to remote Rdb databases
DEC Database Integrator	Provides transparent access to data residing in Rdb, DB2, Oracle or other database systems on a local or remote server
Datatrieve	A tool for managing data interactively or from within an application program
DBMS	The CODASYL database management system
DECforms	A forms management system based on the proposed FIMS standard
Rdb	A relational database management system
DEC DB Gateway for...	Various gateways to access RMS, Oracle, DB2, Sybase, EDA/SQL, DBMS, Mumps or create custom drivers
Rally	Digital's 4th generation language for building applications
RMS	Record Management System

think a degree in computer science is necessary to use the product. Nothing could be further from the truth. These sophisticated options are there for very large production systems or those users requiring ultra high performance. The majority of users run very happily with the system defaults and are oblivious to all the other available options.

1.2.2   Rdb Product Family

A number of products comprise the complete Rdb interoperability family. This book concentrates on the Rdb component, but will explain how these other products integrate with it.

The Rdb *development kit* provides the following capabilities:

- The Rdb kernel
- The RMU management utility and GUI
- The SQL query language
- SQL/Services (VMS, MS-DOS, OSF/1, Mac)
- Remote database access
- Precompilers for SQL
- Dynamic SQL API
- ODBC driver
- SQL/Multimedia routines

The Rdb development kit provides everything needed to develop applications on centralized or remote databases. Another optional product is the Graphical Schema Editor, a tool that enables the database design to be specified graphically rather than using SQL, although the output from this tool is the SQL to create the database. The SQL/Services component of Rdb also allows access to Rdb from a desktop or laptop computer. If a style of distributed database is required, then one or more optional products will be needed. Several optional products work with Rdb and extend its capabilities. DEC Data Distributor can manage the distribution of data among multiple databases, for example and DEC Db Integrator will transparently integrate data from many distributed data managers.

For the majority of systems, Rdb is sufficient because it provides the ability to store and manipulate data locally, access remote databases, or access Rdb from a PC or other operating system, which is adequate for most processing needs.

1.2.3   Inside Rdb

Rdb is a sophisticated relational database with a number of components, which have been designed using a layered and modular approach. Rdb is based upon the architecture shown in Figure 1.2. Although Rdb users need not be aware of what lies underneath, the architecture has two layers, the relational data manager and the record storage system.

Figure 1.2 Rdb Architecture

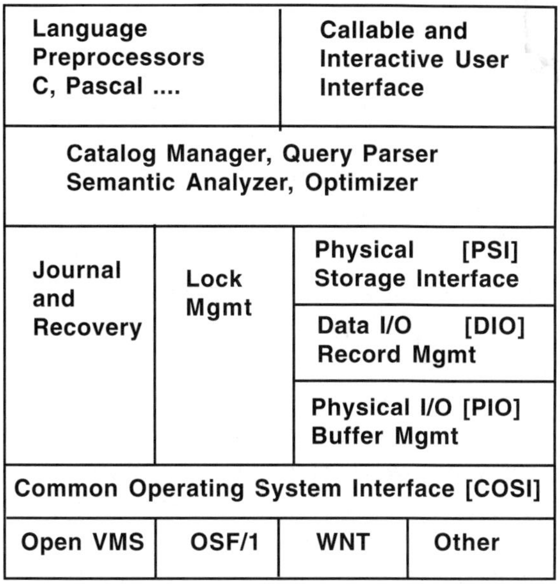

Language Preprocessors C, Pascal		Callable and Interactive User Interface	
Catalog Manager, Query Parser Semantic Analyzer, Optimizer			
Journal and Recovery	Lock Mgmt	Physical [PSI] Storage Interface	
		Data I/O [DIO] Record Mgmt	
		Physical I/O [PIO] Buffer Mgmt	
Common Operating System Interface [COSI]			
Open VMS	OSF/1	WNT	Other

The relational data manager has several components:

- Interactive user interface

- Callable interface

- Query parser

- Semantic analyzer

- Catalog manager

- Optimizer

- Query executor

The record storage system is responsible for managing many tasks. These tasks include:

- Fetching, storing, modifying, and erasing records
- Managing physical storage

- Managing locking and buffers
- Controlling journaling and recovery

Digital Standard Relational Interface (DSRI)

In the early days of Rdb, much emphasis was placed on the Digital Standard Relational Interface, or DSRI. This interface is an architecture and calling standard for Digital relational database products intended to provide a common access method to relational database systems. No matter what language is used to construct the query, it is always converted to the DSRI protocols.

Programming in DSRI is difficult and is similar to programming in assembler language. Today there is a shift away from writing applications in complex interface languages, with emphasis instead on the widely used standard SQL. We encourage this approach because the small performance improvement that results from writing in DSRI is far outweighed by the comparatively rapid development time that results when using SQL. It should be mentioned that the DSRI architecture has facilitated integration of Rdb with a wide range of tools. Figure 1.3 illustrates, as we have said, that all user queries are ultimately converted to the DSRI protocol.

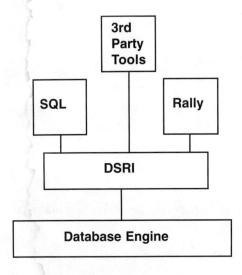

Figure 1.3 DSRI Architecture

RMU Utility

Rdb is managed and controlled using a combination of the data manipulation languages and the RMU management utility (Rdb Management Utility). From V6.1 a GUI interface for this tool is also available, called RMUwin.

The RMU utility is made up of a number of commands which allow the user to manage the database, such as backup, restore, statistics on database performance, journal file management, and restricting access to the database. The complete list is shown below. These commands will be discussed in more detail in subsequent chapters.

Table 1.2 RMU Commands

Command	Description
ALTER	Tool to patch the physical contents of the database
ANALYZE	Shows database usage, indexes, db pages, storage areas
BACKUP	Backs up a database
CHECKPOINT	Forces a database checkpoint
CLOSE	Closes a database to prevent access
CONVERT	Facilitates upgrading to a new software version
COPY_DATABASE	Copies a database
DUMP	Displays database internal structures
LOAD	Loads data into a specific table
MONITOR	Controls the Rdb monitor
MOVE	Moves a database storage area
OPEN	Opens a database for access
OPTIMIZE	Optimize an AIJ file
RECOVER	Recovers a database to a specific point using journal files
RESOLVE	Allows manual commitment or abort of blocked distributed transactions
RESTORE	Restores a database
SET AUDIT	Controls security auditing
SHOW	Displays various information such as current version, statistics on database performance, users and how they are accessing a database
UNLOAD	Unloads data from a specific table
VERIFY	Verifies the database format

Precompilers

Precompilers are available for the various languages as shown in the table below.

	OpenVMS VAX	OpenVMS Alpha	OSF/1
Ada	Yes	Yes	Yes
C	Yes	Yes	Yes
COBOL	Yes	Yes	Microfocus
Fortran	Yes	Yes	Yes
Pascal	Yes		
PL/1	Yes		

For organizations developing software that adheres to current standards, options are available on the SQL precompilers to identify SQL statements that are not in the ANSI/ISO SQL standard.

SQL also includes the SQL Module Language, which will be described in detail in Chapter 17. Using the SQL Module Language, SQL statements are grouped into modules. These modules can be called by any language, regardless of whether an Rdb precompiler is available for that language.

This approach facilitates the writing of Rdb applications for languages without the appropriate precompilers. It also enables a standard set of database access modules to be written, which are then used by everyone. This practice saves considerable time in writing and debugging similar database access code.

There is one additional interface, Dynamic SQL, which is a non-compiled query language. It is used when the nature of the query is not known until execution time.

SQL/Services

Increasingly today, access to an Rdb database is required from various platforms, such as MS-DOS personal computers. SQL/Services, which is supplied by default with Rdb, enables users on OSF/1, MS-DOS, OS/2, Sun and Apple Macintosh platforms to query an Rdb database. This open, published interface is based on Dynamic SQL, so there are no restrictions on the operations that can be performed.

ODBC Driver

Microsoft's ODBC driver is proving very popular with PC users to provide access to various databases from the PC platform. Provided within the SQL/Services component, once installed on the PC, it allows any ODBC compliant application such as Microsoft Access or Forest & Trees to use this method to access the Rdb data.

The Monitor

All activity on the database is monitored by a special process known as the *RDMS_MONITOR*, which is always active. It is a watchdog process that logs all users accessing the database and any abnormal process terminations that have occurred, and it also coordinates recovery.

Hint: The log maintained by the monitor is very useful for detecting problems with the database.

1.3   KEY AREAS OF RDB

When discussing Rdb, it is useful to group its many features into several key areas:

- Performance

- Availability

- Referential integrity support

- Distributed capabilities

- Interoperability

- Multimedia

- Tools

1.3.1   Performance

A relational database system is concerned with performance in two areas: enabling the database designer to produce sophisticated physical designs to overcome performance bottlenecks, and measuring the performance of the database locating the cause of any performance problems. Rdb is strong in both of these areas. They will be discussed in detail later in the book, but it is worth summarizing the key features here.

Overcoming Performance Problems

Whether written in a third-generation language (3GL), such as COBOL, or a fourth-generation language (4GL), such as RALLY, a database application usually supports a finite number of users performing a finite amount of work for a given hardware configuration, that is, for a certain power CPU and a set number of disk drives. As the workload increases, a point is reached where the throughput of the database stops increasing and levels off. Sometimes it even starts to decrease. Further investigation typically shows that the limit of some resource has been reached. For a database application the resource usually is CPU capacity, disk I/O bandwidth capacity, or memory. In addition, a fourth bottleneck typically is hit with database systems – locking contention.

The important question is whether a bottleneck can be overcome once it has occurred. In the case of Rdb it usually can. Rdb on OpenVMS makes full use of Digital's Symmetrical Multi-Processing (SMP) and DECcluster architecture, so adding another CPU board or another VMScluster node usually will result in an increase in database throughput.

Another common bottleneck is disk I/O, which occurs when the I/O rates to the disk exceed the capabilities of the disk drive. In this case a solution is to buy more disk drives. However, this remedy is effective only if the database architecture has the physical capability to enable the database designer to make use of the extra disk drives. With Rdb there are many options. The database itself has a multifile capability. Database tables can be mapped to physical files that can be placed on separate disk drives. The mapping is quite sophisticated—a table can reside in a single file or it can be horizontally partitioned across many physical files so the addition of extra disk drives can be easily accommodated. But Rdb goes further than this.

Sophisticated row-placement options allow the database designer to store rows from different tables physically close to one another. Rows that are normally accessed together are read in from disk in the same disk I/O, thus reducing the overall disk I/O requirements of the application. Hashed index support as well as sorted index support means that for certain kinds of table access, fewer disk I/Os are needed to access the data. The ability to specify index node sizes and fill factors can reduce the disk I/O requirements even more.

If these techniques still do not achieve the required performance, then global buffers can be used, which involves permanently allocating memory to the database buffers. With the 64-bit architecture of the Alpha range of machines which allows mapping of gigabytes of memory, very fast memory resident databases become a reality.

A shortage of memory is not uncommon. The best solution to this problem is to optimize its use with global buffers or if the memory is being consumed by many user processes, running the application under a transaction processing monitor, such as DEC ACMS, or DEC ACMSxd, should be considered.

Hitting a locking bottleneck is an interesting problem. Rdb tries to keep lock contention to a minimum by providing a powerful locking mechanism that will lock at the row level to avoid contention and maximize throughput. On the Alpha range of machines, partitioned lock trees are available which create smaller manageable lock trees. Other features, such as hashed indexes, adjustable locking granularity, variable page sizes, and snapshot transactions, help reduce problems caused by locking.

Analyzing Performance Problems

A database designer or administrator may realize that there is a performance problem but may not know the exact cause. A component of Rdb, the RMU/ SHOW STAT monitoring utility, helps find the cause by obtaining information on the utilization of database tables, indexes, locks, and much more. An additional product, the expert-system-based physical design tool RdbExpert, produces optimized physical database designs. The event-based collector DECtrace is used to record database performance events, and its monitor can display database and other events in real-time. Both RMU and DECtrace are invaluable tools to the database tuner.

1.3.2   Availability

By availability, we mean that portion of time a database is available to run the company's business applications. If critical business applications cannot be run because the database is unavailable, the survival of the company is in jeopardy. Obviously, it is in a company's best interests to use a database system that is highly available.

The threats to availability are unscheduled failures, such as a CPU failure, and scheduled downtime used for database backup and restructuring. Rdb attempts to maintain its availability in the following ways.

Unscheduled Failures

If a node crashes in a single-node system, Rdb will automatically roll back incomplete transactions when the node reboots. This procedure eliminates manual intervention, which could be costly in terms of time. If a VMScluster is being used and a node fails, a surviving node dynamically rolls back transactions that were not completed by users on the failed node. The important points to note here are that database integrity is ensured and that the service does not terminate as long as there are remaining VMScluster nodes. The company's business does not stop. This reliability is the result of using a mixture of high-availability hardware (the VMScluster) and high-availability software (Rdb).

Scheduled Downtime

To minimize scheduled downtime, Rdb uses sophisticated backup technology. A database backup can be run online while people are using the database.

The database does not have to be closed, nor do the users have to limit the types of operation they are performing or the parts of the database they are working on. Rdb ensures that the backups are consistent and that a restore operation will result in a perfectly consistent database. Incremental backups may be run, which only backup database pages that have changed. In addition, Rdb supports the simultaneous backup/restore of a database to/from multiple tape drives, allowing large quantities of data to be backed/restored in a short time. However, large database users, such as those with more than 10 gigabytes, generally do not have the time to restore the entire database. Therefore other options are available, such as if a disk drive is damaged, only the affected area needs to be restored, rather than the whole database or a specific page in the database.

Rdb supports online restructuring as well, so a database administrator need not close the database to users when adding or deleting database table columns or creating and deleting indexes. If a database area fills, disk space will automatically be allocated. The database need not be closed to users while a database administrator manually increases the size of the database. All these features mean that Rdb supports highly available applications.

1.3.3   Referential Integrity Support

Referential integrity support is vital to ensure that the data in the database remains consistent with the company's business rules. For example, it may be inappropriate in a banking application for an account not to be associated with a customer. It is important that such rules be stored in the database itself, not in the applications, otherwise a maintenance headache would result.

Rdb allows the database designer to model constraints in the database so that business rules are enforced. Primary and foreign key support ensures that constraints are automatically created between primary and foreign keys in the database. Rdb also supports triggers. Triggers are switches that operate when some predefined event occurs and are also used to enforce the business rules of a company at the database level.

1.3.4   Distributed Capabilities

Rdb has had distributed capabilities since Version 1.0. A 3GL program or 4GL can transparently access an Rdb database on another node in the network. In fact, more than one database can be accessed from within a 3GL program or 4GL in the network for retrieval or update. With the two-phase commit protocol support that is in Version 4.0, Rdb also guarantees the integrity of distributed transactions. An optional product, DEC Data Distributor, can be used to replicate data throughout the network, and DEC Db Integrator to provide location transparency and distributed query optimization to remote databases.

1.3.5   Interoperability

The SQL/Services component of Rdb allows access to Rdb databases from desktop and laptop computers, such as those running MS-DOS. Optional products including DEC Db Integrator Gateway for ORACLE, SYBASE and DBMS and DB2, enable tools that are normally used with Rdb to be used with ORACLE, DB2 or SYBASE. Other gateways include DEC Db Integrator Gateway for RMS on VMS which allows SQL access to non-relational data structures.

1.3.6   Multimedia

Today users demand more from their database system than storing textual data. Increasingly people want to store objects like pictures, sound or even video. Rdb supports multimedia objects with the BLOB datatype and the routines in SQL/Multimedia which facilitate easier management of these objects. Once one enters the realm of multimedia, traditional storage mediums are inadequate, so for this reason, Rdb supports WORM (write-once read many) devices.

1.3.7   Tools

There are a number of tools for querying Rdb databases and developing applications. RALLY is a fourth-generation application environment. Of course, SQL is used to manipulate data in the database. Because of the open architecture of Rdb, currently, third-party companies have layered hundreds of tools and application packages on it. This number is increasing constantly.

1.3.8   List of Key Features

Let us summarize the key features of Rdb. The following form can be used as a quick reference:

● **Performance**

  – Multifile support

  – Horizontal table partitioning

  – Coincidental record clustering

  – Sorted index retrieval

  – Hashed index retrieval, scattered and ordered

  – Adjustable page size

– Sophisticated query optimizer

– Query outlines to specify how to execute a query

– Ascending and descending indexes

– Row-level locking

– Adjustable locking granularity

– Data compression capability

– Global buffer

– Asynchronous pre-fetch

– Asynchronous batch writes

– AIJ cache on solid-state disk

– Full VMScluster and Symmetrical Multi-Processing (SMP) support

– Performance-monitoring utilities

– Expert-system-based physical design tools

- **Availability**

  – Full VMScluster support

  – Online backup

  – Incremental backup

  – Multithreaded backup/restore

  – Selected area backup/restore

  – No quiet-point backup

  – Restore by page

  – Powerful online restructuring capability

  – Dynamic space allocation

  – Online database parameter changes

  – Circular AIJ, AIJ Backup Server, AIJ Log Server

- **Referential integrity support**

  – Constraints

  – Triggers

  – Primary and foreign key support

- **Other Facilities**

  – Stored Procedures

  – SQL-92 Compliance

  – MIA support

  – Date-time Arithmetic

  – Collating Sequences

  – Multimedia support and callable routines

- **Interoperability**

  – Desktop integration via SQL/Services of OpenVMS, ULTRIX, MS-DOS, OSF/1, OS/2, and Apple Macintosh computers

  – DEC Db Gateways range of products

  – ODBC driver

- **Tools**

  – Graphical Schema Editor (optional)

  – InstantSql to create SQL queries graphically (optional)

  – Many Digital tools for development and end-user query

  – Many third-party tools for development and end-user query

  – Many applications layered on Rdb

- **Distributed capabilities**

  – Remote database access

  – Attachment to multiple schemas for read and write

  – Distributed transaction integrity (2PC)

  – Data replication across network via DEC Data Distributor

  – Distributed queries and optimization via DEC Db Integrator

1.4   LICENSE OPTIONS

Rdb presents various types of licensing options. The five Rdb license options are:

- Full development

- Interactive

- Run time

- Personal use Full or Interactive license

- Concurrent use run-time license

Selecting the most appropriate license can result in considerable cost savings: for example, purchasing the full development license for a small DEC processor on which to do development and then running the production application on a large DEC processor or DECcluster, using the considerably cheaper run time license.

1.4.1   Full Development

The full development license includes all the kernel Rdb software, the dynamic SQL engine, SQL/Services, SQL/Multimedia API, ODBC driver, full database maintenance and administration using the RMU utility, full database definition and manipulation using Interactive SQL and RDO, Callable RDO, Graphical Schema Editor, InstantSQL and all the precompilers. The precompilers include the SQL Module Language and the SQL/Services Client API, which is the component that runs on the client platform. This is the license that is required to develop an Rdb system.

1.4.2   Interactive

The interactive license, also known as the DBA license, provides the base database software, the dynamic SQL engine, SQL/Services server, full database maintenance and administration using RMU, full interactive database definition and manipulation using interactive SQL and the ODBC driver.

Hence this option supports the execution of previously developed applications, database definition, and interactive queries from SQL. It does not support program development using the precompilers.

1.4.3   **Run Time**

With the run-time option comes the base database software, the dynamic SQL engine, the SQL/Services server process, the RMU management utility, interactive SQL and the ODBC driver. The purpose of the run-time option is to support the execution of previously developed applications. It is not possible with this option to perform interactive queries or program development or create or drop databases.

1.4.4   **Personal Use**

A personal use license is available for the development or interactive license. It allows a single specified user to use all the options available with this license. Purchasing a single personal use license can be a very cost-effective alternative if there will only be a single person responsible for managing the database on a large system.

1.4.5   **Concurrent Use**

A concurrent use license is available with the run-time license and it enables one to specify the specific number of users that will be using the database on this system. When the maximum number of specified users has been reached, no other users can attach to the database until one of the current users detaches. Once again, if only a few people will be using the database, this may be a more cost-effective option than purchasing a full run-time license.

This brief introduction has shown that Rdb is a very comprehensive product. The following chapters will discuss the details behind all these components.

2 Data Definition

This chapter introduces the data definition features of SQL. For detailed and exhaustive descriptions of the SQL syntax, the appropriate Rdb manuals, such as the *Rdb SQL Reference Manual*, can be consulted if necessary.

After the database designer has formulated a logical database design through analysis and data normalization, he or she will want to create a database based upon it, using the data definition statements provided by SQL.

The next section will introduce some basic relational terminology. Subsequent sections in this chapter will describe how the database designer can use the data definition features of SQL to create various Rdb objects, such as:

- Databases
- Tables
- Columns
- Domains
- Views
- Storage areas
- Storage maps
- Indexes

The CREATE DATABASE statement defines characteristics that can be applied to the database as a whole. Using Rdb, tables can be created containing columns that may be based upon domain definitions, and virtual tables called *views*, which combine columns from one or more tables, can also be defined. If the database designer wishes to create a multifile database, storage areas can be created that define the files into which the tables and indexes are placed. Storage maps provide the mapping between the storage areas and the objects placed in them. The function of storage areas and storage maps in multifile databases is discussed in detail in Chapter 4; this chapter will discuss basic data definition only in single-file databases. Indexes are structures that are used to access data quickly. Only sorted indexes can be created in single-file databases. In multifile databases, however, hashed indexes also may be created. Indexed access is described in detail in Chapter 5.

Later in this chapter the BANKING database will be introduced, which will form the basis for all the examples in this book. The reader should refer to the description of the BANKING database in Appendix A while studying the examples in the next few sections.

2.1   BASIC RELATIONAL TERMS

In relational databases, such as Rdb, data is stored in tables (sometimes called relations). Examples of these tables are shown in Figure 2.1, including the CUSTOMER and ACCOUNT tables. Usually, a table represents some real-world object that is pertinent to the organization's business. A table may contain a number of rows that are instances of table elements. For example, the CUSTOMER table contains a number of rows, one for each customer. The rows consist of columns, which are data elements and represent attributes of the table element. For example, the CUSTOMER table consists of a number of columns that are attributes of the entity customer, such as the customer's name and address.

In the relational model, a column or number of columns is designated as a primary key. A row must be uniquely identified by its primary key; therefore, a primary key value cannot occur more than once in a table. This also means that a primary key cannot contain null values; i.e. a column that constitutes a primary key must contain a value. In the CUSTOMER table, the primary key is the customer number represented by the column CUSTOMER_NO. Each customer's number is unique throughout the bank. No two customers may have the same number.

Columns in one table typically do not also appear in another table, other than to establish a relationship between tables. These columns are called foreign keys. In the BANKING database, the ACCOUNT table contains a column CUSTOMER_NO. This is a foreign key and establishes a relationship between the CUSTOMER table and the ACCOUNT table. Foreign key relationships, represented by thicker lines, are shown in Figure 2.1.

Figure 2.1   Tables in the BANKING Database

TRANSACTION TABLE

ACCOUNT NO	TRANS DATE	TRANS AMOUNT	DC IND	TRANS CD
8882334992	13 OCT 1994	2000.00	1	SO
0066434427	14 OCT 1994	50.00	1	CD
4522334927	12 OCT 1994	1000.00	2	DD

BRANCH TABLE

BRANCH CODE	BRANCH NAME	BRANCH ADDRESS	MANAGERS NAME
ALT	Alton	33 High St.	D. Thomas
SOT	Southampton	46 Dock Rd.	A. Ball
POT	Portsmouth	23 Navy Ave	I. Stephen

ACCOUNT TABLE

ACCOUNT NO	CUSTOMER NO	BRANCH CODE	BALANCE	OVERDRAFT LIMIT	ACCT TYPE	STATEMENT FREQUENCY	STATEMENT DATE	STATEMENT DAY
882334992	1122334997	ALT	104.89	1000.00	1	2	14 OCT 1994	14
0066424427	1166434467	ALT	200.77	100.00	1	2	11 OCT 1994	11
4522334927	4422334997	ALT	786.50	2000.00	2	3	13 OCT 1994	13
44422765462	1122765467	SOT	987.00	50.00	1	1	14 OCT 1994	14
008764482	1198764487	POT	544.77	1000.00	2	3	12 OCT 1994	12

CUSTOMER TABLE

CUSTOMER NO	SURNAME	FIRST NAME	ADDRESS LINE 1	ADDRESS LINE 2	ADDRESS LINE 3	ADDRESS LINE 4	POST CODE	CREDIT LIMIT	STATUS
1122334997	England	Ken	77 Acacia Rd.	Beech	Alton	Hants	GU34 6RT	10000	1
1166434467	England	Margaret	77 Acacia Rd.	Beech	Alton	Hants	GU34 6RT	15000	1
4422334997	Hobbs	Lilian	56 The Street	Chandlers	Soton	Hants	ST77 7YU	16000	2
1122765467	Lilburn	Jocky	Le Taj	Drury Lane	Holborn	London	WC1 5TR	100	3
1198764487	Jackson	Tony	The Mansion	Posh Road	Upnorth	Cheshire	ZX4 8UJ	1000000	1

Other common terms that are often found in the relational world are selection, projection, and join. A *selection* operation forms a subset of the rows in a table, usually by applying some condition such as the customers who have a status value of one. A *projection* operation removes columns from the rows being retrieved by forming a stream of rows with only specified columns present. A *join*, probably one of the most powerful relational operators, allows data from more than one table to be combined. Typically, data from more than one table is joined by relating certain meaningful columns from the tables. In the BANKING database, for example, a meaningful operation would be the joining of the ACCOUNT and CUSTOMER tables over the CUSTOMER_NO column to produce a report about customers and their accounts.

By using the SQL SELECT statement to achieve this join, specifying a predicate of CREDIT_LIMIT > 10000, and specifying that the columns to be displayed are the SURNAME, ACCOUNT_NO, and BALANCE, we have combined all three relational operations to produce a meaningful result. The SQL SELECT statement is described in more detail in Chapter 3.

2.2 CREATING A SINGLE-FILE RDB DATABASE

The following sections describe how the various objects present in a single-file database can be created. Although the following definitions can be entered interactively at the SQL> prompt, it is good practice to use a text editor to enter them into a file and then to execute the file.

In addition, placing the SQL statements in a file facilitates the process of correction and re-execution and also provides a documented record of the metadata definition.

Hint: Use Digital's Graphical Schema Editor with its graphical user interface to define the database and the objects in it, if you are not familiar with SQL.

2.2.1 Creating a Database

The CREATE DATABASE statement is used to create a database and in its simplest form can be specified as:

```
SQL> CREATE DATABASE FILENAME banking;
```

This statement, using many of the defaults provided by Rdb, creates a database file and a snapshot file. The database file will have a file extension of .RDB, and the snapshot file will have a file extension of .SNP. In the directory there will be two files where the database has been created, BANKING.RDB and BANKING.SNP. This is known as a *single-file* database; that is, the user data is stored in a single file along with the tables and indexes. Another option is to create a *multifile* database, which will be discussed in Chapter 4.

When the database is created, a number of defaults can be used, including:

- The number of database buffers and their size

- The page size

- Whether snapshots are enabled or disabled

For OpenVMS users who wish to create an entry in the repository, CDD/Repository, the statement would be specified as:

```
SQL> CREATE DATABASE FILENAME banking

cont> PATHNAME eurobank:[uk.dict]database.banking;
```

See Chapter 14 for more details about using CDD/Repository.

2.2.2   Creating Domains

The database designer will want to create tables consisting of columns. However, generic data elements called *domains* can be defined, and one or more columns in the database may be based upon these domains. By specifying domains, the database designer can create standard definitions for data elements that share similar characteristics. An example of this in the BANKING database would be the domain STANDARD_DATE, which is used to provide a standard definition for columns that need to be defined as a date field. Such columns would be STATEMENT_DATE and TRAN_DATE.

Generally, it is good practice to define all columns by basing them on domains. For OpenVMS users, these domains may themselves have been defined from definitions in the OpenVMS repository, CDD/Repository. Using domains enables the designer to efficiently add columns to the database definition in the future and to ensure that the correct attributes of the column are defined. Many of the columns in the BANKING database are not based upon domains. The reason is merely to demonstrate the different methods of defining columns.

Domains consist of a name, a datatype, and optional characteristics such as an edit string. There are two ways to create a domain.

First, the designer can use the CREATE DOMAIN SQL statement specifying a datatype. For example:

```
SQL> CREATE DOMAIN standard_date DATE;
```

Second, the designer can define a domain using a field definition in the OpenVMS repository, CDD/Repository. For example:

```
SQL> CREATE DOMAIN standard_date FROM
cont> eurobank:[uk.dict]database.standard_date;
```

In this case STANDARD_DATE is a field in CDD/Repository.

A comment may be added to a DOMAIN to aid clarity. For example:

```
SQL> CREATE DOMAIN CHAR(20);

SQL> COMMENT ON DOMAIN standard_name IS
cont> 'Standard Definition for a Name';
```

Hint: Once the domains have been created, it is a good idea to enter a COMMIT statement to ensure that the definitions are made permanent in the database.

2.2.3 Creating Tables

Once the domains have been defined, the database tables can be created. The CREATE TABLE statement can be used to specify a name for the table, the columns used in the table, and many other table characteristics. On the other hand, for OpenVMS users, the designer also can define a table using a record definition in CDD/Repository. Each column in the table can be based on a previously created domain or explicitly defined with a datatype and any other column characteristic that the database designer wishes.

The database designer also can specify *constraints*. Constraints are rules that can be applied to columns and tables. They are described in more detail in Chapter 9.

An example of creating a table could be:

```
SQL> CREATE TABLE account
cont> ( account_no        NUMERIC (10),
cont> customer_no         CHAR (10),
cont> branch_code         CHAR (4),
cont> balance             NUMERIC (10,2),
cont> overdraft           NUMERIC (10,2),
cont> acct_type           INTEGER,
cont> statement_freq      STANDARD_DATE,
cont> statement_day       INTEGER);
```

For OpenVMS users, an example of creating a table from a CDD/Repository record definition would be:

```
SQL> CREATE TABLE FROM eurobank:[uk.dict]branch;
```

In this example, BRANCH is the name of a record definition in CDD/Repository.

A comment can be added to a table to aid clarity. For example:

```
SQL> COMMENT ON TABLE branch IS 'This is the bank branch table';
```

Hint: Once the tables have been created, it is a good idea to enter a COMMIT statement to ensure the definitions are made permanent in the database.

2.2.4   Creating Sorted Indexes

To improve data retrieval, the database designer may wish to create indexes in the database. Indexing in Rdb is discussed in more detail in Chapter 5. Two types of index can be created in Rdb:

- B-tree sorted indexes

- Hashed indexes (multifile databases only)

B-tree sorted indexes usually are referred to as sorted indexes. To create an index, the CREATE INDEX statement is used. Different options may be added to the statement to determine whether the index is a sorted or hashed index.

Other options may specify, for example, whether duplicate key values are allowed and what index node size is to be used, as well as index compression options. An example of creating a sorted index with no duplicate key values allowed would be:

```
SQL> CREATE UNIQUE INDEX cust_index
cont> ON customer (customer_no);
```

This statement creates a sorted index (by default) on the CUSTOMER table based on the column CUSTOMER_NO. The UNIQUE key word specifies that no duplicate key values will be allowed. To allow duplicate key values, the UNIQUE key word should be omitted. A comment can be added to an index for clarity. For example:

```
SQL> COMMENT ON INDEX cust_index IS 'This helps us locate customers';
```

By default, the CREATE INDEX statement creates a sorted index with ascending index segments. The database designer may wish to create an index with descending index segments. For example:

```
SQL> CREATE UNIQUE INDEX cust_index ON customer (customer_no DESCENDING);
```

An index can be composed of more than one column, which is known as a *multi-segment* index. For example:

```
SQL> CREATE INDEX cust_index ON customer (surname, first_name);
```

Additionally, a database designer can specify the size of each index node in bytes. Varying the index node size can reduce or increase the depth of the index, that is, the number of index levels. Methods of calculating the optimum index node size can be found in the *Rdb Guide to Database Maintenance and Performance*.

An initial fullness also can be specified for an index node, as well as whether the index is to be used for update or for query. USAGE UPDATE specifies that the initial fullness is 70 percent, and USAGE QUERY specifies that the initial fullness is 100 percent. For example:

```
SQL> CREATE INDEX cust_index ON customer (surname,first_name)
cont>     TYPE IS SORTED
cont>     NODE SIZE 400
cont>     USAGE UPDATE;
```

Hint: As with tables, once the indexes have been created, it is a good idea to enter a COMMIT statement to ensure the definitions are made permanent in the database.

2.2.5   Creating Views

Views are virtual tables. They do not physically hold data, but rather act like a window into physical tables that were defined with the CREATE TABLE statement. The database designer uses the CREATE VIEW statement to create views in the database. To the end-user, a view looks like a table and generally can be treated as if it were a table. The major exception is if the user wishes to update or insert rows in a view. Rdb places restrictions on this type of operation in a view.

Views can contain subsets of the rows or columns found in a physical table or a combination of physical tables and can, therefore, be used to replace often-used SELECT and JOIN operations. Views also may be used to enforce security. A user may be allowed to retrieve data through a view, but not from the underlying physical table.

An example of creating a view in the BANKING database would be:

```
SQL> CREATE VIEW customer_mailing
cont> ( customer_no,
cont>    surname,
cont>    first_name,
cont>    address_line1,
cont>    address_line2,
cont>    address_line3,
cont>    address_line4,
cont>    postcode)
cont> AS SELECT  customer_no,
cont>            surname,
cont>            first_name,
cont>            address_line1,
cont>            address_line2,
```

```
cont>           address_line3,
cont>           address_line4,
cont>           postcode
cont> FROM customer;
```

This view specifies a subset of the columns present in the CUSTOMER table. The columns CREDIT_LIMIT and STATUS are omitted. The database designer may consider that these fields contain sensitive information. Therefore, strict protection is placed on the CUSTOMER table, allowing only a very few users to see data in these columns. Many users, however, are allowed access to the view, CUSTOMER_MAILING, shown in Figure 2.2.

Figure 2.2 The CUSTOMER_MAILING View

CUSTOMER TABLE

CUSTOMER NO	SURNAME	FIRST NAME	ADDRESS LINE 1	ADDRESS LINE 2	ADDRESS LINE 3	ADDRESS LINE 4	POST CODE	CREDIT LIMIT	STATUS
1122334997	England	Ken	77 Acacia Rd.	Beech	Alton	Hants	GU34 6RT	10000	1
1166434467	England	Margaret	77 Acacia Rd.	Beech	Alton	Hants	GU34 6RT	15000	1
4422334997	Hobbs	Lilian	56 The Street	Chandlers	Soton	Hants	ST77 7YU	16000	2
1122765467	Lilburn	Jocky	Le Taj	Drury Lane	Holborn	London	WC1 5TR	100	3
1198764487	Jackson	Tony	The Mansion	Posh Road	Upnorth	Cheshire	ZX4 8UJ	1000000	1

CUSTOMER MAILING VIEW

CUSTOMER NO	SURNAME	FIRST NAME	ADDRESS LINE 1	ADDRESS LINE 2	ADDRESS LINE 3	ADDRESS LINE 4	POST CODE
1122334997	England	Ken	77 Acacia Rd.	Beech	Alton	Hants	GU34 6RT
1166434467	England	Margaret	77 Acacia Rd.	Beech	Alton	Hants	GU34 6RT
4422334997	Hobbs	Lilian	56 The Street	Chandlers	Soton	Hants	ST77 7YU
1122765467	Lilburn	Jocky	Le Taj	Drury Lane	Holborn	London	WC1 5TR
1198764487	Jackson	Tony	The Mansion	Posh Road	Upnorth	Cheshire	ZX4 8UJ

The CUSTOMER_MAILING view only specifies one table. It is possible to define views that join data from one or more tables. For example:

```
SQL> CREATE VIEW customer_account_info
cont> ( customer_no,
cont>   surname,
cont>   first_name,
cont>   credit_limit,
cont>   account_no,
cont>   balance)
cont> AS SELECT c.customer_no,
cont>             c.surname,
cont>             c.first_name,
cont>             c.credit_limit,
cont>             a.account_no,
cont>             a.balance
cont> FROM customer c, account a
cont> WHERE c.customer_no = a.customer_no;
```

The CUSTOMER_ACCOUNT_INFO view is shown in Figure 2.3.

Views can be created using a mixture of constructs, such as joins and unions, and can be based upon previously created views. Depending on the constructs used to create the view, Rdb may consider the view to be read-only.

A view is considered to be read-only if:

- Duplicate rows have been removed by using the DISTINCT clause in the SELECT statement.

- A view is created from a join.

- A subquery is specified in the WHERE clause.

- The select list specifies a function such as COUNT.

- The clauses GROUP BY or HAVING are used.

If Rdb considers the view to be read-only because it was created with any of the previous statements, the INSERT, UPDATE, or DELETE statements cannot be used. Rdb will also consider the view to be read-only if columns in the

Figure 2.3 The CUSTOMER_ACCOUNT_INFO View

ACCOUNT TABLE

ACCOUNT NO	CUSTOMER NO	BRANCH CODE	BALANCE	OVERDRAFT LIMIT	ACCT TYPE	STATEMENT FREQUENCY	STATEMENT DATE	STATEMENT DAY
882334992	1122334997	ALT	104.89	1000.00	1	2	14 OCT 1994	14
0066424427	1166434467	ALT	200.77	100.00	1	2	11 OCT 1994	11
4522334927	4422334997	ALT	786.50	2000.00	2	3	13 OCT 1994	13
44422765462	1122765467	SOT	987.00	50.00	1	1	14 OCT 1994	14
008764482	1198764487	POT	544.77	1000.00	2	3	12 OCT 1994	12

CUSTOMER_ACCOUNT_INFO VIEW

CUSTOMER NO	SURNAME	FIRST NAME	CREDIT LIMIT	ACCOUNT NO	BALANCE
1122334997	England	Ken	10000	8882334996	104.89
1166434467	England	Margaret	15000	0066434427	200.77
4422334997	Hobbs	Lilian	16000	4522334927	786.50
1122765467	Lilburn	Jocky	100	44422765462	987.00
1198764487	Jackson	Tony	1000000	0008764482	544.77

CUSTOMER NO	SURNAME	FIRST NAME	ADDRESS LINE 1	ADDRESS LINE 2	ADDRESS LINE 3	ADDRESS LINE 4	POST CODE	CREDIT LIMIT	STATUS
1122334997	England	Ken	77 Acacia Rd.	Beech	Alton	Hants	GU34 6RT	10000	1
1166434467	England	Margaret	77 Acacia Rd.	Beech	Alton	Hants	GU34 6RT	15000	1
4422334997	Hobbs	Lilian	56 The Street	Chandlers	Soton	Hants	ST77 7YU	16000	2
1122765467	Lilburn	Jocky	Le Taj	Drury Lane	Holborn	London	WC1 5TR	100	3
1198764487	Jackson	Tony	The Mansion	Posh Road	Upnorth	Cheshire	ZX4 8UJ	1000000	1

CUSTOMER TABLE

view are formed from arithmetic expressions. In this case, UPDATE and INSERT statements cannot be used.

A useful clause that may be used with views is the WITH CHECK OPTION clause. If this clause is used when creating a view, no rows can be inserted through the view that do not conform to the view's definition. In other words, a row cannot be inserted that does not belong to the set of rows that are displayed through the view.

For example, the following view definition only allows rows to be inserted into the ACCOUNT_TRANSACTION table with a value in the TRAN_AMT column greater than $10,000. The insertion of a row with TRAN_AMT of $55,000 is allowed, but the insertion of a row with a TRAN_AMT of $5,000 is not.

```
SQL> CREATE VIEW big_transactions
cont> AS SELECT * FROM account_transaction
cont> WHERE tran_amt > 10000
cont> WITH CHECK OPTION CONSTRAINT check_view;

SQL> INSERT INTO
cont> big_transactions (account_no, tran_date, tran_amt,
cont> dc_ind, trans_cd)
cont> VALUES
cont> (1223466557, '10-Jun-1990', 55000, 1, 'CD');
1 row inserted

SQL> INSERT INTO
cont> big_transactions (account_no, tran_date, tran_amt,
cont> dc_ind, trans_cd)
cont> VALUES
cont> (1223466557, '10-Jun-1990', 5000, 1, 'CD');
%RDB-E-INTEG_FAIL, violation of constraint CHECK_VIEW caused
    operation to fail
-RDB-F-ON_DB, on database EUROBANK:[UK.DB]BANKING.RDB;1
```

Hint: Once the views have been created, it is a good idea to enter a COMMIT statement to ensure the definitions are made permanent in the database.

Once the database designer has created the database, the domains, the tables, the indexes, and the views, it may become necessary to alter these definitions. This restructuring of the definitions is described in Chapter 10. More sophisticated database definitions that include multiple files are discussed in detail in Chapter 4, and more detail on indexes can be found in Chapter 5.

2.3   CREATING MULTIFILE DATABASES

The creation of multifile databases is fully described in Chapter 4. A multifile database is created using the data definition features of Rdb, similar to single-file databases. A multifile database, however, is composed of a number of physical files. Tables and indexes, which are created using the same methods as for single-file databases, then can be stored in these files. Chapter 4 has more detail on this process.

2.4   DELETING DATABASE METADATA

At some point, the database designer may wish to remove definitions from the database or to remove the entire database. This is achieved using the DROP statement in SQL. The following sections describe how the various Rdb objects may be dropped.

2.4.1   Dropping Databases

The DROP DATABASE statement is used to delete a database. All the files associated with the database are deleted. For example:

```
SQL> DROP DATABASE FILENAME 'eurobank:[uk.db]banking';
```

Hint: Be very careful when using this statement—it cannot be rolled back.

2.4.2   Dropping Domains

The DROP DOMAIN statement is used to delete a domain definition. For example:

```
SQL> DROP DOMAIN standard_date;
```

A domain cannot be dropped if a column in a table refers to it. The column definition must be dropped from the table first. The database must have been attached to prior to issuing this and the following DROP statements.

2.4.3   Dropping Columns

To drop a column from a table, the ALTER TABLE statement should be used. A column cannot be dropped if it is referred to by a view, a constraint, or an index. The view, constraint, or index must be dropped first. An example of removing a column from a table would be:

```
SQL> ALTER TABLE customer DROP COLUMN status;
```

2.4.4   Dropping Tables

The DROP TABLE statement removes a table definition and the data stored in it. For example:

```
SQL> DROP TABLE CASCADE customer;
```

If a view definition, index, or constraint refers to the table, it will be automatically dropped.

2.4.5   Dropping Views

The DROP VIEW statement removes a view definition. For example:

```
SQL> DROP VIEW customer_mailing;
```

2.4.6   Dropping Indexes

The DROP INDEX statement removes an index definition. For example:

```
SQL> DROP INDEX cust_index;
```

2.5   THE MULTISCHEMA DATABASE

If we consider for the moment what in Rdb we understand to be a database, we think of our user data, system metadata and information on physical storage characteristics. The term *schema* is used to mean database, if it is used at all, and no distinction is made between the two terms. In the default scenario this is fine as there is one schema to one database and no confusion can arise.

A schema is an object in itself and can be named and referred to. In a multischema database however, there may be more than one schema and it becomes more necessary to be precise with terminology. In a multischema database, a schema only consists of data definitions and so the data definition and data are separated from the physical attributes of the database. ANSI SQL standard compliance is one of the main reasons for supporting this option.

To create a multischema database the MULTISCHEMA IS ON clause must be present on the CREATE DATABASE statement.

```
SQL> CREATE DATABASE FILENAME banking MULTISCHEMA IS ON;
```

If a database is not created with this extra clause, it can be converted into a multischema database later with the ALTER DATABASE statement. A multischema database may be made to behave like a single schema database at attach time if required with the MULTISCHEMA IS OFF clause.

```
SQL> ATTACH 'DATABASE FILENAME banking MULTISCHEMA IS OFF';
```

The internal Rdb structure is not modified by enabling the multischema option. However, the way SQL references objects will change as we shall see shortly.

To support the multischema database option, an Rdb database now allows multiple schemas to be created within multiple catalogs within an Rdb database. This classification hierarchy is shown in Figure 2.4.

This hierarchy allows for domains, tables and other schema objects to have the same names in different schemas. Thus, schema objects can be classified in ways that model a company's organization without having to use unique table names such as BRANCH_NORTH, BRANCH_WEST, which only serves to complicate the application. The naming rules will be discussed shortly.

When a multischema database is created, a default catalog RDB$CATALOG is created with a default schema RDB$SCHEMA inside it. A database designer can create more catalogs and schemas and in reality would normally do so.

Figure 2.4 The Classification Hierarchy in a Multischema Database

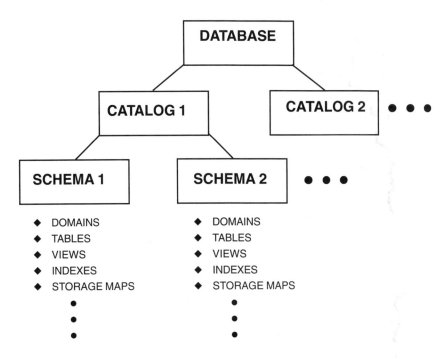

If an existing single schema database is converted into a multischema data-base, all the schema objects created previously would be placed inside RDB$SCHEMA.

To add catalogs to the default multischema database, the CREATE CATALOG statement is used and to add schemas to the multischema database, the CREATE SCHEMA statement is used. The following example shows two catalogs being created:

```
SQL> CREATE CATALOG banking_america;
SQL> CREATE CATALOG banking_europe;
SQL> SHOW CATALOG;
Catalogs in database with filename banking
     BANKING_AMERICA
     BANKING_EUROPE
     RDB$CATALOG
```

The next example shows two schemas being created. Note that a SET CATALOG statement is issued first to specify in which catalog the schema belongs:

```
SQL> SET CATALOG 'banking_america';
SQL> CREATE SCHEMA retail_banking;
SQL> CREATE SCHEMA wholesale_banking;
SQL> SHOW SCHEMA;
Schemas in database with filename banking
    RETAIL_BANKING
    WHOLESALE_BANKING
    RDB$CATALOG.RDB$SCHEMA
```

The next example shows a domain being created. Note that a SET CATALOG and a SET SCHEMA statement are issued first:

```
SQL> SET CATALOG 'banking_america';
SQL> SET SCHEMA 'retail_banking';
SQL> CREATE DOMAIN exposure BIGINT;
SQL> SHOW DOMAIN exposure;
EXPOSURE      BIGINT
    Stored name is EXPOSURE
```

The stored name information line will be discussed shortly. To uniquely specify the objects in a multischema database such as schemas and domains, it is not sufficient to merely specify the name. This is because the same schema name or schema object name can exist in the database more than once. For example, the domain EXPOSURE could be defined in a number of different schemas in a number of different catalogs and the schema RETAIL_BANKING could be defined in a number of catalogs.

There are a number of ways of uniquely identifying the object:

• Use default catalog and schema settings

• Provide the full name of the object

The first method is achieved by using the SET CATALOG and SET SCHEMA statements as shown in the previous examples.

The second method is achieved by providing qualified names, for example:

```
SQL> SHOW DOMAIN banking_america.retail_banking.exposure;
BANKING_AMERICA.RETAIL_BANKING.EXPOSURE      BIGINT
     Stored name is EXPOSURE
```

This could get tedious, so for interactive sessions, at least, it is easier to use default catalog and schema settings.

If we do not name the schema an interesting message results.

```
SQL> ATTACH 'FILENAME banking';
SQL> SHOW DOMAIN exposure;
%SQL-F-SCHNOTDEF, Schema ENGLAND is not defined
```

This is because SQL will implicitly qualify the name of a schema object with the current authorization identifier which identifies the definer of the schema. In the above example, ENGLAND is the definer of the schema.

This fully qualified naming approach will get even more complex if aliases are used. For example:

```
SQL> ATTACH 'ALIAS bank1 FILENAME banking';
SQL> SET ANSI QUOTING ON;
SQL> SHOW DOMAIN
cont>  "BANK1.BANKING_AMERICA".retail_banking.exposure;

"BNK1.BANKING_AMERICA".RETAIL_BANKING.EXPOSURE      BIGINT
     Stored name is EXPOSURE
```

The pair of names in the double quotes is referred to as a delimited identifier in ANSI SQL. ANSI SQL allows a maximum of three levels in an object name but with an alias, catalog name, schema name and schema object name we have four levels. We are saved because ANSI SQL treats a delimited identifier as one level. The SET ANSI QUOTING ON statement is needed to ensure that Rdb interprets the (" ") as a delimited identifier – by default it would treat it as a string literal and the above statement would fail.

Hint: Only use uppercase characters in the delimited identifier or errors will be returned by Rdb.

If the multischema option is disabled or interfaces other than SQL are used, Rdb refers to schema objects by their stored names. These are nonqualified names assigned by Rdb that uniquely identifies the schema object. The stored name is usually constructed by appending a numeric integer to the text part of the name. In the example below, the CUSTOMER tables are uniquely identified by appending a value to one of the schema objects.

```
SQL> ATTACH 'FILENAME banking MULTISCHEMA IS ON';
SQL> SHOW TABLES
User tables in database with filename banking
      BANKING_AMERICA.RETAIL_BANKING.CUSTOMER
      BANKING_AMERICA.WHOLESALE_BANKING.CUSTOMER
SQL> ATTACH 'FILENAME banking MULTISCHEMA IS OFF';
SQL> SHOW TABLES
User tables in database with filename banking
      CUSTOMER
      CUSTOMER1
```

2.6   THE BANKING DATABASE

The examples in this book are based on a fictitious relational database that supports the everyday business of a bank. The example is, of course, oversimplified for clarity. However, it is sufficiently complex to allow the features of Rdb to be fairly described.

The BANKING database consists of four main tables:

- ACCOUNT

- BRANCH

- CUSTOMER

- ACCOUNT_TRANSACTION

The relationship between these entities is simple, as shown in Figure 2.5. A bank's customers may hold a number of accounts of different types; for example, a checking account and a saving account. Other tables and schema objects appear throughout this book and in the SQL database definition in Appendix A; however, for clarity only the major components are described here.

Figure 2.5 The Table Relationships in the BANKING database

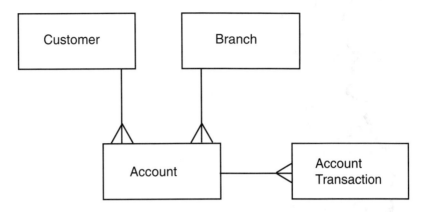

These accounts may be held at the same bank branch or at different branches. A branch usually would be responsible for a number of accounts. Various transactions, such as deposits and withdrawals, can be made against an account. The details of each are recorded by storing a log of the transactions in the ACCOUNT_TRANSACTION table.

2.6.1   The BRANCH Table

Each row in the BRANCH table represents a branch of the bank. There are four columns:

- BRANCH_CODE

- BRANCH_NAME

- BRANCH_ADDRESS

- MANAGERS_NAME

The BRANCH_CODE column holds the unique branch code and is the primary key for this table. The BRANCH_NAME and BRANCH_ADDRESS columns hold the name and address of the branch, and the MANAGERS_NAME column holds the name of the branch manager. No columns are designated as foreign keys in the BRANCH table.

2.6.2   **The CUSTOMER Table**

Each row in the CUSTOMER table represents a bank customer. There are ten columns:

- CUSTOMER_NO
- SURNAME
- FIRST_NAME
- ADDRESS_LINE1
- ADDRESS_LINE2
- ADDRESS_LINE3
- ADDRESS_LINE4
- POSTCODE
- CREDIT_LIMIT
- STATUS

The CUSTOMER_NO column holds the unique customer number and is the primary key for this table. The SURNAME and FIRST_NAME columns hold the customer's name, and the ADDRESS_LINE and POSTCODE columns hold his or her address. The customer's credit limit is held in the CREDIT_LIMIT column and represents the total amount of cash the customer is allowed to owe the bank at any given time. The STATUS column holds the customer's status, for example, whether he or she resides abroad. No columns are designated as foreign keys in the CUSTOMER table.

2.6.3   **The ACCOUNT Table**

Each row in the ACCOUNT table represents a customer account. There are nine columns:

- ACCOUNT_NO
- CUSTOMER_NO
- BRANCH_CODE
- BALANCE

- OVERDRAFT_LIMIT
- ACCT_TYPE
- STATEMENT_FREQ
- STATEMENT_DATE
- STATEMENT_DAY

The ACCOUNT_NO column holds the unique account number and is the primary key for this table. The CUSTOMER_NO column holds the number of the customer who owns this account, and the BRANCH_CODE column specifies the branch at which the account is held. The balance of the account is held in the BALANCE column, and the amount to which the account is allowed to go into the red by the branch manager is held in the OVERDRAFT_LIMIT column. The type of account, such as checking or saving, is specified in the ACCT_TYPE column. The STATEMENT_FREQ, STATEMENT_DAY, and STATEMENT_DATE columns specify how often an account statement is issued to the customer, on which day of the month it is issued, and the date on which the statement was last issued. The CUSTOMER_NO and BRANCH_CODE columns are foreign keys relating the ACCOUNT table to the CUSTOMER and BRANCH tables respectively.

2.6.4 The ACCOUNT_TRANSACTION Table

Each row in the ACCOUNT_TRANSACTION table represents a transaction that has been executed against a customer's account. There are five columns:

- ACCOUNT_NO
- TRAN_DATE
- TRAN_AMT
- DC_IND
- TRANS_CD

The ACCOUNT_NO and TRAN_DATE columns hold the account number and transaction date combination. The TRAN_DATE column holds the date and time that a transaction was executed against the account. The TRAN_AMT column holds the monetary value of the transaction, and the DC_IND column specifies whether the account was debited or credited.

The TRANS_CD column holds the transaction code; for example, DD is a direct debit and SO is a standing order. The ACCOUNT_NO column is a foreign key relating the ACCOUNT_TRANSACTION table to the ACCOUNT table.

2.6.5 The Indexes

The basic BANKING database contains five indexes:

- ACCOUNT_NO_HASH
- ACCOUNT_TXN_SORTED
- BRANCH_CODE_SORTED
- CUST_NO_HASH
- CUST_SURNAME_SORTED

The indexes ACCOUNT_NO_HASH and CUST_NO_HASH are hashed indexes with a key based on the column CUSTOMER_NO. The index CUST_SURNAME_SORTED is a sorted index with an ascending key based on the column SURNAME. The index BRANCH_CODE_SORTED is a sorted index on BRANCH with an ascending key based on the column BRANCH_CODE and the index ACCOUNT_TXN_SORTED is a sorted index on ACCOUNT_TRANSACTION with an ascending key based on the columns ACCOUNT_NO and TRAN_DATE

2.6.6 The Storage Areas

When an Rdb database uses more than one physical file to hold the user data, it is said to be a multifile database. In Rdb terminology, these files are known as storage areas. Storage areas are discussed more fully in Chapter 4. The basic BANKING database has nine storage areas:

- RDB$SYSTEM
- ACCOUNT_AREA
- BRANCH_AREA
- CUSTOMER_AREA

- TXN_AREA_93

- TXN_AREA_94

- TXN_AREA_95

- INDEX_AREA

- LIST_AREA

The RDB$SYSTEM storage area holds the Rdb system relations, which are often referred to as the metadata.

The INDEX_AREA storage area holds the sorted indexes:

- CUST_SURNAME_SORTED

- BRANCH_CODE_SORTED

- ACCOUNT_TXN_SORTED

The CUSTOMER_AREA holds the table CUSTOMER and the hashed indexes:

- CUST_NO_HASH

- ACCOUNT_NO_HASH

The ACCOUNT_AREA storage area holds the table ACCOUNT. The CUSTOMER_AREA and ACCOUNT_AREA storage areas are of MIXED page format whereas all the other storage areas are of UNIFORM page format.

The ACCOUNT_TRANSACTION table is partitioned across the three storage areas:

- TXN_AREA_93

- TXN_AREA_94

- TXN_AREA_95

The BRANCH_AREA storage area holds the BRANCH table and the LIST_AREA storage area is the default area for all lists (segmented strings).

Sorted indexes and hashed indexes are discussed in Chapter 5.

2.6.7   **The Storage Maps**

If a multifile Rdb database is created, there must be a means of specifying which storage areas hold what data. This is achieved with storage maps, which will be discussed more fully in Chapter 4. The basic BANKING database has four storage maps:

- ACCOUNT_MAP
- BRANCH_MAP
- CUSTOMER_MAP
- ACCOUNT_TXN_MAP

The ACCOUNT_MAP specifies that the ACCOUNT table resides in the storage area ACCOUNT_AREA and that it is placed via the index ACCOUNT_NO_HASH. Data-compression techniques are not to be used to compress the ACCOUNT data.

The BRANCH_MAP specifies that the BRANCH table resides in the storage area BRANCH_AREA. By default, data-compression techniques will be used to compress the BRANCH data.

The CUSTOMER_MAP specifies that the CUSTOMER table resides in the storage area CUSTOMER_AREA and that it is placed via the index CUST_NO_HASH. By default, data-compression techniques will be used to compress the CUSTOMER data.

The ACCOUNT_TXN_MAP specifies that the ACCOUNT_TRANSACTION table resides in the storage areas:

- TXN_AREA_93
- TXN_AREA_94
- TXN_AREA_95

By default, data-compression techniques will be used to compress the ACCOUNT_TRANSACTION data.

The BANKING database definition is shown in Appendix A. It is meant to support the examples in the book and, therefore, does not necessarily reflect a fully realistic database.

3   Data Manipulation

When Rdb was first released back in 1984, the only data manipulation language supplied was Digital's own proprietary data manipulation language, RDO (Relational Database Operator). All of the early systems were built using the RDO language, which had proved very popular because it was very easy to understand and use. It also was very similar to another Digital query language, VAX DATATRIEVE, which is still in extensive use around the world.

In 1986 the slightly changed SQL (Structured Query Language), originally developed for the IBM System R prototype, was adopted by the American National Standards Institute. It was later introduced into Rdb. Now SQL is considered the standard data manipulation language for developing applications using relational databases. Over the years SQL has evolved from its initial SQL-86 through to SQL-89 and the ratified SQL-92. There is still much to be incorporated into the language and it continues to evolve with the proposed SQL3 standard.

Currently Rdb is SQL-92 entry level compliant. It should be noted that versions of SQL that are only ISO or ANSI compliant lack in some of the functionality demanded by the market today. Therefore most versions of SQL provide extensions to the language to extend its capabilities.

The purpose of this chapter is to review the query language SQL. It is not meant to be a manual in how to use it; instead it will illustrate some of SQL's capabilities. A comprehensive guide to the language is presented in the Rdb manuals, the *Guide to Using SQL*, and *Rdb Guide to Data Manipulation*.

3.1   SQL DATA MANIPULATION OPTIONS

Various data manipulation options are offered by Rdb, but today the decision is not which language to use, because that has to be SQL, the industry de-facto standard, but which type of SQL language such as precompiled or a callable interface. The options available are:

- Precompilers

- SQL Module Language

- Dynamic SQL

- Interactive SQL

An illustration of how to write application programs using the precompilers, dynamic SQL or the SQL Module Language is given in Chapter 17 on application programming.

3.2   SQL

Digital first provided the SQL query language for Rdb in 1987 as an optional layer of functionality. Once SQL became widely accepted as the preferred relational query language, SQL became a standard component of Rdb. Rdb now complies with the standards like most implementations of the SQL language. It also includes additional capabilities to allow for the enhancements made to Rdb.

The newcomer to SQL should find the language fairly straightforward, although some of the commands may not be immediately obvious. The rule to remember is that every statement must be terminated with a semicolon.

Hint: If still struggling with the command line SQL interface, then try developing queries with the GUI, InstantSQL.

3.2.1   Initial Access

Before any data manipulation can begin, the user must specify which database to attach to, using one of two methods:

- ATTACH statement an Rdb extension

• SQL$DATABASE logical or SQL_DATABASE environment variable

```
SQL> ATTACH   'FILENAME eurobank:[uk.db]banking';
```

The /TYPE qualifier is required when using products like DEC Db Integrator to specify the additional qualifiers it requires.

```
SQL> ATTACH   'FILENAME   /TYPE=DBI/DBNAME=........ '
```

The SQL$DATABASE logical is a very handy alternative when using the interactive query language. It contains the directory and name of the database to access; SQL then uses it to automatically open the database. The disadvantage of using the logical is that it is not possible to specify any of the additional qualifiers, as it is with the ATTACH statement.

To attach to the database in the previous example, the following logical SQL$DATABASE can be defined instead:

```
DEFINE SQL$DATABASE eurobank:[uk.db]banking
```

Hint: Take care when using the interactive query language and the SQL$DATABASE logical. It is very easy to attach to the wrong database.

3.2.2   Attaching to Several Databases

Organizations often need to distribute data across several databases. With the introduction of two-phase commit protocols to ensure data integrity, multiple databases will be used more often. To achieve this in SQL, an alias must be specified in the ATTACH statement to identify which database is being referenced. This is used on all subsequent statements:

```
SQL> ATTACH 'ALIAS bank   FILENAME eurobank:[uk.db]banking';
SQL> ATTACH 'ALIAS insurance FILENAME euroins:[uk.ins]insurance';
```

In the previous example, BANK is the alias and is used on all queries, as shown in the following example:

```
SQL> ATTACH 'ALIAS bank FILENAME eurobank:[uk.db]banking.rdb';
SQL>
```

```
SQL> SELECT surname FROM bank.customer;
  SURNAME
    Hobbs
    Smith
 2 row(s) selected
```

Specific details on accessing distributed databases will be covered in Chapter 12 on distributed databases and Chapter 17 on application programming.

3.2.3 Starting a Transaction

The process for starting a transaction in SQL may seem slightly confusing because two statements are available and also their syntax might not immediately convey the action implied by the statement. The two statements provided are:

- DECLARE TRANSACTION
- SET TRANSACTION

The DECLARE TRANSACTION does not specify at which point the transaction is to start. It merely advises that the transaction will start with the characteristics specified in the DECLARE TRANSACTION statement when the first SQL statement is executed. Remember that the DECLARE TRANSACTION statement merely declares an intention. It does not start anything. For example:

```
SQL> DECLARE TRANSACTION READ WRITE NOWAIT
cont> RESERVING branch FOR SHARED READ;
```

To start a transaction at a specific point the SET TRANSACTION statement should be used. This is the preferred method because it provides the application developer with a means to control precisely when locks on resources are taken. A transaction is started as soon as this statement is executed.

The transaction modes available are:

- READ WRITE
- READ ONLY
- BATCH UPDATE (Exclusive database access V6.0, table V6.1, no journaling)

The following is an example of SET TRANSACTION which is executed immediately:

```
SQL> SET TRANSACTION READ WRITE NOWAIT
cont> RESERVING branch FOR SHARED READ;
```

Hint: The SET TRANSACTION statement makes applications easier to read and provides more control over how the accessed tables should be locked.

If the user attempts to finish the transaction without specifying whether to commit or rollback, by default SQL will COMMIT the data.

3.2.4   Isolation Levels

The SQL standard defines four isolation levels which are explained in detail in the chapter on locking:

- Read Uncommitted
- Read Committed
- Repeatable Read
- Serializable

By default, as specified by the SQL standard, all Rdb transactions are run in mode Serializable but it does support all these levels except Read Uncommitted. The isolation level is changed by specifying the required level on the transaction statement, but it is only valid for a read-write transaction.

```
SQL> SET TRANSACTION READ WRITE ISOLATION LEVEL READ COMMITTED;
```

3.2.5   Retrieval Operations

The primary statement for retrieving data in SQL is the SELECT statement, which forms a stream of records. To report the first and last names of all customers, the equivalent SQL statement would be:

```
SQL> SELECT surname, first_name FROM customer;

  SURNAME        FIRST_NAME
  Hobbs          Lilian
  Smith          Paul
  2 row(s) selected
```

Sort Sequence

Sort sequence is achieved using the ORDER BY clause. The following is used to sort all the customers who have active accounts:

```
SQL> SELECT surname, first_name FROM customer WHERE
cont> status = 1
cont> ORDER BY surname, first_name;

  SURNAME        FIRST_NAME
  Hagan          Steve
  Hobbs          Lilian
  Vona           Fred
  3 row(s) selected
```

If the sorting sequence is not specified, that is, the keyword *ASC* is omitted after the column name, then Rdb assumes ascending order. With the descending clause, *DESC*, SQL will sort accordingly and use a descending index whenever possible, if one is available.

Group By

The GROUP BY clause is used to group together rows that an aggregate function such as SUM or COUNT has been applied to. The example below produces a report for each customer, and their total balance for all the accounts they hold.

```
SQL> SELECT SUM(balance) ,customer_no FROM account GROUP BY
customer_no;

    CUSTOMER_NO
   1691.34        100201
```

Having

Sometimes the GROUP BY clause does not restrict the results sufficiently. In this instance the HAVING clause is added to the query. For example, below we report the total balance for all accounts for a customer, but only those with an ACCT-TYPE of 1.

```
SQL> SELECT SUM(balance) ,customer_no FROM account
cont> GROUP BY customer_no, acct_type HAVING acct_type = 1;
        CUSTOMER_NO
    1691.34                100201
1 row selected
```

Retrieving only *n* records

SQL will display only a specified number of records from the stream rather than all the records, if the LIMIT TO clause is used. For example:

```
SQL> SELECT account_no, customer_no FROM account
cont> WHERE statement_day=10
cont> LIMIT TO 3 ROWS;
        ACCOUNT_NO   CUSTOMER_NO
        1551290       100201
        1561290       100205
        1674321       1002501
3 rows selected
```

Correlation Names

It is common for the same column name to appear in several tables. When these tables are joined, a mechanism is required to determine which columns are being referenced. This problem is overcome by the use of a correlation name. Using the example of joining the ACCOUNT and the TRANSACTION tables using the column ACCOUNT_NO, where A and T are the correlation names, the query becomes:

```
SQL> SELECT A.account_no, T.tran_date, T.tran_amt
cont>   FROM account A, transaction T
cont>   WHERE A.account_no = T.account_no
cont>   ORDER BY A.account_no;
```

```
A.ACCOUNT_NO    T.TRAN_DATE                      T.TRAN_AMT
 1002013127     5-DEC-1993    00:00:00.00          -35.45
 1002013127     30-NOV-1993   21:09:05.00           12.34
 1002013127     1-DEC-1993    23:35:01.01           12.34
 1002035678     1-DEC-1993    23:35:10.01          121.54
 1002035697     1-DEC-1993    23:45:10.01         1571.54
5 rows selected
```

Use of the correlation name is optional. The same effect is achieved by qualifying the query using the full table name instead.

Column Renaming

Another useful feature available in SQL is the ability to rename a column using the AS clause. This is especially useful when creating new data values based on existing columns. In the example show below create the column address by concatenating together columns ADDRESS_LINE1 and ADDRESS_LINE2.

```
SQL> SELECT surname,
cont> substring (address_line1 from 1 for 20) ||
cont> substring (address_line2 from 1 for 20) AS address
cont> from customer;

SURNAME         ADDRESS
 Hobbs          12 Special Street  Chandlers Ford

 Smith          10 Winchester Road Totton
2 rows selected
```

Relational Operators

A list of SQL relational operators can be found in Table 3.1. These SQL relational operators are combined to form queries such as:

```
SQL> SELECT * FROM account WHERE overdraft_limit NOT BETWEEN 750 AND 900;
SQL> SELECT * FROM customer WHERE surname LIKE 'HOBBS%';
```

A very useful clause that may be specified on a SELECT expression is the asterisk (*), which advises SQL to display all columns in the table or joined tables.

Table 3.1 SQL Relational Operators

=	Equal To
<>	Not Equal To
>	Greater Than
>=	Greater Than or Equal
<	Less Than
<=	Less Than or Equal
AND	
OR	
NOT	
BETWEEN	
IS NULL	
LIKE	
NOT IN	
ALL	
EXISTS	
IN	
SOME	
SUBSTRING	Specify the number of characters to display

Partial Matching

To find all the customers who live in the SO postal code area:

```
SQL>  SELECT customer_no, surname, first_name FROM customer
cont>  WHERE postcode LIKE 'SO%';

 CUSTOMER_NO  SURNAME        FIRST_NAME
 100201       Hobbs          Lilian
 1 row(s) selected
```

In SQL the wildcard symbol (%) denotes many characters and the underscore (_) a single character.

Eliminating Duplicate Values

The DISTINCT clause in the SELECT statement is used to eliminate all duplicate values in a query. For example:

```
SQL>  SELECT DISTINCT branch_code FROM account;
    BRANCH_CODE
    ALT
    LON
    SOT
 3 row(s) selected
```

Not Null

Sometimes a column may not initially be given a value. For example, when an account is first opened, the overdraft limit may not be known. It will be entered later when it has been agreed upon.

```
SQL> SELECT account_no  FROM account WHERE overdraft_limit IS NULL;

    ACCOUNT_NO
    1674321890
 1 row(s) selected
```

To insert a NULL value into a record, the NULL clause is used, as is illustrated in the following example:

```
SQL> INSERT INTO account VALUES
cont> ('1674321890','1002501','SOT',0,NULL,1,01,'10-JUN-1990',03);
 1 row(s) inserted
```

Uniqueness or Existence

To identify all the accounts with no transactions, the NOT EXISTS clause is included in the SELECT statement:

```
SQL> SELECT A.account_no FROM account A
cont>  WHERE NOT EXISTS
cont>   (SELECT T.account_no FROM transaction T
cont>  WHERE T.account_no = A.account_no)
cont>
cont>  ORDER BY account_no;
```

```
      ACCOUNT_NO
      1674321890
      9167823415
      9167823445
      9167823487
4 rows selected
```

3.2.6   Joining Tables & Multi Record Joins

To join two or more tables:

```
SQL> SELECT account.customer_no, surname, account_no
cont>   FROM account, customer
cont>    WHERE account.customer_no = customer.customer_no;
    ACCOUNT.CUSTOMER_NO  CUSTOMER.SURNAME  ACCOUNT.ACCOUNT_NO
    100201               Hobbs             1002013127
    100205               Smith             9167823445
    100205               Smith             9167823487
    100201               Hobbs             1002035678
    100201               Hobbs             9167823415
    100205               Smith             1002035697
  6 rows selected
```

```
SQL> SELECT account.customer_no, account.account_no, tran_date
cont>
cont>   FROM customer, account, transaction
cont>
cont>    WHERE customer.customer_no = '100201' AND
cont>     customer.customer_no = account.customer_no AND
cont>     account.account_no = transaction.account_no;

ACCOUNT.CUSTOMER_NO  ACCOUNT.ACCOUNT_NO  TRANSACTION.TRAN_DATE
  100201             1002013127          5-DEC-1993   00:00:00.00
  100201             1002013127          1-DEC-1993   23:35:01.01
  100201             1002013127          30-NOV-1993  21:09:05.00
  100201             1002035678          1-DEC-1993   23:35:10.01
  4 rows selected
```

Joins - Inner, Outer & Full

SQL offers various types of Joins, including the Inner, Outer and Full. An Inner Join is the default join type; that is, only rows which match are retained. A left outer join retains all the rows from the first table and only those from the second table that matched the selection criteria. When a value is not available it is displayed as NULL.

```
SQL> SELECT a.account_no, tran_amt FROM account a
cont> LEFT OUTER JOIN
cont> account_transaction t
cont> ON a.account_no = t.account_no;


     A.ACCOUNT_NO    T.TRAN_AMT
       1567890         -15.00
       1567890         500.00
       1567890        1245.78
       1567890        -402.45
       9551490          NULL
5 rows selected
```

A Right Outer join is the reverse; it reports all rows in the second table and then only those rows from the first table that match.

```
SQL> SELECT a.account_no, tran_amt FROM account a
cont> RIGHT OUTER JOIN
cont> account_transaction t
cont> ON a.account_no = t.account_no;


     A.ACCOUNT_NO    T.TRAN_AMT
       1567890         -402.45
       1567890        1245.78
       1567890         500.00
       1567890         -15.00
4 rows selected
```

3.2.7 Date & Time Arithmetic

The SQL standard defines a number of functions to perform date and time arithmetic. These functions are well worth using because they alleviate the need to write special code or call operating system routines. The dates and times can be defined as:

- DATE 'y-m-d'

- TIME 'h:m:s.sss'

- TIMESTAMP 'y-m-d:h:m:s.sss'

- INTERVAL

Using these functions it is very easy to perform operations like add 30 days to the invoice date.

```
SQL> SELECT invoice_date + INTERVAL '30' DAY FROM account_transaction;

 1994-03-17
```

These functions can only be used on ISO or ANSI datatypes. Existing OpenVMS systems are unlikely to have this datatype because they were probably defined with the DATE VMS datatype. However, this does not prevent these legacy systems from using these functions. All that is required is to use the CAST function to convert it to the DATE ANSI datatype. For example, referring to the example below, the TRAN_DATE is converted to ANSI and then it can be subtracted from the INVOICE_DATE. In this instance there is a 3 year and 2 month difference between these dates so the result is 3-2.

```
SQL> SELECT (invoice_date - CAST(tran_date AS DATE ANSI))YEAR TO MONTH
cont> FROM account_transaction;

 03-02
```

There are infinite possibilities with Date and Time arithmetic; these examples just scratch the surface with what is possible. Another example of where you could use these functions is:

```
SQL> SELECT transaction_duration FROM query_log WHERE
cont> transaction_duration > INTERVAL'1'SECOND;
```

3.2.8   **Statistical Functions**

SQL supports the following statistical functions:

- COUNT (*)

- COUNT (DISTINCT column name)

- SUM

- AVG

- MIN

- MAX

Typical queries are:

How many customers are there?

```
SQL>  SELECT COUNT(*) FROM customer;
     2
 1 row(s) selected
```

How many unique overdraft limits are there?

```
SQL> SELECT COUNT (DISTINCT overdraft_limit) FROM account;
     5
 1 row(s) selected
```

What is the average balance?

```
SQL> SELECT AVG (balance) FROM account;
     8.5483757E+01
 1 row(s) selected
```

What is the maximum overdraft?

```
SQL> SELECT MAX (overdraft_limit) FROM account;
       5000.00
 1 row(s) selected
```

3.2.9   **Value Expressions**

SQL also supports a range of value expressions that can be used within a SELECT statement. We have seen some of these used in examples already and will see more later within this chapter.

- EXTRACT

- TRANSLATE

- SUBSTRING

- CHAR_LENGTH

- OCTET_LENGTH

- COALESCE

- NULLIF

- CASE

What day of the week did the transaction take place?

```
SQL> SELECT EXTRACT(WEEKDAY FROM tran_date) FROM account_transaction;

        3
        4
        6
        6
4 rows selected
```

We will see later in this chapter how you can define your own functions that may be called from within SQL.

3.3   **STRING MANIPULATION**

In Rdb, SQL allows string manipulation with the SUBSTRING qualifier. Included as part of a standard SELECT statement, it allows the columns to be truncated upon display by specifying the number of characters to display. The following example illustrates how to display the customers' numbers, names, and the first ten characters of their addresses.

```
SQL> SELECT customer_no, surname,
cont> SUBSTRING (address_line1 FROM 1 for 10) AS address FROM customer;

CUSTOMER_NO   SURNAME          ADDRESS
  100201        Hobbs          'Nightsky
  100205        Smith          10 Winches
  1678345       Vona           NULL
3 rows selected
```

3.3.1   Standard Key Words

Various standard key words may be used instead of variables in SQL to obtain specific information. They are:

Table 3.2   SQL Key Words

CURRENT_TIMESTAMP	Returns the date and time
CURRENT_USER	Is the current active username. But if during the execution of the SQL statement, definer's right are used, then the definer's username is returned.
SESSION_USER	Current active username
SYSTEM_USER	This is the username used when first attached to the database
CURRENT_DATE	Date in yyyy-mm-nn format
CURRENT_TIME	Time in hh:mm:ss

These key words may be included in any SQL expression where a column name is expected to either display or store data. Typical uses for these two key words are in trigger definitions to obtain useful audit trail information. The following example illustrates a SELECT expression where the two key words are specified in an interactive session:

```
SQL> SELECT customer_no, USER, CURRENT_TIMESTAMP FROM customer;
 CUSTOMER_NO
  100201        HOBBS        20-FEB-1994 13:36:09.49
  100205        HOBBS        20-FEB-1994 13:36:09.49
  1678345       HOBBS        20-FEB-1994 13:36:09.49
3 rows selected
```

```
SQL> SELECT current_date, current_time, current_timestamp from branch;

 1994-02-20          20:27:51          20-FEB-1994 20:27:51.82
1 row selected

SQL> SELECT current_user, session_user, system_user FROM branch;

 HOBBS      HOBBS      HOBBS
1 row selected
```

3.3.2 Cursors

A cursor is a logical table that contains the result of a query. It is a mechanism by which a number of rows are grouped together and then processed individually. It is an essential statement used extensively in all application programs because the SELECT clause on its own does not provide a way to process rows individually. Therefore, the SELECT clause is specified in the cursor declaration to group the rows together before they are individually processed.

SQL provides for two types of cursors:

- Table
- List

A **table** cursor provides access to individual rows in a table. All the examples in this section are table cursors.

A **list** cursor provides access to individual elements in a list. List cursors are used to manipulate the segmented string or list of byte-varying datatype. One unique feature offered with list cursors is that they may be scrolled forwards and backwards.

Further enhancements made to cursors include the ability to specify one of two types of operation on the cursor. For a table cursor, the user can specify:

- Insert-only
- Update-only
- Read-only

An update cursor is the default type of cursor clause.

A list cursor may be either of the following types:

- Read-only

- Insert

A *read-only* cursor only allows data to be read, while an *insert* cursor allows the insertion of data.

A typical example of cursor usage is creating a cursor to identify those accounts that require a statement to be printed. The cursor is created, then each account row is selected in turn and printed.

Four statements are used in cursor processing:

- DECLARE CURSOR – Specifies the name and result selection condition

- OPEN – Forms the cursor

- FETCH – Retrieves one row from the stream

- CLOSE – Deletes the cursor

The following is an example of the four statements:

```
SQL> DECLARE statement_prt CURSOR FOR
cont>  SELECT * FROM account WHERE statement_day = 31;
SQL>

SQL> OPEN statement_prt;

SQL> FETCH statement_prt;

    ACCOUNT_NO   CUSTOMER_NO   BRANCH_CODE   BALANCE
    OVERDRAFT_LIMIT    ACCT_TYPE   STATEMENT_FREQ
    STATEMENT_DATE        STATEMENT_DAY
    9167823487   100205      SOT       354.34
        250.00        1       31
    6-DEC-1989 00:00:00.00          31


SQL> CLOSE statement_prt;
```

Hint: It is important to remember that cursors are useful, but the rows in the cursor can remain locked, depending on the isolation level; (unless it's a snapshot transaction), until the transaction is finished using the commit or rollback statement. Closing the cursor does not release the locks on the rows.

Later in the optimizer chapter we will see how we can influence the strategy used by specifying the FAST FIRST or TOTAL TIME optimization.

```
SQL> DECLARE acurs READ ONLY TABLE CURSOR FOR
cont>   select * from branch optimize for fast first;
```

3.3.3 Segmented Strings or List of Byte Varying

SQL provides support for manipulating the segmented string datatype that SQL refers to as *list of byte varying*. In SQL, segmented strings require special manipulation. This manipulation is achieved by using two types of cursor, a list and a table cursor.

The list cursor specifies the list of values for the segmented string. The table cursor defines the values for all the non-segmented string datatypes.

Storing Data into a Segmented String

The following example illustrates how data is stored in the segmented string ACCOUNT_TEXT in the table ACCOUNT_NOTES:

1 Define a cursor for the table in which the list of byte varying row datatype is defined. In this example it is table ACCOUNT_NOTES.

```
SQL> DECLARE table_cursor INSERT ONLY TABLE CURSOR FOR SELECT *
cont> FROM ACCOUNT_NOTES;
```

2 Create a list cursor into which each segment of the segmented string is placed.

```
SQL> DECLARE list_cursor INSERT ONLY LIST CURSOR FOR SELECT account_text
cont> WHERE CURRENT OF table_cursor;
```

3 Open the cursor and insert a row into the table, omitting the segmented string column. Therefore, in the following example the only data that is specified is the account number because the other row in the table is a list of byte varying datatype.

```
SQL> OPEN table_cursor;
SQL> INSERT INTO CURSOR table_cursor (account_no) VALUES ('1002013127');
```

4 Open the cursor for manipulating the segmented string. Each individual segment of the segmented string is placed into the list cursor.

```
SQL> OPEN list_cursor;
SQL> INSERT INTO CURSOR list_cursor VALUES ('This customer has a
cont> very good');
SQL> INSERT INTO CURSOR list_cursor VALUES ('credit rating');
SQL> INSERT INTO CURSOR list_cursor VALUES ('Requested a Loan on
cont> 03-MAY-1994');
```

5 Finally, close the cursor when all activity upon the table has finished.

```
SQL> CLOSE list_cursor;
SQL> CLOSE table_cursor;
```

Retrieving Data from a Segmented String

As we previously stated, to read the data that is stored inside a segmented string, two cursors must be defined and a loop must fetch each segment of the segmented string. There is no loop in the following example, only a repeat of the fetch command:

1 Create a cursor that can only be read from for the table ACCOUNT_NOTES

```
SQL> DECLARE read_table_cursor READ ONLY TABLE CURSOR FOR SELECT *
cont> FROM ACCOUNT_NOTES;
```

2 Create another cursor that is read-only for the column account_text, which is a segmented string. Using as the current row the position in the table cursor

```
SQL> DECLARE read_list_cursor READ ONLY LIST CURSOR FOR
cont> SELECT account_text
cont> WHERE CURRENT OF read_table_cursor;
SQL> OPEN read_table_cursor;
```

3 Fetch a row from the table cursor.

```
SQL> FETCH read_table_cursor;
      ACCOUNT_NO   ACCOUNT_TEXT
      1002013127            1:115:8

SQL> OPEN read_list_cursor;
```

4 Open the list cursor for the segmented string column account_text and read the first segment.

```
SQL> FETCH read_list_cursor;
 ACCOUNT_TEXT
 This customer has a very good
```

5 Fetch the next segment for this segmented string.

```
 SQL> FETCH read_list_cursor;
 ACCOUNT_TEXT
 credit rating

SQL> FETCH read_list_cursor;
 ACCOUNT_TEXT
 Requested a Loan on 03-MAY-1990
```

6 Close the cursors.

```
SQL> CLOSE read_table_cursor;

SQL> CLOSE read_list_cursor;
```

3.3.4   Storing Data

Data is stored in the database using the INSERT clause. In SQL, first all the column names are specified, then the actual value.

```
SQL> INSERT INTO branch
cont> (branch_code, branch_name, branch_address, managers_name)
cont> VALUES
cont> ('NW','England & Hobbs PLC', 'The High Street, Ampton',
cont>    'Mr J Smith');
1 row(s) inserted
```

3.3.5   Modify

The UPDATE statement is very powerful because in one expression, the user can specify which row to amend and the amendment. For example:

```
SQL>  UPDATE customer SET
cont>   credit_limit = '900' WHERE  customer_no = '100205';
1 row(s) updated
```

The query also can be specified using a cursor.

```
SQL>  DECLARE update_cust CURSOR FOR
cont>     SELECT credit_limit FROM customer
cont>       WHERE customer_no = '100205'
cont>       FOR UPDATE OF credit_limit;

SQL>  OPEN update_cust;

SQL>  FETCH update_cust;

 CREDIT_LIMIT

 9.0000000E+02

SQL>  UPDATE customer
cont>   SET credit_limit = '900'
cont>     WHERE CURRENT OF update_cust;
1 row(s) updated
```

3.3.6   Deletions

Data is removed in SQL using the DELETE statement. Its structure is similar to the UPDATE statement seen previously:

```
SQL>  DELETE FROM customer WHERE customer_no = '100205';
1 row(s) deleted
```

Or using cursors

```
SQL>  DECLARE delete_cust CURSOR FOR
cont>     SELECT * FROM customer WHERE customer_no = '100205';
SQL>  OPEN delete_cust;
```

```
SQL>   FETCH delete_cust;
 CUSTOMER_NO   SURNAME              FIRST_NAME
   ADDRESS_LINE1               ADDRESS_LINE2
     ADDRESS_LINE3               ADDRESS_LINE4
      POSTCODE    CREDIT_LIMIT    STATUS
 100205                Smith                Paul
   10 Winchester Road           Tighten
     Portsmouth                Hampshire
       PO12 6TY    9.0000000E+02        1

SQL>   DELETE FROM customer WHERE CURRENT OF delete_cust;
1 row(s) deleted
```

3.4   MULTISTATEMENT PROCEDURES

It is possible to write two types of procedures in Rdb:

• Single statement procedures

• Multistatement procedures

As their names suggest, a single statement procedure allows access to a database through a single SQL statement, whereas a multistatement procedure allows access to a database through multiple SQL statements. This is achieved through the concept of a *compound statement*, that is, a collection of a number of SQL statements within a BEGIN...END block. This is a concept not unfamiliar to programmers who use structured languages. A multistatement procedure can contain a number of these BEGIN...END blocks and they may be nested inside one another as shown below:

```
BEGIN
  sql statement 1
  sql statement 2
     BEGIN
       sql statement 3
       sql statement 4
     END
  sql statement 5
     .
     .
END
```

Why bother doing this? A good reason is to simplify the logic in an application program. An application program that makes calls to SQL Module Language procedures can call a multistatement procedure that executes complex logic before returning control to the calling program. If single statement procedures were used, the program would have to call many procedures many times and would have to deal with all the conditional logic.

With a multistatement procedure, one call might suffice and as we shall see shortly, a multistatement procedure may contain conditional logic. Multistatement procedures can also be written by one developer and reused by many. We shall see later how multistatement procedures may be stored as schema objects within an Rdb database.

An interesting question raised by the provision of multistatement procedures in Rdb is that of *atomicity*; Rdb designers are used to the fact that single SQL statements are atomic, that is, an SQL statement either executes to completion or not at all. For example, a row can never be partly inserted. This is quite apart from Rdb transactions that are themselves atomic and may contain a number of SQL statements which may or may not succeed.

What happens in the case of the compound statements mentioned above? Does Rdb treat a BEGIN...END block as a unit of atomicity or can the BEGIN...END partially execute? In fact either case is possible and it is a design decision made by the developer which determines what actually will happen as discussed next.

3.4.1   NOT ATOMIC Compound Statements

Compound statements that are not atomic contain SQL statements that are atomic though the compound statement as a whole is not. This is the default. If an error occurs while executing SQL statements in the compound statement, any successful SQL statement will not be rolled back. In the following example where the INSERT fails and is rolled back, the DELETE statement has already successfully executed and so is not rolled back. The UPDATE is never executed.

```
BEGIN
   DELETE FROM account...
   INSERT INTO account......fails!
   UPDATE account...
END;
```

3.4.2   ATOMIC Compound Statements

Compound statements that are atomic contain SQL statements that are atomic and the compound statement as a whole is atomic. If an error occurs while executing SQL statements in the compound statement, all SQL statements that have executed will be rolled back. In the following example where the INSERT fails and is rolled back, the DELETE statement has already successfully executed and is also rolled back. The UPDATE is never executed.

```
BEGIN ATOMIC
    DELETE FROM account...
    INSERT INTO account......fails!
    UPDATE account...
END;
```

3.4.3   Compound Statements and Transaction Demarcation

A compound statement can contain SET TRANSACTION, COMMIT and ROLLBACK statements but only if the compound statement is non-atomic.

```
SQL> BEGIN
cont> SET TRANSACTION READ WRITE RESERVING branch FOR SHARED WRITE;
cont>   UPDATE BRANCH SET managers_name = 'Steve Horn'
cont>       WHERE branch_code = 'ALT';
cont>   COMMIT;
cont> END;
```

Note also that a compound statement cannot refer to more than one database alias and that not all SQL statements can appear inside a compound statement. The *Rdb SQL Reference Manual* lists the SQL statements than may be placed inside a compound statement.

3.4.4   Variable Declaration and Assignment in Compound Statements

In order to test multistatement procedures that will be embedded in SQL modules or precompiled programs and to write multistatement procedures in interactive SQL, variables can be declared and have values assigned to them:

```
SQL> DECLARE :bnam CHAR(20);
SQL> DECLARE :cust_status INTEGER;
```

The above example shows two simple variable declarations. These variables can be assigned values and used in other statements as in the examples below:

```
SQL> BEGIN
cont>   DECLARE :bnam CHAR(20);
cont>   SET :bnam = 'Bramley';
cont>   DELETE FROM branch WHERE branch_name = :bnam;
cont> END;
```

```
SQL> BEGIN
cont>   SET :bcnt = (SELECT COUNT(*) FROM branches);
cont>   SET :bnam = NULL;
cont> END;
```

SELECT ... INTO

The following example shows the use of SELECT...INTO with a variable:

```
SQL> BEGIN
cont> DECLARE :tot_bal INTEGER;
cont> SELECT SUM(account_balance) INTO :tot_bal FROM account;
cont> INSERT INTO funds_history (run_date, funds)
cont>   VALUES (CURRENT_DATE, :tot_bal);
cont> END;
```

A variable exists for the duration of the compound statement in which it is declared, again, a concept that will be familiar to anyone using structured programming languages. In the example below, the variable *BNAM* is declared within the scope of the inner compound statement. When an assignment is made to it in the outer compound statement, a failure occurs because it no longer exists, unless it is defined as a GLOBAL variable.

```
SQL> BEGIN
cont>   BEGIN
cont>    DECLARE :bnam CHAR(20);
cont>    SET :bnam = 'Bramley';
cont>   END;
cont>   SET :bnam = 'Winchester';
cont> END;
```

```
%SQL-F-UNDEFVAR, Variable BNAM is not defined
```

Similarly, inner variable declarations hide outer ones. In the example below the outer variable declaration of *BNAM* has been assigned the value "Ropley", but the inner variable declaration of *BNAM* has not been assigned a value. Consequently, the update places an undefined variable value into the *BRANCH* row which is then displayed as "....................". This is because the inner declaration hid the outer declaration.

```
SQL> BEGIN
cont>   DECLARE :bnam CHAR(20);
cont>   DECLARE :bcode CHAR(4);
cont>   SET :bcode = 'ROP';
cont>   SET :bnam = 'Ropley';
cont>    BEGIN
cont>     DECLARE :bnam CHAR(20);
cont>     UPDATE branch SET branch_name = :bnam
cont>        WHERE branch_code = :bcode;
cont>    END;
cont> END;
SQL> SELECT branch_name FROM branch WHERE branch_code = 'ROP';

  BRANCH_NAME

  ....................
1 row selected
```

3.4.5   Flow Control in Compound Statements

As in any programming languages, statements can be placed in compound statements to modify the logic flow. There are a number of flow control statements and these are:

- CASE
- IF
- LOOP
- LEAVE
- FOR

CASE

This statement is used to execute a number of alternative statements depending on the result of a value expression.

```
SQL> BEGIN
cont>   SET :cust_status_line =
cont>    (CASE :cust_status
cont>       WHEN 1 THEN 'Living in Great Britain';
cont>       WHEN 2 THEN 'Living in Europe';
cont>       WHEN 3 THEN 'Living in North America';
cont>       WHEN NULL THEN 'Status Unknown';
cont>       ELSE 'Living in Hampshire';
cont>     END CASE; )
cont> END;
```

IF

This statement is used to execute statements conditionally depending on the result of a predicate.

```
SQL> BEGIN
cont>  IF :account_type = '2' THEN
cont>    IF :account_balance < 0 THEN
cont>       BEGIN
```

```
cont>           SET :cust_current_desc = 'Poor Customer';
cont>           END;
cont>     END IF;
cont>     ELSEIF :account_balance > 0 THEN
cont>        BEGIN
cont>             SET :cust_current_desc = 'Jolly Fine Customer';
cont>        END;
cont>     ELSE
cont>        BEGIN
cont>             SET :cust_current_desc = 'Not Sure';
cont>        END;
cont>     END IF;
cont> END;
```

LOOP

The LOOP statement is used to execute statements repetitively. The loop can be made to end when a condition is reached or a LEAVE statement is executed. This statement is extremely useful for loading test data into a database. The example below loops around loading branch rows as long as the WHILE condition is true.

```
SQL> BEGIN
cont>   DECLARE :i INTEGER;
cont>   DECLARE :c CHAR (4);
cont>   SET :i = 1;
cont>   SET :c = 1;
cont>   BEGIN
cont>      WHILE :i <= 9999
cont>      LOOP
cont>          INSERT INTO branch (branch_code) VALUES (:c);
cont>          SET :i = :i +1;
cont>          SET :c = :i;
cont>      END LOOP;
cont>   END;
cont> END;
```

The example below loops around loading branch rows as long as the IF condition is true and then a LEAVE statement is executed.

```
SQL> BEGIN
cont>   DECLARE :i INTEGER;
cont>   DECLARE :c CHAR (4);
cont>   SET :i = 1;
cont>   SET :c = 1;
cont>    BEGIN
cont>       branch_store_loop:
cont>      LOOP
cont>            INSERT INTO branch (branch_code) VALUES (:c);
cont>            SET :i = :i +1;
cont>            IF :i > 100 THEN LEAVE branch_store_loop;
cont>            END IF;
cont>            SET :c = :i;
cont>       END LOOP;
cont>    END;
cont> END;
```

FOR

The FOR statement allows you to easily process rows in a record stream. RDO fans will be used to this construct.

```
SQL> BEGIN
cont>   DECLARE :cred_flag CHAR(1);
cont>   FOR :cust AS EACH ROW OF
cont>     SELECT * FROM customer
cont>   DO
cont>     IF cust_status = 3 THEN
cont>       BEGIN
cont>       SET :cred_flag = 'D';
cont>       END;
cont>     END IF;
cont>   END FOR;
cont> END:
```

3.4.6   Getting Diagnostics in Compound Statements

If a statement in a compound statement returns an exception condition, the multistatement procedure is terminated. GET DIAGNOSTICS can be used to return the status of the last SQL statement as well as other information.

```
SQL> BEGIN
cont>   DECLARE :rows_updated INTEGER;
cont>   UPDATE branch SET managers_name = 'Steve Hagan'
cont>     WHERE branch_code > '8999';
cont> GET DIAGNOSTICS :rows_updated = ROW_COUNT;
cont> END;
```

In the above example, the value of the number of rows updated is returned. Other possibilities, to name but a few, include:

- Row count

- Transaction access mode

- Transaction isolation level

3.4.7   Debugging Compound Statements

Unlike many 3GL compilers, there is no symbolic debugger for SQL. Debug information for the values of variables must be obtained with the TRACE statement. To turn on debugging, the logical name RDMS$DEBUG_FLAGS must be set.

```
$ DEFINE RDMS$DEBUG_FLAGS 'Xt'
```

Note that the string Xt is case sensitive – XT or xT will not work! When the logical name is set, TRACE can be inserted into the SQL statements.

```
SQL> BEGIN
cont> DECLARE :j INTEGER;
cont>   WHILE :j <> -100
cont>     LOOP
cont>       SET :j = :j - 1;
```

```
cont>      TRACE 'The value of j is ', :j;
cont>      END LOOP;
cont> END;
~Xt: The value of j is -1
~Xt: The value of j is -2
~Xt: The value of j is -3
~Xt: The value of j is -4
```

As in the example above, once the SQL statements are executed, a line of debug information is displayed.

3.5　　　**STORED PROCEDURES**

SQL modules can be held as schema objects inside the database like a table or view and typically consist of multistatement procedures. There are a number of good reasons for doing this, including:

- Function encapsulation

- Inheritance of privilege

- Client/server processing

From an encapsulation of function perspective, stored procedures enable the designer to place an action or group of actions together in the database. This can effectively *hide* the complexity of the group of actions. Developers can then easily *re-use* procedures.

From an inheritance of privilege perspective, the definer of a procedure must have access to the base objects referenced in the procedure. However, the invoker of a procedure can inherit the access rights of the procedure definer so procedure invokers can execute set actions even though they have no access to the base objects referenced in the procedure. Another option is that the procedure invoker must have access to the base objects referenced in the procedure when the procedure is executed. Note that the definer of a stored module must have CREATE privilege and an invoker must have EXECUTE privilege granted on the module holding the procedure to be called.

From an client/server perspective, by using stored procedures complex SQL logic can be held at the server in the database. Holding one copy of the procedure definition can simplify maintenance, and security can be implemented more easily. Less SQL code is passed between the client and the server.

Procedures are not actually held as stand-alone objects in the database. They are created as part of a CREATE MODULE statement. This means that the database administrator cannot CREATE or DROP individual procedures. However, the database administrator can SHOW individual procedures and a procedure is called, not a module. A database administrator can CREATE, DROP or SHOW individual modules in the database. To drop a procedure, the sequence of events is:

1 DROP the module

2 Delete procedure from source module file

3 CREATE the module

4 Use RMU/EXTRACT to retrieve source module/procedure definition

The following is an example of creating a module:

```
SQL> CREATE MODULE branch_module LANGUAGE SQL
cont> PROCEDURE update_branch (:bcode CHAR(4));
cont>   BEGIN
cont>     UPDATE branch
cont>       SET branch_name = 'Alton' WHERE branch_code = :bcode;
cont>     END;
cont> PROCEDURE DELETE_BRANCH (:bcode CHAR(4));
cont>   BEGIN
cont>     DELETE FROM branch where branch_code = :bcode;
cont>   END;
cont> END MODULE;
```

The following is an example of showing a module:

```
SQL> SHOW MODULES
Modules in database with filename BANKING
 Module name is: BRANCH_MODULE

SQL> SHOW MODULE branch_module
 Module name is: BRANCH_MODULE
 Header: branch_module LANGUAGE SQL AUTHORIZATION ENGLAND
 No description found.
 Owner is: ENGLAND
 Module ID is: 13
 Procedures in Module:
     DELETE_BRANCH
     UPDATE_BRANCH
```

The following is an example of showing a procedure:

```
SQL> SHOW PROCEDURE DELETE_BRANCH
Procedure name is: DELETE_BRANCH
 Procedure ID is: 15
 Source: DELETE_BRANCH (:bcode CHAR(4));
    BEGIN
       DELETE FROM branch where branch_code = :bcode;
    END
 No description found.
 Module name is: BRANCH_MODULE
 Module ID is: 13
 Function owner is: NONE
 Number of parameters is: 1

Parameter Name    Data Type     Domain
--------------    ---------     ------
BCODE             CHAR(4)
    Parameter position is 1
    Parameter is IN (read)
    Parameter is passed by REFERENCE
```

A stored procedure is simply invoked by issuing a CALL statement; however, note that a CALL statement cannot be issued in a compound statement. The implication of this is that currently a stored procedure may not call a stored procedure.

```
SQL> CALL delete_branch('2323');
```

Because of the objects that a stored procedure will typically reference, it has dependencies upon these various objects such as tables and columns. If these objects were to change then the behavior of the stored procedure could be affected. To manage this, Rdb uses dependency tracking to keep a record of the objects a stored procedure depends upon in new system relations. Rdb records what objects the stored procedure references (called *referenced objects*). Referenced objects can include:

- Domain

- Table

- View

- Column

- Constraint

Depending on the type of dependency, an attempt to alter a referenced object may fail. Alternatively, the stored procedure may be invalidated.

3.6   EXTERNAL FUNCTIONS

A function in SQL refers to a routine that returns a value. In SQL there are two types of function. First, there are built-in functions that are essentially internal code to Rdb and are not modifiable by anyone other than the Rdb engineering group. Examples of built-in functions would be AVG() and SUBSTRING(). Second, there are external functions. External functions are 3GL programs that are executed as part of a value expression in an SQL statement and are external code to SQL. They are typically written by Rdb sites and other groups outside Rdb engineering.

Because an external function is a 3GL program, almost limitless possibilities exist as to its use, bounded only by a developer's imagination. As well as being code written by an Rdb site, an external function can be an OpenVMS library routine. The only major restriction is that an external function cannot call back to the database.

Functions are manipulated via:

- CREATE FUNCTION

- DROP FUNCTION

The following example creates an external function named encrypt and drops an external function named decrypt.

```
SQL> CREATE FUNCTION encrypt (IN CHAR(80) BY REFERENCE)
cont> RETURNS CHAR(80);
cont> LOCATION 'cypher$lib'
cont> LANGUAGE C GENERAL PARAMETER STYLE;

SQL> DROP FUNCTION decrypt;
```

Creating an external function consists of a number of steps:

1 Write and compile the code.

2 Create a linker options file.

3 Create a shareable image.

4 Check it using a testbed program.

5 Create an external function definition.

The steps required to creating a shareable image in OpenVMS are as follows:

Compile the function

```
$ cc encrypt.c
```

On a VAX system create an options file with the external function name a UNIVERSAL symbol

```
$ create encrypt.opt
 UNIVERSAL = encrypt
```

Link a shareable image

```
$ link/shareable encrypt encrypt.opt/opt
```

As external functions are executed as part of a value expression in an SQL statement, there are many places where they can be embedded. For example:

```
SQL> INSERT INTO secret_accounts(account_num, account_name)
cont> VALUES ('99886543', encrypt('Margaret Moneybags'));

SQL> SELECT account_num, decrypt(account_name) FROM accounts;
```

Other possibilities include using external functions within column constraints, triggers and COMPUTED BY clauses.

As was mentioned earlier, an OpenVMS library routine can be used as an external function; for example, the following external function definition uses the mathematics library function *mth$gsind* to compute the sine of an angle specified in degrees:

```
SQL> CREATE FUNCTION sine (IN DOUBLE PRECISION)
cont> RETURNS DOUBLE PRECISION;
cont> EXTERNAL NAME mth$gsind
cont> LOCATION 'sys$share:mthrtl'
cont> LANGUAGE GENERAL GENERAL PARAMETER STYLE;
```

The following table definition uses this external function in a COMPUTED BY field:

```
SQL> CREATE TABLE sine_table
cont> (degrees DOUBLE PRECISION,
cont> sine_num COMPUTED BY sine(degrees));
```

If we were now to insert some rows and display them we would see the following:

```
SQL> INSERT INTO sine_table (degrees) VALUES (0);
1 row inserted
SQL> INSERT INTO sine_table (degrees) VALUES (10);
1 row inserted
SQL> INSERT INTO sine_table (degrees) VALUES (45);
1 row inserted
```

```
SQL> INSERT INTO sine_table (degrees) VALUES (90);
1 row inserted
SQL> COMMIT;
SQL> SELECT * FROM sine_table;
          DEGREES              SINE_NUM
  0.000000000000000E+000   0.000000000000000E+000
  1.000000000000000E+001   1.736481776669304E-001
  4.500000000000000E+001   7.071067811865476E-001
  9.000000000000000E+001   1.000000000000000E+000
4 rows selected
```

If we wished to be really clever we could have used the CAST function to display the sine value in a more friendly integer format!

Because external function code is not stored internal to the database, security is a concern and external images should be made safe from tampering. One approach on OpenVMS is to use the OpenVMS INSTALL utility. Another approach is to use appropriately created concealed and system executive logical names.

3.7   WHAT'S NEXT FOR SQL?

The SQL standard is continually evolving. It began as SQL-86 then SQL-89 and today the latest version is SQL-92, known as SQL2. The next working version of the standard is known as SQL3 and the main areas of enhancement are:

- Call level interface

- Stored modules

- Object oriented extension

- Further relational extensions

- Procedural extensions

It is unlikely that this standard with be ratified before 1996.

4   Storage Structures

In Chapter 2 we saw how a single-file Rdb database could be created. This chapter describes how multifile Rdb databases are created and then gives an overview of the on-disk structure used by Rdb.

4.1   WHY USE MULTIFILE DATABASES?

In a single-file database, all the tables containing the user data and the indexes are stored in one operating system file, which usually resides on a single disk drive. Disk drives are capable of sustaining a maximum physical I/O rate. This rate depends on the type of disk drive, the amount of data transferred in the physical I/O, and the amount of disk head movement that needs to be performed, often known as a disk seek.

If we place a single-file database on a single disk drive (assuming it would fit) and steadily increase the work performed on the database, we would reach a point where the rate of requests to perform physical I/O to the database exceeds the rate at which the disk drive can service these requests. At this point, a queue of physical I/O requests begins to build up, and a disk bottleneck occurs. The rate at which the database is able to perform work stops increasing. The addition of a larger central processing unit has no benefit—the bottleneck is with the disk drive.

Hint: In the OpenVMS environment, the OpenVMS MONITOR utility is used to monitor the disk I/O rates and the disk queues. The following commands are used to do so.

```
MONITOR DISK
MONITOR DISK/ITEM=QUEUE_LENGTH
```

Rdb allows a database designer to specify multifile databases. In a multifile database, the tables and indexes usually are placed in more than one file, which are placed on more than one disk drive. By doing this, the physical I/O requests to the database are spread over a number of disk drives, increasing the rate at which physical I/Os are handled by the system. Rdb names these files storage areas. A storage area can hold:

- A table

- A number of tables

- Part of a table (a table partition)

- An index

- A number of indexes

- Part of an index (an index partition)

Figure 4.1 shows the relationship between tables and disk drives where the tables are stored in a single storage area residing on a single disk drive.

Figure 4.2 shows the relationship between tables and disk drives where the tables are stored in their own storage area and each storage area resides on its own disk drive.

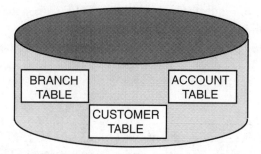

Figure 4.1 Mapping Many Tables to a Single Storage Area

Figure 4.2 Mapping Tables to Their Own Storage Areas

Figure 4.3 Mapping a Single Table to Many Storage Areas

Figure 4.3 shows the relationship between a table and a number of disk drives where the table is partitioned across four storage areas residing on four disk drives.

The configuration in Figure 4.3 clearly will be able to support more concurrent table-level access than the configuration in Figure 4.1.

4.2   **CREATING MULTIFILE DATABASES**

To create a multifile database, the database designer uses the CREATE STORAGE AREA clause in the CREATE DATABASE statement. In this situation, a root file is created that contains Rdb housekeeping information. It also contains pointers to files that contain tables and indexes.

The root file is created with a file extension of .RDB, and the data files with an extension of .RDA. If an Rdb database is composed of a .RDB file and .RDA files, it is said to be a multifile database. A storage area may be specified to hold the metadata definitions. This storage area is given the name RDB$SYSTEM.

A number of storage area slots may be reserved to enable the database administrator to add storage areas to the database at some future point with the ADD STORAGE AREA clause of the ALTER DATABASE statement. This operation may be performed without shutting down the database.

Hint: It is a good idea to reserve a small number of slots as insurance in case it becomes necessary to add an area urgently.

The database designer must be able to specify which storage areas are used for which tables. To do this, the CREATE STORAGE MAP statement is used. To specify which storage areas are used for indexes, the STORE clause is used as part of the CREATE INDEX statement.

4.3   CREATING STORAGE AREAS

When creating storage areas, a file specification is given, specifying the location of the storage area files. An example of such a file specification in the OpenVMS environment would be:

```
$222$dua23:[uk.db]bank_cust
```

Although this is clearly a hardcoded filename, moving the storage area to another directory and/or device is easily achieved with the RMU/ MOVE_AREA command. If the disk 222dua23 is logging errors, for example, the storage area BANK_CUST may be moved to another disk.

```
$ RMU/MOVE_AREA banking bank_cust/DIRECTORY=$222$dua25:[uk.db]
```

Hint: Do not use the operating system's native file copy command with multifile databases. Because the file specification of a storage area is held in the root file, Rdb may think that a storage area is stored in one position when in fact it has been copied to another. This will make the storage area inaccessible.

Once the attributes of the storage areas and the root file have been decided, the multifile database now may be created. The CREATE STORAGE AREA clause is issued as part of the CREATE DATABASE statement.

```
SQL> CREATE DATABASE FILENAME $222$dua23:[uk.db]banking
cont>   RESERVE 10 STORAGE AREAS
cont>   CREATE STORAGE AREA rdb$system
cont>      FILENAME $222$dua24:[uk.db]bank_system
cont>   CREATE STORAGE AREA customer_area
cont>      FILENAME $222$dua25:[uk.db]bank_cust
cont>      ALLOCATION IS 1000 PAGES
cont>   CREATE STORAGE AREA account_area
cont>      FILENAME $222$dua26:[uk.db]bank_acct
cont>      PAGE FORMAT IS MIXED;
                 .
                 .
                 .
```

This CREATE DATABASE statement performs a number of functions. A storage area named RDB$SYSTEM is created in a file named BANK_SYSTEM.RDA to hold the Rdb system tables. A storage area named CUSTOMER_AREA is created in the file BANK_CUST.RDA, and a storage area named ACCOUNT_AREA is created in a file named BANK_ACCT.RDA. Ten storage area slots are reserved for the future addition of storage areas to the database.

Many qualifiers may be added to the CREATE STORAGE AREA clauses; for example, an initial file allocation has been specified for the storage area CUSTOMER_AREA and the storage area ACCOUNT_AREA has been specified with PAGE FORMAT IS MIXED. Page formats will be discussed shortly. Other qualifiers that may be added to the CREATE STORAGE AREA statement include:

- Extent parameters

- Page size

- SPAM intervals

- Thresholds

- Page or row locking

- Snapshot parameters

4.3.1   Creating Storage Maps

To specify which tables use which storage areas, the database designer uses storage maps. To specify which indexes use which storage areas, however, the STORE clause is used in the CREATE INDEX statement. Mapping indexes to storage areas is discussed in Chapter 5.

Previously, it was seen that storage areas are added as part of the CREATE DATABASE statement. In the context of this statement, domains, tables, and storage maps may be created. They may be added outside the CREATE DATABASE statement by attaching to the database and submitting the commands, but it is important to note that the CREATE STORAGE MAP statement should have been executed while the tables are still empty; that is, no data has been loaded into them. A storage map used by the BANKING database could be created as follows:

```
Tables and Domains have been created
            .
            .
            .
SQL> CREATE STORAGE MAP customer_map FOR customer
cont>   STORE IN customer_area;
```

This is a simple mapping with the CUSTOMER table placed in the CUSTOMER_AREA storage area. The relationship between the table, map, and area is shown in Figure 4.4.

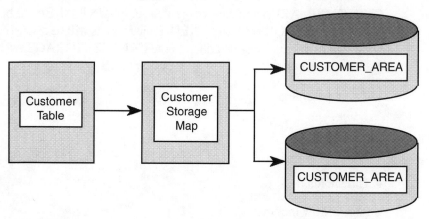

Figure 4.4 The Relationship Between a Table, a Map and Its Areas

A table is mapped by only one storage map. A storage map maps only one table. However, a table may be mapped to one or many storage areas.

Qualifiers may be placed on the CREATE STORAGE MAP statement. For example:

```
SQL> CREATE STORAGE MAP account_map FOR account
cont> STORE IN account_area
cont> DISABLE COMPRESSION;
```

In this example, the database designer has specified that the data in the ACCOUNT table is not to be compressed by Rdb.

The way data is stored inside the storage area also may be specified by the database designer. Typically, the method of storing the table rows with respect to an index is specified. For example:

```
SQL> CREATE STORAGE MAP account_map FOR account
cont> STORE IN account_area
cont> DISABLE COMPRESSION
cont> PLACEMENT VIA INDEX account_index;
```

The placement of rows relative to indexes is discussed in Chapter 5. The relationship between the table, map, index, and area is shown in Figure 4.5. A STORE clause in the index definition specifies in which storage area the index is to be placed.

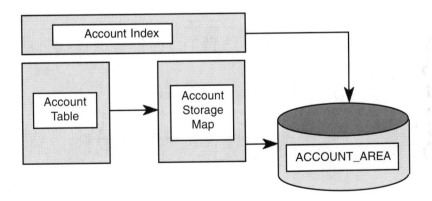

Figure 4.5 The Relationship Between a Table, an Index, a Map, and an Area

4.3.2   **Uniform and Mixed Page Formats**

The database designer may choose to create storage areas with UNIFORM or MIXED page formats. A database page is the structure used to store and locate data in an Rdb database.The choice of page format is determined by its use in terms of the data to be stored in it and how that data is to be accessed.

UNIFORM Page Format

The database designer should choose UNIFORM page format when the tables to be stored are likely to be accessed sequentially. In addition, sorted indexes are usually placed in storage areas with UNIFORM page format. Hashed indexes may not be, however. If the storage area is created with a UNIFORM page format, the database pages in the storage area will only hold rows from a specific table or index nodes from a specific index. Rdb assigns groups of pages, known as clumps, in the storage area. These clumps will only hold rows from a specific table or index nodes from a specific index. Figure 4.6 shows a storage area with a uniform page format. Space management (SPAM) pages will be explained later in this chapter.

Typically, a table or sorted index will require a number of clumps to reside in, which may or may not be adjacent in the storage area. The size of a clump is a function of the buffer length (a database-wide parameter) and is calculated by dividing the buffer length by the page size.

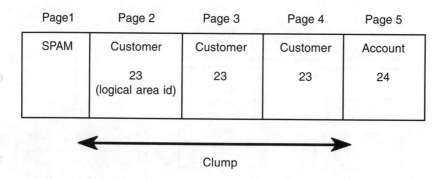

Figure 4.6 A Uniform Format Storage Area

Note that the buffer length is specified on the CREATE DATABASE statement. It cannot be changed with the ALTER DATABASE statement but can be increased during an RMU/RESTORE operation. An SQL EXPORT followed by an SQL IMPORT may be used to increase or decrease the buffer length. This does not apply to the number of database buffers. These may be set on a per-user basis (strictly speaking, per attach) by setting the logical name RDM$BIND_BUFFERS to the number of buffers desired, or by setting the value on a database-wide basis with the ALTER DATABASE statement.

Sequential scans of a table, in other words non-indexed access, is very efficient when using UNIFORM page format. Rdb does not look for the data in the clumps that it knows contain data from other tables. This saves physical I/Os to disk. Figure 4.6 shows a storage area that has been created with a UNIFORM page format. The RDB$SYSTEM storage area mentioned previously is always created with a UNIFORM page format. If a page format is not specified on the CREATE STORAGE AREA command, the default action is to create a storage area with UNIFORM page format.

MIXED Page Format

If the database designer creates a storage area with MIXED page format, each page in the storage area may be used to store rows from any table in the area, sorted index nodes, and hash buckets. Hash buckets are structures used by hash indexes and are described in Chapter 5.

The database designer must be careful not to assign many tables and indexes to such an area, otherwise each page may end up with a hodgepodge of rows and index nodes that are ill-equipped for any query. The goal is to store only a few objects in an area with a MIXED page format, including only objects that tend to be accessed together. This will optimize certain important queries.

If the database designer wishes to use hashed indexes, the storage area must be created with a MIXED page format. Hashed indexes only speed up queries if the full value of the hash key is known. If this kind of access to a table is required, a hashed index may be created for the table. The database designer would store the table and the hashed index in a storage area with MIXED page format. In the BANKING database, for example, the customer rows are normally accessed by the column CUSTOMER_NO. In this case, the CUSTOMER_NO column is always specified in full by the query, and the end-user typically is looking for a row in the CUSTOMER table that exactly

Figure 4.7 A Mixed Format Storage Area

Page1	Page 2	Page 3	Page 4
SPAM	Customer (23)	Customer	Customer
	Account (24)	Account	Account
	Account (24)	Account	Account
	Account (24)	Account	Account

System Records

matches the customer number supplied. The database designer may create a hashed index on the CUSTOMER table based on the column CUSTOMER_NO and store the CUSTOMER table and the hashed index in the same storage area with a MIXED page format, in this case CUSTOMER_AREA.

Typically, the database designer will wish to store rows from different tables on the same page. In our BANKING database example, it would be possible to store the ACCOUNT rows belonging to a customer physically next to the CUSTOMER row on the same database page. For transactions that joined CUSTOMER rows and their ACCOUNT rows together to satisfy a particular query, this will result in very high performance because, hopefully, only one physical disk I/O would be needed to retrieve the CUSTOMER row. The associated ACCOUNT rows, residing on the same page, will be retrieved at the same time. Organizing data in this manner is known as coincidental clustering. Figure 4.7 shows a storage area with a mixed format where a customer row and all its accounts reside on the same database page. Note that rows with different logical area identifiers (23 and 24) may be stored on the same database page. In the uniform format area, they had to be stored on database pages in different clumps.

4.3.3 Partitioning Data in Multifile Databases

The fact that the database designer may create storage areas on separate disk drives to spread the disk I/O load has already been mentioned. Suppose, though, a table is subject to particularly heavy access. Placing the storage area that holds the table on a single disk drive may still result in a disk I/O bottleneck.

The I/O rate that the disk drive is able to sustain is not large enough to support the access requirements of the table. In this situation the database designer may partition the table over a number of storage areas, which then are placed on separate disk drives. This way, the disk I/O bottleneck is overcome. The database designer also may place snapshot files on their own disk drives to alleviate disk I/O problems. Snapshot files are described later in this chapter. Chapter 5 discusses how indexes may be partitioned.

The rows of a table may be grouped by rows in particular storage areas according to column values and the storage map specified. These storage areas then may be created on separate disk drives. In the BANKING database, for example, suppose the database designer wished to partition the CUSTOMER table. The database designer could create a number of storage areas in which to place the partitions. Suppose it was decided to create three partitions. These could be named:

- CUSTOMER_AREA_1

- CUSTOMER_AREA_2

- CUSTOMER_AREA_3

The database designer then may create a storage map that specifies which CUSTOMER rows are stored in which storage area. For example:

```
SQL> CREATE STORAGE MAP customer_map FOR customer
cont> STORE USING (customer_no)
cont>    IN customer_area_1 WITH LIMIT OF ('3000000000')
cont>    IN customer_area_2 WITH LIMIT OF ('6000000000')
cont>    OTHERWISE IN customer_area_3;
```

When CUSTOMER rows are added to the database, they will be stored in the appropriate storage area, depending on the value of the CUSTOMER_NO column. When the rows are retrieved, only the appropriate storage areas will be accessed, depending on the retrieval method. Figure 4.8 shows the relationship between the customer table and the three storage areas created to hold it.

Hint: These three storage areas may be created initially on the same disk drive and then moved to other disk drives with RMU/MOVE_AREA when the single disk becomes a disk I/O bottleneck.

Figure 4.8 Mapping the CUSTOMER Table to Three Single Storage Areas

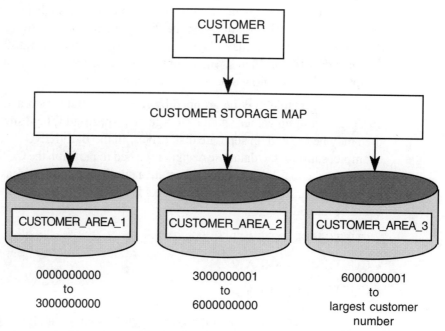

Hint: In the case of sequential scans of the database, even though a particular range of the column CUSTOMER_NO may be specified, Rdb will scan all the partitions. This is because Rdb would not physically move CUSTOMER rows between partitions when the value of CUSTOMER_NO was modified. Therefore, scanning only one partition would not guarantee that all the rows satisfying the condition would be found.

If in the future the database designer decides that more partitions are needed to support access to the table, the SQL EXPORT and SQL IMPORT commands may be used to restructure the database. The ALTER STORAGE MAP statement also may be used to restructure partitions, as will be discussed in detail in Chapter 10. Using ALTER STORAGE MAP is a quicker and simpler option.

An important point to note is that partitioning is done at the physical level, not the logical level. This means that partitioning is transparent to the application program or end-user. The database designer can manipulate the physical storage areas that constitute a table without having to modify application programs.

4.4   DISPLAYING DATABASE PAGES

Once the database storage areas have been created, the RMU/DUMP command is used to display the contents of the database pages in them. This may be used in the following ways:

- RMU/DUMP/AREA

- RMU/DUMP/LAREA

- RMU/DUMP/SNAPSHOTS

The RMU/DUMP/AREA command allows the database designer to examine pages from database storage areas.

The RMU/DUMP/LAREA command displays pages from logical areas within a database storage file. The database designer examines pages allocated to a table with this command.

The RMU/DUMP/SNAPSHOTS command is used by the database designer to examine pages in snapshot files.

In a single-file database, there is only one data storage file which has the file extension .RDB. In a multifile database, there may be many storage files with file extension of .RDA. The .RDB file contains pointers to these. To examine pages in a specific storage area, the storage area name must be used in the RMU/DUMP command. For example:

```
$ RMU/DUMP/AREA=customer_area  eurobank:[uk.db]banking
```

In this example, database pages from the storage area CUSTOMER_AREA are displayed.

Tables in a database have their own logical areas. Each table has one logical area, which cannot be shared with other tables. Indexes for a table also are associated with a logical area. All the indexes for one table share a logical area in a single-file database. A logical area consists of groups of pages reserved for rows for a particular table.

In a single-file database or multifile database with UNIFORM page format storage areas, the first page of a logical storage area is the area bit map page, or ABM. Area bit maps are discussed later in this chapter. A storage area with a MIXED page format does not use area bit map pages, and the RMU/DUMP/LAREA command cannot be used to display logical areas for such storage areas.

The RMU/DUMP/LAREA command might be used to examine pages in the logical area associated with the CUSTOMER table. For example:

```
$  RMU/DUMP/LAREA=customer  eurobank:[uk.db]banking
```

4.5   THE DATABASE PAGE STRUCTURE

Now that the placement of tables in storage areas has been discussed, we can explore the contents of the storage areas. Database storage areas are composed of *database pages*, which may be one or more disk blocks in size. On OpenVMS systems a disk block is 512 bytes long. Page size in a database storage area is normally specified in units of disk blocks.

Hint: On OpenVMS systems, if a database storage area consists of one block page, then the number of pages divided by 2000 gives the storage area size in Megabytes.

A database page typically holds rows from tables or index structures. Certain types of pages hold special control information, which will be discussed later. A database page, besides holding the user's data, also holds certain fixed and dynamic information. This information may be broken down as follows:

• Page header

• Line index

• Transaction sequence number (TSN) index

• Free space

Figure 4.9 The Format of a Database Page

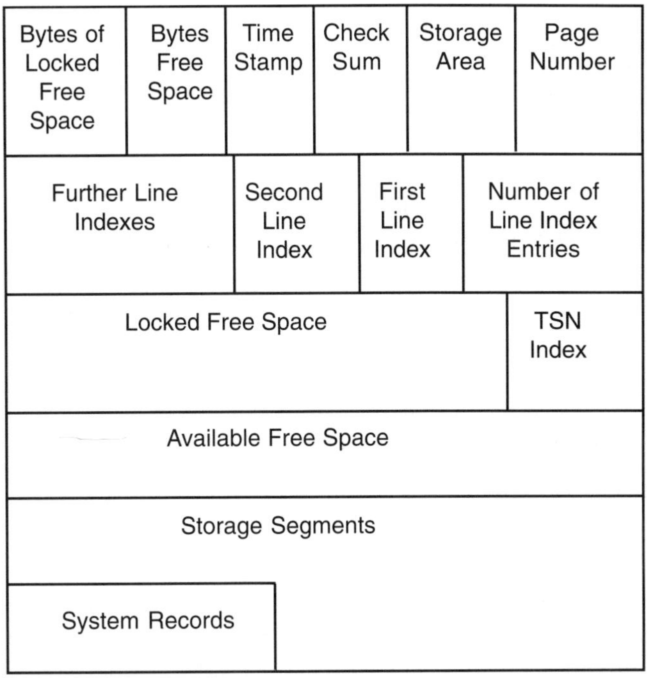

Bytes of Locked Free Space	Bytes Free Space	Time Stamp	Check Sum	Storage Area	Page Number
Further Line Indexes		Second Line Index	First Line Index	Number of Line Index Entries	
Locked Free Space				TSN Index	
Available Free Space					
Storage Segments					
System Records					

- Locked free space

- Page tail

- System record

Figure 4.9 shows the layout of these different components.

4.5.1   The Page Header

Every page in a database storage area is numbered. The *page header* contains the page number and the storage area number, as well as a checksum value to maintain the integrity of a database page. Also stored in the page header is the time and date that the page was last written back to the database; that is, the last time the page was modified. If the page contains data and fixed overhead, then the page header also contains the value of the free space remaining on the database page. If data has been deleted from a page, free space becomes available on the database page but is marked as locked. In this case, the page header contains a value specifying the amount of locked free space on the page. Locked free space will be described shortly.

4.5.2   The Line Index

The *line index* grows and shrinks as rows are stored on and deleted from the database page. Each line index entry points to a row. Strictly speaking, rows should be called storage segments because a row is only one of the objects that may be stored on a database page. The line index entries consist of the offset address and length of the storage segment. The line index mechanism may be thought of as a method of indirect addressing. The storage segments may be physically moved within the database page, but the line index entry that points to the storage segment remains constant.

4.5.3   Transaction Sequence Number Index

Each storage segment is associated with a *transaction sequence number* (TSN), which allows Rdb to remember the last transaction that updated the storage segment. Transaction sequence number entries and line index entries are stored so that the *n*th line index entry and the *n*th transaction sequence number entry relate to the same storage segment. The transaction sequence number entries follow the line index entries. If a new storage segment is stored on a page, the transaction sequence number entries are shuffled along the page until there is space to store the new line index entry.

4.5.4   Locked Free Space

The part of the database page that separates the last transaction-sequence-number index and the storage segments, called *free space*, is available to store new storage segments. Just because there is free space does not guarantee that a storage segment will be stored, however. There may appear to be enough free space but the database designer may have specified threshold values that cause Rdb to search elsewhere for space. Thresholds are discussed later in this chapter.

As storage segments are added to the database page, free space is used up. Line index entries and transaction sequence number entries also encroach on free space from the opposite direction until there is none left. When this happens Rdb must find a new database page with available free space to add new storage segments.

Suppose Rdb deletes a storage segment. Before the transaction has committed, there is no guarantee that the transaction will not abort and roll back the deleted storage segment. Therefore, Rdb must guarantee that the deleted storage segment can be stored back on the original database page; that is, it must ensure that there is sufficient free space on the original database page. Rdb does this by using the concept of *locked* free space. When a storage segment is deleted, the space that becomes free is locked. It cannot be used by any transaction other than the transaction that deleted the storage segment. In fact, the space does not become available for use by other transactions until the user whose transaction locked the space has detached from the database by issuing a DISCONNECT statement. This may seem strange, but the method is designed to reduce contention among users for free space.

Hint: When deleting rows with a program that stays attached to the database for a long time, locked free space will not be available to other users. In the case of systems that use dedicated database server processes that attach to a database and stay attached, it may be advisable to detach from the database and then attach again to unlock the free space at periodic intervals. This situation is more common in transaction processing systems that provide a continuous service to users. With Digital's transaction processing monitors, such as DEC ACMS, this may be done in such a way that users are unaware that the reattachments to the database have occurred.

4.5.5   Storage Segments

Typically, a database page holds a number of storage segments. If a storage segment is too large to fit on a page, Rdb splits it into primary segment and a number of secondary segments.

Why would a user's storage segment be too large to fit on a page? There are probably two main reasons. First of all, a table in the database may have rows consisting of many columns, making the row length disproportionately long compared to other tables in the database. The database designer may decide not to place this table in its own storage area with a large page size. Instead, the database designer decides that a small amount of fragmentation is acceptable, and places the table in an area with other tables.

A more common cause for fragmentation is the expansion of rows that already reside on a database page. Rdb gives the database designer the option of compressing or not compressing data. Data frequently is compressed as the size of the storage areas and the disk requirements (and, presumably, the financial outlay) are reduced.

Suppose, though, a table contains four 30-byte columns to hold address data. If only a fraction of these columns are used to store the address data, considerable space is saved through data compression. But suppose after the storage segments have been stored, the addresses are modified in a way that they take up more space on the page. A point will be reached when there is not enough room on the page to accommodate the expanded storage segment. In this case, Rdb will fragment the row, and the secondary segment will be stored on a new database page where there is space. When storing a row, Rdb allows for an extra 10 bytes of space in case the row becomes fragmented in the future. This is to allow a primary fragment to be formed. It is useful to know if fragmentation is occurring in the database. To retrieve fragmented rows could take two or more disk I/Os, as opposed to one disk I/O for a row that is not fragmented. The level of fragmentation in the database should be checked with the RMU/ANALYZE command.

Note that adding columns to a table definition and placing values in rows containing null will also eventually cause rows to expand and potentially fragment.

Suppose that no database page is found with available space in which to store a new row. This is not a problem with Rdb. Its dynamic space management comes to the rescue and the database storage area automatically extends. Database pages with free space become available without the intervention of the database administrator or system manager and without the user being aware that a database storage area has extended.

Hint: It is a good idea to pre-allocate space, if possible, when creating storage areas. Although Rdb dynamically extends a storage area, there is no guarantee that the operating system will allocate a disk extent that is contiguous with existing extents. This may result in more disk head movement and a small performance penalty. To see if a storage area has extended, the RMU/DUMP/HEADER command is used. The number of times each storage area has extended will be reported. Note that it is very important to correctly size storage areas used for hashed indexes. This is discussed in more detail in Chapter 5.

Typically, the types of storage segment that are stored on a database page are:

- Storage segments stored by a user (table rows)

- List segments (segmented-strings)

- Index node segments

The storage segments are stored with header information and a fragment indicator.

The user-stored segments contain user data. List storage segments contain a pointer to the actual segments, which hold the user data. Lists are designed to hold large amounts of unstructured data, such as graphics, voice, or image data. Rdb does not know or care about the contents of the list; it merely knows the length of the segments. The length of a segment is anything from 0 to 64 Kbytes and is specified by Rdb with the special name RDB$LENGTH. The value of a segment is given the special name RDB$VALUE. These names are used to manipulate lists.

In Rdb lists are stored by default in the RDB$SYSTEM storage area. However, it is possible to define an alternative default list storage area on the CREATE DATABASE statement. The CREATE STORAGE MAP statement allows the database designer to specify that:

- lists from different tables are to be stored in the same storage area

- lists from a single table are to be stored in their own storage area

- different lists from the same table be stored in different storage areas

An example of manipulating segmented strings was given in Chapter 3.

Index node segments are stored on a database page the same way as any other type of segment. An index node segment contains at least three index key entries. The two types of index node segments are sorted and hashed.

If a table is stored in a UNIFORM page format storage area, the sorted index or indexes are stored in a logical area within the storage area. Each sorted index has its own hierarchical tree structure consisting of a collection of index nodes that are linked together. A database storage area with a MIXED page format may contain a number of rows from tables and their hashed indexes. These may be located together. See Chapter 5 for more information on hashed index placement.

4.5.6 The Page Tail

The page tail comes at the end of the storage segments and usually contains snapshot file information, which is described later in this chapter.

4.5.7 System Record

Each page in an area with MIXED page format contains a system record pointed at by line index entry zero. If there are no hash buckets on the page, the system record typically will take up 5 bytes of space. If a page contains a hashed index, the system record will then contain a pointer to the hash bucket, with the pointer usually adding an extra 6 to 10 bytes to its length. The system record will contain as many pointers as there are hashed indexes defined on that database page.

4.5.8 The Database Key

Now that the format of a database page has been explained, it is possible to explain the concept of a *database key*. A database key or *dbkey* is a pointer to a storage segment on a page. It is used for fast, direct access to a row and may be specified in SQL statements such as SELECT and INSERT. The database key contains the database logical area number, the page number within the area, and the line number. The length of a database key is typically 8 bytes when referring to base tables and longer when referring to database views. Digital provides a formula for calculating the length of the database key in bytes when a view is involved.

The formula is:

8 * number of tables named in the view

The length of time for which a database key stays valid may be specified when the program attaches to the DATABASE or on the CREATE DATABASE statement. The choice is:

- SCOPE IS TRANSACTION – The duration of a transaction (default)

- SCOPE IS ATTACH – The duration of a database attachment

The behavior of Rdb with respect to the re-use of database keys differs depending upon which of the above options is taken.

If a user attaches to the database with a scope is transaction and deletes a record, the database key of that record can be re-used as soon as that user commits the transaction. Clearly, if the user rolls back the transaction the record will not be deleted and the database key will not be available for re-use.

If a user attaches to the database with a scope is attach and deletes a record, the database key of that record cannot be re-used until the user detaches from the database.

Note that if all users of the database attached with scope is transaction, then the database key scope is transaction for all users. If on the other hand only one user attaches with scope is attach, then the database key scope is attach for all users. In fact, as long as one user is attached with scope is attach, database keys will not be re-used on the database.

Suppose a user, therefore, attaches with scope is attach and deletes rows from the database and then detaches. The space freed up by the deleted records is available for re-use, however, if users are active with scope is attach, the database key will not be available for reuse. In this case, although the space freed up by a deleted record is re-used, a new database key must be allocated which will require a line index entry (4 bytes) and a TSN index entry (4 bytes).

Hint: Do not write applications where the application expects the value of the database key to be stable across database attaches. It probably will be; however, this is not guaranteed by Digital. An SQL IMPORT will almost certainly cause the value of a row's database key to change.

4.6   SPACE AREA MANAGEMENT (SPAM) PAGES

When Rdb is inserting storage segments (rows from tables or index nodes) in the database, it must find database pages that contain enough free space to hold the new storage segments. When a database is created, the storage areas contain pages that have ample free space. Once many storage segments have been inserted, it is important that Rdb does not waste time, processing power, and disk I/O reading database pages into a buffer to insert new storage segments, only to find that these pages do not contain enough free space. This could be disastrous for performance, with many physical I/Os to disk being performed to find free space for each storage segment. To ensure that this situation does not occur, Rdb uses a sophisticated space management scheme based around *space management pages*, often known as SPAM pages.

A space management page contains a map of a range of database pages, with each entry specifying the free space that is available for each database page in the range. Figure 4.10 shows space management page entries pointing to the appropriate data pages.

Figure 4.10 SPAM Entries Pointing to Data Pages

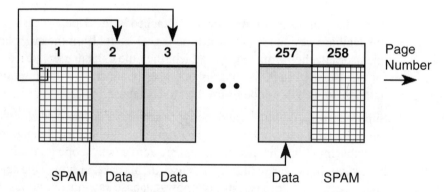

Space management pages are used in single-file and in multifile databases and in database storage areas with UNIFORM and MIXED page format. In multifile databases that contain storage areas with UNIFORM page format space management is handled the same way as it is in single-file databases. In this situation, only one storage segment type may be stored on a database page, simplifying the space management page entries. Rdb always knows the size of the storage segment that is to be stored. However, if compression is enabled for a table, the actual space taken up by a row will vary for each row depending on how effective the compression has been. Also, non-unique sorted indexes may contain duplicate nodes of a different size to the higher level nodes. Even in uniform page format storage areas, therefore, storage segments may be of varying sizes and as we shall see shortly, threshold values may need to be specified.

In multifile databases that contain storage areas with MIXED page format, more than one storage segment type may be stored on a database page. In this situation, Rdb cannot know the size of the next storage segment to be stored. Therefore, to manage space in MIXED page format areas, by default, Rdb uses the concept of threshold values. Threshold values may be specified as part of the CREATE STORAGE AREA and ALTER STORAGE AREA statements. The space management pages do not hold the exact value of the free space available in a database page; rather they hold a value that indicates when certain thresholds have been exceeded. Holding the exact value would place an unacceptable processing burden on Rdb and is unnecessary.

The database designer also may specify the interval between space management pages as part of the CREATE STORAGE AREA clause. Each space management page manages a number of database pages. Therefore, the structure is one space management page, followed by the database pages it manages, followed by the next space management page.

The specification of the number of space management pages in a storage area has an impact on performance because it either increases or decreases the time spent searching for free space. The database designer has control over the number of pages managed by a space management page, that is the interval between them, for MIXED page format storage areas but not UNIFORM page format storage areas.

4.6.1 Space Management in Storage Areas with UNIFORM Page Format

In a single-file database or multifile database with UNIFORM page format storage areas, the space management page is the same size as the data page it manages; that is, it is the same number of 512-byte disk blocks. Therefore, a space management page contains a finite number of entries, the number being limited by its size. This also regulates the frequency at which a space management page must occur in a storage area. Given a database page size and, therefore, a space management page size, the intervals between the space management pages in a database storage area are found from Table 4.1.

Table 4.1 SPAM Intervals for Various Page Sizes

Page Size (Blocks)	SPAM Interval (Pages)
1	531
2	1089
3	1647
4	2205

These cannot be changed. Each entry in a space management page contains an entry for each database page it manages and an entry specifying a fullness threshold value. Each of these entries is two bits long. For UNIFORM page format, by default, database storage areas may take a value 0 (neither bit set) or 3 (both bits set). The value 0 denotes that a database page is not full, and the value 3 denotes that a database page is full. For database storage areas with MIXED page format, by default, this entry may take different values.

A database designer may, however, override the default case and specify threshold values for areas containing UNIFORM page format. The threshold values for UNIFORM page format areas are set on the CREATE STORAGE MAP statement or the CREATE INDEX statement. How thresholds work will be discussed shortly.

Hint: If a storage area is created with an initial allocation of 1000 pages, each one block long, Table 4.1 shows that two space management pages will be needed. These space management pages do not count against the storage area's initial allocation, so if the RMU/DUMP/HEADER command is used to check the size of the storage area, a value of 1002 pages will be found even though the initial allocation was specified as 1000 pages. So these extra pages are space management pages, not poor arithmetic on the part of Rdb.

Two other types of pages are found in database storage areas with UNIFORM page format. These are *area bit map* (ABM) pages and *area inventory pages* (AIP). Together, they optimize sequential searches in a table by informing Rdb which space management pages manage which database pages for a particular logical area. This avoids a situation where Rdb could be checking space management pages that are not relevant. The function these two page types perform is critical for good performance in very large storage areas.

4.6.2   Space Management in Storage Areas with MIXED Page Format

The space management page entries in storage areas with MIXED page format (or in UNIFORM page format if threshold values have been set) are updated whenever the total amount of data stored on a database page managed by a particular entry exceeds a threshold value. Consider what happens when rows are inserted into a table. Rdb decides that it will store a particular row on a particular database page, known as the *target* page. The way Rdb chooses the target page depends on whether explicit placement (using the PLACEMENT VIA clause in the storage map) is specified or not. If the target page is full, Rdb typically checks the other pages in the database buffer for free space. If they are full, Rdb looks at the space management page that manages the target page to find if another page contains enough free space in which to store the row. If there is not enough free space on the database pages in that SPAM interval, the search for free space continues. Rdb only has to look at the space management pages to find free space; it does not have to search the data pages themselves. This is a very good strategy where large storage areas are involved.

The interval between the space management pages in a MIXED page format storage area may be specified by the database designer. The interval between space management pages and the threshold values is specified as part of the CREATE STORAGE MAP and ALTER STORAGE MAP statements.

Hint: If the database designer decides that new INTERVAL and THRESHOLD values should be applied to an existing database the RMU/MOVE_AREA command may be used.

The default number of database pages managed by a space management page in a MIXED page format area is 216. Figure 4.11 shows the layout of space management pages and database pages in this situation. Of course, the database designer may choose an interval other than the default as long as it does not exceed the maximum interval, which is a function of the page size of the storage area. The minimum value for the interval is 216 pages, which is the

Figure 4.11 SPAM Intervals in Storage Areas

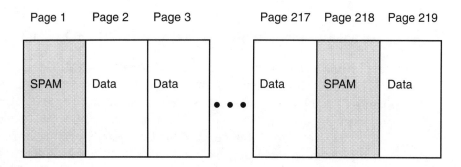

default. Digital provides a formula for calculating the maximum value for the interval:

((Page size in blocks * 512) - 22) * 4

Therefore, a page size of one block allows a maximum interval of 1960 database pages, and a page size of two blocks allows a maximum interval of 4008 pages.

4.6.3   How Space Management Page Thresholds Work

We said that the space management page entries in storage areas with MIXED page format (or UNIFORM page format if threshold values have been set) are updated whenever the total amount of data stored on a database page managed by a particular entry exceeds a threshold value. The database designer may specify up to three threshold values. By default, they are 70%, 85%, and 95% for MIXED page format areas. (For UNIFORM page format areas the default is in fact (0,0,0) which means that a page is marked as full once there is not enough space to store an uncompressed record.)

Explaining how space management page thresholds work is easiest with an example. Suppose that the BANKING database has been created such that the database designer has specified that the threshold values for the ACCOUNT_AREA are 70%, 80%, and 90%.

These threshold values define four ranges of guaranteed free space on a database page in the ACCOUNT_AREA. The free space available in a database will fall into one of these ranges at some point. Given these threshold values, the ranges of guaranteed free space are:

- 30% free space (0% to 70% full)

- 20% free space (70% to 80% full)

- 10% free space (80% to 90% full)

- 0% free space (90% to 100% full)

If a space management page entry shows that a database page is in the 90% to 100% full range, Rdb will not attempt to use that database page to store a storage segment. Imagine that Rdb wishes to insert a row in the ACCOUNT table in the ACCOUNT_AREA storage area and the size of the row is 25% of a data page. Rdb will not be interested in any database page other than those pages in the first threshold-fullness range because database pages in the second threshold-fullness range only have 20% guaranteed free space.

Then suppose that an application program, which adds new customer accounts to the database, starts to insert rows in the ACCOUNT table. The rows in the ACCOUNT table are stored according to the appropriate storage map, in this case ACCOUNT_MAP. This storage map specifies that the rows are to be placed via the hashed index ACCOUNT_INDEX (see Chapter 5 where hashed indexes and placement is described). Essentially, when Rdb inserts a row, a hashing algorithm chooses a target page in which to attempt to store that row.

Suppose database page 23 in this storage area is empty apart from the fixed overhead described earlier in this chapter. The application program inserts a row and the hash algorithm calculates that the row should be stored on that empty database page. During the application program run, a number of rows hash to this database page. Rdb inserts rows into this target page. So long as the target page can hold the inserted rows, everything goes smoothly.

However, eventually a point will be reached when the database page is full (the third threshold level is crossed). Rdb then must look elsewhere for a database page to hold the row. If no other database pages in the buffer contain enough free space, the SPAM page that controls the interval in which the target page belongs is now searched for a database page that contains enough free space to hold a new row.

Say, for example, that Rdb finds database page 42 and inserts rows in it. Eventually, a point will be reached when database page 42 becomes 65% full, leaving only 35% of the free space available on the page. However, the database page is still in the first threshold-fullness range; that is, it is less than 70% full.

Then the user begins to insert a group of new customer accounts. A row is inserted and the hash algorithm calculates a target page, as it did before. Suppose database page 23 is the target page again. That page is full, so Rdb must look for free space. It looks at the space management page, as before, and finds page 42 – our 65% full database page. If the row takes up 13% of the available space on an empty page, in our example there would be enough free space (30% guaranteed) in which to store the row. It is, therefore, stored on database page 42, which now becomes 78% full. That leaves 22% free space. Now, however, database page 42 is in the second threshold-fullness range, which guarantees that 20% of the database page is still available. The application inserts another row, and page 42 is chosen again because the space management page entry shows that 20% free space is available there. This amount is enough, so the row is inserted. Database page 42 is now 91% full, so it falls into the fourth threshold-fullness range as threshold level three is crossed.

If the application program continues to insert rows whose target page is calculated to be 23, Rdb will continue to check the space management page. Database page 42 is now in the fourth threshold-fullness range, however. With the next entry, Rdb ignores this page, therefore, and instead looks for a space management page entry pointing to a database page that guarantees enough free space for the data. Keep in mind that the database designer could store more than one table in an area. If the application program tried to insert a row from a different table that only required 6% free space, our target page would still not have been chosen because it is in the fourth threshold-fullness range.

Calculating optimal threshold values in a storage area is not a trivial operation. If the database designer is not sure which threshold values would be good choices, the defaults should be taken. Choosing incorrect threshold values may degrade performance. A good way to choose optimal threshold values is to calculate what the thresholds should be and then create a small test database with these threshold values set for the required storage areas. Some rows should be inserted and then the database pages analyzed with the RMU/DUMP command to see if the expected behavior matches the actual behavior. Remember that Rdb uses the uncompressed size of a row to calculate the free space necessary to insert that row. So if data compression is being used, the designer may expect a row to fit on a page where it does not. If the threshold values need to be changed, this can be done with the RMU/RESTORE or RMU/MOVE_AREA command.

Hint: Use RMU/DUMP/HEADER/OPT=DEBUG to see how threshold percent values translate into threshold byte values. The SPAM_T1, SPAM_T2 and SPAM_T3 fields are the ones to check.

4.6.4   Snapshot Files

Besides having files for user data and housekeeping information, Rdb databases also hold another type of file. Called the *snapshot* file, it has a file extension of .SNP. A single-file Rdb database has one snapshot file; a multifile database has one snapshot file for each storage area. The database designer may specify the size of each snapshot file and its location but not whether such files exist. Snapshot files are always present and are necessary to support such activities as READ ONLY transactions and the online backup facility. If READ ONLY transactions and online-backups are not needed, the snapshot mechanism may be disabled. This means that the snapshot files are present although they are not used. To understand why Rdb uses snapshot files, it is necessary to understand the concept of a snapshot transaction.

4.6.5   Snapshot Transactions

A snapshot transaction, also called a *read-only* transaction, is started by issuing a SET TRANSACTION statement with a READ ONLY clause. For example:

```
SQL> SET TRANSACTION READ ONLY;
```

A snapshot transaction ensures that the data in the database is always seen the way it was when the transaction started. This is true regardless of however long the transaction is active. It is almost as if Rdb takes a photograph of the database when the transaction starts, freezing the database in time; hence the name snapshot transaction. This consistent view of the data is one of the advantages of using snapshot transactions.

In the default state, snapshots are enabled. Transactions that update the database when snapshots are enabled write the *before* images of the updated rows into the relevant snapshot file. Rows, of course, are not the only objects that could be updated. Index nodes are also written to the snapshot file. A snapshot transaction is able to read these before images in the snapshot file and it does not need to hold read locks to maintain consistency. Because of this fact, the second major advantage of using snapshot files becomes apparent. Snapshot transactions do not participate in lock conflict situations with updating transactions. An end of year report, for example, could run for hours analyzing masses of data in the database without being involved in lock conflicts with updating transactions.There is one instance where snapshot transactions are involved in lock conflicts with other transactions. This occurs when another transaction has started that has reserved the database areas in EXCLUSIVE mode. In this case a snapshot cannot start. The converse is also true.

To ensure that snapshot transactions only see data modified by transactions that complete before the snapshot transaction starts, Rdb uses the concept of a transaction sequence number (TSN). These numbers were mentioned earlier while discussing the structure of a database page. When a transaction starts, a transaction sequence number is assigned to it. If a storage segment is updated by the transaction, the transaction sequence number is associated with that storage segment. If a SHOW TRANSACTION statement is issued after a snapshot transaction starts, the transaction sequence number values held by the storage segments that the snapshot transaction can and cannot see are returned. For example:

```
SQL> SET TRANSACTION READ ONLY;
SQL> SHOW TRANSACTION;
  Transaction information:
     Statement constraint evaluation is off

On the default alias
Transaction characteristics:
     Read only
Transaction information returned by base system:
a snapshot transaction is in progress
- all transaction sequence numbers (TSNs) less than 144 are visible
- all TSNs greater than or equal to 144 are invisible
- session ID number is 24
```

Figure 4.12 A Snapshot Transaction with Updating Transactions

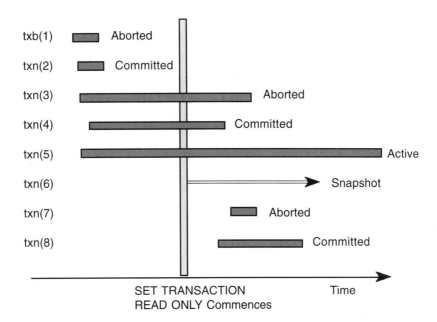

The example shows that this snapshot transaction can see the storage segments updated by transactions with transaction sequence numbers of less than 144. It cannot see the storage segments updated by transactions with transaction sequence numbers greater than or equal to 144. The fact that the transaction characteristics information shows it is read-only proves this is a snapshot.

From the previous example, we deduce that transactions with transaction sequence numbers of less than 144 had completed before the snapshot transaction started. Figure 4.12 shows a snapshot transaction starting.

In the figure, the snapshot transaction only sees the changes made by *txn(2)* because it completed before the snapshot transaction started. *Txn(1)* rolled back its changes, so the snapshot transaction does not see them. In this example, *txn(2)* would have been a transaction with a transaction sequence number of less than 144. The snapshot transaction cannot see *txn(3)* and *txn(4)* because these transactions completed after the snapshot transaction started. The snapshot transaction cannot see *txn(5)* because it has not yet completed and, therefore, will complete after the snapshot transaction started. The snapshot transaction cannot see *txn(7)* and *txn(8)* because they started after it.

4.6.6   **Disabling Snapshot Transactions**

From the previous discussion, it is evident that snapshot files could experience
high disk I/O activity. Snapshots may be placed on separate disk devices to
spread the disk I/O load, but Rdb also can disable the snapshot mechanism. If
a transaction is started that reserves an area in EXCLUSIVE mode, it must by
definition be the only transaction accessing that area. Therefore, no snapshot
transactions may be started on that area, in which case there is no need for the
EXCLUSIVE transaction to write any before images to the relevant snapshot
file because they are never needed. Typically, load programs should use
EXCLUSIVE mode.

Another method of disabling the snapshot mechanism is by using the ALTER
DATABASE statement. For example:

```
SQL> ALTER DATABASE FILENAME eurobank:[uk.db]banking SNAPSHOT IS DISABLED;
```

The snapshot mechanism may be re-enabled in a similar fashion:

```
SQL> ALTER DATABASE FILENAME eurobank:[uk.db]banking SNAPSHOT IS ENABLED;
```

If the snapshot mechanism is disabled, snapshot transactions are converted to
READ WRITE retrieval mode transactions. For example:

```
SQL> ALTER DATABASE FILENAME eurobank:[uk.db]banking SNAPSHOT IS DISABLED;
SQL> SET TRANSACTION READ ONLY;
SQL> SHOW TRANSACTION;
Transaction information:
     Statement constraint evaluation is off

On the default alias
Transaction characteristics:
     Read only
Transaction information returned by base system:
a read-write transaction is in progress
- updates have not been performed
- transaction sequence number (TSN) is 192
- snapshot space for TSNs less than 192 can be reclaimed
- session ID number is 32
```

Note that the SHOW TRANSACTION statement now shows that "a read-write transaction is in progress."

4.6.7   Altering Snapshot Files

The size of snapshot files and the number of pages by which they dynamically extend may be changed with the ALTER DATABASE statement by specifying the storage area whose snapshot file needs to be changed. For example:

```
SQL> ALTER DATABASE FILENAME eurobank:[uk.db]banking
cont> ALTER STORAGE AREA CUSTOMER_AREA
cont> SNAPSHOT ALLOCATION IS 300 PAGES
cont> SNAPSHOT EXTENT IS 100 PAGES;
```

4.6.8   Deferred Snapshots

By default, all transactions that update the database write before images into the snapshot files. If there are disk I/O bottlenecks in the system and the application has many update transactions and few READ ONLY transactions, performance may be improved by using the deferred snapshot capability of Rdb. If this capability is used, updating transactions do not write to the snapshot files unless a READ ONLY transaction is active.

If an update transaction is active and a read-only transaction starts, it will be forced to wait until the update transaction has completed. Subsequent update transactions will write before images to the snapshot files. If the snapshot transaction then completes, new update transactions will not write to the snapshot file until another snapshot transaction attempts to start, and the scenario is repeated.

The ALTER DATABASE statement is used to select the deferred snapshot capability. For example:

```
SQL> ALTER DATABASE FILENAME eurobank:[uk.db]banking
cont> SNAPSHOT IS ENABLED DEFERRED;
```

The deferred snapshot capability may be turned off and the snapshot mechanism returned to its normal mode of execution with the ALTER DATABASE statement. For example:

```
SQL> ALTER DATABASE FILENAME eurobank:[uk.db]banking
cont> SNAPSHOT IS ENABLED IMMEDIATE;
```

Hint: To check whether snapshots are deferred or immediate, the RMU/ DUMP/HEADER command should be used.

4.7   READ-ONLY AREAS

An Rdb storage area may be set to be read-only, in which case the performance of operations that retrieve data from the storage area may improve because certain overheads, such as locking, are removed. Of course, data cannot be inserted, updated, or deleted in a read-only area.

To designate a storage area as a read-only area, the ALTER DATABASE statement is used. For example:

```
SQL> ALTER DATABASE FILENAME eurobank:[uk.db]banking
cont> ALTER STORAGE AREA customer_area
cont> READ ONLY;
```

This example shows how to alter the storage area so that write operations may be performed:

```
SQL> ALTER DATABASE FILENAME eurobank:[uk.db]banking
cont> ALTER STORAGE AREA customer_area
cont> READ WRITE;
```

4.8   WRITE ONCE READ MANY (WORM) AREAS

With the extremely cost-effective storage now available on WORM optical devices, Rdb allows for the placement of lists (segmented strings) on them. Note that non-list data cannot be written to a WORM device except via RMU commands. A WORM device is treated similarly to any read-write device and so special qualifiers pertinent to WORM devices must be used when performing various database administration functions, including:

- RMU/MOVE_AREA
- RMU/COPY_DATABASE
- RMU/RESTORE/ONLY_ROOT

These qualifiers are /WORM and /NOSPAMS. The /WORM qualifier is used to convert a read-write area to a WORM area, setting the storage area allocation and logical end-of-file as appropriate. The /NOSPAMS qualifier ensures that the creation of SPAM pages is disabled in the WORM area as it makes no sense to have SPAMS in what will essentially be a read-only area.

Apart from holding list data, Rdb support for WORM devices can be useful when storage areas become stable and are not updated. These storage areas can be archived to a WORM device with the RMU/MOVE_AREA command. This means that the data is stored on cost-effective storage media but remains online and accessible to the programs that accessed it when it was held on read-write media, with the exception that it is now read-only.

A problem with holding large amounts of list data on WORM devices is that any changes to such data could swamp the after-image journal file. To avoid this, the logging of WORM data changes can be optionally disabled, for example:

```
SQL> CREATE DATABASE FILENAME banking
cont>   CREATE STORAGE AREA txn_area_93
cont>   ALLOCATION 1000 PAGES
cont>   WRITE ONCE JOURNAL IS DISABLED;
```

After-image journaling is described in Chapter 9.

5 Table Access

Once data has been put into a database, the data must be accessible or it is useless. Many tools are used to access the data in Rdb databases.

5.1 INDEXED ACCESS

A user may use interactive SQL to manipulate the data in an ad-hoc fashion or a variety of end-user decision-support tools, such as Microsoft's Access or the Trinzic Corporation's Forest & Trees to name but two.

A user also may run pre-written applications that use embedded SQL in programs. Usually, these do not provide an ad-hoc interface. Instead, they are menu driven or possess a graphical user interface (GUI) so the user can select from a variety of options. These options generally would map onto business functions; for example, a user may choose an option to update a customer account or query a customer's last five account transactions.

The latter example is typical of a *transaction processing* application, where users are performing discrete, predefined functions. In other words, the database designer knows the types of transactions that will be run against the database, the data they access, their frequency, and priority. The former example, end-user decision support, is by its nature ad-hoc. Therefore, the work that will be performed by the database cannot be strictly determined. Ad-hoc querying and decision-support work tend to result in large amounts of data being filtered, returning to the end-user data that meets certain criteria. Transaction processing applications tend to manipulate small quantities of data, but the number of users and the transaction rates often are high.

When asked to return some data, Rdb could sequentially scan an entire table or tables to find the appropriate rows. The correct data would be returned. In a small database the performance may be acceptable, but if the database holds a few gigabytes of user data, the performance almost certainly will not be acceptable.

Consequently, Rdb maintains structures called indexes. Indexes are used to dramatically speed up the retrieval of data based upon some search criteria. If we wanted the account with the number 4523346786, for example, sequentially scanning the ACCOUNT table until the correct row was found could result in many disk I/Os. By using an index based on the column ACCOUNT_NO, direct access to the appropriate row is gained with perhaps only one disk I/O being involved. Indexes may speed up data retrieval, but they usually adversely affect the insertion, deletion and sometimes updating of data.

The database designer, therefore, has to make a careful choice when deciding which indexes to create in the database. Too many indexes may affect the performance of applications that insert data. Too few indexes may severely degrade the performance of applications that retrieve data. Also, the more indexes the database designer creates, the more disk space is required. Obviously, in read-only databases that support retrieval operations only, the database designer does not have to perform a balancing act. Many indexes can be created, with disk space requirements as the only concern.

How can an organization have read-only databases? How did the data get into them in the first place? Read-only, or reference databases, are common. Many organizations do not want ad-hoc work done on the production databases that are supporting the second-by-second changes in the organization's business. These organizations, therefore, periodically extract sections of the database to give to ad-hoc users. Digital's DEC Data Distributor, described in Chapter 12, may be used for this task. *Data warehousing* has become a popular term used to describe these reference databases.

There is no value in creating indexes without information on which transactions need what data, how often transactions execute, and whether they are important to the organization's business; that is, their priority relative to other transactions. (This information is often determined through a transaction analysis.) Without it, the database designer may end up creating indexes that are never used for retrieval and forgetting to create indexes that are needed for an organization's most important transactions. The database designer also may end up creating inappropriate hashed indexes instead of sorted indexes. In the authors' opinion, too many companies miss out this vital analysis.

Rdb uses three methods to access data:

- Sequential retrieval

- Indexed retrieval

- Database key retrieval

This chapter is primarily concerned with indexed retrieval, although database key retrieval is mentioned briefly later in the chapter. In sequential retrieval, Rdb searches all the rows in a table to find those rows which match the specified search criteria. It is a fast process for small tables, but slower for large tables. There are also locking implications, as described in Chapter 7. If there are no suitable indexes on a table, the rows in the table will be accessed sequentially. Because of *asynchronous pre-fetch*, a new feature introduced with Rdb Version 6.0, the sequential retrieval of rows may now be performed more quickly. Asynchronous pre-fetch is discussed later in this chapter.

Two types of indexed retrieval are available in Rdb:

- Sorted index

- Hashed index

Most relational database systems available today support sorted index retrieval and some support hashed index retrieval. Sorted index retrieval is a good general-purpose method of indexed retrieval, while hashed index retrieval is best where only certain types of queries are to be performed. Sorted index retrieval works well for exact match retrieval, that is, where the complete value of a key is known. It also is useful for finding whether a row with a certain key value exists in a table. If a number of rows are to be retrieved based on a range of key values or if only the first part of the key is known, then sorted index retrieval also performs well.

Hashed index retrieval also performs well for exact match key retrieval. In fact, it generally performs better than sorted index retrieval in this area, especially if a table has many rows. It is also very efficient at finding whether a row with a certain key value exists in a table. Hashed index retrieval cannot be used for partial key searches, range retrievals, or with operators other than the equality operator. Sequential retrieval may perform best if there are few rows in a table.

5.2   THE STRUCTURE OF SORTED INDEXES

A sorted index structure looks like an inverted tree and is somewhat similar to that of indexed sequential files. This tree structure contains index key nodes and duplicate key nodes. The index key nodes contain unique index keys and pointers to other nodes. Because they contain the key values, a query that requires only key data can be satisfied without having to retrieve the rows from the actual table. Duplicate key nodes are present if the key word UNIQUE was not specified in the CREATE INDEX statement. If an index contains duplicate key values, they are held in duplicate nodes. Figure 5.1 shows a sorted index structure.

Figure 5.1 shows a *balanced hierarchical structure*, with three index nodes linked by database keys. Level 1 nodes point to the rows in the table or to duplicate index nodes. Level 2 and 3 nodes point to lower-level index nodes. The Level 3 node (the index root) is at the top of the index tree. The duplicate index nodes contain pointers to rows with identical key values. If there are many rows with the same key values, more than one duplicate index node may be needed and these duplicate index nodes are chained together.

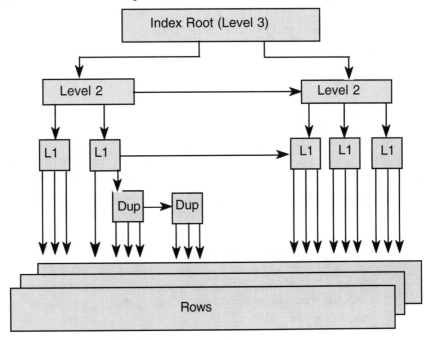

Figure 5.1 A Sorted Index Structure

Figure 5.2 A Duplicate Node Structure

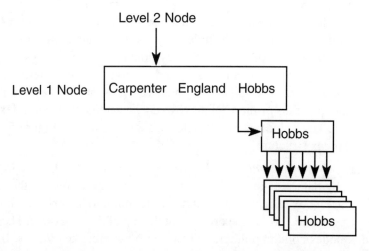

Figure 5.2 shows a duplicate node structure in more detail. Only single instances of the key values Carpenter, England, and Hobbs exist; however, there are a number of rows with the key value Hobbs. Therefore, a duplicate node is seen pointing to a number of table rows with the key value Hobbs.

5.2.1 Creating a Sorted Index

Not surprisingly, the CREATE INDEX statement is used to create an index. In Chapter 2, we saw how to create a simple sorted index that, for example, may be found in a single-file database. In a single-file database, all the indexes for a particular table are stored in a single logical area in the .RDB file. For a multifile database, however, the database designer specifies a storage area in which to create the index. The index can be partitioned across a number of storage areas or it can share a storage area with the rows from the table.

The following example shows how the database designer creates a sorted index in a specified storage area:

```
SQL> CREATE INDEX cust_index
cont> ON customer (surname, first_name)
cont> TYPE IS SORTED
cont> STORE IN cust_area;
```

In this example, a sorted index named CUST_INDEX is created in the storage area CUST_AREA on columns *surname* and *first_name*.

The database designer can partition indexes in a way that is similar to partitioning tables. For example:

```
SQL> CREATE UNIQUE INDEX cust_no_index
cont> ON customer (customer_no)
cont> TYPE IS SORTED
cont> STORE USING (customer_no)
cont> IN customer_area_1 WITH LIMIT OF('3000000000')
cont> IN customer_area_2 WITH LIMIT OF('6000000000')
cont> OTHERWISE IN customer_area_3;
```

In this example, a sorted index, CUST_NO_INDEX, is created and partitioned in three storage areas depending on the value of CUSTOMER_NO. Partitioning an index in this way enables the database designer to spread the disk I/O to an index across multiple disk spindles. There are other beneficial effects that can be obtained from partitioning an index as there is a separate index tree maintained for each partition dealing with its own subset of rows. This often means that each tree has fewer levels of nodes than the equivalent non-partitioned index. This is a physical implementation and, to the outside world, there appears to be one logical index. Because of the partitioning, index lock conflicts may also be reduced. The partitioned index created in the above example is shown in Figure 5.3.

A sorted index is accessed in a number of ways. If a unique index key is specified in the query, Rdb uses it to locate the row and access it directly from

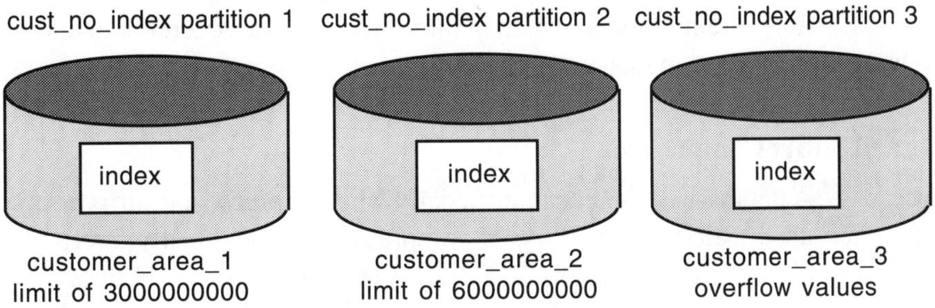

Figure 5.3 A Partitioned Index

the table. This technique is called *direct index access*. If the query specifies a partial key, for example, the first two columns of a three-column key, or a duplicate key, Rdb will scan the index until the appropriate keys are found, then the rows are read from the table. This technique is called retrieval by index. When the columns required by the query form part of the index key, there is no need to access the table itself. In this case, Rdb performs *index-only retrieval*.

Hint: The index-only retrieval method requires fewer logical and physical I/O operations to satisfy the query. Retrieval by index uses more CPU and disk I/O resource.

5.2.2   Sorted Index Key Compression

Sorted indexes can use a considerable amount of disk space especially if they are defined on large tables or the keys themselves are of substantial length. To reduce the disk space requirements of sorted indexes, four types of index compression are available.

- Prefix and suffix compression

- SIZE IS segment truncation

- MAPPING VALUES compression

- Run-length compression

Note that the reduction in disk space requirements is as a result of less index nodes being needed which in turn may result in a decrease in disk I/O requirements but an increase in locking.

Prefix and Suffix Compression

A database designer cannot specify whether prefix and suffix compression are used; Rdb uses this type of compression automatically. Prefix compression alone is applied to the Level 1 index nodes whereas both prefix and suffix compression are applied at the other levels. Prefix compression works by removing bytes from the front of the index key that are the same as the previous index key. Suffix compression removes redundant trailing bytes from the key.

SIZE IS Segment Truncation

SIZE IS segment truncation may be used for CHAR or VARCHAR datatypes. The database designer may specify on the CREATE INDEX statement that the first *n* bytes of the key be used in the index, as it is this first *n* bytes that are unique. This means that if the key size is *k*, then *k* - *n* bytes may be saved for each index entry. For example, the database designer might specify that the first five characters of the branch name provide uniqueness.

```
SQL> CREATE UNIQUE INDEX branch_name_idx
cont> ON branch
cont> (branch_name SIZE IS 5)
cont> TYPE IS SORTED
cont> STORE IN index_area;
```

If specifying that the first 5 bytes be used for the index entry in the above example actually results in an attempt to store a duplicate value being made, an error will be returned and the insert or update operation will fail. Note that the designer can specify that this be a non-unique index if required.

MAPPING VALUES Compression

Where SIZE IS segment truncation may be used only for CHAR or VARCHAR datatypes, MAPPING VALUES compression may only be used for TINYINT, SMALLINT and INTEGER datatypes. The specification of MAPPING VALUES allows Rdb to encode the numeric data in a more compact internal form hence saving disk space.

```
SQL> CREATE UNIQUE INDEX bank_annual_business_idx
cont> ON bank_annual_business
cont> (branch_code,
cont>  bus_year MAPPING VALUES 1950 TO 2001)
cont> TYPE IS SORTED
cont> STORE IN history_area;
```

Run-length Compression

Rdb Version 6.0 onwards enables space characters from text datatypes and binary zeros from non-text datatypes to be compressed. Quite dramatic space saving for indexes can be achieved with this technique.

Run-length compression compresses a sequence of space characters from text datatypes and binary zeros from non-text datatypes. It is most useful when there are a lot of consecutive spaces or binary zeros. Run-length compression can be used with sorted or hashed indexes. An example of a sorted index creation using run-length compression follows:

```
SQL> CREATE UNIQUE INDEX all_branch_index ON branch
cont> (branch_code,
cont>      branch_name,
cont>      branch_address,
cont>      managers_name)
cont>     ENABLE COMPRESSION
cont>          (MINIMUM RUN LENGTH 2)
cont> STORE IN cust_area;
```

The MINIMUM RUN LENGTH is the minimum length of the sequence that Rdb should compress and MINIMUM RUN LENGTH is 2 means that Rdb should compress each sequence of 2 or more space characters or binary zeros. A sequence is compressed to the minimum run length plus one byte contains compression information, that is, the number of space characters compressed in this sequence.

As an example, consider how this compression works on the *managers_name* key column which is 20 bytes in length using a run-length compression of 2.

Without run-length compression the contents of this key column might be:

```
Dan*de*Lion*********
```

Where a * character represents a space. With run-length compression this key column will now be:

```
Dan*de*Lion**#
```

Where a # character represents the compression information. This key column is now 14 bytes in length which is a considerable space saving.

Hint: Care is needed when using a minimum run length of one to ensure that the key column size is not increased! For example, a key column containing the character string AB*TT*GHT*GG*GHT may, after compression, contain AB*#TT*#GHT*#GG*#GHT.

By compressing index keys, as well as saving disk space, disk I/O is reduced because more keys can be held in an index node and therefore less index nodes are needed. This may result in a sorted index tree with fewer levels. However, note that fewer index nodes may mean more lock contention in the index in multi-user systems and the designer should be prepared for this occurring.

System Metadata Index Compression

Run-length compression can be so effective at reducing space usage that Rdb now gives the designer the opportunity to compress the system indexes residing in the system metadata. Unless applications frequently execute concurrent DDL operations, system index compression is recommended.

```
SQL> CREATE DATABASE FILENAME banking
cont> SYSTEM INDEX COMPRESSION IS ENABLED;
```

5.2.3   Clustering Rows with a Sorted Index

If a sorted index is created on a table and rows are inserted into the table, Rdb will store the rows in the database in no fixed order. The database designer can specify that Rdb should try to store the rows in the order in which they appear in the index. Although Rdb will attempt to do so, there is no guarantee that the order the rows are stored in will match the index order.

The following factors influence the level of success Rdb will have:

- The technique initially used to load the table

- The volatility of the data in the table

If clustering rows via a sorted index is required, the initial load of the table must be performed by sorting the data in ascending key order prior to the load.

Hint: The VAX SORT utility can be used to sort the data as required.

By sorting the data, the database designer ensures that every row inserted is physically stored after the previous row, which has a lower key value, and before the next row, which has a higher key value. Thus, the order in which the rows are stored will be the same as the order in which they appear in the index.

Suppose the database designer is loading the CUSTOMER table and that the rows from this table are clustered via the sorted index CUST_INDEX, which has a key consisting of the customer's surname and first name.

The database designer sorts the data into ascending key order and loads it into the CUSTOMER table. The physical order in which the rows are stored in the database should be the same as the order in which the rows appear in the index. Imagine that the rows in the table are not deleted and new rows are inserted whose key values fall within the range of the key values already present. In this case, Rdb cannot insert the new rows in the appropriate physical position relative to the old rows because there is not enough free space where they should go. In this situation, the clustering efficiency will be degraded. If rows are regularly deleted from the table as well as inserted, there may be enough appropriate free space to maintain clustering efficiency. Otherwise the table must be regularly unloaded, sorted and reloaded to maintain optimum efficiency.

If the clustering is efficient, range retrieval queries use significantly fewer disk I/Os because the target rows are physically close to one another.

Hint: Consider the technique of at least pre-sorting data when there are queries that require all similar alphabetic names together, for example, all surnames with SMITH.

5.3   THE STRUCTURE OF HASHED INDEXES

Hashed indexes are a more restrictive type of index than sorted in that there are fewer scenarios in which they can be used. However, when they can be used, they perform very efficiently indeed, fetching the target rows with the minimum of overhead. Hashed indexes may only be used in database storage areas with MIXED page format. As was mentioned earlier in the book, hashed index structures only work if the full key value is known and the equality operator (=) is used. Hashed indexes enable a row to be accessed with only one or two I/Os, depending on whether the rows are in a different storage area from the hashed index or in the same storage area. Compared to a sorted index, this is a saving in I/Os. If a large sorted index is used with many levels of index structure, a number of I/Os may be necessary to search the index tree. Hashed index structures also tend to result in less locking overhead than sorted indexes because it is not necessary to lock many levels of index nodes when using them.

Prior to Rdb Version 6.0, there was only one hashing algorithm possible known as *Hashed Scattered*. Rdb Version 6.0 introduced a second hashing algorithm known as *Hashed Ordered*. Depending on, amongst other factors, the type of index key and data distribution, one of the hashing algorithms may give better results than the other. Hashed Scattered is still the default mechanism and is still considered to be the algorithm that should be used in the majority of cases. Hashed Ordered may only be used if certain criteria are met.

Hashed Scattered

With Hashed Scattered, a hashing function is performed on the hashed index key that may be composed of a single column or a number of columns from the table. The result produces a database page number in the appropriate storage area that is dependent upon the number of database pages initially allocated in the storage area and the value of the hashed index key. For example, consider the hashed index ACCOUNT_INDEX, which uses the single column ACCOUNT_NO as a key.

We may find that an account number of 1223454432 hashes to database page 545 in the ACCOUNT_AREA storage area. Another account number, 4997866554, may hash to database page 23. The Hashed Scattered algorithm does not typically result in a uniform distribution of page numbers and we would expect that account numbers with consecutive values will probably hash to completely different database page numbers, which means they will be stored physically far apart. Unlike sorted indexes, therefore, retrieving account numbers with similar values probably will require a physical disk I/O for each retrieval. Indeed, the randomizing effect of the Hashed Scattered hashing function means that database buffer caching is likely to be ineffective.

Suppose a storage area contains a total number of database pages that is identical to the number of rows to be inserted and that the index key value for each row is unique. Is it reasonable to expect that the randomizing effect of the hashing function will result in one row per database page? With Hashed Scattered, the answer is probably not. We would most likely find that some index keys hashed to the same database page. This is known as a *collision* and the rows that hashed to the same page are known as *synonyms*. We probably would also find that some database pages remained empty. It is, therefore, very important that the database designer carefully choose such parameters as the storage area initial page allocation and page size when using hashed indexes. Correct hashed index page sizing is critical for performance and, as a general rule, hashed indexes need a more careful eye kept on them by the database administrator while in production use to make sure that they remain in tip-top condition.

Hashed Ordered

The Hashed Ordered algorithm in contrast does result in a uniform distribution. It is likely to produce a good and uniform distribution of page numbers for data with key values that are uniformly distributed across a range, that is, each key value occurs the same number of times. An order numbering system which allocated an order number that was the latest order number plus one would provide an example of a uniform data distribution.

To use the Hashed Ordered algorithm, however, the index key must conform to certain rules, including:

- The hashed index must be a single segment index and thus must be created on at most one column from the table.

- This table column on which the Hashed Ordered index is created must be of integer, date, timestamp or interval datatype.

- The range of index key values should be uniform with each key value occurring the same number of times.

- The index must be created ascending.

To demonstrate the uniform distribution produced by a Hashed Ordered index and the non-uniform distribution produced by a Hashed Scattered index the following graphs were produced showing the number of rows resident on database pages after executing a load program that incremented the key by one. Note that as page one is a space area management page, it is not shown.

In Figure 5.4 rows are randomly placed on the database pages. The number of rows in a page ranges from zero through to three.

In Figure 5.5 rows are uniformly placed on the database pages. The number of rows in a page is always one.

Figure 5.4 A Hashed Scattered Distribution

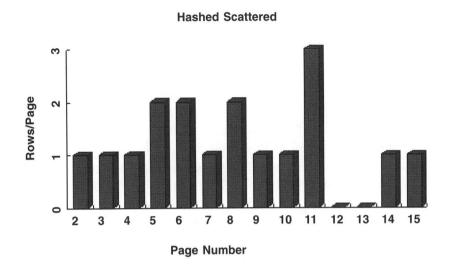

Figure 5.5 A Hashed Ordered Distribution

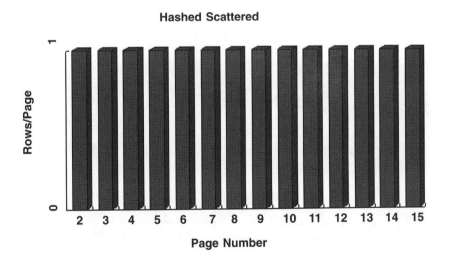

A hashed index structure consists of three types of record:

- A system record

- A hash bucket record

- A duplicate node record

The system record points at each hash bucket on a database page so that the appropriate hash bucket can be quickly located. In other words, the system record on a database page has an entry for each hashed index in the storage area that uses that database page.

A hash bucket, if it exists on a database page, contains the key value of the row that hashed to that page. So, if a row from the ACCOUNT table with an account number of 5686542245 hashed to page 77, a hash bucket will exist on page 77 containing the key value 5686542245. The hash bucket also will contain a database key pointing to the row itself. It may be that the row is not stored on the same database page as the hash bucket. The reasons for this will be explained shortly. If a hashed index is not created with the UNIQUE clause, that is, if duplicate key values are allowed and duplicates exist, the hash bucket will not contain the database key of the row but will contain the database key of a duplicate node record.

A duplicate node record has a fixed size of 92 bytes and will hold the database keys of the duplicate rows to a maximum of ten rows. If there are more duplicate rows, another duplicate node record is used and the duplicate node records are chained together. Figure 5.6 shows the structure of a hashed index that contains unique key values only and Figure 5.7 shows the structure of a hashed index that contains duplicate key values.

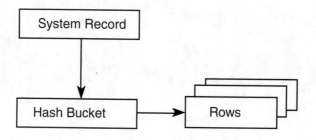

Figure 5.6 A Unique Hashed Index Structure

Figure 5.7 A Non-Unique Hashed Index Structure

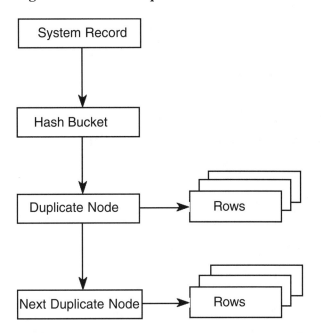

5.3.1   Creating a Hashed Index

The CREATE INDEX statement is used to create a hashed index the same way it is used to create a sorted index. In Chapter 2, we saw how to create a simple sorted index that, for example, may be found in a single-file database. It is impossible to create a hashed index in a single-file database because a hashed index must be placed in a storage area created with a MIXED page format. A hashed index can be partitioned across a number of storage areas or it can share a storage area with the rows from a table.

The following example shows how the database designer can create a hashed index in a specified storage area:

```
SQL> CREATE INDEX account_index
cont> ON account (account_no)
cont> TYPE IS HASHED SCATTERED
cont> STORE IN account_area;
```

In this example, a hashed index named ACCOUNT_INDEX is created in the storage area ACCOUNT_AREA. The hashing algorithm used will be Hashed Scattered. To create a Hashed Ordered index:

```
SQL> CREATE INDEX commodity_index
cont> ON commodity (commodity_num)
cont> TYPE IS HASHED ORDERED
cont> STORE IN deal_area;
```

Hashed indexes can be partitioned the same way as tables. For example:

```
SQL> CREATE UNIQUE INDEX cust_no_index
cont> ON customer (customer_no)
cont> TYPE IS HASHED SCATTERED
cont> STORE USING (customer_no)
cont> IN customer_area_1 WITH LIMIT OF('3000000000')
cont> IN customer_area_2 WITH LIMIT OF('6000000000')
cont> OTHERWISE IN customer_area_3;
```

In this example, the hashed index CUST_NO_INDEX is created and partitioned in three storage areas depending on the value of CUSTOMER_NO.

5.3.2   Storing and Retrieving Rows Stored via a Hashed Index

Let us look at the CUSTOMER table in the BANKING database. Assume that if we examine the storage map CUSTOMER_MAP, which specifies where the CUSTOMER table is stored, we find that the placement is specified via a hashed index, CUSTOMER_INDEX. The CUSTOMER table and the hashed index CUSTOMER_INDEX are stored in the same storage area, CUSTOMER_AREA, and the hashed index uses only the SURNAME column for simplicity.

Suppose that we wish to insert a row into the CUSTOMER table. The value contained in the column SURNAME, the key value, is hashed by the Rdb hashing algorithm. The result is a database page number within the storage area CUSTOMER_AREA. Assume that the customer surname that we want to insert is HOBBS and that the hash algorithm returns us a database page number 23.

This page number is the database page on which the hash bucket will be created. If that page has enough free space according to the appropriate entry on the space management page, the row is stored on that page. If no other row from the table is stored on the page, Rdb also must create a hash bucket and modify the system record on the database page so that it contains an entry for the hashed index, CUSTOMER_INDEX. In fact, the system record will now contain an entry that is the database key of the the hash bucket. The logical area identifier component of the database key is that of the hashed index.

Assuming that the CUSTOMER_INDEX allows duplicate key values, the hash bucket will contain a pointer to a duplicate record. If another CUSTOMER row with the same key value is then inserted, Rdb checks for sufficient free space on the database page. If there is free space, the hash bucket is merely updated to reflect the count of rows that contain this key value and another database key entry is added. Figure 5.8 shows what the database page looks like after a second row has been inserted. Of course, in the simplest case duplicates would not be allowed in the index and duplicate nodes would not exist.

Figure 5.8 shows a database page with the system record pointing to a hash bucket, which contains an entry for a customer with the surname of HOBBS. Because duplicates are allowed in the index and two rows contain a key of HOBBS, the hash bucket entry points to a duplicate node that, in turn, points to the rows.

Suppose we want to retrieve a customer with the surname of HOBBS. Rdb will hash the surname, and database page 23 will be returned. Rdb will retrieve this database page and check the system record for a pointer to the appropriate hash bucket. First, the database key of the duplicate record is found, then the database key of the actual row, which is fetched. Hopefully, this is all achieved in a single disk I/O operation because all the information resides on the same database page. If the row does not exist, Rdb will have used only a single I/O operation to determine this.

If we continue to add rows with the same key value, the free space on the database page eventually will be used up and there will be an overflow onto another database page. In this case, Rdb already used a single disk I/O to retrieve the hash bucket and now may need another disk I/O to fetch the actual row if the page containing the row has not been brought into the buffer. Figure 5.9 shows an overflow onto another database page. A customer with a surname of ENGLAND has been inserted on the page (ENGLAND hashed to the

Figure 5.8 A Hashed Index and Rows on the Same Page

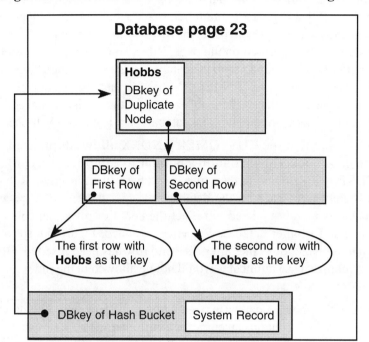

same page as HOBBS) and, because there was not enough free space on page 23, the row was stored on page 24, the next page with free space. Note that as only one row of the key value ENGLAND has been inserted, no duplicate node has been created – the hash bucket entry points directly to the row.

The database designer should try to avoid this situation. Apart from causing Rdb extra disk I/Os inserting and fetching rows, the problem is likely to get worse. As rows overflow onto another database page with free space, this database page fills and then contains insufficient free space to accommodate the rows that hash to it. This is not a satisfactory state of affairs. The database designer can use RMU/ANALYZE/PLACEMENT to investigate such overflow.

Note that the table can be put in a different storage area than the hashed index. In this situation, an extra disk I/O will be needed to retrieve a row. However, the database designer does have more flexibility in the choice of storage-area design parameters, which then can be specified independently for each storage area.

Figure 5.9 A Hashed Index and Rows on the Same Page

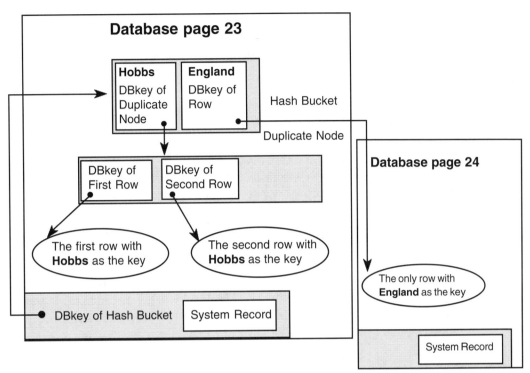

5.3.3   Ensuring That Hashing Is Efficient

It was mentioned that hash overflow degrades performance. It is important to create storage areas with the correct page size and allocation to optimize hashed index performance.

The database designer should consider the following variables when choosing hashed index access to a table:

- Row size

- Initial page allocation

- Page size

- Space management page threshold values

- The space management page interval

- Hash key size

- The projected number of unique and duplicate hash key values

- The cardinality of the relevant table (the number of rows)

- Whether shadow clustering is being used

- Whether data and index keys are compressed or not

- Key value distribution

Chapter 11 contains equations to relate these variables. Their details are outside the scope of this book; however, the page size and initial page allocation should be mentioned. Too small a page will result in insufficient free space to hold the hashed index structures and a sensible number of rows. Too small an initial page allocation for the database storage area will cause it to dynamically extend. The page hashing algorithm uses the initial database page range to compute the target page so even though a storage area has extended, the new database pages cannot become target pages for the hash algorithm. Rows may be stored in the extension, but their hash buckets will always be in the initial allocation of pages. Therefore, at least two disk I/Os will be needed to retrieve these rows, assuming the pages are not already in a database buffer.

5.3.4   Hashed Index Key Compression

Index key compression has already been mentioned in relation to sorted indexes. Hashed index keys may also be compressed. However, the compression techniques that may be used are more limited. The available techniques are:

- MAPPING VALUES compression

- Run-length compression

These techniques have already been described and so will not be discussed further.

5.3.5   Concurrent Index Definition

There are occasions when the database administrator might wish to create a number of indexes concurrently on a table. An example might be at the end of the online day when extra indexes need to be created to facilitate overnight batch processing or the creation of a 10Gb database. Similarly, there may be situations when more than one user simultaneously wishes to create an index on a table.

Prior to Rdb Version 6.0, creating more than one index on a table simultaneously was difficult to do. Usually, one of the index creations was forced to wait on a lock until the other one finished. Rdb Version 6.0 introduced new syntax to the SET TRANSACTION statement to support the concurrent creation of indexes:

```
SQL> SET TRANSACTION READ WRITE
cont> RESERVING branch FOR SHARED DATA DEFINITION;
```

If a transaction is started with the SHARED DATA DEFINITION clause, querying and updating the reserved table are not allowed and other users can only create indexes on this table. They are not allowed to execute any other data definition language statements. The PROTECTED key word cannot be used with the DATA DEFINITION clause. The EXCLUSIVE key word may be used but this then forces single user access to the table so indexes cannot be then created concurrently, which defeats the whole object of what we are trying to do!

5.3.6   Dropping and Disabling Indexes

There will be occasions when the database administrator will wish to drop a sorted or hashed index from the database. If the index is large, this operation may take a considerable length of time. For example, for a sorted index it usually involves the removal of every index node in the sorted index structure or for a hashed index every page in the mixed area will be scanned.

Some optimizations were previously added to Rdb to speed up the DROP INDEX statement for sorted indexes. If the index creation statement contained a STORE clause that explicitly placed the index in a uniform page format storage area, then the index or index partition will be allocated its own unique logical area. In this case, Rdb merely marks this logical area as deleted when the DROP INDEX statement is issued. This is a fast operation. If the index was created in a mixed page format storage area, this optimization is not possible and every page on which a node is stored must be retrieved.

If the database administrator wishes to remove an index but because of reasons of time or concurrency it is not possible, the index may be disabled.

A disabled index is not used by the optimizer and it is not maintained; that is, it is not updated. It can be dropped later at the database administrator's convenience but it cannot be enabled again. To disable an index, add the syntax MAINTENANCE IS DISABLED to the ALTER INDEX statement.

```
SQL> ALTER INDEX branch_idx MAINTENANCE IS DISABLED;
```

5.4   THE DATABASE BUFFER POOL

It has been assumed up to now that if Rdb needs to retrieve a database page, it must perform a physical I/O to disk in order to read the page. Performing a disk I/O is relatively time-consuming, so reducing disk I/Os will reduce the time it takes to perform a database operation. Rdb uses the concept of a buffer pool to achieve this. A buffer is an area of memory used to hold database pages during read and write operations to the database. A buffer pool is a number of these buffers and this number may be specified by the database designer.

There are two buffering mechanisms in Rdb:

- Local

- Global

The traditional mechanism is local which is still the default. Global buffering is offered as an option. A description of local buffering follows. Global buffering is described shortly.

In the case of Rdb, a local buffer pool is created every time an attach is made to a database. Usually, this means that each Rdb user has his or her own private buffer pool.

Hint: When Digital's ACMS transaction processing monitor is being used, a few server processes are attached to the database. In this case, each server process is allocated a buffer pool for each database it is attached to (often just one). Many people may be using the transaction processing system, and the effect is that these users share the server's buffer pool. This is beneficial for performance and will be further discussed in Chapter 15. Also note that many 4GL environments perform multiple attaches to a database and therefore a number of buffer pools are created for a user process.

5.4.1   The Buffer Length

The length of a database buffer is a parameter that can be specified by the database designer when the database is being created with the CREATE DATABASE statement. To alter the buffer size, the SQL EXPORT and SQL IMPORT commands are normally used. It is also possible to increase the buffer size during an RMU/RESTORE operation.

The buffer size is specified as a number of 512-byte blocks. If the buffer size is not specified, the default value of three database pages is used where a database page refers to the largest page found in the database. The default database page size is two disk blocks, so, by default, a database buffer is six disk blocks long (remember that a disk block is 512 bytes). This relationship is seen in Figure 5.10.

Figure 5.10 The Relationship Between Disk Blocks and Buffers

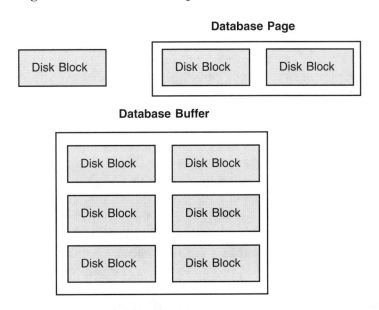

Hint: The buffer pool is kept in the user's process virtual memory and is pageable. Always ensure that the user's OpenVMS operating system working set is sufficiently large enough to accommodate the buffer pool, otherwise the resulting paging may degrade performance.

5.4.2   The Number of Buffers

Once the buffer size has been decided, the number of buffers in the buffer pool needs to be considered. The default value for the number of buffers is 20. The database designer can specify the number of database buffers in the buffer pool when the database is being created with the CREATE DATABASE statement. However, unlike the buffer size, the number of buffers in the buffer pool can be easily changed with the ALTER DATABASE statement. More importantly, by defining an OpenVMS process logical name or an OSF/1 environment variable, RDM$BIND_BUFFERS, the number of buffers in the buffer pool may be made to take on different values for each database user.

For example, the following DCL command can be executed for an OpenVMS user, perhaps in the user's login command file:

```
$ DEFINE RDM$BIND_BUFFERS 200
```

5.4.3   Local Buffer Pool Operation

When Rdb needs to retrieve a row, it makes a request for the appropriate database page. Before reading the database page on disk, it checks to see if the page is in the buffer pool. If it is, Rdb has just saved a disk I/O operation. If it isn't, Rdb has wasted a negligible amount of CPU (special techniques are be used to efficiently search buffer pools) and now must read the page from the disk. When Rdb reads the page, it does not read a single page, but rather a buffer full of pages. These pages then stay in the buffer pool until the buffer pool becomes full, in which case they may be discarded or written back to disk if the buffer has been modified. A distinction should now made between physical I/O and logical I/O. A *physical* I/O is an access to a disk drive, whereas a *logical* I/O is an access to a memory buffer. A logical I/O is much less costly in terms of elapsed time than a disk I/O, because memory access is much quicker than disk access. A request for a database page can be satisfied by a logical or physical I/O being performed. It is part of the database designer's challenge to minimize physical I/O and maximize logical I/O.

As each physical I/O is performed, a buffer in the database buffer pool is used to hold the retrieved database pages. Eventually, no buffers are available to hold new pages because they have all been used. In this situation, Rdb will reuse the buffer that has been used the least, that is, the buffer that contains the database pages that Rdb has not accessed for the longest time. This technique is known as a *least-recently used* algorithm. It is elegant in its simplicity and very effective. It guarantees that the database pages that are being used the most will be held in memory for the user. Frequently used database pages usually will be those that hold sorted index nodes.

If a user has modified a row in a page and a second user wishes to gain access to a row that is in the first user's buffer, Rdb signals the user to flush the buffer to disk. If a user ends a transaction with a COMMIT statement, Rdb flushes all the modified database pages to the storage areas on disk (unless the Fast Commit feature is enabled). If the user starts a new transaction without deattaching from and reattaching to the database, the buffers will still hold the database pages acquired during the last transaction.

5.4.4   Large Versus Small Local Buffers

Should a large number of small buffers be used or a small number of large buffers? There is no correct answer. It depends on the type of processing that is being done, among other factors. Of course, it is possible to have a high number of large buffers. Typically, however, the memory limit on the system regulates this. If a large number of buffers is used, more index nodes will stay resident in the buffer pool and a reduction in disk I/O operations will result.

This process is more useful for sorted index nodes. Hashed index buckets, by definition, are randomly accessed and are unlikely to be re-used often in a buffer. With a large number of buffers, database pages may not need to be written to disk until the user commits the transaction. This operation is asynchronous in nature, meaning that the disk I/Os happen together instead of one after the other. As a general rule of thumb, a small number of large buffers is beneficial for sequential operations against the database, whereas a large number of small buffers is beneficial for random operations against the database. This is summarized in Table 5.1.

Table 5.1 Suggested Buffer Pool Profiles

Main Transaction Type	Buffers Needed
Random	Few Small
Hierarchical Retrievals	Many Small
Sequential Searches	Many Large

Hint: When many users are updating a database and large buffers are used, the probability of different users requesting database pages that are in each other's buffers will increase. This will result in increased buffer flushing, which will reduce overall database performance.

5.4.5   Global Buffering

One of the main disadvantages of the local buffering approach is that cached data is never shared between database attaches. Many users may read in the same page from disk to a buffer but each user will need to perform a disk I/O to do so. Also, because no sharing takes place, each user will keep their own copy of the database page in their buffer pool. This non-sharing of cached data can lead to many disk I/Os being issued for the same pages and more memory being used to hold the multiple copies in the local cache.

If we consider the case where a 4GL product makes multiple attaches to a database, we can see that each attach that needed the same page would cause the same process to issue a disk I/O and the same process would hold a copy of the page in memory multiple times.

The above situation could be considered inefficient only if users were sharing database pages and it might be that some applications do not have users sharing data in this way. However, consider index nodes. If many users are constantly navigating through a sorted index tree then there is a strong possibility that they will be reading the same pages containing index nodes and the local buffer case has again become inefficient even though data rows are not being shared.

To eliminate much of this inefficiency, Rdb has introduced global buffers. The concept is fairly straightforward. Instead of every user's database attach being allocated a private set of local buffers, every attach may now share buffers from a global buffer pool. If a user reads a page from disk into a buffer, that buffer containing that page is available to any other attach against that database. This means that no matter how many users need to read that page, only one disk I/O is performed to bring it into memory the first time it is requested. Unless it is overwritten, the page in that buffer will continue to be available to all the users of that database. Another advantage of this approach is that only one copy of the page is held in memory with a consequent saving in memory usage. Note, however, that a global buffer pool is per machine.

So disk I/O is saved and memory is saved – what is the downside? Because the buffer pool is now a shared resource, synchronization in the form of locking must be applied. This will use up extra CPU; however, with Rdb Version 6.0, high performance locks, known as *recoverable latches* are used. The result is that there really is no downside to global buffers and Rdb database designers and administrators should strongly be considering their use.

Hint: Do not rush into global buffers. Although they are simple to enable they require specific system resource. On an OpenVMS system, for example, they will require the number of global pages to be increased. Check the Rdb documentation, adjust your system parameters and then experiment with global buffering. Not adjusting system parameters is likely to result in a fall at the first hurdle!

Global or local buffering may be specified for an individual database but not both as the buffering technique is a database-wide parameter. Every node that accesses the database will maintain a global buffer pool for that database.

To enable global buffers, the ALTER DATABASE statement is used.

```
SQL> ALTER DATABASE FILENAME banking GLOBAL BUFFERS ARE ENABLED
cont> (NUMBER IS 1000, USER LIMIT IS 50);
```

This statement enables global buffering for the BANKING database and specifies that 1000 global buffers will be created in the database's global buffer pool (per node). The USER LIMIT IS parameter will be discussed shortly.

If an RMU/DUMP/HEADER command is issued, information about the global buffering for this database is displayed.

```
$ RMU/DUMP/HEADER banking
       .
       .
    Buffers...
     - Global buffers are enabled
     - Global buffer count is 1000
     - Maximum global buffer count per user is 50
     - Default database buffer count is 20
     - Recovery buffer count is 20
     - Buffer size is 6 blocks
       .
       .
```

This RMU/DUMP/HEADER display shows the global buffering information stored in the database root file. To show the values actually in use on a node, the RMU/SHOW USERS command can be used.

```
$ RMU/SHOW USERS banking
    Rdb V6.0 on node ORION 11-FEB-1994 18:40:54.33

        database EUROBANK:[UK.DB]BANKING.RDB;1
          * database is opened by an operator
            - global buffer count is 1000
            - maximum global buffer count per user is 50
            - 980 global buffers free
            - 1 active database user

            - 0000005F:1 - _FTA7:, ENGLAND - active user
            - image $DKA100:[SYS$COMMON.][SYSEXE]SQL$.EXE;1
            - 20 global buffers allocated
```

The values actually in use on a node and the values stored in the root file may differ. We shall see how shortly. Firstly, though, the parameter USER LIMIT needs some explaining. Global buffering gives the database designer two new parameters. The NUMBER IS parameter is the number of buffers in the global buffer pool for a database. The USER LIMIT IS parameter specifies the maximum number of global buffers that can be allocated to a database attach at any point in time.

How many buffers then is an attach given? Firstly, it is given the number of buffers specified by the NUMBER OF BUFFERS IS parameter on the CREATE or ALTER DATABASE statement, or if no value was specified the Rdb default of 20 buffers is used. For some processes, however, the logical name or environment variable RDM$BIND_BUFFERS may have been specified and its value will override the NUMBER OF BUFFERS IS parameter.

This behavior is identical to the local buffer case. The difference comes about with the USER LIMIT parameter. This sets an effective limit to the number of global buffers that can be allocated to an attach. It overrides both the NUMBER OF BUFFERS IS parameter and RDM$BIND_BUFFERS.

The usual relationship between these parameters is shown in Figure 5.11. It is normal practice to specify a user limit that is not less than the other parameters.

Figure 5.11 The Relationship Between Global Buffer Parameters

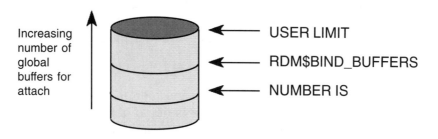

Any attach may in fact gain access to any buffer in the buffer pool, all of which are available to it. It is these buffer quota parameters that ultimately determine the number of buffers that an attach can use at a given point in time. In the ALTER DATABASE statement above, the number of global buffers in the global buffer pool is set at 1000 with a user limit set at 50. This means that 20, that is 1000 divided by 50, attaches at most are guaranteed against this database or 20 users assuming one attach per user. Any user is in fact able to read any of the 1000 buffers but at any point in time a user can only modify a maximum of 50 buffers. These 50 buffers are known as the user's allocate set.

It has been stated that the global buffer parameters are database wide and are set on the CREATE or ALTER DATABASE statement. Indeed, they may be also set during an RMU/RESTORE operation. Suppose, however, we have a system that is comprised of a large processor with a great deal of memory and a small processor with limited memory and we want to share a database across both these nodes. In this scenario perhaps we would wish to specify many global buffers for the large processor and few for the small processor. How do we achieve this? The answer is to use the RMU/OPEN command. The RMU/OPEN command allows the specification of the number of buffers in the global buffer pool and the user limit.

```
$  RMU/OPEN/GLOBAL_BUFFERS=(TOTAL=5000,USER_LIMIT=100) banking
```

A typical approach would be to use the CREATE or ALTER DATABASE statement to set the parameters to values suitable for the small processor and then override these values using RMU/OPEN for the large processor. This is why the values actually in use on a VMScluster node and the values stored in the root file may differ and why RMU/DUMP/HEADER and RMU/SHOW USERS may report different values.

Hint: It is good practice to always use OPEN IS MANUAL on operational databases and make them accessible or unavailable with RMU/OPEN and RMU/CLOSE. This will ensure that the global buffer pool is held together as described shortly.

How should a database designer or administrator decide on values for the buffer parameters? The total number of global buffers for a database is usually determined by the availability of memory. For example, if a processor has 64 Mb of memory configured, of which 30% is available for a database's global buffer pool and the default buffer size of 3 pages (6 blocks or 3Kb) is used, then the total number of global buffers in the pool is:

> total memory * % memory available / buffer size

> $(64 * 0.30)/0.003 = 6400$

Of course, the opposite approach can be taken – decide how many global buffers are needed and ask your boss to buy you the extra memory!

But where do the other parameters fit in? The USER LIMIT parameter defines the total number of guaranteed attaches that will be supported. In other words, if each attach is allocated a number of buffers equal to the user limit (the maximum possible for an attach), there will be an upper limit of guaranteed attaches. For example, if our global buffer pool consists of 6400 buffers and the user limit is specified to be 100, Rdb will guarantee to allow 64 attaches. If a user attempts to execute a 65th attach, it will fail as the global buffer pool will now be all allocated.

Hint: The Rdb monitor log or the RMU/SHOW USER command can be used to see if the global buffer pool is nearly exhausted.

In reality, a database designer or administrator will probably set the NUMBER OF BUFFERS IS parameter to be less than the USER LIMIT parameter. Certain important classes of processes will then have their buffer allocation increased up to the user limit by the use of RDM$BIND_BUFFERS.

So how does global buffering actually work? This is best described with an example. Imagine two processes attached to a database. Each process has an allocate set of 3 buffers. The buffer size is 6 blocks and the page size is 2 blocks. The global buffer pool is 6 buffers in size. Initially the global buffer pool contains no database pages as shown in Figure 5.12.

Figure 5.12 The Global Buffer Pool Initial State

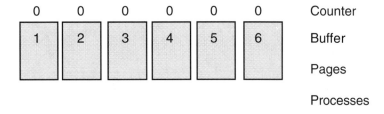

User 1 reads pages 2 to 4 into global buffer 1 and User 2 reads pages 38 to 43 into global buffers 2 and 3. The reference counters for global buffers 1, 2 and 3 are incremented. A reference counter indicates how many processes (attaches) are referencing a global buffer. The situation at this point is shown in Figure 5.13.

Figure 5.13 The Global Buffer Pool After Users Have Read Data

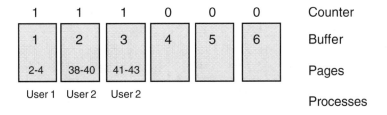

The users continue to read data. User 1 reads pages 8-10 into global buffer 4 and pages 14-16 into global buffer 5. User 2 then reads 47-49 into global buffer 6. The reference counters are all incremented accordingly. This is shown in Figure 5.14. Note that there are now no free buffers.

Figure 5.14 A Full Global Buffer Pool

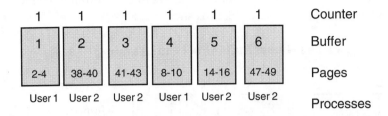

User 1 now wants page 83; however, User 1 has reached his maximum allotment (3 buffers) and so the least recently used (LRU) algorithm chooses a victim buffer to discard from User 1's allocate set, in this case buffer 1.

User 2 now wants page 9. She has also reached her maximum allotment and so a buffer must be discarded from her allocate set, in this case buffer 2. However, in this case page 9 is already in a buffer in the global buffer pool. The reference counter on buffer 2 is set to 0 and the reference counter on buffer 4 is set to 2.

Figure 5.15 The Sharing of a Global Buffer

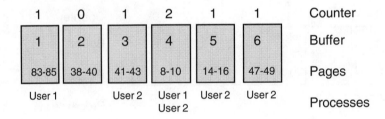

What actually happens to a discarded global buffer when a user's allocate set is full; that is, the user is using all of their buffers?

As described previously, for local buffers, when a buffer is needed, the least recently used algorithm (LRU) chooses a target buffer and effectively discards its contents by overwriting it with the new database pages just read in from disk. If the buffer had been modified, it is written back to disk.

The pages in the overwritten buffer are now unavailable and if they are needed they must be read back from disk using physical disk I/O.

For global buffers the situation is somewhat different. A modified least recently used algorithm comes into play. If the user's allocate set is full and they need a new buffer of information, a target buffer must be chosen as in the local case. However, the information in it may stay in the global buffer pool.

An optimization in global buffering ensures that an unallocated empty buffer in the buffer pool is used to receive new pages from disk before an unallocated buffer containing database pages. In this way, the discarded buffer is merely returned to the buffer pool to make space in the user's allocate set for the new buffer. It is available to be re-read by the user or by any other user without incurring disk I/O.

This optimization does not happen if the entire global buffer pool is allocated to database attaches. In this case the target buffer is overwritten with the new pages from disk and the old information is discarded. To access this information again, disk I/O will be incurred.

After users have been reading database pages into the global buffer pool for a while it becomes an effective cache with frequently used database pages staying in memory in the buffer pool. If the global buffer pool is large enough to accommodate all of the needed database pages, it effectively then provides an in-memory database delivering very good performance.

But what happens to this global buffer pool when no one is attached to the database? If the database OPEN attribute is AUTOMATIC then the last person to detach from the database will cause the global buffer pool to be released from memory. When a user attaches to the database again, the global buffer pool will be created again. Thus all the hot cached data will have been lost. This is obviously not desirable. To avoid this situation, the OPEN attribute should be set to MANUAL with ALTER DATABASE and RMU/OPEN and RMU/CLOSE used to manage access to the database. Now if the last user detaches, the global buffer pool will not evaporate but will be held together by the RMU/OPEN. A subsequent RMU/CLOSE will discard the global buffer pool.

In this way, the global buffer pool and the useful data in it may be kept available until the database really must be shutdown. Figure 5.16 shows the results of an experiment performed with global buffers and the use of RMU/OPEN.

Figure 5.16 The Benefit of Using RMU/OPEN for Global Buffers

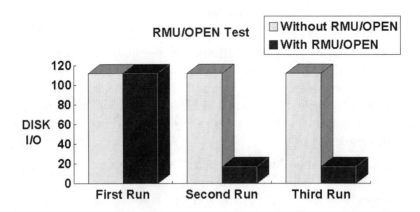

The experiment consists of a program that retrieves data from the database. The first time it is run, the same number of physical accesses to disk occur whether the database is opened manually with RMU/OPEN or it is opened automatically by the first user attach. The program, having detached from the database, is then run again. Now there are significant differences. The run where the database is opened manually with RMU/OPEN uses far fewer disk I/Os than the case where the database is opened automatically. This is because in the automatic database open case, when the user detaches, the buffer pool is released from memory, as described above. All the data must be read again from disk, whereas it remains in the global buffer pool in the manual open case. No matter how many times this experiment is run, the results will be the same.

As a general statement, the authors believe that global buffering is likely to benefit most Rdb based applications. If it is decided to investigate the effectiveness of global buffering futher, a site should first decide on a test strategy to compare local and global buffer pool performance. A good idea is to ensure that for both cases a user is allocated the same number of buffers and also the number of buffers in the global buffer pool and the total number of local buffers is equal. Tests can then be run and RMU/SHOW STATISTICS displays observed to compare results. However, before global buffering is enabled, the site should ensure that the appropriate OpenVMS SYSGEN and user parameters are adjusted accordingly.

These parameters include:

- GBLSECTIONS

- GBLPAGES

- GBLPAGFIL

- VIRTUALPAGECNT

- PGFLQUOTA

- Rdb Monitor and user process account quotas

The *Rdb Guide to Database Performance and Tuning* documentation provides much useful information concerning these parameters.

Hint: The RMU/DUMP/HEADER command now provides information that can assist in estimating global page requirements. A Derived Data section calculates information on the Rdb global section size for both global buffers disabled and enabled.

5.4.6   Transferring Database Pages To and From the Buffer Pool

It has been previously mentioned that Rdb generally moves data between the database storage areas and the buffer pool (whether local or global) in units of a buffer. Rdb Version 6.0 contains optimizations to ensure that these transfers are made as efficiently as possible to ensure the maximum performance.

There are two new features that arrived in Rdb Version 6.0:

- Asynchronous pre-fetch of database pages

- Asynchronous batch write of database pages

and one that arrived in Rdb Version 6.1:

- Optimized page transfers

Asynchronous Pre-Fetch

The asynchronous pre-fetch feature is designed to improve the efficiency of sequential scans of a storage area. Usually, when Rdb wishes to read in database pages to a buffer, the user process stalls while the transfer takes place. Asynchronous pre-fetch attempts to reduce these process stalls by ensuring that the page is read into the buffer asynchronously before the process requests it. Currently, asynchronous pre-fetch is only active for sequential scans although it is likely that the use of this feature will be extended in the future to pre-fetch data for other kinds of retrieval.

The basic idea is simple. While Rdb is performing normal processing, pages that Rdb believes will be needed by the sequential scan are read into the buffer pool. When the process subsequently requests those pages, it finds that the pages are in memory and no stall occurs. This is obviously a useful feature and by default it is switched on. However, it can be disabled by setting an OpenVMS process or system logical name or OSF/1 environment variable.

```
$ DEFINE RDM$BIND_APF_DISABLED 1
```

The number of buffers that can be pre-fetched is known as the depth. By default the depth is eight buffers or the allocate set divided by four, whichever is the smaller. This can be overridden.

```
$ DEFINE RDM$BIND_APF_DEPTH 10
```

The page on which Rdb realizes a sequential scan is occurring is called a *triggering page*. When a triggering page is discovered, asynchronous pre-fetching of pages starts.

The asynchronous pre-fetch feature works in different ways depending on whether the area is of mixed or uniform page format. A sequential scan of a mixed page format area will look at each page in turn so the asynchronous pre-fetch mechanism can easily calculate the next page to pre-fetch – it is the triggering page number plus one. Rdb then, in a single read operation, pre-fetches the depth of buffers. If a triggering page is found while the depths-worth of buffers is being processed, asynchronous pre-fetch continues.

The situation in a uniform page format area is slightly more complex. A sequential scan of a uniform page format area will not look at each page in turn as different clumps may be allocated to different logical areas. In this case the asynchronous pre-fetch mechanism must calculate the next page to pre-fetch by examining the area inventory page (AIP), area bitmap page (ABM) and space area management page (SPAM). Rdb then, pre-fetches the depth of buffers but uses a single read operation for each buffer. To monitor the asynchronous pre-fetch feature a new asynchronous PIO screen is available with Rdb Version 6.0.

Asynchronous Batch Write

The asynchronous batch write feature is designed to improve the efficiency of database writes to storage areas. Usually, when Rdb wishes to write out database pages to a buffer, the user process stalls while the transfer takes place. The asynchronous batch write feature attempts to reduce the stalls associated with writing to the database. Prior to Rdb Version 6.0, a user's process would collect together pages that needed to be written back to disk and then write them together, during which the process would stall. Improvements were made in successive versions of Rdb prior to Rdb Version 6.0. For example, whereas Rdb Version 4.0 wrote buffers synchronously one by one, Rdb Version 4.1 wrote out buffers in batches. Rdb Versions 4.2 and 5.1 enhanced this capability with user specified batch sizes. With Rdb Version 6.0, these batch writes are asynchronous and so the process normally does not have to wait for them to complete which reduces process stalls.

The idea behind the asynchronous batch write feature is that, at any given time, a portion of the buffers in the user's allocate set are being asynchronously written without stalling the user's process. Rather than waiting until every buffer in the allocate set needs writing, the philosophy behind asynchronous batch write is to start asynchronously writing buffers to disk when a certain threshold has been crossed. In other words, once the number of unmodified buffers has dropped below a specified value, the asynchronous writing of buffers is initiated. The group of unmodified buffers is known as the clean region. The size of the clean region in buffers is specified by an OpenVMS logical name or OSF/1 environment variable.

```
$ DEFINE RDM$BIND_CLEAN_BUF_CNT 8
```

A modified buffer encroaching upon the clean region causes the asynchronous writing of buffers to commence. Another logical name may be used to specify number of buffers that will be asynchronously written.

```
$ DEFINE RDM$BIND_BATCH_MAX 10
```

In the above settings for the logical names, Rdb Version 6.0 will asynchronously write a batch of ten buffers to disk whenever the user's attach has less than eight clean buffers in its buffer pool.

Setting these values will require some experimentation. Too large a value for RDM$BIND_BATCH_MAX may adversely affect other processes whose disk I/Os may get queued behind the batch writer. Too small a value may cause the process not to benefit much from the asynchronous batch write feature, especially where the batches are being written across multiple disk drives.

As well as user application processing, the asynchronous batch write feature is likely to benefit database administrator tasks such as RMU/LOAD and RMU/RECOVER and especially work performed by database recovery processes.

The asynchronous batch write feature is switched on by default but can be disabled by setting a logical name.

```
$ DEFINE RDM$BIND_ABW_DISABLED 1
```

Optimized Page Transfer

The last feature concerned with efficiently transferring database pages is the optimized page transfer feature. This feature, under a set of restricted conditions, allows processes on a single node to share and update pages in memory without having to continually write them away to disk every time they are modified. This feature is automatically enabled and can reduce disk I/O for write intensive applications. However, for it to be enabled, the database must conform to the following set of conditions.

- Global buffering is in use

- Fast commit processing is in use

- After-image journaling is in use

- Access is from a single machine

With the optimized page transfer feature, a process does not have to write a modified page to disk if another process wishes to access it. This can be very beneficial where the users of an application continually update a data page, for example, a stock system where stock levels keep changing.

6 The Optimizer

When retrieving rows from an Rdb database, the programmer or end-user usually does not stop to think about whether the data is being accessed in the most efficient manner. In fact, deciding the most efficient way to retrieve data is a very complex task.

Luckily, Rdb tackles this problem with a sophisticated piece of software called the *optimizer*. The optimizer uses information such as the structure of the query, the indexes available, and the number of rows in a table (the cardinality) to decide the best method for retrieving the data. This is known as choosing the optimum strategy. This process is extremely important because choosing a good strategy over a bad strategy could save seconds or hours when querying a large database. The optimizer is one of the components that differentiates a relational database system from database systems based on the network or hierarchical model. In network or hierarchical database management systems, the programmer or user must specify exactly which access path must be used to retrieve data. In a relational database system, the optimizer decides which is the best access path to retrieve data.

6.1 METHODS OF RETRIEVING DATA

When the optimizer resolves a query, it chooses from a number of different access methods to retrieve the data. Prior to Rdb Version 4.0, the optimizer would choose one of four retrieval methods.

- Sequential retrieval

  All the pages in the logical area of the database are checked sequentially. This can be time-consuming in a large database, especially if a table has been stored with MIXED page format as opposed to UNIFORM page format.

- Index retrieval

  A hashed or sorted index obtains the database key of the row, which is used to retrieve the row itself.

- Index-only retrieval

  Only the index is retrieved if the columns requested in the query are held in the index. Rdb does not need to access the data in the table itself.

- Database key (dbkey) retrieval

  If the database key of the row is known, it is accessed directly without using indexes or sequential scans.

When one of these strategies is chosen, Rdb makes its choice prior to retrieving the data. One of the disadvantages of this approach is that if a method is selected but retrieval time turns out to be longer than anticipated, the choice cannot be reversed.

6.1.1   Dynamic Optimization

Rdb Version 4.0 introduced four new optimizer strategies under the general heading of *dynamic optimization*, making a total of eight strategies available. When data is retrieved using the dynamic optimization strategy, several indexes can be used to retrieve the data. The key difference between the static optimizer and the dynamic optimizer is that the latter makes use of background and foreground processes, where these two processes can run synchronously in parallel or individually.

The purpose of the background process is to scan one or more indexes, and return the matching rows as a list of dbkeys, which are passed to the foreground stage. The list of dbkeys is held in memory or in a temporary table. When multiple indexes must be scanned, the optimizer prioritizes them by their selectivity factor; that is, the indexes most likely to return dbkeys are searched first. The foreground process then takes this list of dbkeys and actually retrieves the record. There are four dynamic optimization methods:

- Background only

  One or more indexes is used because no single index contains all the columns required for the query.

- Index only

  Selected when an index contains all the columns necessary to satisfy the query.

- Sorted order

  A specific order is required by virtue of an ORDER BY, DISTINCT or GROUP BY clause and index-only retrieval is not possible.

- Fast first

  Retrieval of the first few records is very quick.

The method chosen to retrieve the data will ultimately govern how long Rdb takes to execute the query, the amount of CPU used, and the number of disk I/Os performed. Because of this, it is critical that Rdb chooses the best method. Originally only the optimizer could make this choice, not the programmer or end-user, but all of that has now changed. We will see shortly how the optimizer can be forced to use the FAST FIRST or TOTAL TIME strategy or a specific strategy with the query outline. Remember though, that if no indexes or the incorrect indexes are created on a table, the optimizer can only perform a sequential access. In versions of Rdb prior to V6.0 this was not an efficient strategy, but with asynchronous pre-fetch the response time has improved dramatically and sequential retrieval should not necessarily be considered inefficient.

A transaction analysis, shown in Chapter 11, tells the database designer which indexes to create on which tables using which columns. Performing a transaction analysis lets the designer understand which transactions the database must be optimized for; that is, which indexes must be created (indexes speed up retrievals and slow down inserts).

Hint: In our experience, many database performance problems are the result of non-optimum strategies being chosen by the optimizer. This happens because indexes are not created at the proper time because they use the wrong set of columns, or because incorrect index types are created (hashed instead of sorted). In all these cases, if the designer had performed a rigorous transaction analysis, the problems may not have occurred.

6.2   CHOOSING A STRATEGY

When the optimizer analyzes a query, it performs a number of tasks. First, it chooses a possible access method for each table based on the indexes that are defined for the table and the columns that are specified in the query. Then it estimates the cardinality of the rows to be accessed based on the selection criteria of the query and the access method being explored. A cost in terms of time is then worked out for this particular method. The cost may be greater or less than previously explored strategies (solutions). If it is less, previous solutions that cost more are discarded; if it is more, this current method is discarded.

6.2.1   Index Cardinality

Rdb knows the approximate number of rows in a table and the cardinality of each index that is not unique. For example, in the BANKING database the CUSTOMER table has a column marked STATUS. If the STATUS column could only take three possible values and the designer had defined an index based on this column alone, the index cardinality of this index would be three. On the other hand, consider an index defined on the SURNAME field alone. If there were 10,000 customers in the bank, the cardinality of this index could be between 7000 and 10,000 because of duplicate surnames. The index cardinalities, then, are a measure of the number of unique values in a non-unique index. The CUST_INDEX in the BANKING database is a multi-segment index made up of the SURNAME and FIRST_NAME columns, so the index cardinality probably will be higher than if the index was based on the SURNAME alone.

The optimizer understands index cardinalities, so it can choose the best non-unique index to use, possibly saving many disk I/Os. Maintaining index cardinality adds a small overhead to certain write transactions, but it is more than worth the effort.

6.2.2   Dynamic Optimization Strategy

Dynamic optimization methods are chosen when b-tree or hashed indexes are available. The first step is to select the background indexes by identifying all the useful indexes and then eliminate those indexes which contain the same attributes. The cost of scanning each background index is determined and this influences the order in which the indexes are scanned. All the strategies except background-only use foreground and background indexes. Rdb switches between these indexes while retrieving data, depending on the retrieval speed and the actual number of rows found that satisfied the query.

6.2.3   Checking the Optimizer Strategy

You will recall that many performance problems are caused by missing or incorrect indexes. It is possible to check what strategy the optimizer has chosen for a particular query and also its estimated cost. To produce a formatted display of the chosen strategy, set the OpenVMS logical name RDMS$DEBUG_FLAGS to be "S". For example:

```
$ DEFINE rdms$debug_flags "S"
```

This will display the output on the developer's terminal or workstation. If required to direct the output to a file, the OpenVMS logical name RDMS$DEBUG_FLAGS_OUTPUT is defined in addition. For example:

```
$ DEFINE rdms$debug_flags_output "my_output.dat"
```

For dynamic optimization, two additional options for the debug flags are available:

E Displays the dynamic optimization execution trace

\ Forces the optimizer to switch between the foreground and background indexes once ten dbkeys are placed in the buffer; used during testing only.

Some examples of checking optimizer strategies follow. In the first example, the optimizer cannot use an index so the access method chosen is sequential:

```
SQL> SELECT surname, first_name, credit_limit FROM customer;
~S#0018
Get    Retrieval sequentially of relation CUSTOMER
  SURNAME         FIRST_NAME        CREDIT_LIMIT
  Hobbs           Lilian            10000.00
  Smith           Paul                900.00
    .
    .
```

In the next example, a condition is specified (conjunct) but there is no index on first name so a sequential access method is chosen again:

```
SQL> SELECT surname, first_name, credit_limit FROM customer
cont>   WHERE first_name = 'Lilian';
~S#0035
Conjunct    Get  Retrieval sequentially of relation CUSTOMER
 SURNAME        FIRST_NAME       CREDIT_LIMIT
 Hobbs          Lilian           10000.00
1 row selected
```

The index BRANCH_INDEX is used in the following example because the BRANCH_CODE column is the only column in the index.

```
SQL> SELECT *  FROM branch WHERE branch_code = 'SOT';
~S#0024
Get    Retrieval by index of relation BRANCH
  Index name  BRANCH_INDEX [1:1]      Direct lookup
 BRANCH_CODE   BRANCH_NAME      BRANCH_ADDRESS  MANAGERS_NAME
  SOT          Southampton      10 High Street  Mr Jones
```

A query is made against the ACCOUNT table in the next example, but the condition used is the greater than (>) operator, so the hashed index ACCOUNT_INDEX cannot be used.

```
SQL> SELECT customer_no FROM account
cont>   WHERE account_no > 1234567890;

 Conjunct   Get   Retrieval sequentially of relation ACCOUNT
    CUSTOMER_NO
    1122334455
       :
       :
  1122334455
 13 rows selected
```

The final example shows a query being made against the ACCOUNT table where the equality operator (=) is used. For this reason, the hashed index ACCOUNT_INDEX is selected:

```
SQL> SELECT customer_no FROM account WHERE account_no = 1551290;
~S#0039
Leaf#01 FFirst ACCOUNT Card=8
  BgrNdx1 ACCOUNT_INDEX [1:1] Fan=1
~E#0039.01(1) BgrNdx1 EofData   DBKeys=1 Fetches=0+0 RecsOut=1 #Bufs=1
~E#0039.01(1) FgrNdx FFirst     DBKeys=1 Fetches=0+0 RecsOut=1 'ABA
~E#0039.01(1) Fin     Buf       DBKeys=1 Fetches=0+0 RecsOut=1
  CUSTOMER_NO
  100201
1 row selected
```

It is important to note that the optimization of Rdb queries is *dynamic*; that is, a query is optimized every time one is submitted to Rdb. Suppose a program is run to access data, and afterwards the database administrator creates an index. If the program is run again, the index will be considered by the optimizer and may be used. Recompiling a program is not necessary to make use of the new index structures available.

6.2.4   Checking the Optimizer Cost

The logical name RDMS$DEBUG_FLAGS is set to display statistics concerning the number of solutions tried by the optimizer and rejected before query execution. The statistics show the estimated number of rows that will be returned, which is displayed as the cardinality of the chosen solution. The cost of the chosen solution is the estimated number of I/Os (physical or logical) that will be performed to execute the query. To display these statistics, set the OpenVMS logical name RDMS$DEBUG_FLAGS to be "0". For example:

```
$ DEFINE rdms$debug_flags "0"
```

The following is an example of the display:

```
SQL> SELECT customer_no FROM account
cont> WHERE account_no = 1234567890;
Solutions tried 2

 Solutions blocks created 1
 Created solutions pruned 0
 Cost of the chosen solution      2.0769231E+00
```

```
Cardinality of chosen solution      2.4253564E-01
Solutions tried 0
Solutions blocks created 0
Created solutions pruned 0
 CUSTOMER_NO
 1122334455
1 row selected
```

Here we can see that the optimizer has estimated that approximately two I/Os could be necessary to satisfy the query. The estimated cardinality implies that no more than one row will be returned.

6.2.5   Pre-Version 4.0 Optimizer Strategy Examples

Seeing examples of queries and the resulting optimizer strategy can help you to understand the optimizer.

Sequential Retrieval

The sequential retrieval strategy results in a sequential walk of the entire relation, which could be costly in terms of performance if the table walked is very large. However, Rdb V6.0 has an asynchronous pre-fetch facility to read database pages in advance which can reduce the time required to read all the pages. Nevertheless, all sequential retrievals should be justified because while the table is being read it is locked in protected mode which can prevent other users from accessing data in the table. Sequential retrieval is usually considered undesirable, but bear in mind that there are instances where sequential access is perfectly reasonable and may be the best retrieval method available.

```
SQL> SELECT account_no FROM account WHERE statement_day > 25;
~S#0040
Conjunct      Get     Retrieval sequentially of relation ACCOUNT
         ACCOUNT_NO
            1561290
            9561490
            9167890
            1551290
4 rows selected
```

Index Retrieval

In index retrieval, an index is used to identify the records that satisfy the record selection expression. Not all the required information is specified within the index, however, so the actual row must be retrieved to display all the information. An index retrieval method implies quick access to the data.

```
SQL> SELECT account_no,balance FROM account
cont>  WHERE account_no= 1002035678;
Get Retrieval by index of relation ACCOUNT Index name ACCOUNT_INDEX
00000001 Segments in low Ikey    00000001 Segments in high Ikey

     ACCOUNT_NO              BALANCE
     1002035678              -508.78
1 row selected
```

Index-Only Retrieval

The only difference between an index-only retrieval and the previous strategy is that in index-only the column BALANCE is not displayed. As a result, the optimizer decides that since only the ACCOUNT_NO is required and this information is already in the index, it is not necessary to retrieve the actual row from the database. Improved performance is the result. The index-only strategy is used when the optimizer can report all the requested information without having to retrieve any of the actual rows from the database.

```
SQL> SELECT surname FROM customer ORDER BY surname;
~S#0045
Index only retrieval of relation CUSTOMER
  Index name   CUST_INDEX [0:0]
 SURNAME
 Grice
 Hagan
 Hobbs
 Smith
4 rows selected
```

6.2.6   Dynamic Optimizer Strategy Examples

In this chapter, there is not enough space or time to explain the detailed workings of the optimizer using dynamic optimization methods. Instead, some examples of queries that have used the dynamic optimization strategy are included to illustrate how the different methods are selected.

Interpreting the Dynamic Optimizer Display

The information output by the dynamic optimizer can be very useful, especially during database tuning. So what does the following output mean?

```
SQL> SELECT surname, first_name, balance
cont>  FROM customer c, account a WHERE surname='Hobbs' AND
cont>  credit_limit > 100 AND c.customer_no = a.customer_no
cont>    ORDER BY postcode;
~S#0015       15th Strategy in this session
Sort
Cross block of 2 entries
  Cross block entry 1
    Bgr Only Retr on table Customer.
   Leaf#01 BgrOnly CUSTOMER Card=4 (4 rows in table)
     Bgr Idx CUST_INDEX
   BgrNdx1 CUST_INDEX [1:1]  Fan=11 (est 11 entries per node)
  Cross block entry 2
    Bgr Only Retr on table Account.
   Leaf#02 BgrOnly ACCOUNT Card=8 (8 rows in table)
     Bgr Idx ACCT_CUST
   BgrNdx1 ACCT_CUST [1:1] Fan=14 (est 14 entries per node)
~E#0015.01(1)  BgrNdx1 EofData DBKeys=1 Fetches=0+0 RecsOut=0 #Bufs=1
~E#0015.02(1)  BgrNdx1 EofData DBKeys=4 Fetches=0+0 RecsOut=0 #Bufs=4
~E#0015.02(1)  Fin    Buf    DBKeys=4 Fetches=0+0 RecsOut=4
~E#0015.01(1)  Fin    Buf    DBKeys=1 Fetches=0+0 RecsOut=1

  C.SURNAME        C.FIRST_NAME A.BALANCE
  Hobbs            Lilian            1234.56
  Hobbs            Lilian             456.78
```

```
Hobbs            Lilian          -1207.56
Hobbs            Lilian          -64.45
4 rows selected
```

~E#0015.01 indicates the execution for leaf #01. *EofData* means that the index was traversed to the end, and *DBKeys* is the number of dbkeys found, which in this example is 1. *Fetches of 0+0* means that no I/O was incurred to walk the index and no I/O to retrieve database pages. This means that all the information was in the database buffer. *RecsOut* is the total number of rows delivered; again this is zero and *#Bufs* is an estimate of how many page buffers will be read for the dbkeys in the list, which in this example is only 1 buffer because we only found 1 dbkey.

~E#0015.02(1) refers to the execution for the second leaf where four dbkeys have been identified that match the searching criteria.

~E#0015.02(1) Fin indicates the execution for leaf #02 in the final reading phase. 4 dbkeys were found that matched the criteria, no I/O was incurred to retrieve and 4 records were output.

When the indexes are scanned the numbers within the brackets indicate how the index is scanned, [0:0] means that the entire index was scanned; [1:1] means an equivalence test or there is a low and high value. Referring to our example, the optimizer tells us that it used CUST_INDEX as [1:1] which would be to evaluate the *surname = 'Hobbs'* part of the query.

If the values are [0:1], then this means there is no low value and one high value. That is, the surname is less than 'S'.

```
SQL> SELECT surname FROM customer WHERE surname < 'S';
~S#0003
Index only retrieval of relation CUSTOMER
   Index name   CUST_INDEX [0:1]
```

Reversing the query, values are [1:0] because there is a low value but no high value.

```
SQL> SELECT surname FROM customer WHERE surname > 'S';
~S#0004
Index only retrieval of relation CUSTOMER
   Index name   CUST_INDEX [1:0]
```

Hint: Use the Fetches <no>+<no> as a measure of the amount of I/O used to execute the query.

Background-Only

The objective of the background-only method is to reduce the total time required to execute the query. Unlike the fast-first method, where the objective is to return the first few records very quickly, this method is selected when one or more indexes could be used, but none contains all the fields required for the query. In the following example, only one index, CUST_INDEX, is available on the columns SURNAME and FIRST_NAME.

```
SQL> SELECT surname, first_name FROM customer
cont>   WHERE surname = 'Hobbs'
cont>   ORDER BY postcode;
~S#0046
Sort
Leaf#01 BgrOnly CUSTOMER Card=4
   BgrNdx1 CUST_INDEX [1:1] Fan=11
~E#0046.01(1) BgrNdx1 EofData  DBKeys=1 Fetches=0+0  RecsOut=0 #Bufs=1
~E#0046.01(1) Fin     Buf      DBKeys=1 Fetches=0+1  RecsOut=1

  SURNAME          FIRST_NAME
  Hobbs            Lilian
1 row selected
```

Index-Only Strategy

The index-only method is used when one or more indexes exist that contains all the columns required to execute the query. However, to use this method there must be at least one other index that does not contain all the columns. In the following example, two indexes are available, one called CUST_SUR_STATUS on columns status and surname, the other CUST_STATUS on column status.

```
SQL> SELECT surname, status FROM customer
cont> WHERE surname <='Z' AND surname >='A' AND status = 0;
~S#0050
Leaf#01 NdxOnly CUSTOMER Card=4
   FgrNdx    CUST_SUR_STATUS [1:1] Fan=9
   BgrNdx1   CUST_STATUS [1:1]     Fan=17
~E#0050.01(1) FgrNdx NdxOnly DBKeys=0 Fetches=0+0 RecsOut=0
0 rows selected
```

Sorted Method Strategy

The sorted method is used when:

- A query requests a sorted order.

- Index-only cannot be used.

- An index with the correct order exists.

- At least one index is used for filtering.

In the following example, two indexes are available, CUST_INDEX on columns surname and first name, and CUST_STATUS on column status.

```
SQL> SELECT surname, first_name, status FROM customer
cont> WHERE surname >='Hobbs' AND status = 1 ORDER BY surname;
~S#0051
Leaf#01 Sorted CUSTOMER Card=4
   FgrNdx    CUST_INDEX [1:0]   Fan=11
   BgrNdx1   CUST_STATUS [1:1] Fan=17

 SURNAME      FIRST_NAME        STATUS
 Hobbs        Lilian            1
~E#0051.01(1) FgrNdx Sorted  DBKeys=2 Fetches=0+0 RecsOut=2
 Smith        Paul              1
2 rows selected
```

Fast-First Strategy

The fast-first method is used to deliver a few records very quickly. This strategy is often chosen by the optimizer during interactive queries when it suspects that the query may be terminated early. Apart from interactive queries, fast-first also is used on queries with EXISTS, FIRSTN, or LIMIT TO *x* ROWS clauses.

```
SQL> SELECT surname, first_name, status FROM customer
cont> WHERE surname >='Hobbs' AND status = 1 AND
cont>  customer_no > '100203' AND first_name <='Lilian';
~S#0052
Leaf#01
  CUSTOMER Card=4
    BgrNdx1 CUST_STATUS [1:1]  Fan=17
    BgrNdx2 CUST_UNIQUE [1:0]  Fan=14
    BgrNdx3 CUST_INDEX [1:0]   Fan=11
~E#0052.01(1) Estim    Ndx:Lev/Seps/DBKeys 2:1/2/2 1:1/1\5 3:_7
~E#0052.01(1) Fin    Seq    DBKeys=4  Fetches=0+0  RecsOut=0
0 rows selected
```

Debug Flags Strategy

The logical RDMS$DEBUG_FLAGS can take a number of values. The table below details the most useful.

Table 6.1 - RDMS$DEBUG_FLAGS Logical Possible Values

Value	Description
C	Cardinality Values
E	Dynamic Optimization Execution Trace
O	Optimizer Costs
S	Retrieval Statistics Strategy
Ss	Generate a query outline
\	Dynamic Optimization fill buffer with only 10 dbkeys

6.3   INFLUENCING THE OPTIMIZER

In an ideal world it should not be necessary to influence the optimizer to take a different course of action to the one that it thinks is best. However, experi- ence has shown that sometimes the user knows best and for that reason Rdb provides three methods to influence the optimizer strategy:

- Enforce a FAST FIRST strategy

- Enforce a TOTAL TIME strategy

- Query outline

6.3.1   FAST FIRST or TOTAL TIME

There are certain occasions when you may want the optimizer to use the FAST FIRST (FFirst) or TOTAL TIME (BgrOnly) strategy. This can be simply achieved by including these key words in the SELECT clause or in a cursor declaration. Remember though that once specified in an application, this method will always be used, so only include it in an application if it is really necessary.

In the example shown below the optimizer decides that a FFirst strategy should be used.

```
SQL> SELECT surname, first_name FROM customer
cont>   WHERE surname>='Hobbs' AND status = 1 AND
cont>   customer_no > '100203' AND first_name <='Lilian';
~S#0016
Leaf#01 FFirst CUSTOMER Card=4
  BgrNdx1 CUST_UNIQUE [1:0] Fan=14
  BgrNdx2 CUST_INDEX [1:0] Bool Fan=6
~E#0016.01(1) Estim   Ndx:Lev/Seps/DBKeys 1:1/2/2 2:_7
~E#0016.01(1) Fin     Seq    DBKeys=4  Fetches=0+1  RecsOut=0
0 rows selected
```

By adding the OPTIMIZE FOR TOTAL TIME clause the strategy is changed to BgrOnly.

```
SQL> SELECT surname, first_name FROM customer
cont> WHERE surname>='Hobbs' AND status = 1 AND
cont>   customer_no > '100203' AND first_name <='Lilian'
cont>   OPTIMIZE FOR TOTAL TIME;
~S#0017
Leaf#01 BgrOnly CUSTOMER Card=4
   BgrNdx1 CUST_UNIQUE [1:0] Fan=14
   BgrNdx2 CUST_INDEX [1:0] Bool Fan=6
~E#0017.01(1) Estim    Ndx:Lev/Seps/DBKeys 1:1/2/2 2:_7
~E#0017.01(1) Fin     Seq    DBKeys=4  Fetches=0+0  RecsOut=0
0 rows selected
```

6.3.2   Query Outlines

One of the often touted advantages of using a relational database is the fact
that the user does not need to know how to retrieve the data; they simply
specify the query and the optimizer chooses the access path. For the majority
of queries and applications this approach is ideal. However, some users have
found that the access strategy chosen by the optimizer varies between versions
which can result in a sub-second query taking many seconds, or even minutes
if you are very unlucky. Another common problem is when a table is very
volatile and the number of rows in the table varies. In this instance, the number
of rows in the table will determine the strategy chosen by the optimizer. Both
of these examples illustrate the need to stabilise the optimizer strategy, which
is achieved by defining query outlines.

**Hint: Query outlines should only be defined as a last resort because one
requires considerable knowledge of the optimizer to ensure that the query
does not perform worse when the outline is used.**

A query outline is created by defining the two logicals
RDMS$DEBUG_FLAGS and RDMS$DEBUG_FLAGS_OUTPUT. Then the
query is executed and the outline for the query is modified to produce the
desired results. Finally it is executed in SQL and for all subsequent queries
that will be used.

In the following example the normal retrieval strategy is to use the index. An outline is created which changes the retrieval strategy to sequential. Of course a sequential retrieval strategy is not one the authors would normally recommend.

```
$ DEFINE RDMS$DEBUG_FLAGS "Ss"
$ DEFINE RDMS$DEBUG_FLAGS_OUTPUT    query_outline.sql
SQL> SELECT branch_name FROM branch WHERE branch_code = 'SOT';
```

This results in the creation of the following outline, which is edited to change the access path to sequential.

```
SQL- Rdb Generated Outline : 19-DEC-1993 16:17
CREATE OUTLINE     QO_102BBBD9A2DE99C7_00000000
id '102BBBD9A2DE99C76134EFB3D5CB4BA8'
mode 0
as (
  query (
   subquery (
    BRANCH 0      access path sequential
    )
   )
  )
compliance optional   ;
COMMIT;
```

Using SQL, the outline is stored with the system metadata.

Now when the query is executed the optimizer output displays the name of the query outline used to resolve this query.

```
SQL> SELECT branch_name FROM branch WHERE branch_code = 'SOT';
~S: Outline QO_102BBBD9A2DE99C7_00000000 used
~S#0007
Conjunct    Get    Retrieval sequentially of relation BRANCH
 BRANCH_NAME
 test
1 row selected
```

The nice aspect of this feature is that the query outline only applies to this specific query; therefore the one shown below which is very similar to the outline query but not identical, will use the index for retrieval.

```
SQL> SELECT branch_name FROM branch WHERE branch_code = 'SOT'
cont>  AND branch_code IS NOT NULL;
~S#0006
Get    Retrieval by index of relation BRANCH
  Index name  BRANCH_INDEX [1:1] Bool    Direct lookup
 BRANCH_NAME
 test
1 row selected
```

Sometimes it might be desirable to change the strategies for a query depending on the circumstances. For example, whether the query is run during the online day or as part of overnight batch processing. This can be achieved by defining multiple outlines for the same query, where each outline has a unique negative number, known at the *mode*. Each outline for a query is allocated a unique negative number. When the query is run, the outline chosen is determined by the value of the logical:

RDMS$BIND_OUTLINE_MODE

Another option available to the designer of the query outline is to specify what is known as a partial outline. Unlike a full outline which details how the entire query must be executed, a partial outline specifies the strategy for certain components or elements, such as one of the tables in the query. Outlines such as these are less likely to be invalidated, and may offer all the query optimization control required. An outline is automatically invalidated if metadata changes occur which affect the outline, such as an index is dropped that is referenced in the outline.

It is a good idea not to start defining outlines until a database design is stable, because certain metadata changes will invalidate the outline, which means it will have to be dropped and redefined.

This chapter introduced the optimizer and explained how the chosen strategy is observed using the RDMS$DEBUG_FLAGS logical name. Use of the RDMS$DEBUG_FLAGS logical name should be mandatory in every program test and documentation. Since the optimizer code is enhanced in every release of Rdb, it is vital that no attempts be made to fool the optimizer, otherwise the strategy may change when a new release is installed. Influencing the optimizer should only be attempted via query outline. The *Rdb Guide to Database Maintenance and Performance* has more detailed information about the optimizer.

7   Transaction Management

Rdb is a multi-user database system, meaning that many users can be attached to a database, reading and updating rows simultaneously. When this is the case, a number of users most likely will be interested in the same tables and rows at the same time. Rdb manages this shared access to data with a locking scheme. If shared access were not managed it would not be long before the database contained inconsistent data. In fact, the data would gradually become invalid, meaning information derived from it could not be trusted. Eventually the database would not reflect the state of the business, making it virtually useless. One of the organization's most important assets would have to be written off.

To demonstrate how database data could become inconsistent, we can draw upon a well-known problem that can occur in a database if shared access to its data is improperly managed. This problem is known as the *buried* or *lost update* problem. Suppose two users are updating customer accounts in the BANKING database. The first runs an online program that starts transaction *txn(1)*. This transaction reads a customer account and displays the data on the terminal screen. The user wishes to subtract $50 from the balance, which stands at $200. The user, therefore, instructs the program to debit the account by $50. The program displays the new account information on the terminal screen and asks the user to confirm the transaction. The new balance displayed of $150 looks correct, so the user confirms the transaction and the program updates the account on the database.

Everything is fine. Unfortunately, a second user also has decided to update the same account. The second user runs the online program and starts a transaction, *txn(2)*. Just after the first user has read the account row with *txn(1)*, the second does the same with *txn(2)*. Both users see exactly the same information on the terminal screen. The second user wishes to credit the account balance with $100. Unfortunately, this occurs after *txn(1)* has finished. The balance of

$200 is credited with $100, overwriting the balance of $150 stored by the first user. Clearly, the information added to the database by the first user is lost forever and the information held on this customer account is incorrect. The sequence of events is shown in Figure 7.1, with time progressing from left to right.

The correct balance value for this account should be $250 after executing these transactions. Rdb ensures that the inconsistency just discussed cannot occur by using a locking scheme. We shall see later in this chapter how a locking scheme prevents the buried update inconsistency.

Another classical problem occurs when one transaction is reading rows sequentially down a table while another transaction is allowed to insert rows into the table. We shall look at such a problem shortly.

7.1   TRANSACTIONS

All operations in Rdb are performed within transactions, whether they are data manipulation operations (DML) or data definition operations (DDL). Within a transaction, all of the operations are performed or none of them are performed. Consistency is maintained during a transaction; that is, the user's view of the data is stable. Of the various degrees of consistency, Rdb, by default, implements degree 3 consistency which is the ANSI standard default for a READ/WRITE transaction. To adhere to degree 3 consistency a transaction must meet the following requirements:

- All reads must be repeatable. If a transaction is reading a row, another transaction may not update that row until the first transaction finishes.

- An updated row cannot be read until the updating transaction finishes. No transaction can read the *in-flight* updates of another transaction.

- If a transaction updates a row, no other transaction may update that row until the first transaction finishes. In other words, all updates can be correctly rolled back.

These requirements mean that writers must wait for readers to finish before they can update. In fact, locks are never relinquished or demoted until the transaction ends with a commit or rollback. A more relaxed regime will be discussed later in this chapter.

Figure 7.1 The Buried Update Problem

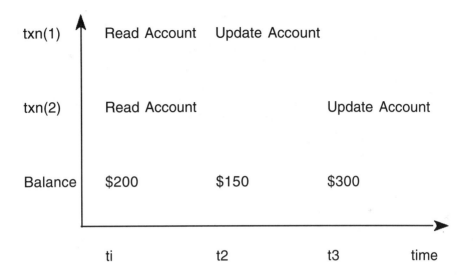

The locking scheme in Rdb is used for a number of purposes. Firstly, locks are used to control data at the logical level. Users can control these locks to a point using the SET TRANSACTION statement.

Secondly, locks are used to control data at the physical storage level. For example, database pages must be locked because different users may wish to manipulate rows on the same page. Prior to Rdb Version 6.0, page level locking was not controllable by the database designer. From Rdb Version 6.0 onwards, page level locking can be set for individual storage areas. Prior to Rdb Version 6.0 page locks were really just a mechanism to assist in buffer locking and synchronization. Now they can be thought of as real page locks.

Third, locking is used to communicate events between processes, such as when a node in a VMScluster accessing a database fails during a VMScluster state transition.

7.2 RDB LOCKING

The Rdb locking scheme is a sophisticated approach to ensuring that data integrity is maintained in a multi-user environment. In the OpenVMS environment, Rdb uses the OpenVMS Ddistributed Lock Manager to implement its locking scheme. To understand how Rdb overcomes problems such as the buried update problem, it is useful to use this environment as an example. The OpenVMS Distributed Lock Manager controls locks and resources. Every request for a lock is associated with a particular resource, such as a particular row. A lock is considered to control two types of access: the access permitted by the holder of the lock, the access mode, and the access permitted to other users, the share mode. The access modes may be *read* or *write*. The share modes may be:

● Concurrent: Readers and writers may share the resource.

● Protected: Only readers may share the resource.

● Exclusive: No one may share the resource.

Rdb considers many objects to be resources, including:

● The database itself

● A storage area (physical area)

● A table (logical area)

● A database page

● A table row

● An sorted index node

● A hash bucket

● A system record

A lock may be granted for any resource as long as it does not conflict with locks already held by other users. Locks also may be promoted or, in certain circumstances, demoted to a different lock mode. This is called *lock conversion*. Lock mode compatibility is shown in Table 7.1.

Table 7.1 Lock Mode Compatibility

Mode of	**Mode of Currently Granted Locks**					
Requested Lock	**NL**	**CR**	**CW**	**PR**	**PW**	**EX**
CR	Yes	Yes	Yes	Yes	Yes	No
CW	Yes	Yes	Yes	No	No	No
PR	Yes	Yes	No	Yes	No	No
PW	Yes	Yes	No	No	No	No
EX	Yes	No	No	No	No	No

Key: NL - Null Lock; CR - Concurrent Read; CW - Concurrent Write

PR - Protected Read; PW - Protected Write; EX - Exclusive Lock

If a conflict does occur, a user's lock cannot be granted. In this case, the user trying to unsuccessfully apply the lock may wait until it can be granted or terminate the lock request. The SET TRANSACTION statement includes a WAIT and NOWAIT qualifier with which the programmer may specify the desired course of action. If the WAIT qualifier is used, a time limit can also be specified.

If the NOWAIT qualifier is to be used, any lock conflict will immediately cause Rdb to return an error status. If the WAIT qualifier is used, the transaction will wait until the lock can be granted. It may be that in a well-designed database the transaction is forced to wait less than a second. In this instance, it often makes sense to take a WAIT approach, avoiding the associated overhead involved in trying access again, if the transaction would only have to wait a short time before the lock was granted. There also is no guarantee that a subsequent try would result in the lock being granted. Therefore, in most cases, choosing WAIT is the best strategy.

Chapter 12 describes how a wait time can be specified for a transaction.

7.2.1   Deadlocks

In a deadlock situation, locks can be neither granted nor converted. Take a situation where User A has a protected update lock on resource P, and User B has a protected update lock on resource Q. Now suppose User A attempts to place a protected update lock on resource Q. It cannot be granted, because the locks are incompatible. User A must wait until User B has released his lock. If User B now tries to place a protected update lock on resource P, she will be forced to wait for the same reasons. It is clear that both users, who are said to be in a deadlock state, will wait indefinitely. Figure 7.2 shows a deadlock state.

Figure 7.2 A Deadlock State

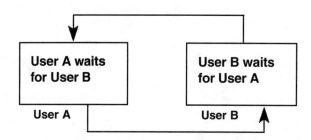

The OpenVMS distributed lock manager initiates a deadlock search once a lock request has been waiting for a predetermined length of time. This pre-determined time is the value of the OpenVMS system (SYSGEN) parameter DEADLOCK_WAIT and by default is set at ten seconds. The deadlock search is done to determine whether the waiting lock request is part of a deadlock. A victim is chosen if a deadlock is detected. The victim is always the youngest transaction, that is, the transaction that has existed for the shortest time. The victim's lock request is denied, and an error status is returned from Rdb indicating a deadlock failure. It is usual for the application to roll back the transaction, releasing all its locks, and to try the transaction again. It is possi-ble to be in distributed deadlocks where the relevant transactions originate from different nodes on the network. Distributed deadlocks are described in more detail in Chapter 12.

Hint: There is a myth that a process receiving a deadlock message automatically releases its locks and the other process continues its work. This is not true. When a deadlock error message is received the program or 4GL code must detect this fact and explicitly release its locks by ending the transaction, usually with a rollback.

7.2.2   The Buried Update Problem Revisited

If we look at the buried update problem again and apply a lock scheme similar to that used by Rdb, we can devise a simple solution. Suppose that when a transaction retrieves a customer account, Rdb places a protected read lock on the account row. Since protected read locks are compatible (see Table 7.1), both transactions can retrieve the same customer account row. However, when the first transaction tries to update the customer account row, Rdb must attempt to place a write lock on it. Write locks are not compatible with protected read locks (see Table 7.1), so the first transaction is forced to wait. The second transaction also attempts to update the customer account, but it, too, is forced to wait for the same reason. Consequently, we have a deadlock state. One of the transactions will be chosen as a victim and will receive an error message. The application program usually will abort the transaction at this point. The first transaction then will acquire its write lock and successfully complete. The integrity of the customer account will have been maintained as a buried update will not have been allowed to happen.

7.3   TABLE LOCKING

Three factors determine the locking for tables and rows:

- The SET TRANSACTION statement

- The verb being executed

- The retrieval method

- The transaction isolation level

7.3.1   The SET TRANSACTION Statement

Table locks are determined by the SET TRANSACTION statement. Transactions have many characteristics associated with them, which can be specified as part of the SET TRANSACTION or DECLARE TRANSACTION statements. Most of the characteristics affect the type of locking that is performed. The access mode that the transaction requires is one of the characteristics that can be specified.

The access modes that can be specified are:

• READ ONLY

• READ WRITE

• BATCH UPDATE

If snapshot files are enabled on the database, the clause READ ONLY can be specified on the SET TRANSACTION statement to start a snapshot transaction. Snapshot transactions are discussed in detail in Chapter 4. Snapshot transactions can only be used to retrieve data. From a locking point of view, they do not interfere with updating transactions. Thus, a user retrieving data from a table with a snapshot transaction does not lock out a user updating data in the same table. On the other hand, the user executing the snapshot transaction is not locked out by the updating user. This can dramatically increase concurrency in the table. Snapshot retrieval transactions are handy when writing reports based on database tables. Not only is the data presented consistently, no lock conflict occurs when rows are updated in the same table that is being searched, no matter how long the report takes to generate.

Note: Snapshot transactions will conflict with exclusive transactions.

READ WRITE transactions can update, as well as read data. READ WRITE transactions use locks determined by the tables and access modes specified in the RESERVING clause of the SET TRANSACTION statement.

BATCH UPDATE transactions also can update data as well as read it. These transactions lock the whole database, so no table or row-level locking needs to be done. BATCH UPDATE transactions should only be used in very special circumstances, such as the bulk loading of data, when the database has been backed up and load failure is not a concern. Unlike EXCLUSIVE UPDATE transactions, BATCH UPDATE transactions do not write to the run unit journal and therefore cannot be rolled back.

Share modes also can be specified as part of the SET TRANSACTION and DECLARE TRANSACTION statements. By specifying a share mode, a transaction limits the access by other transactions. The RESERVING clause is used to specify how the tables are to be shared.

If a lock is incompatible with other locks already in use, the SQL operation may terminate immediately or it may be delayed until the lock can be granted. The action taken is determined by a WAIT or NOWAIT qualifier on the SET TRANSACTION or DECLARE TRANSACTION statement.

The ANSI SQL standard defines the concept of *transaction isolation levels*. Isolation levels affect locking and are specified as part of the SET TRANS-ACTION or DECLARE TRANSACTION statement; however, they will be specifically dealt with shortly.

Some examples of the above mentioned SET TRANSACTION statements follow. The following statement starts a snapshot transaction.

```
SQL> SET TRANSACTION READ ONLY;
```

The following example reserves two tables. The transaction may wish to read the CUSTOMER table and update the ACCOUNT table.

```
SQL> SET TRANSACTION READ WRITE
cont>     RESERVING customer FOR SHARED READ
cont>            account FOR SHARED WRITE;
```

The next statement accesses two databases. Data will be read from the CUSTOMER table in one database and stored in the CUSTOMER table of another database. BANK and INSURANCE are known as aliases and specify the databases that are to be accessed.

```
SQL> SET TRANSACTION
cont>     ON bank USING (READ ONLY
cont>     RESERVING bank.customer FOR SHARED READ)
cont>     AND ON insurance USING (READ WRITE
cont>     RESERVING insurance.customer FOR SHARED WRITE);
```

The example that follows shows a transaction that will not wait for a lock conflict to be resolved. In the case of such a conflict, an error will be returned.

```
SQL> SET TRANSACTION READ WRITE
cont>  RESERVING branch FOR PROTECTED WRITE NOWAIT;
```

7.3.2   The Verb Being Executed

If no RESERVING clause is specified, the verbs executed during the transaction determine the table locks. That is, if the transaction only reads rows, the table will be treated as if it were reserved for shared read. Once an update occurs, the table will be treated as if it were reserved for shared write. A user need not specify a SET TRANSACTION because Rdb will provide a default READ WRITE transaction.

Hint: To ensure complete control over the transaction and to document the type of transaction started, the authors advise that a SET TRANSACTION statement always be issued.

7.3.3   The Retrieval Method

Once data is stored in a database, someone undoubtedly will want to retrieve it. Typically, the user retrieves a number of rows based upon some condition, such as all ACCOUNTS with a BALANCE greater than $10,000. In transaction processing, the search condition often is an exact key match, and only one row is retrieved. Depending on the structure of the query and the indexes defined on the table, the Rdb optimizer will choose one of the following retrieval strategies, which will determine the locking.

- Sequential

- Sorted index

- Hashed index

- Database key (dbkey)

Sequential Retrieval

In sequential retrieval, the rows in the table are read sequentially until all the rows satisfying the search condition are returned. Rdb locks each row before reading it. In accordance with degree 3 locking, these locks cannot be removed or demoted until the transaction issues a COMMIT or ROLLBACK. Consequently, many locks could be used if a large number of rows are processed. To avoid locking every row, Rdb changes to a table lock. To ensure that no other user can update a row, the table is locked with a protected read lock or a protected write lock, depending on whether the SET TRANSACTION statement specified a shared read or a shared write transaction.

The table lock is promoted after the SET TRANSACTION statement, that is, once the strategy is known. Therefore, a user may successfully issue a SET TRANSACTION statement only to find it is necessary to wait for another user to finish before access to the table is allowed.

Sorted Index Retrieval

If sorted indexes are present on a table, the optimizer may choose a sorted index retrieval strategy. In this situation, Rdb does not alter an existing table lock. Instead, both rows and index nodes are likely to be locked. It is possible, therefore, for lock conflict to occur in an index as well as in the data itself.

Rows and index nodes are locked in similar fashion. SHARED READ transactions place protected read locks on index nodes and rows, as in this transaction example.

```
SQL> SET TRANSACTION RESERVING accounts FOR SHARED READ;
```

SHARED WRITE transactions place an exclusive write lock on the index nodes and rows that are being modified, such as in the following transaction example.

```
SQL> SET TRANSACTION RESERVING accounts FOR SHARED WRITE;
```

Table 7.1 shows that protected and exclusive write locks are not compatible with protected read, protected write, and exclusive locks. Therefore, other users may be denied access to the locked index node or row until an updating transaction has committed or rolled back. This situation does not apply if only readers are accessing index nodes and rows. Their transactions take out protected retrieval locks that are compatible, as can be seen in Table 7.1.

If a table has only a few rows, probably few index nodes are present. In this case, conflict is likely. This situation is aggravated if the database designer has created the index with large index nodes because there are fewer nodes to hold all the index entries. A table with many rows probably has many index nodes, which decreases the chance of conflict. The index node size is an important point for the database designer to consider. Smaller index nodes can result in less locking contention when many users are updating the database, but they also result in deeper index trees, which could necessitate more disk I/Os to traverse the index.

Hint: The database designer can use the powerful RMU command RMU/ ANALYZE/INDEX/PLACEMENT to check the number of index levels and path lengths in an index. If necessary, the ALTER INDEX statement can be used to change the index node size and other index attributes.

If a transaction does not update a column that is part of the index, the index node will not get an update lock. If an index contains many nodes, the different index node levels are navigated until the lowest level, the Level 1 node, is reached. The nodes at this level point to the rows or duplicate nodes. As the different index levels are navigated, protected retrieval locks are placed on the nodes until the Level 1 index node is reached. A protected retrieval lock or an exclusive lock is placed on this node depending on whether the index is updated or not.

Hint: It is important to avoid situations in which users are updating or inserting rows based upon a similar range of key values, such as rows with serially increasing order numbers. Another example would be a key including a column with the current system time. In this situation, the users inserting or updating rows will be locking the same index nodes and increasing the probability of conflict. In both these situations, a hashed index may be useful.

Sorted Indexes With Non-Unique Keys

In sorted indexes where duplicate key values are not allowed, Level 1 index nodes contain database keys that point to the rows. Rdb creates duplicate index nodes if a sorted index allows duplicate key values and if table rows are inserted with duplicate key values. When duplicate nodes exist, the Level 1 index node entry points to the duplicate index node instead of a table row. The duplicate index node contains the database key for each table row that has identical key values. Duplicate index nodes also may be chained together. A duplicate index node structure was shown in Figure 5.2.

As we have mentioned, Rdb will lock these duplicate index nodes where necessary. Lock conflicts may occur between transactions accessing them.

Hashed Index Retrieval

As we learned in Chapter 5, a hashed index is a special kind of index that can be used to retrieve rows when the whole value of the key is known; that is, all the values of the columns that make up the key are known. A hashed index can provide fast access to rows if the exact match operator (=) is used. Other operators, such as greater than (>), less than (<), and BETWEEN, cannot use hashed index structures to improve the performance of a query.

A hashed index consists of a set of storage segments called *hash buckets*. These hash buckets contain database keys that point to the rows whose keys hash to the database page managed by the hash bucket. Hash buckets are not totally dissimilar to sorted index Level 1 nodes, and a lock placed on a hash bucket can restrict access to other rows pointed to by that hash bucket.

Since hash buckets usually hold fewer database keys than Level 1 nodes, there will be less contention than in sorted index nodes. More important, by definition, the hashing of the row keys may result in the random distribution of rows depending on the algorithm chosen. Therefore, the situation described earlier concerning inserting and updating rows with serially increasing key values should not be a problem with hashed indexes. System records on a database page pointing to hash buckets also are subject to locking and may be a source of conflict.

Database Key Retrieval

A row can be directly retrieved using its database key. In this case only the row is locked. If the row is updated in a way that causes an index update to occur, the index will have to be read and the appropriate locks acquired. Database keys were explained in Chapter 4.

7.3.4   Transaction Isolation Levels

Earlier in this chapter it was mentioned that, by default, Rdb provides degree 3 consistency which is also known as isolation level serializable. This ensures that the highest levels of data integrity are enforced by a very strict locking scheme. Unfortunately, locking is the natural enemy of performance and concurrency and strict locking schemes will reduce transaction concurrency. There may be situations where a relaxation of the locking scheme will not affect the integrity of the data in the database but an increase in concurrency can be made. Rdb provides the capability for the database designer to relax the degree of consistency provided by the locking scheme. The degree of consistency is referred to in Rdb as the isolation level.

The isolation level determines the amount that transactions can be affected by one another. There are three isolation levels supported in Rdb.

- Serializable

- Repeatable Read

- Read Committed

Another isolation level, Read Uncommitted, allows dirty data to be read, however, this is not supported by Rdb. The isolation level is specified as part of the SET TRANSACTION or DECLARE TRANSACTION statement and is only valid for READ WRITE transactions.

```
SQL> SET TRANSACTION READ WRITE ISOLATION LEVEL REPEATABLE READ;
```

The isolation level serializable represents the highest degree of consistency and is the default transaction mode. Different isolation levels determine the types of phenomenon that may occur when transactions are being run concurrently. These phenomena are:

- Nonrepeatable Read

- Phantom

Suppose a transaction *txn(1)* reads a row twice and between those two reads another transaction *txn(2)* updates values in that row and commits the update, then the second read of *txn(1)* will return a different result from the first read. This is known as a nonrepeatable read phenomenon and often leads to the buried update problem mentioned earlier in the chapter. It is shown diagrammatically in Figure 7.3.

In this example, both transactions read a balance of £1000. *Txn(1)* updates the balance by adding £500 to make it £1500 and commits the update. *Txn(2)* then adds £200 to what it believes is the current balance value (£1000) and commits the update. The update made by *txn(1)* has been overwritten by *txn(2)* and in this case data integrity has been compromised.

Suppose a transaction *txn(1)* performs a range retrieval, summing up a column in a number of rows and comparing the result of this summation with another

Figure 7.3 The Nonrepeatable Read Phenomenon

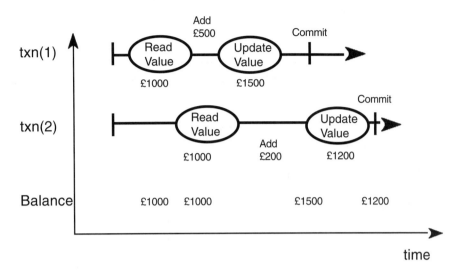

location holding the total. Suppose a transaction *txn(2)* inserts a new row after *txn(1)* has passed, updates the location holding the total and commits. *Txn(1)* will find that the result of its summation and the value in the location holding the total do not agree. This is known as a phantom phenomenon. It is shown diagrammatically in Figure 7.4.

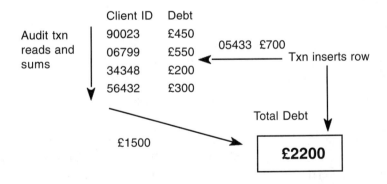

Figure 7.4 The Phantom Phenomenon

These phenomena can be prevented by the selection of an appropriate isolation level. Isolation level serializable will prevent both phenomena from occurring and it is equivalent to degree 3 consistency. Isolation level repeatable read will not allow the nonrepeatable read phenomenon to occur but will allow phantoms. Isolation level read committed allows both the nonrepeatable read phenomenon and the phantom phenomenon to occur. This is summarized in Table 7.2.

Table 7.2 Phenomena Allowed By Different Isolation Levels

Isolation Level	Nonrepeatable Reads Allowed	Phantoms Allowed
Serializable	No	No
Repeatable Read	No	Yes
Read Committed	Yes	Yes

It can be seen from the above discussion that starting a transaction with an isolation level other than serializable can be dangerous as data integrity might be compromised. However, if the database designer knows that his or her database and the applications that use it will not be affected by nonrepeatable read or phantom phenomena, some extra concurrency and therefore performance might be gained by running under more relaxed isolation levels.

7.3.5   Page Level Locking

With Rdb Version 6.0 the database designer was given the choice of using row level locking (as before) or specifying that locking should only be done at the page level. The fact that Rdb applied locks on pages was not controllable by the database designer prior to Version 6.0. Page locking was used transparently to ensure that the integrity of the database pages users had in their buffers was maintained.

Using page level locks instead of row level locks has advantages and disadvantages. The advantage is that one lock is used to lock the page and hence all the rows on the page as opposed to potentially many row level locks. This is a saving in system resource. The disadvantage is that concurrency may be reduced. If different users wish to update different rows on the same page and row level locking is in force, they will be allowed to do so. If page level locking is in force, the first user will take out a page lock on the page and the second user will be forced to wait for the page until the first user has committed their transaction. This is shown in Figure 7.5 and Figure 7.6. In Figure 7.5 two users are updating rows on a database page whereas in Figure 7.6 only one user is able to and the other user is forced to wait.

Figure 7.5 Using Row Level Locks, Two Users Can Both Update Rows

Database Page

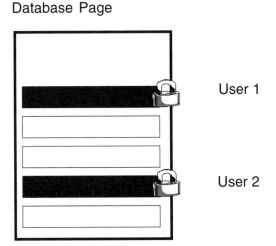

Figure 7.6 Using Page Level Locks, User 2 Must Wait for User 1

Database Page

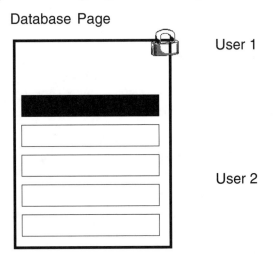

Page level locking is therefore most effective when users are unlikely to be accessing the same pages. An example of this might be where a parent row and its child rows are physically clustered together on a page. In the BANK-ING database this might be a customer and their accounts. In this case it is probable that a bank clerk is dealing exclusively with a customer and their accounts and so page level locking makes sense.

Page level locking is applied at the storage area level and is specified on the **CREATE** or **ALTER DATABASE** statement.

```
SQL> ALTER DATABASE FILENAME banking
cont> ALTER STORAGE AREA customer_area
cont> LOCKING IS PAGE LEVEL;
```

The default is row level locking. A **SHOW STORAGE AREA** statement or an RMU/DUMP/HEADER command will return information on the type of locking in use for a storage area.

```
SQL> SHOW STORAGE AREA CUSTOMER_AREA

     CUSTOMER_AREA
          Access is:        Read write
          Page Format:          Uniform
     :
     :

          Locking is Page Level

$ RMU/DUMP/HEADER banking
  :
Storage area CUSTOMER_AREA
    Area ID number is 2
    Filename is "EUROBANK:[UK.DB]CUSTOMER_AREA.RDA;1"
    Access mode is READ/WRITE
    Pages...
      - Page format is uniform
      - Page size is 2 blocks
      - Initial data page count was 501
      - Current physical page count is 502
      - Page-level locking is enabled
    :
```

Hint: As row or page level locking can only be specified by storage area, this is another consideration when deciding whether to group tables and indexes together in storage areas. Note that page level locking cannot be used for single-file databases or RDB$SYSTEM storage area in multifile databases.

Figure 7.7 The ALG Tree

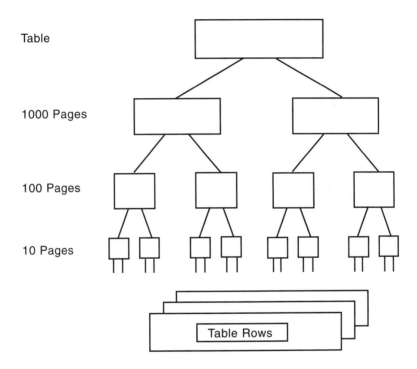

7.3.6   Adjustable Locking Granularity

We have seen that two users manipulating rows in the same table use a number of locks to ensure data integrity. To reduce the number of locks used, Rdb uses a technique called *adjustable lock granularity*. This technique assumes an inverted tree of resources known as the ALG tree. Each level in the tree corresponds to a resource. The farther down the tree the finer the granularity of resource.

This principle is shown in Figure 7.7, where the top of the ALG tree (the root) corresponds to a logical database area (Level 4), the next level down (Level 3) corresponds to groups of 1000 consecutive pages, the next level down (Level 2) corresponds to groups of 100 consecutive pages, the next level down (Level 1) corresponds to groups of 10 consecutive pages and the bottom leaf (Level 0) to the database rows themselves.

A transaction will attempt to take a strong lock out at Level 4 first of all. If there is contention the transaction will attempt to take out a strong lock at Level 3 while demoting the lock at Level 4 to a weak lock, then Level 2 and so on until the row is locked. This means that in a high contention environment it is possible that five locks are used to lock one row.

ALG is most effective where users manipulate rows in the same table but the rows are on different groups of pages.

The ALG mechanism uses CPU resources to manage the ALG tree and uses virtual memory in which to hold the locks. If a small number of rows are accessed by a transaction and other transactions also access a small number of rows in the same group of pages, it is probably best to disable ALG. This situation sometimes is found in transaction processing applications when a small part of the database is being accessed by transactions that manipulate only a few rows. To disable ALG for an individual database use the ALTER DATABASE statement.

```
SQL> ALTER SCHEMA FILENAME banking
cont>    ADJUSTABLE LOCK GRANULARITY IS DISABLED;
```

Contention in the ALG tree can be spotted with RMU/SHOW STATISTICS using the stall message screens. If what looks like a database key with a negative line number is seen, this is ALG tree lock contention. In this case the 'line number' field is set to -4, -3, -2 or -1 to represent the level. The page number field is set to the first page in the group of pages and the logical area identifies the table or index being locked.

7.4   RMU/SHOW LOCKS

The investigation of lock related problems will almost certainly involve the RMU/SHOW STATISTICS command with its screens of lock related information and lock stall messages. This command is described in Chapter 11.

However, the RMU command, RMU/SHOW LOCKS may facilitate the investigation of process locking activity and we will discuss this command in this chapter as it is purely lock related.

The command, on the whole, returns information that is VMScluster node specific. Various flavors of the command can be tried with different qualifiers such as /PROCESS, /MODE or /LOCK_ID.

```
RMU/SHOW  LOCKS/PROCESS=00000063/MODE=BLOCKING
```

```
SHOW LOCKS/PROCESS/BLOCKING  Information
```

```
Resource: record 9597:23
          ProcessID   Process Name      Lock ID     System ID Requested
Granted
Waiting:  00000063    _FTA7:.........   050003DF    00000000     PR NL
Blocker:  00000062    _FTA8:.........   05000356    00000000     EX EX
```

The above example requests information on processes blocking the named process. In this case, process 00000062 has an exclusive lock on the resource, record 9597:23, and this process is blocking process 00000063.

```
RMU/SHOW  LOCKS/LOCK=050003DF
```

```
SHOW LOCKS/LOCK  Information
```

```
Resource: record 9597:23
          ProcessID Process Name      Lock ID     System ID  Requested
Granted
Owner:    00000063   _FTA7:.........  050003DF    00000000     PR  NL
Blocker:  00000062   _FTA8:.........  05000356 00000000        EX  EX
```

The above example displays information about the specified lock. Note that the lock ID can be obtained from an RMU/SHOW STATISTICS stall messages screen and then, using the L key, this information can be instantly displayed.

7.5   PRESTARTED TRANSACTIONS

Since the early versions of Rdb, an optimization has been employed to reduce disk I/O to the database root file known as prestarted transactions. When a read/write transaction is committed or rolled back a new read/write transaction is started for that attach. The same transaction sequence number (TSN) is given to the new prestarted transaction as was given to the previous read/write transaction. Generally, this optimization is fine, however, in certain circumstances it can result in the snapshot file growing excessively.

This is because of the way in which Rdb reclaims snapshot file space, that is, overwrites old, irrelevant data. The read/write transaction that has been active for the greatest length of time has a TSN value that is the basis for a concept known as the *cutoff TSN*. If Rdb finds a row in the snapshot file whose TSN is less than the cutoff TSN, Rdb can overwrite this row and hence re-use the space. Unfortunately, because of the prestarted transaction optimization, a TSN value may stay in the database for a long time if the process does not detach. This means that a cutoff TSN may stay at this same value for a long time and therefore snapshot file space will not be reclaimed and the snapshot file will potentially grow. This phenomenon is most likely to affect applications that use server processes that stay attached to the database for long periods of time, for example, DEC ACMS or ACMSxp.

Originally, there were two methods for forcing a new read/write transaction to receive a new TSN. First, the process could detach from the database and then re-attach at specific time intervals or after a number of transactions had been processed or at some other application defined event. Second, the process could commit, start a read-only transaction, roll back and then start a read/write transaction again. This would force a new TSN.

Now, new syntax is available to allow the database designer to disable the prestarted transaction optimization. This can be specified on an a ATTACH, CONNECT, DECLARE ALIAS, CREATE DATABASE and IMPORT statement.

```
SQL> ATTACH 'FILENAME banking
cont>   PRESTARTED TRANSACTIONS ARE OFF';
```

The database designer will need to determine if there is a significant drop in performance caused by this optimization being disabled.

7.6   **FAST COMMIT TRANSACTION PROCESSING**

When a user executes a COMMIT verb, the default scenario and the scenario everyone expects is that Rdb writes all the modified (also known as *marked*) buffers to stable storage, that is, to disk. In fact, a buffer pool is considered well sized when the only time a modified buffer is written to disk is in response to a commit. By default, the reasons why a modified buffer are written back to disk are:

- A commit verb is issued

- Page contention

- Buffer pool overflow

Page contention occurs when a user wishes to access data held on the same page that another user has in their buffer. In this case, the user holding it must write the page back to disk so both users may see the same version. Buffer pool overflow occurs when a user wishes to read in a page and there are no more buffers free in their local buffer pool (or allocate set if global buffers are enabled). In this case a least recently used algorithm chooses a buffer to discard and if that buffer has been modified it must be written back to disk. Only writing buffer back to disk when a commit occurs and avoiding the other two cases benefits performance as Rdb writes out buffers on a commit in a very efficient fashion.

Hint: Use the RMU/SHOW STATISTICS physical I/O (PIO) display to observe the reasons for buffer flushing and the frequency of it.

Ensuring that all the modified buffers are written to disk on a commit has the advantage that, in the event of a failure, Rdb only has to roll back incomplete transactions. It never needs to consider the committed transactions that completed successfully – they are safely stored on disk, and in the after-image journal file if after-image journaling is enabled. In other words, recovery is very fast.

To summarize therefore what happens when Rdb executes a commit:

1 The run unit journal (RUJ) buffers are written to the RUJ file.

2 The modified database buffers are written to the storage area files.

3 If enabled, AIJ buffers are written to the AIJ file.

4 Commit information is written to the root file.

There are applications where writing the database pages to disk at commit time may be an overkill and may not be the most efficient approach. Consider an application where each user is reponsible for continually updating their own set of database rows. An example might be a commodities dealing system where individual users are responsible for particular commodities or maybe particular clients. They continually update the same group of database pages and at the end of every transaction these pages are written back to disk which can cause a high disk I/O load.

Fast commit processing is a technique that can be used to avoid this. With fast commit processing enabled, a process does not write modified buffers to the database storage areas when a commit is issued. Instead, it writes to the AIJ file which must be in use, keeping the pages in the buffers. Writes to the RUJ file are also avoided. This raises the question - when are the modified pages written to the database storage areas? The answer is when a checkpoint occurs.

A checkpoint is an event that causes the process's modified buffers to be written to the database storage areas. A variety of circumstances cause a checkpoint to occur as will be described shortly, but invariably a checkpoint occurs at a lower frequency than a commit, otherwise there would be no benefit derived.

To summarize therefore what happens when Rdb executes a commit with fast commit processing enabled:

1 The modified database buffers are not written to the storage area files

2 AIJ buffers are written to the AIJ file.

3 Commit information is written to the root file.

Note that the run unit journal (RUJ) buffers are not written to the RUJ file.

The reasons why a modified buffer are written back to disk with fast commit processing enabled are:

- A checkpoint is issued

- Page contention

- Buffer pool overflow

The explanation for page contention and buffer pool overflow is the same as previously described, however, as the fundamental idea behind fast commit processing is to reduce disk I/O, avoiding page contention and buffer pool overflow becomes even more important.

Another question now becomes apparent – namely what happens if a failure occurs with the database page updates now not stored safely in the database storage areas on disk? They are in fact stored away safely on stable storage but they are in the AIJ. Therefore, as well as rolling back a failed transaction, a recovery process must also read the commited updates stored in the AIJ file since the last checkpoint and write them to the database. This has an important ramification – recovery can now be much slower especially if the interval between checkpoints is long. Also a database recovery operation will freeze other users until it completes. This, of course, is of no consequence if a stable operational environment is present.

Note that by recovery we refer to the recovery initiated by, for example, a process failure where a database recovery process is created. We are not referring to a RMU/RECOVER operation.

The database administrator can specify how long the interval between checkpoints is, or to look at this another way, how frequently should a checkpoint be issued?

A long interval between checkpoints will minimize the disk I/O activity on the database storage area disks but at the expense of a longer recovery time. A short interval between checkpoints will reduce the benefits of fast commit processing as the buffers will be frequently written. The frequency of process checkpoints can be selected with any one or any combination of the following:

- The amount the AIJ can grow in blocks

- The elapsed time in seconds

- The number of transactions completed

When any condition becomes true, the process checkpoints and all the counters are effectively reset. The first two counters are specified database-wide; however, the third may be specified per process. It is only set by a logical name RDM$BIND_CKPT_TRANS_INTERVAL.

To turn on fast commit processing, the ALTER DATABASE statement may be used.

```
SQL> ALTER DATABASE FILENAME banking
cont> JOURNAL FAST COMMIT ENABLED
cont> (CHECKPOINT INTERVAL IS 200 BLOCKS,
cont> CHECKPOINT TIMED EVERY 120 SECONDS);
```

The above example will cause a process to checkpoint when the AIJ has grown at least 200 blocks since the last checkpoint or 120 seconds has elapsed since the last checkpoint, whichever is the sooner. Note that checkpoints do not occur in the middle of a transaction, however, the database administrator can force all the processes to checkpoint immediately for a given database with the RMU/CHECKPOINT command:

```
RMU/CHECKPOINT banking
```

Hint: The effectiveness of the checkpointing intervals can be observed with the RMU/SHOW STATISTICS checkpoint statistics display.

7.6.1   Commit To Journal Optimization

If fast commit processing is enabled for a database, a further optimization may be used – journal optimization. This reduces disk I/O to the database root file by assigning users a range of transaction sequence numbers instead of assigning them one at a time. Enabling journal optimization is achieved with additional syntax when enabling fast commit processing.

```
SQL> ALTER DATABASE FILENAME banking
cont> JOURNAL FAST COMMIT ENABLED
cont> (CHECKPOINT INTERVAL IS 200 BLOCKS,
cont> CHECKPOINT TIMED EVERY 120 SECONDS,
cont> COMMIT TO JOURNAL OPTIMIZATION,
cont> TRANSACTION INTERVAL IS 512);
```

The transaction interval specifies the range of transaction sequence numbers to be assigned. To use this feature two criteria must be met:

• Fast commit processing must be enabled.

• Snapshots must be disabled or enabled deferred.

8   Security

Since their database is so crucial to many organizations, it is important to restrict its use. The database cannot offer free-for-all access, especially when it contains confidential corporate information. The goal of Rdb security is to make sure users are authorized before they are allowed access to the database.

An Rdb database is secured using the GRANT and REVOKE commands in SQL. Most database security is enforced with commands, but some security also is available with the operating system's own file-security mechanism. Using the options available in the operating system to secure the database is not recommended because it secures the database only at the physical file level, whereas Rdb security restricts access down to the column level. In addition to the security measures just mentioned, this chapter will highlight some of the other ways that Rdb enforces security using the OpenVMS operating system. Differences in implementing security on other operating system platforms will be described in Chapter 19.

8.1   USING OPENVMS SECURITY

When an Rdb database is created, OpenVMS file security is placed on the physical files that make up the database. By default, these files are seen only by the owner of the database or anyone else using system-owned utilities, such as Rdb.

8.1.1   Security Identifiers

Rdb security is implemented by allocating security identifiers to database access privileges at the database, table, or column level.

Three types of security identifiers may be specified:

- UIC (user identification code)
- General
- System-defined

It is possible to combine these three security identifiers and define stringent security. Combining identifiers is shown in the following example:

```
[DEV,3]+REMOTE
```

UIC Identifiers

UIC (User Identification Code) identifiers are a component of the OpenVMS operating system and are allocated by the system manager when a user's account is created. The UIC takes the form of an identifier that uses a combination of numbers or words. Typical UIC identifiers are:

```
[DEV,3]
[10,456]
```

In this example, the group is DEV and the unique number within that group is 3. This enables the group of development users to be denoted by [DEV,*], the * denoting all users in that group. Each user has a unique number within that group. UICs offer a convenient method of grouping users and giving them unique identifiers. OpenVMS automatically attaches the UIC identifier to all files created by the user.

General Identifiers

A general identifier is created by the system manager and is allocated when usernames are created. The identifiers are held in the system rights database and are allocated either to an individual or to a group of users. Typical identifiers are:

```
PROGRAMMERS
CLERICAL
FINANCE
```

System-defined Identifiers

System-defined identifiers can also be used to restrict access to the database.

Table 8.1 - SQL Privileges

SQL Privileges	Priv Type	Description
ALL		Grant all privileges.
ALTER	func, db, tab, mod	Change database parameters or alter a table.
CREATETAB	db, tab	Create a table, domain, storage map, index, view, module & function
DBADM	db	Use ALTER SCHEMA and RMU commands from Version 4.0.
DBCTRL	func, db, tab, mod	Create, delete or modify access privileges.
DELETE	db, tab	Delete rows from a table.
DISTRIBTRAN	db	Allow participation in a distributed transaction.
DROP	db, func, tab, mod	Drop a domain, table, view, index, function or module.
EXECUTE	mod, func	Execute a module or function.
INSERT	db, tab	Insert rows into a table.
OPERATOR	db	Use RMU/ANALYZE and other RMU commands from Version 4.0.
REFERENCES	db, tab, col	Create a constraint based on another table
SECURITY	db	Enable security auditing.
SHOW	db, tab, mod	Reserve for future use.
SELECT	db, tab	Read data from a table.
UPDATE	db, tab, col	Allow column updating in a table.

Valid system identifiers are:

```
BATCH
INTERACTIVE
REMOTE
DIALUP
```

Rdb security is complete when the SQL database privileges, listed in Table 8.1, have been allocated to the appropriate security identifiers.

8.2   SECURITY STRATEGY

A security strategy should be defined before database security is specified. The golden rule is that security should always be maintained by the database system, not left to the operating system. Rdb security should be used whenever possible, because it prevents unauthorized access to the database, regardless of how the database is accessed.

The next consideration is how secure the database should be. If the database must be highly secure, each table must specify which users are allowed access to its rows. Each table also should contain a catch all UIC of [*,*], which denies the general public any privileges. If the database is to be relatively open, on the other hand, the database should provide access to everyone at the schema level, securing only the tables that require restricted access. Whatever the security requirements, strategy must be defined first, then the database security must be created and maintained.

Hint: Once a standard set of security rules have been defined, they should be included with the database creation command procedures to ensure that they are always included whenever a database is created.

8.3   **RDB SECURITY**

Rdb security is implemented at the database, table, and column levels, by allocating one or more of the database privileges listed in the SQL privileges table. Privileges are granted to the user only when a match is found for the user against the list of system identifiers specified within Rdb.

When defining security on an OpenVMS system, users with certain operating system privileges such as SYSPRV and BYPASS can override the protections defined within the database.

Figure 8.1 Security within Rdb

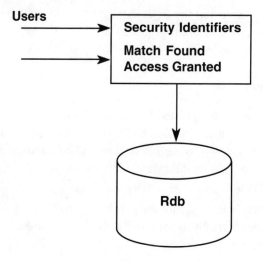

8.3.1   **ANSI-Style Security**

An Rdb database can be protected using the alternative ANSI-style GRANT statement instead of the default ACL scheme used by Rdb. A major difference between the two security approaches is that ANSI checks all the security identifiers for a match on the list of identifiers and performs an OR operation on the result. The ANSI display format also is different. The SQL approach, known as ACL protection, searches the list of identifiers in the order in which the security identifiers are specified. As soon as the first match is found, the search stops.

The following example is a list of security identifiers and the SQL database privileges granted.

```
[20,3]   Access=INSERT,SELECT
[100,*]  Access=SELECT
[50,*]   Access=INSERT,SELECT
[100,2]  Access=INSERT
```

Suppose User [100,2] accesses the database. Using the ACL security scheme, Rdb searches the list until [100,*] is identified, granting the user SELECT privilege only, which is the right to read data. With the ANSI protection scheme, the outcome would be different because Rdb matches on both [100,2] and [100,*], which results in the user being granted both INSERT and SELECT privilege. The following is an example of the ANSI-style display for the table ACCOUNT. The WITH GRANT OPTION clause means that anyone with the INSERT and SELECT privilege may grant it to other users.

```
SQL> GRANT select ON TABLE account TO PUBLIC;
SQL> GRANT select ON TABLE account TO [100,34];
SQL> GRANT select,insert ON TABLE account TO [100,34] WITH GRANT OPTION;
SQL> SHOW PROTECTION ON TABLE account;


Protection on Table ACCOUNT
[100,34]:
   With Grant Option:      SELECT,INSERT
   Without Grant Option:   SELECT,INSERT
```

```
[DAVE]:
  With Grant Option:    SELECT,INSERT,UPDATE,DELETE,SHOW,CREATE,ALTER,
                        DROP,DBCTRL,OPERATORDBADM,REFERENCES
  Without Grant Option: NONE

[*,*]:
  With Grant Option:    NONE
  Without Grant Option: SELECT
```

To use ANSI-level security, the PROTECTION IS ANSI clause must be specified when the Rdb database is created using the CREATE DATABASE command, otherwise SQL ACL security is implemented by default. The previous example also illustrates the additional user class of PUBLIC, which is specified in the ANSI standard.

The following explanations apply to both the ANSI and ACL protection scheme, although identifiers such as [DEV,*] are disallowed in ANSI. All the subsequent examples are in the ACL format.

8.3.2   Database-Level Security

When a database is created, Rdb allocates the following protections by default:

```
SQL> CREATE DATABASE ALIAS bank_id FILENAME eurobank:[uk.db]banking;

SQL> SHOW PROTECTION ON DATABASE ALIAS bank_id;

Protection on Alias BANK_ID
(IDENTIFIER=[40,12],ACCESS=SELECT+INSERT+UPDATE+DELETE+SHOW+
    CREATETAB+ALTER+DROP+DBCTRL+OPERATOR+DBADM)
(IDENTIFIER=[*,*],ACCESS=NONE  )
```

This example shows that the creator of the database, [40,12], has all access privileges, whereas other users have no rights to access the database.

Hint: In a production environment where security is of utmost importance, it is good practice to create and maintain the database from a special account with its own unique UIC that is used only by the DBA, rather than from a general user account.

The following example illustrates how to include security at the database level so that User [200,33] or INTERACTIVE users can only retrieve data.

```
SQL> GRANT SELECT ON DATABASE ALIAS rdb$dbhandle TO [200,33];

SQL> SHOW PROTECTION ON DATABASE rdb$dbhandle;

 Protection on Alias RDB$DBHANDLE
(IDENTIFIER=[200,33],ACCESS=SELECT)
(IDENTIFIER=[40,12],ACCESS=SELECT+INSERT+UPDATE+DELETE+SHOW+CREATETAB+
    ALTER+DROP+DBCTRL+OPERATOR+DBADM)
(IDENTIFIER=[*,*],ACCESS=NONE  )

SQL> GRANT SELECT,SHOW ON DATABASE ALIAS rdb$dbhandle TO INTERACTIVE;

SQL> SHOW PROTECTION ON DATABASE  Rdb$dbhandle;

 Protection on Alias RDB$DBHANDLE
(IDENTIFIER=INTERACTIVE,ACCESS=SELECT+SHOW)
(IDENTIFIER=[200,33],ACCESS=SELECT)
(IDENTIFIER=[40,12],ACCESS=SELECT+INSERT+UPDATE+DELETE+SHOW+CREATETAB+
    ALTER+DROP+DBCTRL+OPERATOR+DBADM)
(IDENTIFIER=[*,*],ACCESS=NONE)
```

To remove an entry, the REVOKE command is used. In the following example, the entry for User [200,33] is removed at the database level.

```
SQL> REVOKE ENTRY ON DATABASE ALIAS rdb$dbhandle FROM [200,33];
```

Hint: Users who cannot remember their SQL authorization identification should use RDB$DBHANDLE instead.

8.3.3   Table Level

Database level security is generally inadequate to protect a database. Table level security is the preferred method because it provides finer granularity as to which parts of the database the user can access. In the following example, User [200,33] is given the privilege to insert and update rows in the BRANCH table. However, before being given access rights at the table level, a user must have already received them at the database level.

```
SQL> GRANT SELECT,UPDATE,INSERT ON TABLE branch TO [200,33];

SQL> SHOW PROTECTION ON branch;

Protection on Table BRANCH
  (IDENTIFIER=[200,33],ACCESS=SELECT+INSERT+UPDATE)
  (IDENTIFIER=[40,12],ACCESS=SELECT+INSERT+UPDATE+DELETE+SHOW+
    CREATETAB+ALTER+DROP+DBCTRL+OPERATOR+DBADM)
  (IDENTIFIER=[*,*],ACCESS=NONE)
```

8.3.4   Column Level

Privileges also can be applied to columns to prevent them from being updated. In the next example, the MANAGERS_NAME columns may be changed on the table BRANCH only by User [200,33]. At the table level, however, User [200,33] may create new columns.

```
SQL> GRANT UPDATE ON COLUMN branch.managers_name TO [200,33];

SQL> SHOW PROTECTION ON TABLE branch;
  Protection on Table BRANCH

  (IDENTIFIER=[200,33],ACCESS=SELECT+INSERT)
  (IDENTIFIER=[40,12],ACCESS=SELECT+INSERT+UPDATE+DELETE+SHOW+
    CREATETAB+ALTER+DROP+DBCTRL+OPERATOR+DBADM)
  (IDENTIFIER=[*,*],ACCESS=NONE)

SQL> SHOW PROTECTION ON COLUMN branch.managers_name;

Protection on Column BRANCH.MANAGERS_NAME
  (IDENTIFIER=[200,33],ACCESS=UPDATE)
  (IDENTIFIER=[*,*],ACCESS=NONE)

SQL> UPDATE branch SET managers_name = 'Miss K Jones'
cont>    WHERE branch_code = 'ALT';
 1 row updated
```

Any attempt to update other columns in the BRANCH table will result in the following message:

```
SQL> UPDATE branch SET branch_name = 'New Alton'
cont> WHERE branch_code ='ALT';
 %RDB-E-NO_PRIV, privilege denied by database facility
```

8.4 **ALTERNATIVE SECURITY MECHANISMS**

Security does not necessarily have to be enforced using the security commands GRANT and REVOKE. Some other features also are used to enforce security, including:

- Views
- Read-only areas
- Triggers
- Stored procedures
- Functions

8.4.1 **Views**

Besides accessing the database through a table, a user can gain access through a view. The advantage of this approach is that to the user, the view seems to be identical to a table, but it specifies exactly which columns in the table the user can see. This is a very effective means of restricting a user's view of the data. When taken one step further, this approach forces all access to the data through the view because access to the table has been denied. The disadvantage of this approach is that a view that references more than one table cannot be used for updating purposes, only inquiries. Once a view has been defined, Rdb treats it as if it were a table; therefore, the security identifiers are applied to a view as if it were a table.

8.4.2 **Read-Only Areas**

One feature infrequently used in Rdb is the ability to define a database storage area as a read-only storage area. A read-only area is a very effective means of ensuring that absolutely no one writes to a storage area. This technique is used to best advantage on storage areas containing data that must not be changed under any circumstances. Storage areas such as these would only be opened for write access under controlled circumstances, such as when new data must be added.

Read-only is a security feature that cannot be overridden by anyone, even with all the OpenVMS privileges. Once a read-only area, always a read-only area, unless it is changed to read-write by the database administrator.

8.4.3   Triggers

Triggers, described in detail in the data integrity chapter, are used in database security for the following:

- Audit trails

- Forcing an error when illegal update actions are performed

A trigger applies to all users; therefore it is an effective blanket-security mechanism that cannot be overridden. One advantage of using triggers is that their operation is transparent to the database user. For example, users inserting rows into a table are unaware that an automatically activated trigger writes an audit-trail record every time a row is created.

The ERROR clause is also an excellent overriding security mechanism. Suppose a user breaks through the table security using a very privileged account that enables him to delete the row. The trigger is activated, forcing an error and preventing the row deletion from completing.

8.4.4   Stored Procedures

Stored procedures, described in detail in the data manipulation chapter, and available since V6.0 of Rdb, can be viewed as another means of securing the database. If all access to the database is via these procedures then this is a very effective method of restricting the operations a user may perform on the database because each procedure can have its own security defined.

Although a user will call the procedure by name, security is defined on the module containing the procedure. A user must have EXECUTE privilege to call a procedure as illustrated in the example below. Therefore don't forget to specify who may call the procedure, otherwise users will receive an unexpected error message.

```
SQL> CALL branch_name ('SOT', :bname);
%RDB-E-NO_PRIV, privilege denied by database facility
```

The procedure BRANCH_NAME is defined in the module SHOW_BRANCH_NAME

```
SQL> GRANT EXECUTE ON MODULE show_branch_name TO [HOBBS];
```

```
SQL> DECLARE   :bname char(30);
SQL> CALL branch_name ('SOT', :bname);
 BNAME
 Southampton
```

8.4.5 External Functions

To call external functions from within SQL the user must have been granted the right to execute the function, as by default only the creator is given access. Without access rights the user will receive the 'privilege denied by database facility' message.

```
SQL> SHOW PROTECTION ON FUNCTION sqrt
Protection on Function SQRT
   (IDENTIFIER=[250,1],ACCESS=EXECUTE+SHOW+ALTER+DROP+DBCTRL)
   (IDENTIFIER=[*,*],ACCESS=NONE)
```

8.5 DEPT. OF DEFENSE OR C2 SECURITY

Considerable interest has arisen recently in the security of relational database systems. Since the database is a focal point for information on an organization, it is imperative to deny unauthorized users access to the data and to record any unauthorized access. Since no commercial security standards are available, database systems suppliers have opted to comply with the U.S. Department of Defense security classification. This is detailed in the *Department of Defense Trusted Computer System Evaluation Criteria*, commonly known as the Orange Book because of the color of the cover. This document specifies the functionality, testing, and documentation requirements for a secure system.

The Orange Book defines four security divisions, A, B, C, and D, two of which are subdivided into classes. Rdb is Class C2-compliant, which is known as controlled access protection. The divisions and classes specified in the Orange Book are:

- Division D – Minimal protection
- Division C – Discretionary protection
  - Class C2 – Controlled access protection
  - Class C1 – Discretionary access

- Division B – Mandatory protection

  - Class B3 – Security domains

  - Class B2 – Structures protection

  - Class B1 – Labelled protection

- Division A – Verified protection

For Rdb to be C2-compliant, it must have the following capabilities:

- Object re-use

- User identification and authentication

- Discretionary access control

- Security auditing

Object re-use prohibits all new database objects from containing data that the user is not authorized to see. In simple terms, this means that OpenVMS clears all memory pages before giving them to Rdb. Whenever a row in a table is deleted, Rdb overwrites the data with the transaction identification. Overwriting makes it impossible to see the previous data and protects all the in-memory data structures used by Rdb.

User identification and authentication means that users may not access the database until they have identified and authenticated themselves. This is achieved in Rdb by:

- OpenVMS UICs

- OpenVMS environment identifiers (for example, REMOTE, INTERACTIVE)

- OpenVMS class identifiers (for example, ORDER)

- SELECT privilege to access the database

To implement C2 security, a database probably will need to be considerably enhanced in order to specify all the users who may be granted access.

The two relevant privileges are:

- DISTRIBTRAN, which allows a 2-phase commit protocol to be specified

- SECURITY, which permits a user to perform the new RMU auditing commands

Hint: The database creator by default is given full access to the database, other users no access at all. Therefore, it is recommended that production databases be created from a special maintenance account rather than from their default account. This helps ensure that full access to the database is available only from specific accounts rather than the database administrator's routine account.

8.6   **CONTROLLING RMU COMMANDS**

Database manipulation is not the only access that is restricted. Security is also concerned with unauthorized database management. An Rdb database is managed via the RMU utility. Using some of these commands it is possible to alter the integrity of the database. Therefore it is important to secure their use with the RMU/SET PRIVILEGE command. Each RMU command has an associated RMU privilege that must be granted before it may be executed; in addition, some of the commands also require operating system privileges to execute them. To find out which users may execute an RMU command use the SHOW PRIVILEGE command as shown in the following examples.

```
$ RMU/SHOW PRIVILEGE eurobank:[uk.db]banking
Object type: file,
Object name: EUROBANK:[UK.DB]BANKING.RDB;1, on 13-NOV-1993 17:57:16.79
 (IDENTIFIER=[40,12],ACCESS=READ+WRITE+RMU$ALTER+RMU$ANALYZE+
     RMU$BACKUP+RMU$CONVERT+RMU$COPY+RMU$DUMP+RMU$LOAD+RMU$MOVE+
     RMU$OPEN+RMU$RESTORE+RMU$SHOW+RMU$UNLOAD+RMU$VERIFY)

 (IDENTIFIER=[*,*],ACCESS=READ+WRITE+RMU$ALTER+RMU$ANALYZE+
     RMU$BACKUP+RMU$CONVERT+RMU$COPY+RMU$DUMP+RMU$LOAD+RMU$MOVE
     +RMU$OPEN+RMU$RESTORE+RMU$SHOW+RMU$UNLOAD+RMU$VERIFY)
```

As can be seen from the above example there is quite a comprehensive list of RMU privileges, which provide sufficient flexibility to ensure that only the required commands are available to various users.

Granting the user a right to issue an RMU command is a simple process as illustrated below with the RMU/SET PRIVILEGE. One simply specifies the user; in the example below it is [ENGLAND] and the access right, in this instance RMU$ANALYZE.

```
$ RMU/SET PRIVILEGE /ACL=(IDENTIFIER=[ENGLAND], ACCESS=RMU$ANALYZE)
        eurobank:[uk.db]banking

$ RMU/SHOW PRIVILEGE eurobank:[uk.db]banking
Object type: file,
Object name: EUROBANK:[UK.DB]BANKING.RDB;1 on 13-NOV-1993 18:35:31.78

(IDENTIFIER=[ENGLAND],ACCESS=RMU$ANALYZE)
(IDENTIFIER=[HOBBS],ACCESS=READ+WRITE+CONTROL+RMU$ALTER+RMU$ANALYZE+
     RMU$BACKUP+RMU$CONVERT+RMU$COPY+RMU$DUMP+

     RMU$LOAD+RMU$MOVE+RMU$OPEN+RMU$RESTORE+RMU$SECURITY+

     RMU$SHOW+RMU$UNLOAD+ RMU$VERIFY)
```

Typically, one gives the right to execute many RMU commands to a user, such as [HOBBS] in the example above. If the syntax shown here is used then the commands become very long and prone to error. An easier option is to use the editor, invoked with the /EDIT option, which displays all the users and their access rights. It is then very easy to change the values.

When a user does not have the right to execute an RMU command, the following message is returned.

```
$ RMU/OPEN   NEW_BANK
%RMU-F-NOPRIVERR, no privileges for attempted operation
```

8.7   SECURITY AUDITING

Security auditing is concerned with logging access to the database. Rdb permits that three audit classes may be specified:

- DACCESS – Data access

- PROTECTION – Changes to security ACLs

- RMU – RMU commands

Using the RMU/SET AUDIT command makes it possible to log all access to the database. This information is recorded in one of two ways, either directly to the operator console, which is known as an alarm, or to the OpenVMS security log file, which is known as an audit. The latter is the best method to implement audit trails because it does not interfere with the daily routine of the operators managing the computer system. This method leaves the operators' console free to display messages that require their attention, rather than informational messages.

Hint: C2 security features are managed only by Rdb users who have the Rdb SECURITY privilege. It is impossible to bypass this security mechanism with the OpenVMS BYPASS privilege.

The following command enables security auditing on the database, which is recorded in the OpenVMS security audit log.

```
$ RMU/SET AUDIT /TYPE=AUDIT /ENABLE=RMU /START eurobank:banking
```

Once this command has been issued, any user issuing an RMU command will be logged in the security audit file. A security alarm also could be set. In this instance, the following display shows what typically would appear on the operator's console for the data access class:

1 Data access – alarm example

```
%%%%%%%%%% OPCOM 27-SEP-1994 16:16:19.08
%%%%%%%%%% Message from user HOBBS on RDB4ME
Rdb Security alarm (SECURITY) on RDB4ME, system id: 63534
Database name:      EUROBANK:BANKING.RDB;1
Auditable event:    Attempted table access
Event time:         27-SEP-1994 16:16:19.06
PID:                21E018A9
User name:          HOBBS
Object name:        BRANCH
Object type:        TABLE
Operation:          Select Record
Access requested:   SELECT
Sub status:         Rdb required privilege
Final status:       %SYSTEM-S-NORMAL
Rdb privilege used: SELECT
```

2 Protection access – alarm example

```
%%%%%%%%%% OPCOM 14-SEP-1994 11:28:16.14
%%%%%%%%%% Message from user HOBBS on RDB4ME
Rdb Security alarm (SECURITY) on RDB4ME, system id: 63534
Database name:       EUROBANK:BANKING.RDB;1
Auditable event:     Protection change
Event time:          14-SEP-1994 11:28:16.01
PID:                 21E00AE8
User name:           HOBBS
Object name:         EUROBANK:BANKING.RDB;1
Object type:         SCHEMA
Grantee:             [100,23]
New ACE privileges: SELECT
Old ACE privileges:
Final status:        %SYSTEM-S-NORMAL
```

3 RMU access –alarm example

```
%%%%%%%%%% OPCOM 14-SEP-1994 11:15:44.97 %%%%%%%%%%
Message from user HOBBS on RDB4ME

Rdb Security alarm (SECURITY) on RDB4ME, system id: 63534

Database name:       EUROBANK:BANKING.RDB;1
Auditable event:     Attempted RMU command
Event time:          14-SEP-1994 11:15:44.95
PID:                 21E00AE8
User name:           HOBBS
RMU command:    RMU/BACKUP eurobank:banking.rdb;1 backup1_mon/LOG
Final status:        %SYSTEM-S-NORMAL
```

These examples illustrate ways of logging all access, but it is possible to restrict logging to an individual or a group of users. In fact, the data access audit class will be logged only if the users to be logged are specified. Auditing all access to the branch table by users with the code [200,33] or an identifier of HOBBS, for example, is achieved by specifying the following RMU/SET AUDIT commands.

```
$ RMU/SET AUDIT/ENABLE=DACCESS=TABLE=BRANCH /PRIV=ALL -
      /TYPE=ALARM   eurobank:banking

$ RMU/SET AUDIT/ENABLE=IDENT=('[200,33]') eurobank:banking

$ RMU/SET AUDIT/ENABLE=IDENT=[HOBBS]    eurobank:banking
```

Under normal circumstances, all the audit records are written to the OpenVMS audit journal file. These audit records may be analyzed at any time by using the qualifier /AUDIT on the RMU/LOAD command. Rdb will read the OpenVMS audit log, extract those records for the specified database, and load them into an Rdb database, creating a special table for the data if required. After the records have been loaded into an Rdb database, they may be examined and reported upon using any tool that can query an Rdb database.

In the following example, we first see the records being loaded into the database using the RMU/LOAD AUDIT command. A new table called AUDIT_RECS is created in the banking database, containing the database audit records in the OpenVMS AUDIT$JOURNAL file.

Then an SQL query is executed to find the users who issued an RMU/BACKUP command.

```
$ RMU/LOAD /AUDIT eurobank:banking audit_recs   audit$journal
%RMU-I-DATRECSTO, 155 data records stored

SQL>SELECT rdbvms$user_name,rdbvmsRMU_command FROM audit_recs
cont> WHERE rdbvmsRMU_command CONTAINS '/BACKUP';

rdbvms$USER_NAME     rdbvmsRMU_COMMAND
OPER_LMH             RMU/BACKUP/LOG banking full_bkp_1009

OPER_KE              RMU/BACKUP/LOG banking full_bkp_1109
```

In these examples, we can see that user OPER_LMH issued the backup command for the backup filename 'full_bkp_1009', whereas user OPER_KE performed that task for the filename 'full_bkp_1109'. This illustrates a very small percentage of the information that is logged into the audit trail. Other useful information that is recorded includes the date and time, the status of command, the type of event, the action performed, the new ACL, and the old ACL.

Hint: When the audit records are loaded into the database, they are not removed from the audit log. Therefore, a new audit log should be created after each load to avoid duplicate records being loaded.

Rdb provides comprehensive security using either the ANSI or the ACL approach. The ability to implement security down to the field level helps ensure that only authorized users may update corporate data. Data is such an important company asset that the number of people allowed to change it must be restricted.

9   Database Integrity

One of the most important benefits a database management system can provide is the ability to maintain database integrity. The integrity of a database is maintained when it contains no corrupt or invalid data. By corrupt data, we mean data with an incomplete internal format. Invalid data is data that does not conform to the business rules for the system, such as a branch code in the account table that does not match the code in the master branch table. In the unlikely event that a breakdown in database structure integrity occurs, utilities are provided to rebuild the database. There are two areas to consider in database integrity:

- Data integrity

- Database structure integrity

9.1   DATA INTEGRITY

By data integrity, we mean ensuring that the data stored in the database abides by certain rules defined by the business functions. The rules that data must conform to are defined in Rdb using a combination of:

- Constraints

- Primary and foreign keys

- Triggers

Another facet to data integrity is ensuring that the data manipulated in a transaction is either kept or thrown away to maintain database consistency. This is achieved in Rdb using:

- After-image journaling

- Before-image journaling

- DECdtm (distributed transaction monitor) for coordinating distributed database transactions

9.2   CONSTRAINTS

A constraint in SQL is a rule that is applied to a single column or collection of columns. It ensures that no matter how the data is stored or updated, whether by interactive SQL or an application program, no updates or stores can be made unless they comply with the constraint, as Figure 9.1 illustrates. SQL allows the following rules to be specified on a column:

- UNIQUE

- CHECK

- NOT NULL

Constraints can be defined as part of a table, column or domain definition.

An important decision to make when defining the constraint is when it should be evaluated, at commit time or at statement execution time. This is known in the SQL syntax as DEFERRABLE or NOT DEFERRABLE. Performance can easily degrade if the wrong option is chosen. A good rule of thumb is to use the NOT DEFERRABLE option so that the constraint is evaluated immediately which is not the default. The only time one would need the deferrable option is if a program was loading data and information required to evaluate the constraint was not available until the transaction committed.

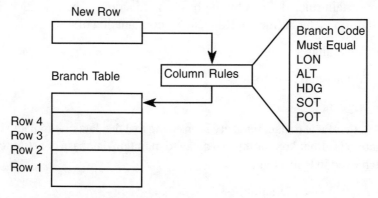

Figure 9.1 Constraint Rules on a Column

The following two examples illustrate how to define both types of constraints.

```
SQL> CREATE TABLE customer (
cont>     customer_no CHAR (10)
cont>             CONSTRAINT  customer_primary_customer_no
cont>             PRIMARY KEY     NOT DEFERRABLE,

SQL> ALTER TABLE account_transaction
cont>       ALTER account_no
cont>             CONSTRAINT wrong_acct_for_trans
cont>             REFERENCES account (account_no)  DEFERRABLE;
```

Hint: Although it is optional, it is good practice to define a sensible constraint name because if the constraint is violated, this is the name that will be included in the error message.

The following are typical column-constraint definitions. The branch code must be one of the specified codes, the branch name must be unique, and the branch address cannot be omitted.

```
SQL> CREATE TABLE branch
cont>     (branch_code CHAR(4)
cont>     CONSTRAINT check_the_branch_code
cont>       CHECK
cont>         (branch_code IN ('LON','ALT','HDG','SOT','POT'))
cont>           NOT DEFERRABLE,
cont>     branch_name CHAR(20)
cont>     CONSTRAINT unique_branch_name
cont>       UNIQUE
cont>           NOT DEFERRABLE,
cont>     branch_address CHAR(120)
cont>     CONSTRAINT no_branch_address
cont>       NOT NULL
cont>           NOT DEFERRABLE,
cont>     managers_name CHAR(20));
```

Figure 9.2 Primary and Foreign Key Definition

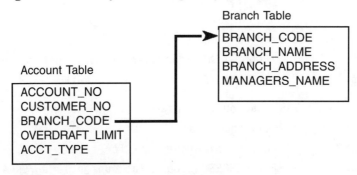

9.3   PRIMARY AND FOREIGN KEYS

It is very common today to define primary or foreign keys on a column within a table definition. Including the primary key clause automatically ensures that the columns referred to are unique and not null.

When a foreign key is defined using the REFERENCES clause on a column or the clause FOREIGN KEY on a table, it ensures that the value of a field in table A matches a value in table B, which contains the master list of allowed values. Figure 9.2 illustrates this point.

Using the BANKING example, the BRANCH CODE in the table BRANCH is defined as a primary key. The ACCOUNT table also uses the BRANCH code. Therefore, a foreign key relationship is defined between BRANCH and ACCOUNT to ensure that no row is defined in the ACCOUNT table that contains a BRANCH code not already defined in the BRANCH table.

Hint: When defining column constraints, Rdb may require additional indexes to be specified to speed evaluation, especially on large tables.

The following example illustrates the table definitions for ACCOUNT and BRANCH required to implement this relationship.

```
SQL> CREATE TABLE branch
cont> (branch_code CHAR(4)  CONSTRAINT dup_branch_code
cont>    PRIMARY KEY   NOT DEFERRABLE,
cont> branch_name CHAR(20),
cont> branch_address CHAR(120),
cont> managers_name char(20));
```

```
SQL> CREATE TABLE account
cont> (account_no BIGINT
cont> CONSTRAINT account_primary_account_no PRIMARY KEY
cont>    NOT DEFERRABLE,
cont> customer_no CHAR(10),
cont> branch_code CHAR(4) CONSTRAINT check_acct_branch_code
cont>    REFERENCES branch (branch_code)
cont>       NOT DEFERRABLE,
cont> overdraft_limit NUMERIC (10,2),
cont> acct_type INTEGER);
```

By creating this relationship, a constraint definition has automatically been created that the SHOW TABLE command identifies.

```
SQL> SHOW TABLE account;
Information for table ACCOUNT


Columns for table ACCOUNT:
Column Name          Data Type        Domain
-----------          ---------        ------
ACCOUNT_NO           BIGINT
 Primary Key constraint ACCOUNT_PRIMARY_ACCOUNT_NO
CUSTOMER_NO          CHAR(10)
 Foreign Key constraint WRONG_CUSTOMER
BRANCH_CODE          CHAR(4)
 Foreign Key constraint WRONG_BRANCH_CODE
BALANCE              BIGINT(2)
OVERDRAFT_LIMIT      BIGINT(2)
ACCT_TYPE            INTEGER
STATEMENT_FREQ       INTEGER
STATEMENT_DATE       DATE VMS    STANDARD_DATE
STATEMENT_DAY        INTEGER
```

```
Table constraints for ACCOUNT:
ACCOUNT_PRIMARY_ACCOUNT_NO
Primary Key constraint
Column constraint for ACCOUNT.ACCOUNT_NO
 Evaluated on COMMIT
Source:
    ACCOUNT.ACCOUNT_NO PRIMARY KEY

CHECK_ACCT_BRANCH_CODE
 Foreign Key constraint
 Column constraint for ACCOUNT.BRANCH_CODE
 Evaluated on COMMIT
 Source:
     ACCOUNT.BRANCH_CODE REFERENCES Branch (Branch_code)

Constraints referencing table ACCOUNT:
WRONG_ACCT_FOR_TRANS
 Foreign Key constraint
 Column constraint for ACCOUNT_TRANSACTION.ACCOUNT_NO
 Evaluated on COMMIT
 Source:
 ACCOUNT_TRANSACTION.ACCOUNT_NO REFERENCES account(account_no)
```

The examples so far have illustrated integrity checks placed at the column level. The foreign or primary key, on the other hand, can be specified at the table level, as the following illustrates.

```
SQL> CREATE TABLE account
cont> (account_no        BIGINT,
cont> customer_no        CHAR(10),
cont> branch_code        CHAR(4),
cont> overdraft_limit    BIGINT,
cont> acct_type          INTEGER,
cont> CONSTRAINT account_primary_account_no
cont>      PRIMARY KEY (account_no),
cont> CONSTRAINT check_acct_branch_code
cont>      FOREIGN KEY (branch_code)
cont>    REFERENCES branch (branch_code)
cont>  );
```

When a foreign key is defined at the table level, the FOREIGN KEY clause may be used. There is no difference between defining the foreign key at the column or table level. However, if multiple columns make up the primary key, the key can only be defined at the table level.

Hint: Use the Graphical Schema Editor to specify a number of foreign key constraints rapidly. Simply draw a line with the mouse between the primary and foreign key columns and the constraint is defined.

9.4   USING INDEXES TO MAINTAIN INTEGRITY

In some cases, data integrity may be maintained by defining some constraints upon the indexes that are created on the tables. For instance, specifying the UNIQUE clause ensures that no non-unique index key columns are inserted into the table. Another useful clause on an index definition is MAPPING VALUES which ensures that all the values in the index map onto the range supplied.

Therefore, in the BANKING example, an index is defined on the ACCOUNT table on the field STATEMENT_DAY, so all the entries in the index must be in the range 1 to 31.

```
CREATE INDEX statement_day
   ON ACCOUNT
    (statement_day MAPPING VALUES 1 TO 31)
     TYPE IS SORTED;
```

9.5   INTEGRATION WITH THE REPOSITORY

Using CDD/Repository V5.3 it is possible to define the constraints in the Repository and then create the table using a CREATE TABLE FROM PATHNAME statement. Otherwise the table definition must be altered afterwards, using the ALTER TABLE command to include these constraint statements as shown below:

```
SQL> CREATE TABLE branch FROM eurobank:[uk.dict]banking.branch;
```

```
SQL> ALTER TABLE branch
cont>   ADD CONSTRAINT check_branch_code
cont>      PRIMARY KEY (branch_code);
```

When the constraints are defined using this method, the primary key constraint will be considered a table constraint and not a column constraint. So, showing the table BRANCH will not include the primary key on the individual column; instead, it is held at the table level. This has no impact upon how the constraint is evaluated. It is highlighted to make the user aware that the table constraints must be checked. Otherwise, the user might think that the constraint does not exist.

```
SQL> SHOW TABLE branch;

Columns for table BRANCH:
Column Name          Data Type          Domain
_____          _____          _____

BRANCH_CODE          CHAR (4)
BRANCH_NAME          CHAR (20)          STANDARD_NAME
BRANCH_ADDRESS       CHAR(120)
MANAGERS_NAME        CHAR (20)          STANDARD_NAME

Table constraints for BRANCH:
 BRANCH_PRIMARY_BRANCH_CODE
 Primary Key constraint
 Table constraint for BRANCH
 Evaluated on COMMIT
 Source:
    PRIMARY KEY (Branch_code)
```

9.6   TRIGGERS

So far, we have seen how constraints can prevent the insertion or amendment of data that does not conform to specific rules. Implementing triggers inside the database helps the user change data while still ensuring it conforms to certain rules or automatically perform some actions when something occurs. Triggers can be used to perform:

Figure 9.3 Cascading Update Trigger

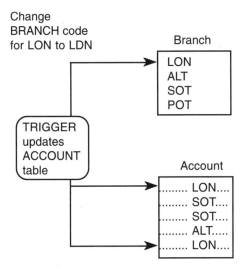

- Cascading updates (see Figure 9.3)

- Cascading deletes (see Figure 9.4)

- Summation updates

- Hidden deletes

- Security functions

- Limited auditing

To further explain how triggers can be used, suppose a company reorganizes. As a result, some of the branch offices are merged, which means the branch coding system must be revised. It would not be possible to change the BRANCH CODE using constraints because the existing relationships between account and branch would be invalidated.

A trigger mechanism is required. This mechanism allows the master branch code to be changed, automatically updating all the tables that include the old branch code and replacing it with the new code. The integrity of the database is maintained by ensuring that the data conforms to the business requirements.

Figure 9.4 Cascading Delete Trigger

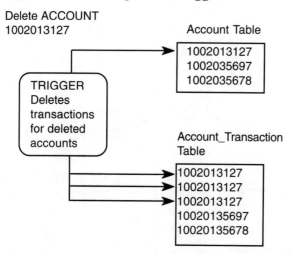

The following trigger example illustrates this point.

```
SQL> CREATE TRIGGER change_branch_code
cont>   BEFORE UPDATE OF branch_code ON branch
cont>    REFERENCING OLD AS old_branch_code
cont>            NEW AS new_branch_code
cont>
cont>    (UPDATE account A
cont>     SET  A.branch_code = new_branch_code.branch_code
cont>     WHERE A.branch_code = old_branch_code.branch_code)
cont>
cont>    FOR EACH ROW;
```

The FOR EACH ROW clause means that the trigger will be performed for every row that satisfies the WHERE condition.

Triggers can be defined to take effect upon any of the following types of actions:

• Insertions

• Updates

• Deletions

The advantage of using triggers is immediately apparent. The trigger mechanism catches all types of changes to the database, regardless of how they were initiated, because the trigger is set off at a low level inside the database. Because the triggering code is completely transparent to the user, a trigger can perform many types of actions, such as:

- INSERT – Automatically creating an entry in another table

- DELETE – Automatically deleting the transaction records for the appropriate account row when an account is deleted

- UPDATE – Automatically updating the branch codes in other tables when a branch code is changed

A trigger also can be used to force an error to prevent a row from being deleted. This feature is useful when rows in a table must not be removed from the database under any circumstance.

Hint: Creating comprehensive referential integrity of the data in the database, however, can only be achieved using a combination of constraints and triggers.

9.7   DATABASE STRUCTURE INTEGRITY

Relational databases contain many different types of internal structures, which must be completely accurate if the system is to function properly. Sometimes, these internal structures can become corrupt because of a hardware malfunction. For this reason, Rdb provides the RMU/VERIFY utility to verify the internal Rdb structures of the database. The RMU/ALTER command is available to correct some of the internal structure problems reported by RMU/VERIFY, but it should only be used by someone experienced with the internal structure of Rdb.

9.7.1   RMU/VERIFY

RMU/VERIFY is used to verify the following structures:

- Checksums on database pages

- Constraints

- Database page structure

- Indexes, sorted and hashed

- Root file

- Snapshots

- Storage areas

Hint: Use the /LOG option to see which structures are being verified and how long it took to verify each area.

A common approach taken with the RMU/VERIFY utility is to request Rdb to verify everything. This can be very time consuming and may be quite unnecessary. Therefore if the database is at least several gigabytes in size, consider performing verifies with only some of the qualifiers such as checking the page checksums or only the indexes but not their data as well. Remember though that full verifies must still be done.

For large databases, the /INCREMENTAL qualifier is used to verify the pages in the database that have changed since the last full verify. Remember that when performing an incremental verify, the /ALL qualifier must be included, otherwise the page date and time stamps used to determine which pages to check will not be updated.

Once RMU/VERIFY detects an irreparable inconsistency in the internal database structures, the database must be rebuilt from backups and journal files because no utility is currently available to allow the database administrator to patch the database. Sample output from a very simple verify follows.

```
$ RMU/VERIFY/LOG eurobank:[uk.db]banking


%RMU-I-DBBOUND,bound to database "EUROBANK:[UK.DB]BANKING.RDB;1"
%RMU-I-BGNROOVER, beginning root verification
%RMU-I-ENDROOVER, completed root verification
%RMU-I-BGNAIPVER, beginning AIP pages verification
%RMU-I-OPENAREA, opened storage area RDB$SYSTEM for protected retrieval
%RMU-I-ENDAIPVER, completed AIP pages verification
```

```
%RMU-I-BGNABMSPM, beginning ABM pages verification
%RMU-I-OPENAREA, opened storage area CUSTOMERS_AREA for protected retrieval
%RMU-I-ENDABMSPM, completed ABM pages verification
%RMU-I-CLOSAREAS, releasing protected retrieval lock on all storage areas
%RMU-S-ENDVERIFY, elapsed time for verification :  0 00:00:15.81
```

Hint: The database should be verified frequently so a corrupt database structure does not exist in too many database backups.

9.7.2   Repairing Internal Structures

Depending on the nature of the corruption, it may be possible to repair a problem without having to restore the database. An index could be dropped and then redefined, for example.

Another useful utility is RMU/REPAIR, which is used to repair damaged space management (SPAM) pages. The main utility used to correct internal structure problems is RMU/ALTER, however.

RMU/ALTER

The command RMU/ALTER is a low-level patch utility that allows the user to physically amend the internal structures of the database, such as the bytes on a database page. It is a very powerful and useful utility that carries a DATABASE HEALTH WARNING.

This utility must only be used by people who thoroughly understand the internal structures of Rdb; otherwise it is the quickest route to database corruption. Fortunately, the command cannot be run unless the user has the OpenVMS privilege SYSPRV and has been granted the RMU privilege RMU$ALTER. But once this security hurdle is passed, a user can change anything inside the database.

The following is important advice for anyone attempting to use this utility:

1 Read the manuals thoroughly so you understand all about RMU/ALTER and the internal Rdb structures.

2 Backup the database to be amended.

3 Use a copy of the database to be amended or find a small test database.

4 Start an RMU/ALTER session on the test database, determine precisely which commands should be used, and check that the database is accessible afterwards.

5 Apply the proposed changes to the database only when you are sure that they will work.

6 Backup the database when you are finished so the process does not have to be repeated again.

In the hands of the right person, this utility can save an organization many hours in costly recovery times.

When the RMU/ALTER utility is invoked, the user passes into the ALTER command line environment, which has its own comprehensive set of commands. Some of these commands are specified in Table 9.1.

Hint: Don't forget to set the RADIX to decimal so that conversions to hexadecimal are not required.

Table 9.1 Popular Commands Within RMU/ALTER

Command	Description
AREA	Specify physical storage area
ATTACH	Specify database to attach to
COMMIT	Keep all changes
DEPOSIT	Change value in database structure
DETACH	Detach from database
DISPLAY	Display specified data structure or value
LOG	Log all commands and output
PAGE	Specify database page to alter
RADIX	Set radix to decimal or hexadecimal
ROLLBACK	Undo changes
VERIFY	Verify database page

9.8   **BACKUPS AND JOURNALING**

Rdb provides its own mechanisms for making backups and journaling changes made to the database. It is important that these utilities are not substituted by alternatives that exist in the operating system such as BACKUP in OpenVMS and tar in OSF/1.

When databases are backed up, internal information is set by the Rdb RMU commands BACKUP and RESTORE. This internal information is used to rebuild the database and guarantee the integrity of the data.

The journal files are used to either roll back a transaction or recover the database to a given point in time in conjunction with the database backup.

9.8.1   **Backups**

An Rdb database should be backed up using the RMU/BACKUP utility that is provided with Rdb. This utility makes it possible to:

• Take online backups

• Back up entire databases

• Back up only the pages that have changed since the last full backup, which is known as an *incremental* backup

• Back up specified storage areas

• Back up several areas concurrently to multiple tape drives

• Automatically create the backup file in compressed format

The default backup method is a complete backup of the database with no users attached. This is achieved with the RMU/BACKUP command shown below.

```
$ RMU/BACKUP/LOG eurobank:[uk.db]banking  week_34_bank.rbf
```

Online Backups

However, with so many 7 by 24 companies, many organizations do not have the luxury of a period of time when no one is using their database. By using the snapshot file, a consistent view of the database is available when an online backup is started. This means that backups can be taken with users changing the data because all changes are written to the database and the previous version of the data is written to the snapshot file. The backup process then checks whether the version of the row it requires is taken from the storage area or the snapshot area. Using this approach does not in any way significantly degrade the performance of the backup utility. An online backup can be performed on any database that has snapshots enabled and the qualifier /ONLINE is specified.

```
$ RMU/BACKUP/ONLINE/LOG eurobank:[uk.db]banking week_34_bank.rbf
```

The online backup will begin once all users have committed their outstanding transactions. While RMU is waiting for all outstanding transactions to complete the following message is displayed:

```
%RMU-I-QUIETPT, waiting for database quiet point
```

Provided users are finishing their transactions quickly, the online backup should start promptly. Unfortunately sometimes there is always one user who decides not to complete their transaction. While the backup is waiting to start, new transactions cannot commence, so not only is the backup waiting for this troublesome user, but also other database users. To avoid this situation the additional qualifier /LOCK_TIMEOUT should be included. This tells RMU to wait x seconds for the quiet point lock and if it is not acquired in that time, then RMU aborts the backup operation.

```
$ RMU/BACKUP/ONLINE/LOG/LOCK_TIMEOUT=10
      eurobank:[uk.db]banking   week_34_bank.rbf

%RMU-I-QUIETPT, waiting for database quiet point
%RMU-F-TIMEOUT, timeout on quiet
-COSI-W-CANCEL, operation cancelled
```

No-Quiet Point Backups

If finding a quiet point for the backup to begin proves difficult, then the backup can still be taken using the qualifier /NOQUIET_POINT. Although this method means that the backup can be taken immediately, the restore operation is likely to be more complicated because one or more AIJ files will be required to recover the database to a guaranteed integrity point.

```
$ RMU/BACKUP/ONLINE/LOG/NOQUIET_POINT
      eurobank:[uk.db]banking   week_34_bank.rbf
```

Figure 9.5 Multi-threaded Backup to Tape

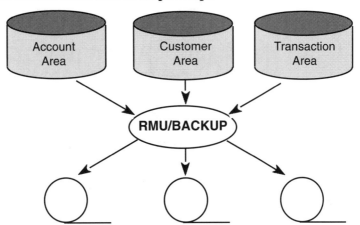

Backup to Tape or Disk

Backups can be written either to a single disk file or to multiple tape drives, but unless the database is very small, most database backups these days are written directly to tape drives. In fact this is the preferred method for backup, because it is the fastest and there are a wealth of options to ensure the integrity of the tapes created. Amongst the options is the ability to label tapes, specify the order in which the tapes must be placed in the stacker unit and write a journal file. Therefore it's worth reading the manuals carefully to select the appropriate options.

The fastest way to backup to tape is to use the multi-threaded option which allows RMU to write to multiple tape drives in parallel.

Incremental Backups

The larger a database grows, the more impractical it becomes to take full backups because they take too long, or one simply doesn't have the tapes available. An incremental backup only backs up pages in the database that have changed since the last full backup. Rdb V6.0 boasts a fast incremental backup mechanism where it can determine from the SPAM pages in each storage area which database pages need to be backed up. The advantage of this method is that if very little data has changed in a database and it is confined to a few storage areas, an incremental backup is completed very quickly. It also results in a small backup file.

Figure 9.6 Typical Database Backup Strategy for the Banking System

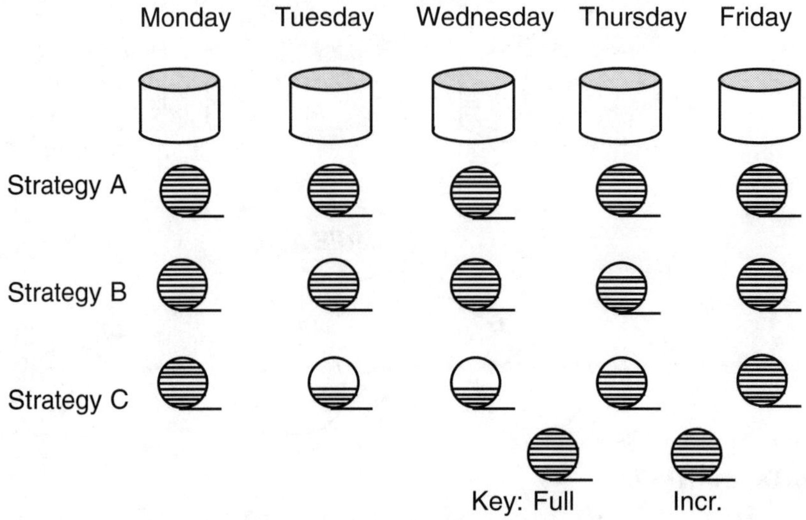

A typical incremental backup command could be:

```
$ RMU/BACKUP/INCREMENTAL/LOG eurobank:[uk.db]banking week_34_bank_incr.rbf
```

Remember to keep incremental backup files safe because they must be used in conjunction with a full backup to rebuild a database.

Backup Strategy

The flexibility of the backup mechanism means that a database strategy can be designed that suits each organization's environment, as illustrated in Figure 9.6. This example shows several different strategies and also illustrates that an incremental backup file can vary in size depending on the volume of data changed.

Another useful backup strategy is illustrated in Figure 9.5, where RMU/BACKUP is used to back up several database storage areas simultaneously to tape.

Backup by Area

Another alternative to an incremental backup is to back up specific database areas, but it can only be used if after-image journaling is enabled. *This option must be used very carefully otherwise it may be impossible to restore the database.*

Hint: When using this strategy, always verify the database can be restored before it is formally adopted.

To facilitate easy backup of a specific storage area, the INCREMENTAL=BY_AREA qualifier should be used on the BACKUP command with an INCLUDE or EXCLUDE specifying the storage areas that must be included or excluded. A sample command to back up only the ACCOUNT_AREA from the BANKING database into a file called mon_inc2 follows.

```
$  RMU/BACKUP/LOG/INCREMENTAL=BY_AREA/INCLUDE=(ACCOUNT_AREA)
       eurobank:[uk.db] banking eurobank:[db.backups]mon_inc2
```

Backup by area should not be used to provide a fast method for backing up the database.

9.8.2 Journaling

Rdb provides two types of journaling:

- After-image

- Before-image

After-image journaling lists all changes that have been made to the database. From V6.0 there may be one or multiple AIJ files, but whichever method is used there will only be one after-image journal file open at any time for an individual database. After-image journaling is completely integrated with the backup facility to enable the database to be restored to a specified point.

Run-unit journaling lists the changes that a user has made within a transaction. One run-unit journal file is open for every user who has an open transaction.

After-Image Journaling

A routine backup is a snapshot of the database at a given point, but often what is required is the ability to *restore* the database to a given point, such as Monday at 11:05:39 a.m. To achieve this precise level of database recovery, after-image journaling is used.

After-image journaling can be enabled or disabled at any time, provided you have exclusive access to the database. It is generally wise to enable it, especially on volatile databases when recovery is required to a specific point without loss of data. After-image journaling is enabled at the database level. Its role is to log all the changes that have been made to the database, collecting them in a journal file with an extension of .AIJ. Only one AIJ file is open at any point for a database. During recovery, however, it is common to use a number of AIJ files to rebuild the database.

Prior to Rdb V6.0, there would have been only one AIJ file. There were a number of performance restrictions with this approach and this resulted in the introduction of multiple AIJ files. Using multiple AIJ files is straightforward, but make sure to adopt good management procedures at the same time. Although everything is done automatically, it is wise to understand the new mechanism and how many AIJ files you are using, where they are located and how often to back them up.

When deciding whether to enable after-image journaling, consider the benefits and the need to maintain data integrity. Performance overhead should not be a consideration, because the journaling mechanism is now very efficient, especially if the electronic cache is being used. Therefore, it is rare that the journaling mechanism degrades performance. The minimal impact on the system is far outweighed by the ability to restore the database to a precise point with guaranteed integrity.

Hint: To achieve optimum performance always use at least 3 fixed size AIJ files.

When the database is created first specify how many AIJ slots are needed. It is always a good idea to specify a few more slots than actual AIJ files. This will mean that if you have to add an additional AIJ file, this can be done online while users are active on the system. In the example below the database is modified to support nine journal files.

```
SQL> ALTER DATABASE FILENAME eurobank:[db.db]banking
cont>    RESERVE 9 JOURNALS;
```

Once the journals have been reserved, the next step is to create the AIJ journal files. Each file must be uniquely named and can be individually sized.

```
SQL> ALTER DATABASE FILENAME eurobank:[db.db]banking
cont> JOURNAL IS ENABLED
```

```
cont> ADD JOURNAL bank_aij1 FILENAME
        aij_disk1:[aijfiles]bank_aij1
cont> ALLOCATION IS 800 BLOCKS BACKUP FILENAME
        aij_bkps:[aijfiles]bank_aij1_bck
cont> ADD JOURNAL bank_aij2 FILENAME
        aij_disk2:[aijfiles]bank_aij2
cont>  ALLOCATION IS 800 BLOCKS BACKUP FILENAME
        aij_bkps:[aijfiles]bank_aij2_bck
cont> ;
```

The previous example shows that each journal file has a BACKUP
FILENAME.

There are three further options available with AIJ files that can improve performance:

• Backup server

• Log server

• Cache on solid state disk

The role of the BACKUP SERVER is to automatically backup the contents of
the AIJ files, thus allowing the AIJ files to be used continuously. This option
should be used in highly available systems.

```
SQL> ALTER DATABASE FILENAME eurobank:[db.db]banking
cont> JOURNAL IS ENABLED
cont> (BACKUP SERVER AUTOMATIC);
```

To improve throughput to the AIJ file, the LOG SERVER can be enabled.
Instead of using one of the processes attached to the database to write to the
AIJ file, now the log server has the task, thus enabling the user's process to
complete their AIJ writing very quickly.

```
SQL> ALTER DATABASE FILENAME eurobank:[db.db]banking
cont> JOURNAL IS ENABLED
cont> (LOG SERVER IS AUTOMATIC );
```

If the system contains any solid state disks, an AIJ electronic cache can be
created on this device. It is a very small file, but it allows quick writing to the
AIJ file. The log server must also be enabled to use this option.

```
SQL> ALTER DATABASE FILENAME eurobank:[db.db]banking
cont> JOURNAL IS ENABLED
cont> (LOG SERVER IS AUTOMATIC ,
cont>  CACHE FILENAME disk_ese1:[aijfiles]the_aij_cache );
```

Hint: For high throughput systems, it is really beneficial to enable the electronic cache but it only works on solid state disks. No perceived benefit will be seen if defined on a traditional disk.

Monitoring AIJ Activity

When the system is comprised of multiple AIJ files, the status of these files can be monitored using the AIJ information screen in RMU/SHOW STATISTICS. This is a very informative screen and it's really worth taking time to understand the display. From the screen can determine:

- Whether AIJ is enabled

- The size of each AIJ file

- The current end of file for each AIJ file

- Time before the database will shut down

- If log server is automatic or manual

- If backup server is enabled

- Whether electronic cache (ACE) is enabled

- Whether fast commit is on or off

- The state of the AIJ file

- How many spare AIJ slots are available

From the screen here, we can see that four AIJ files are currently in use. One of these files needs to be backed up and the other three files have size of 513 and 8000 blocks. The file that is being used presently for writing is BANK_AIJ1 and at the moment we have only written up to block 93 of a 512 block file.

```
Node: RDB4ME    Rdb 6.0-0 Performance Monitor  26-FEB-1994 14:34:25
Rate: 3.00 Seconds     AIJ Information        Elapsed: 00:43:13.79
Page: 1 of 1         EUROBANK:[DB.UK]BANKING.RDB;1     Mode: Online
─────────────────────────────────────────────────────────────────

Journaling: Enabled  Shutdown: 60  Notify: Disabled   State: Accessible
ALS: Manual   ABS: Disabled   ACE: Disabled FC: Disabled CTJ: Disabled

After-Image.Journal.Name... SeqNum AIJsize CurrEOF Status. State......
BANK_AIJ                      2       513     93     Current Accessible
BANK_AIJ2                     1    *BACKUP NEEDED*    Written Accessible
BANK_AIJ3                   Unused  8000    Empty    Latent  Accessible
BANK_AIJ4                   Unused   513    Empty    Latent  Accessible
Available AIJ slot 1
Available AIJ slot 2
Available AIJ slot 3
Available AIJ slot 4
Available AIJ slot 5
Available AIJ slot 6
Available AIJ slot 7
```

9.8.3   AIJ File Is Full

In very active transaction-processing-style systems, the AIJ files will fill up rapidly. When multiple files are in use, the system will automatically switch over to the next available AIJ file. Once all the AIJ files have been filled with data, until their contents are backed up, the database will stall. This stall can be avoided by using the AIJ backup server but if this feature is not enabled then the fastest solution to remove the stall is to add a new AIJ file or backup one or more AIJ journal files.

The first hint that the AIJ file has filled up is users will stall and the stall messages screen in RMU/SHOW STATISTICS will display the following:

```
Node: RDB4ME    Rdb 6.0-0 Performance Monitor  26-FEB-1994 14:34:25
Rate: 3.00 Seconds          Stall Messages    Elapsed: 00:43:13.79
Page: 1 of 1         EUROBANK:[DB.UK]BANKING.RDB;1     Mode: Online
─────────────────────────────────────────────────────────────────
Process.ID  Since......
Stall.reason.................................... Lock.ID.
00000038:4  18:06:31.19 - waiting for 800-block available AIJ (59 minutes)
```

In this example the system requires the creation of an AIJ file, that has a minimum size of 800 blocks so that system processing can continue. It is advisable to create a considerably larger AIJ file than that recommended by the system, otherwise the problem may recur again. The message also advises that unless the AIJ file is created within the next 59 minutes, the system will be shut down automatically.

Adding a new AIJ file can be achieved using one of two methods and it is not necessary to remove any users from the system. They can remain attached to the database and once the new AIJ file is created they will continue working. The two methods available to add the AIJ file are via SQL or RMU. Remember that if your system only has a run-time environment then SQL may not be available and in this instance will have to use RMU. There is no preferred method; either is suitable.

```
SQL> ALTER DATABASE FILENAME eurobank:[db.db]banking
cont> ADD JOURNAL BANK_AIJ3 FILENAME aij_disk1:[aijfiles]bank_aij3
cont> ALLOCATION IS 2000 BLOCKS;

$ RMU/SET AFTER_JOURNAL  /ADD=(NAME=bank_aij3, FILE=aij_disk1:[aijfiles]
      bank_aij3,  ALLOCATION=2000 ) eurobank:[db.db]banking
```

The RMU/SET AFTER command is a very useful command for managing AIJ files because not only can it be used to add AIJ files but it also allows one to enable or disable after-image journaling, enable the electronic cache, suppress an AIJ file and numerous other options.

9.8.4   AIJ Backups

We have already seen that the AIJ files can be automatically backed up via the backup server. If this method is not being used then they must be backed up manually using RMU/BACKUP/AFTER.The contents of the AIJ files are transferred into an AIJ backup file and this file can now be used for recovery.

```
$ RMU/BACKUP/AFTER eurobank:[db.db]banking bank_bkp1
```

9.8.5   Optimizing AIJ Files

If your AIJ files are large then it is worth considering optimizing them to improve recovery time. By applying the RMU/OPTIMIZE/AFTER command to the quiet-point AIJ file, it creates a new AIJ file where:

- All rolled back transactions are removed

- All duplicate updates for the same row are removed

- The rows are sorted into dbkey order to improve recovery time

The optimize process creates a new AIJ file; however, it is important to retain the original AIJ file. The reason for retaining the original file is because if you need to recover to a specific point in time or have to do a restore by area, these are not possible with optimized AIJ files.

9.9 RESTORE

With the RMU/RESTORE command, an Rdb database is restored from the backup file that was created using RMU/BACKUP. In its basic form, RMU/RESTORE will restore the database to its directory. Then, using the RMU/RESTORE/INCREMENTAL qualifier, an incremental backup file that contains only the database pages that have changed since the last full backup is overlaid onto the restored database. From V6.0 the restore command will automatically recover the AIJ files.

Hint: As recovery is automatic don't forget to include the /NORECOVER qualifier if you want to manually recover AIJ files or recover from AIJ backup files.

If automatic recovery is not required then apply the AIJ files using the RMU/RECOVER command. This complete process is illustrated in Figure 9.7.

The backup strategies described in Figure 9.6 would use after-image journaling to rebuild the database to a specific point in the period between backups.

When a restore operation is executed many messages are displayed and it is now very important to check these, especially when automatic recovery has been invoked. In the following example of a restoration of the BANKING database, automatic recovery has been disabled with the /NORECOVERY qualifier because we have to restore an incremental backup, then a backed up AIJ file, followed by an AIJ file.

Normally restoration will just involve a full backup and the AIJ files. In this instance it is recommended that automatic recovery is used; i.e., give a simple RMU/RECOVER/LOG command, and let Rdb do the rest.

Figure 9.7 Typical Procedure to Restore a Database

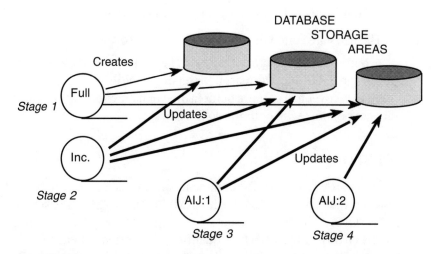

Another possibility with database restoration that is not shown here is the ability to recover the database to a specific point in time. Using the /UNTIL command we can recover the database to a specific point in time. This option may be necessary if a crash occurred at a specific time and you need to rebuild the system to just before this time. It is fair to say that this type of restoration is not very common, because we normally require all data to be restored. But suppose there was an application program fault that corrupted the database and the DBA knew at what time it occurred. The DBA could then rebuild the database to the time just before the corruption occurred.

Also remember that the examples shown here cover a full database recovery but can also recover a specific storage area or specific pages in the database. Some lines have been omitted to reduce the size of the example.

```
$ RMU/RESTORE/LOG/NORECOVERY bank_full_backup

%RMU-I-RESTXT_04, Thread 1 uses devices EUROBANK:

%RMU-I-AIJRSTBEG, restoring after-image journal "state" information

%RMU-I-AIJRSTJRN, restoring journal "AIJ_FILE1" information

%RMU-I-AIJRSTNMD, journal has not yet been modified

%RMU-I-AIJRSTSUC, journal "AIJ_FILE1" successfully restored from file
    'EUROBANK:[BACKUPS] AIJFILE1.AIJ;1'

%RMU-I-AIJRSTJRN, restoring journal "AIJ_FILE2" information
```

%RMU-I-AIJRSTNMD, journal has not yet been modified

%RMU-I-AIJRSTSUC, journal "AIJ_FILE2" successfully restored from file
    "EUROBANK:[BACKUPS]AIJFILE2.AIJ;1"

%RMU-I-AIJRSTEND, after-image journal "state" restoration complete

%RMU-I-RESTXT_00, Restored root file EUROBANK:[DB.UK]BANKING.RDB;1

%RMU-I-LOGRESSST, restored storage area EUROBANK:[DB.UK]BANK_SYSTEM.RDA;1

%RMU-I-LOGRESSST, restored storage area EUROBANK:[DB.UK]BANK_CUST.RDA;1

                 ....(some information removed)

%RMU-I-LOGRESSST, restored storage area EUROBANK:[DB.UK]BANK_SYSTEM.RDA;1

%RMU-I-RESTXT_05,   rebuilt 1 space management page

%RMU-I-RESTXT_06,   restored 6 inventory pages

%RMU-I-RESTXT_07,   rebuilt 141 logical area bitmap pages

%RMU-I-RESTXT_08,   restored 855 data pages

%RMU-I-RESTXT_01, Initialized snapshot file
    EUROBANK:[DB.UK]BANK_SYSTEM.SNP;1

%RMU-I-LOGINIFIL,   contains 192 pages, each page is 2 blocks long

%RMU-I-RESTXT_01, Initialized snapshot file
    EUROBANK:[DB.UK]BANK_CUST.SNP;1

%RMU-I-LOGINIFIL,   contains 10 pages, each page is 2 blocks long

                 ....(some information removed)

%RMU-I-AIJWASON, AIJ journaling was active when the database was backed up

%RMU-I-AIJRECFUL, Recovery of the entire database starts with AIJ file
    sequence 0

%RMU-I-AIJRECBEG, recovering after-image journal "state" information

%RMU-I-AIJRSTAVL, 2 after-image journals available for use

%RMU-I-LOGMODSTR,   activated after-image journal "AIJ_FILE1"

%RMU-I-AIJISON, after-image journaling has been enabled

%RMU-W-DOFULLBCK, full database backup should be done to ensure future
    recovery

%RMU-I-AIJRECEND, after-image journal "state" recovery complete

%RMU-I-LOGINIFIL,   contains 109 pages, each page is 2 blocks long

%RMU-I-AIJWASON, AIJ journaling was active when the database was backed up

%RMU-I-AIJRECFUL, Recovery of the entire database starts with
    AIJ file sequence 0

```
%RMU-I-AIJRECBEG, recovering after-image journal "state" information
%RMU-I-AIJRSTAVL, 2 after-image journals available for use
%RMU-I-LOGMODSTR,  activated after-image journal "AIJ_FILE1"
%RMU-I-AIJISON, after-image journaling has been enabled
%RMU-W-DOFULLBCK, full database backup should be done to ensure future
     recovery
%RMU-I-AIJRECEND, after-image journal 'state' recovery complete
```

The first step of the restoration process is now complete; the next step is to restore the incremental backup.

```
$ RMU/RESTORE/INCREMENTAL/LOG/NORECOVERY  bank_incr_backup
%RMU-I-RESTXT_04, Thread 1 uses devices EUROBANK:
     EUROBANK:[DB.UK]BANKING.RDB;1, restore incrementally? [N]:Y
%RMU-I-RESTXT_00, Restored root file EUROBANK:[DB.UK]BANKING.RDB;1
%RMU-I-LOGRESSST, restored storage area EUROBANK:[DB.UK]BANK_SYSTEM.RDA;1
%RMU-I-LOGRESSST, restored storage area EUROBANK:[DB.UK]BANK_CUST.RDA;1
%RMU-I-LOGRESSST, restored storage area EUROBANK:[DB.UK]BANK_ACCT.RDA;1
%RMU-I-LOGRESSST, restored storage area EUROBANK:[DB.UK]BANK_TRANS.RDA;1
%RMU-I-LOGRESSST, restored storage area EUROBANK:[DB.UK]BANK_INDEX.RDA;1
%RMU-I-RESTXT_09,   initialized 0 space management pages
%RMU-I-RESTXT_10,   restored 0 inventory pages
%RMU-I-RESTXT_11,   initialized 0 logical area bitmap pages
%RMU-I-RESTXT_12,   restored 18 data pages
%RMU-I-RESTXT_13,   initialized 0 data pages
%RMU-I-LOGRESSST, restored storage area EUROBANK:[DB.UK]BANK_SYSTEM.RDA;1
%RMU-I-RESTXT_09,   initialized 0 space management pages
%RMU-I-RESTXT_10,   restored 0 inventory pages
%RMU-I-RESTXT_11,   initialized 0 logical area bitmap pages
%RMU-I-RESTXT_12,   restored 8 data pages
%RMU-I-RESTXT_13,   initialized 0 data pages
%RMU-I-RESTXT_01, Initialized snapshot file
     EUROBANK:[DB.UK]BANK_SYSTEM.SNP;1
%RMU-I-LOGINIFIL,   contains 192 pages, each page is 2 blocks long
%RMU-I-RESTXT_01, Initialized snapshot fileEUROBANK:[DB.UK]BANK_CUST.SNP;1
%RMU-I-LOGINIFIL,   contains 10 pages, each page is 2 blocks long
```

```
%RMU-I-RESTXT_01, Initialized snapshot file EUROBANK:[DB.UK]BANK_ACCT.SNP;1
%RMU-I-LOGINIFIL,   contains 10 pages, each page is 2 blocks long
%RMU-I-RESTXT_01, Initialized snapshot file
    EUROBANK:[DB.UK]BANK_TRANS.SNP;1
%RMU-I-LOGINIFIL,   contains 10 pages, each page is 2 blocks long
%RMU-I-RESTXT_01, Initialized snapshot file
    EUROBANK:[DB.UK]BANK_INDEX.SNP;1
%RMU-I-LOGINIFIL,   contains 109 pages, each page is 2 blocks long
%RMU-I-AIJWASON, AIJ journaling was active when the database was backed up
%RMU-I-AIJRECFUL, Recovery of the entire database starts with AIJ file
    sequence 0
```

The restoration of the incremental backup is complete. Each AIJ file is allocated a sequence number and the recovery command indicates the number required in the first file. If unsure as to which file to use first then use the RMU/DUMP/AFTER command as shown below. We can see from the following example that this is not the first AIJ file to use because it contains AIJ sequence number 4.

```
$ RMU/DUMP/AFTER/NODATA    AIJFILE1.AIJ;1
*──────────────────────────────────────────────────
* Rdb 6.0-0                      27-FEB-1994 22:52:16.25
*
* Dump of After Image Journal
*    Filename: EUROBANK:[UK.DB]AIJFILE1.AIJ;1
*
*──────────────────────────────────────────────────

1/1        TYPE=0, LENGTH=510, TAD=27-FEB-1994 20:37:53.68
    Database EUROBANK:[UK.DB]BANKING.RDB;1
    Database timestamp is 27-FEB-1994 19:38:37.42
    Facility is 'RDMSAIJ ', Version is 601.0
    AIJ Sequence Number is 4
    Last Commit TSN is 95
    Synchronization TSN is 0
    Type is Normal (unoptimized)
    Open mode is Initial
    Backup type is Active
    I/O format is Record
```

The correct file has been found and the RMU/RECOVER command now applies the AIJ files. When there are multiple AIJ files only one RMU/RECOVER command is issued and it then prompts for each AIJ file as required as is shown in the following example.

It is suggested that the DBA carefully read and check each of the messages displayed. For example, in the following recovery sequence we can see that the first AIJ uses sequence 0, then AIJ sequence 2. This is possible because this file is a backed-up AIJ file. Then it prompts for the next AIJ file with a sequence number of 3.

```
$ RMU/RECOVER/LOG AIJ_BKP1.AIJ;1

%RMU-I-LOGRECDB, recovering database file EUROBANK:[DB.UK]BANKING.RDB;1

%RMU-I-LOGOPNAIJ, opened journal file EUROBANK:[BACKUPS]AIJ_BKP1.AIJ;1

%RMU-I-AIJONEDONE, AIJ file sequence 0 roll-forward operations completed

%RMU-I-AIJONEDONE, AIJ file sequence 2 roll-forward operations completed

%RMU-I-LOGRECOVR, 5 transactions committed

%RMU-I-LOGRECOVR, 0 transactions rolled back

%RMU-I-LOGRECOVR, 7 transactions ignored

%RMU-I-AIJACTIVE, 1 active transaction not yet committed or aborted

%RMU-I-LOGRECSTAT, transaction with TSN 91 is active

%RMU-I-AIJSUCCES, database recovery completed successfully

%RMU-I-AIJNXTSEQ, to continue this AIJ file recovery, the sequence number
    needed will be 3

_AIJ_file:AIJ_FILE3.AIJ;1

%RMU-I-LOGOPNAIJ, opened journal file EUROBANK:[BACKUPS]AIJ_FILE3.AIJ;1

%RMU-I-AIJONEDONE, AIJ file sequence 3 roll-forward operations completed

%RMU-I-LOGRECOVR, 4 transactions committed

%RMU-I-LOGRECOVR, 0 transactions rolled back

%RMU-I-LOGRECOVR, 0 transactions ignored

%RMU-I-AIJNOACTIVE, there are no active transactions

%RMU-I-AIJSUCCES, database recovery completed successfully

%RMU-I-AIJNXTSEQ, to continue this AIJ file recovery, the sequence number
    needed will be 4

%RMU-I-AIJALLDONE, after-image journal roll-forward operations completed
```

```
%RMU-I-LOGSUMMARY, total 9 transactions committed

%RMU-I-LOGSUMMARY, total 0 transactions rolled back

%RMU-I-LOGSUMMARY, total 7 transactions ignored

%RMU-I-AIJSUCCES, database recovery completed successfully

%RMU-I-AIJFNLSEQ, to start another AIJ file recovery, the sequence number
      needed will be 4
```

AIJ recovery is now complete. Readers should not be concerned that AIJ recovery is a complex process because from V6.0 it is automated, unless requested otherwise.

9.10 RESTORE BY AREA

If one area in a database becomes corrupt, it is not necessary to restore the whole database. The /AREA qualifier can be used to restore individual storage areas from full backup or incremental backup files. This option is very useful when a disk is lost and the database has to be put back online as quickly as possible. Instead of restoring the entire database, the last full backup file can be used with the RMU/RESTORE/AREA command issued to extract the specified storage area from the backup file. This area then can be extracted from the incremental backup file using the RMU/RESTORE/INCREMENTAL/AREA.

Finally, the database can be recovered to the state it was in just prior to failure by applying the after-image journal files to the database using the RMU/RECOVER/AREA command. As databases become larger, the ability to recover small parts of the database becomes essential.

The following is a typical example of restoring a full database, then a specific area:

```
$ RMU/RESTORE/LOG/NORECOVERY   sunday_full
$ RMU/RESTORE/LOG/INCREMENTAL/AREA banking mon_inc2 ACCOUNT_AREA
```

Hint: When specifying the /AREA command, it is important to also specify which areas to recover in the storage area list. Failure to do this will result in a successful recovery, but no data will have been restored.

9.11   AIJ RECOVERY BY AREA

When a specific database is restored from a backup file, it can be brought up-
to-date by using RMU/RECOVER/AREA. The RMU utility only applies
changes for a specific storage area, ignoring changes to other areas.

9.12   RECOVERING A DATABASE PAGE

Sometimes an individual page or a few pages in the database may become
corrupt. Depending on the application it may not be possible or even feasible
to recover the entire database. In this instance a rapid restoration method is
required and can be found in the restore by database page option.

Rdb knows which pages have to be restored, this information being held in the
root file. It can be viewed using the command RMU/DUMP/HEADER. To
recover the corrupt pages only in the database use the RMU/RESTORE/
JUST_PAGES command and specify which areas are to be recovered as shown
below. This command however must be used in conjunction with the backup file.

```
$ RMU/RESTORE/JUST_PAGES/AREA bank_full_backup

%RMU-W-USERECCOM, Use the RMU/RECOVER command. The journals are not
     available

RMU/RECOVER/AREA/JUST_PAGES   aij_bkp1.aij;1

%RMU-I-AIJONEDONE, AIJ file sequence 0 roll-forward operations completed

%RMU-I-AIJONEDONE, AIJ file sequence 2 roll-forward operations completed
        _AIJ_file:AIJ_FILE3.AIJ;2

%RMU-I-AIJONEDONE, AIJ file sequence 3 roll-forward operations completed

%RMU-W-NOTRANAPP, no transactions in this journal were applied
        _AIJ_file:AIJ_FILE3.AIJ;1

%RMU-W-AIJSEQPRI, AIJ file sequence number 3 created prior to expected
sequence 4

%RMU-I-AIJONEDONE, AIJ file sequence 3 roll-forward operations completed

%RMU-I-AIJALLDONE, after-image journal roll-forward operations completed

%RMU-I-AIJSUCCES, database recovery completed successfully

%RMU-I-AIJFNLSEQ, to start another AIJ file recovery, the sequence number
     needed will be 4
```

9.13   CHANGING DATABASE PARAMETERS ON RESTORE

When restoring a database, it is possible to change the following database parameters:

- The after-image journal file names and number of reserved AIJ journals
- The number of VMScluster nodes
- The directory in which database files reside
- The maximum number of users allowed to be attached to the database
- The number of buffers
- Increase the size of the buffer
- Page size, snapshot file location, and threshold values for a specific storage area

Hint: If there are too many qualifiers to change them individually, the /OPTIONS qualifier should be used to specify an options file that can include all the parameters you wish to change.

9.14   RUN-UNIT JOURNALING

A run-unit journal file is created for every user-process attach. These files contain an image of the data before the user changes it. The run-unit journal file is kept until the user finishes the transaction, at which time its contents are erased. If the user should choose to roll back the transaction, the contents of the RUJ file will be used to return the database to its original state, before the transaction began.

Hint: Many RUJ files will be created on a system. To prevent them all from going to the same disk, the logical RDMS$RUJ should be used to move the run-unit journal file for a given process to another directory.

To change the directory where the RUJ file for a process is stored:

```
$ DEFINE RDMS$RUJ eurobank:[uk.journal]
```

9.14.1   Placement

The journal files are automatically placed, on OpenVMS systems, in the directory [RDM$RUJ] unless redirected by the logical RDMS$RUJ. If this directory does not already exist, Rdb will create it automatically on the same disk as where the user's SYS$SCRATCH is pointing to.

9.14.2   Naming Convention

The run-unit journal file's naming convention is the database name and timestamp with an extension of RUJ. The format is:

```
<database name>$<timestamp number>.RUJ
```

With this naming convention, it is no longer possible to purge the run-unit journal files because each has a unique identifier.

9.15   VMSCLUSTER FAILOVER

If a node (machine) in a VMScluster fails, a cluster state transition occurs. If users have transactions open during VMScluster state transition, the database journal files will be identified and Rdb will automatically roll back the transactions that were active on the failed node, using one of the surviving OpenVMS cluster nodes. This maintains the integrity of the database and allows users on other machines in the VMScluster to continue working once the cluster state transition is complete.

If all the nodes in the OpenVMS cluster fail, when the system is next available, the first user to access the database will have his or her process stalled while all the unapplied run-unit journal files are recovered first. With this powerful capability, it is important to ensure that RUJ files are placed on disks to which all the nodes in the OpenVMS cluster have access.

9.16   DISTRIBUTED TRANSACTIONS

Although distributed transactions will be covered in Chapter 12, you should know that Rdb can maintain the integrity of a database during a transaction that updates multiple distributed resource managers, such as two Rdb databases, or an Rdb database and an RMS file. Most systems only maintain integrity within one type of resource manager, not multiple types. DECdtm will maintain the integrity of databases involved in distributed transactions.

The following additional RMU commands are available to support distributed transactions and maintain integrity within the database:

- RMU/RESOLVE – Resolves blocked transactions

- RMU/RECOVER/RESOLVE – Resolves blocked transactions on roll-forward

Since data is a corporate asset, it is imperative that its integrity is not compromised. For this reason, Rdb provides a range of commands and facilities that guarantee the database is not compromised.

10   Database Restructuring

Before relational database systems were introduced, CODASYL and hierarchial database systems were popular. Changing the structure of these two systems required major effort, however. Something as simple as changing the field length from 10 to 12 characters involved major work and usually would take days or even weeks. Changes were so time-consuming because all the data had to be extracted from the old database. A new database with revised structures had to be created, then the old data would be loaded into the new database in the new format. This was not a task to be taken lightly, especially since all the programs required to make the change had to be thoroughly tested. The unload and load programs offered ample opportunity to corrupt all the data in the database, as illustrated in Figure 10.1.

If a company is to succeed today, it must be flexible enough to change to meet market forces and demands. One of the main reasons for the dramatic success of the relational database is that the physical database structure and metadata definitions can be changed more easily. Of course, not all changes are instantaneous; there still are times when it is necessary to unload and load the data. But with relational technology, these occasions are few and far between. Rdb provides a number of methods for altering the metadata, or the data that describes the data stored in a database, and, consequently, the physical database structures. The data structures usually are changed due to:

- Revised metadata definitions

- Changes in the physical position of tables and indexes in relation to the storage areas

- Movement of physical storage areas to a new location

- Revised physical creation parameters

**Figure 10.1 Changing Database Definitions Prior to
   Relational Databases**

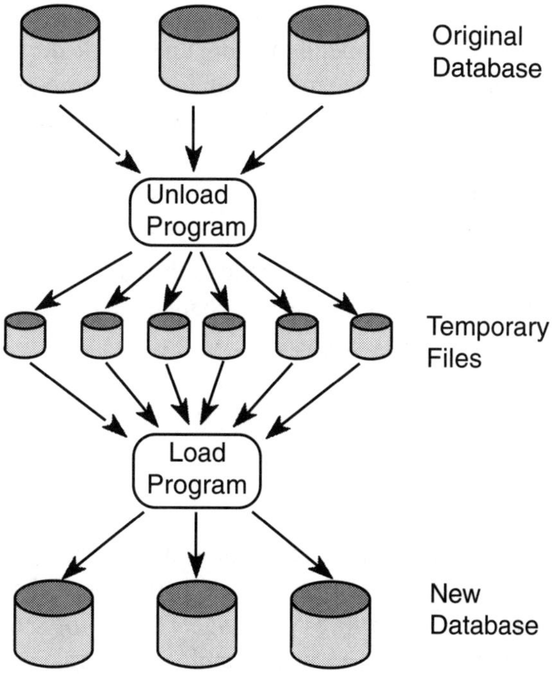

This chapter will review the tools and methods available to the database designer and administrator to change the structure of the Rdb database with minimum impact on the users or application programs. The following commands and tools are used to restructure the database.

- SQL ALTER

- RMU/UNLOAD and RMU/LOAD

- SQL EXPORT and IMPORT

- RMU/RESTORE

- RMU/COPY_DATABASE

- RMU/MOVE_AREA

10.1   CHANGING THE METADATA DEFINITIONS

Most changes in database structure occur because the data within it changes. New data must be included and redundant data is removed. Initially, changes in the data content will amend the domain or table definition. Unfortunately, changes do not stop there. An existing index may require amendment or the index definitions may be affected if a new index is required. The change also could affect the storage map definition if a new table is included or if the partitioning for an existing table requires amendment. Metadata changes do not just affect the data definitions.

Many types of changes may be made to the Rdb database. The following list indicates three SQL commands that change the metadata; however, note that this list is by no means complete.

- CREATE

- ALTER

- DROP

It is possible to make many changes to the database online while users are accessing the data. Of course, the one restriction is that users cannot access data that someone is trying to change. The ability to perform concurrent metadata changes means that new tables, domains, and indexes can be included in the design while the database is being used. This reduces the amount of time that metadata changes require exclusive access to the database. For computer systems that operate 24 hours a day, this feature is essential to perform maintenance on the database.

10.1.1   Creating New Metadata Definitions

We have already seen in Chapter 2 how domains, tables, indexes, and views are added to an Rdb database. The process of creating new tables is identical to that for defining a new database. New domains or tables are added to a database using the CREATE command described in Chapter 3 . Once they are created and committed, the new metadata definitions are available for use.

New storage areas can be created at any time using the ALTER DATABASE statement and the ADD STORAGE AREA clause. This command is not executed inside a transaction. Therefore, once it is completed, there is no rolling back;

the new storage area can only be deleted using the DROP STORAGE AREA clause, as shown in the following example. Remember that first a full backup of the database should be taken. Also remember that there must be free storage area slots.

```
SQL> ALTER DATABASE FILENAME eurobank:[uk.db]banking
cont> ADD STORAGE AREA new_transactions;

SQL> ALTER DATABASE FILENAME eurobank:[uk.db]banking
cont> DROP STORAGE AREA new_transactions
```

10.1.2   Amending Existing Metadata

Amendments to existing metadata definitions are made using the SQL ALTER command. This action allows changes to be made to:

- Domains

- Tables

- Indexes

- Storage maps

Domains

Domains are amended by the ALTER DOMAIN command. With this command, Rdb permits modification of datatypes, the multinational collating sequence, the default value, and the SQL and DATATRIEVE formatting strings. The ability to change the datatype is a very powerful feature inside a relational database. Provided the existing data is not invalidated, many changes can be defined. Text strings can be lengthened or shortened, for example. The following example changes the length of a domain:

```
SQL> ALTER DOMAIN standard_name CHAR(25);
```

Changing a domain automatically cascades the new definition into all the tables that have used it. The only exception is when an index has been defined on a domain. In this instance, the domain can only be altered once the index has been dropped.

Hint: It should be noted here that shortening a text string does not change the physical contents of the string until the data is modified. Rdb keeps the original data, so it is possible to return to the previous data definition without loss of data if no rows in the table are modified.

Tables

Alteration of table definitions is probably the most frequent type of change to an Rdb database. The reason for this is because so many of the table attributes can be changed. New columns and constraints may be added and existing column definitions may be modified or dropped, including their constraints. Using the BANKING example, suppose bank officials decide to offer a phone banking service for a six-month trial period. To help determine if the service should be one of the bank's standard services, the officials decide that every time a customer makes a transaction with this new facility, the column PHONE_TRANSACTIONS in the CUSTOMER table is incremented by one. The first step is to include the new column in the CUSTOMER table:

```
SQL> ALTER TABLE customer ADD COLUMN phone_transactions TINYINT;
```

Suppose the trial proved to be such a success that a TINYINT was inadequate. The column could be amended to a SMALLINT:

```
SQL> ALTER TABLE customer ALTER phone_transactions SMALLINT;
```

At the end of the trial period, the column could be removed using:

```
SQL> ALTER TABLE customer DROP COLUMN phone_transactions;
```

This is just one example of how a business may change its metadata in response to the demands of the marketplace.

Indexes

Indexes are frequently changed within Rdb databases. Typically, they are either dropped (deleted) or new indexes are created. The modifications that may be applied to an existing sorted index are:

● Changing the node size

● Adjusting the percentage fill factor

- Stating the access mode as either query or update

- Disabling maintenance

- Changing the storage area in which the index is stored

Why are changes continually made to the indexes? There are many reasons. It might be necessary, for example, to define additional access paths, rebuild the index to improve performance, or change the access path because access requirements have changed.

An example of amending the CUST_SURNAME_SORTED in our BANK-ING database would be:

```
SQL> ALTER INDEX cust_surname_sorted
cont> NODE SIZE 450
cont> PERCENT FILL 75;
```

Storage Map

The storage map controls how rows in a table are physically stored in the Rdb database. With the changing nature of many businesses today, data frequently is moved inside the database. For instance, information may be required in a different sequence, so a new index is created. To achieve optimum retrieval, the rows in the table should be placed via this new index.

The ALTER STORAGE MAP command in SQL allows the following changes to be made to the data:

- SPAM thresholds

- Placing data via a new index

- Stopping data placement via an index

- Enabling or disabling compression

- Reorganizing data so all data is affected

The last point is one of the most significant clauses in the ALTER STORAGE MAP statement because it physically moves the data according to the new placement requirements. This is an invaluable feature because it improves performance that has deteriorated due to data-placement problems. Figure 10.2 shows how an ALTER STORAGE MAP statement using the REORGANIZE clause makes it possible to increase the number of storage areas and partition the data across all the areas, old and new, moving the data to be

**Figure 10.2 Using the ALTER STORAGE MAP to Physically
Reorganize Data in the BANKING Database**

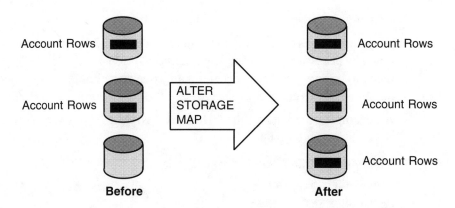

positioned according to the new placement. If desired, a hashed index could
have been created and the data clustered around the hashed index.

The following example uses the BANKING database. The CUSTOMER rows
are moved from the CUSTOMER_AREA storage area, where they are stored
randomly, into the default system area RDB$SYSTEM, where they are placed
next to the new index CUST_FIRST_NAME. This probably is not a design
decision that would be implemented in a real database.

- Define a new index on CUSTOMER and place in storage area
  RDB$SYSTEM

```
SQL> CREATE INDEX cust_first_name ON customer
cont> (first_name DESCENDING, surname ASCENDING)
cont> TYPE IS SORTED NODE SIZE 300
cont> STORE IN rdb$system;
```

- Display the current dbkeys for the CUSTOMER rows

```
SQL> SELECT customer_no, dbkey FROM customer;
 CUSTOMER_NO DBKEY
  100201   37:5:0
  100205   37:5:1
  1678345  37:5:2
3 rows selected
```

- Show the current storage map for the customers

```
SQL> SHOW STORAGE MAP customer_map;
    CUSTOMER_MAP
 For Table: CUSTOMER
 Compression is: ENABLED
 Store clause: STORE IN CUSTOMER_AREA
```

- Amend the storage map to move the CUSTOMER rows to RDB$SYSTEM and place via the new index

```
SQL> ALTER STORAGE MAP customer_map
cont> STORE IN rdb$system
cont> PLACEMENT VIA INDEX cust_first_name
cont> REORGANIZE PAGES;
```

- Display the dbkeys of the CUSTOMER rows that have now moved to logical area 51

```
SQL> SELECT customer_no, dbkey FROM customer;
 CUSTOMER_NO DBKEY
 100201   51:539:0
 100205   51:539:1
 1678345  51:539:2
3 rows selected
```

Hint: In this example, the REORGANIZE clause will move the data only if the STORE clause is specified; otherwise Rdb does not know in which areas to place the rows.

The REORGANIZE clause also is useful when the storage area in which a hashed index is defined has extended. When this occurs, the hashing algorithm will only use the initial allocation size to determine the range of pages over which data can be spread. Therefore, once the extension area is used to store rows from the table, additional I/O is required to retrieve the row, eliminating many of the benefits of using hashed indexes. When this situation occurs, using the REORGANIZE clause avoids the need to unload and reload the data.

10.1.3   Deleting Existing Metadata

So far, we have only considered adding or amending the metadata definitions, but restructuring also could involve deleting data structures. SQL provides the DROP statement to delete the following metadata structures:

- CATALOG
- COLLATING SEQUENCE
- CONSTRAINT
- DOMAIN
- FUNCTION
- INDEX
- MODULE
- PATHNAME
- OUTLINE
- SCHEMA
- STORAGE MAP
- TABLE
- TRIGGER
- VIEW

Some of these commands already have been described in Chapter 2.

Hint: To maintain the integrity of the Rdb database, Rdb imposes some restrictions on the sequence in which metadata definitions may be deleted.

The DROP statement is not the only command available for removing metadata definitions. The ALTER TABLE statement, for example, also includes a DROP COLUMN or DROP CONSTRAINT clause to remove these metadata types from the database. The following example would drop the column statement date from the account table:

```
SQL> ALTER TABLE account
cont> DROP COLUMN statement_date;
```

10.2   CHANGING THE PHYSICAL CREATION PARAMETERS

Restructuring the Rdb database does not always involve changing the metadata definitions. Sometimes, amendments are required to the database-wide creation parameters, such as buffers, journal files, and storage area allocations. A number of parameters may be modified with a number of different techniques. Essentially, the parameters may be changed using:

- Operating system logical names or environment variables

- ALTER DATABASE

- IMPORT/EXPORT

- RMU/RESTORE

Table 10.1 lists many of the database-wide parameters that may be changed and notes which utility implements the modifications. Note that the column for RMU/MOVE is also valid for RMU/COPY_DATABASE.

A typical example from the BANKING database follows. This illustrates amending the database parameters to set the number of buffers allocated to a database attach to 100.

```
SQL> ALTER DATABASE FILENAME eurobank:[uk.db]banking
cont> NUMBER OF BUFFERS IS 100;
```

Table 10.2 lists many of the database-wide parameters that may be changed while users are attached to the database.

Table 10.3 lists many of the data definitions that may be changed while users are attached to the database.

10.2.1   Increasing Storage Area Size

Rdb automatically increases the size of a storage area if extra space is required. This dynamic space allocation lets Rdb continue functioning until the disk is full. At this point, even Rdb cannot pull disk space out of a hat. If the Rdb database administrator noticed that extra space was required and the disks were nearly full, either new storage areas could be created and the storage map changed to use these additional areas, or the database could be restored

Table 10.1 Database-Wide Parameter Changes

Parameters	Logical	ALTER DATABASE	IMPORT/ EXPORT	RMU/ RESTORE	RMU/ MOVE
Adjustable Locking	N	Y	Y	N	N
AIJ Journal Name	N	Y	N	Y	Y
AIJ Allocation	N	Y	N	N	N
AIJ Extent	N	Y	N	N	N
AIJ On or Off	N	Y	N	Y	Y
Buffers, Number of	Y	Y	Y	Y	Y
Buffer Length	N	N	Y	Y	N
Carry Over Locks	N	Y	Y	N	N
Collating Sequence	N	N	Y	N	N
Commit to Journal Opt	N	Y	N	N	N
Database Page Size	N	N	Y	Y	Y
Extension Pages	N	Y	Y	Y	Y
Fast Commit On or Off	N	Y	N	N	N
Global Buffering On or Off	N	Y	Y	Y	N
Open Automatic/Manual	N	Y	Y	Y	N
Recovery Buffers	N	Y	Y	N	N
Restricted Access	N	Y	Y	N	N
RUJ Extent	Y	N	N	N	N
Storage Area Placement	N	N	Y	Y	Y
Snapshots On or Off	N	Y	Y	N	N
Snaps Immediate/Deferred	N	Y	Y	N	N
Snapshot File Allocation	N	Y	Y	N	N
Snapshot File Extent	N	Y	Y	N	N
Thresholds	N	N	Y	Y	Y
Users	N	Y	Y	Y	Y
VMScluster Nodes	N	Y	Y	Y	Y

Table 10.2 Database-Wide Parameter Changes with Attached Users

Parameters	Allowed or Disallowed
Adjustable Locking	N
AIJ Journal Name	N
AIJ Allocation	Y
AIJ Extent	Y
AIJ On or Off	Y
AIJ Add	Y
AIJ Alter	Y
AIJ Drop	Y
Buffers, Number of	Y
Buffer Length	N
Carry Over Locks	N
Collating Sequence	Y
Commit to Journal Opt	N
Fast Commit On or Off	N
Global Buffering On or Off	N
Global Buffer Variables	Y
Lock Timeout Interval	Y
Recovery Buffers	Y
Reservation of Journal Slots	N
Reservation of Storage Area Slots	N
Snapshots On or Off	N
Snaps Immediate/Deferred	N
Snapshot File Allocation	N
Snapshot File Extent	N
Statistics Collection On or Off	N
Storage Area Extension On or Off	Y
Storage Area Allocation	Y
Storage Area Read or Write	Y
Storage Area Lock Levels	N
Users	N
VMScluster Nodes	N

Table 10.3 Data Definition Changes with Attached Users

Object	Allowed or Disallowed	Notes
Constraints	Y	Not while a transaction is accessing the associated tables
Domains	Y	
Functions	Y	
Indexes	Y	Not while a transaction is accessing the associated tables, but users can now concurrently create indexes
Modules	Y	Not while a transaction is calling or has called the stored procedure
Outlines	Y	
Protection	Y	
Storage Maps	Y	
Tables	Y	
Triggers	Y	Not while a transaction is accessing the associated tables or using trigger
Views	Y	

using RMU/RESTORE, using parameters on the RESTORE command to create the additional space that would be required.

A common requirement is to be able to truncate the size of a snapshot file that has grown beyond its normal size. This can happen for various reasons; perhaps a load program was executed in a non-exclusive transaction while snapshots were enabled or perhaps a process such as an ACMS server process was attached to the database for a long time issuing read/write transactions so that Rdb was unable to reclaim snapshot file space.

The snapshot file can be truncated online while other users are attached to the database; however, if any read-only transaction is active, the ALTER statement will be forced to wait until it completes.

```
SQL> ALTER DATABASE FILENAME eurobank:[uk.db]banking
cont> ALTER STORAGE AREA BRANCH_AREA
cont> SNAPSHOT ALLOCATION 300;
```

10.2.2   **RMU/RESTORE**

Most people associate RMU/RESTORE with restoring their database when a problem occurs. Few people consider using it as a database-restructuring tool. RMU/RESTORE can allow the specification of database or storage-area-wide parameter amendments. Not only is it possible to change simple values, such as the number of database users or the after-image journal file size, it also can be used to change the storage area values, such as page size, allocation, or extension. This flexibility means that while a database is being restored, it is possible to refine the database at the same time. A simpler approach is often the use of RMU/MOVE_AREA and RMU/COPY_DATABASE commands to restructure the database. In this case no intermediate storage is required. Table 10.1 defines many of the database-level changes permitted. In addition, changes can be made for each of the following storage areas:

- Blocks per page

- Directory location

- Snapshot directory

- Threshold values

Note that the buffer size can also be specified on an RMU/RESTORE; however, it must be at least the size of the largest page in the database.

Hint: When restoring a database made up of a number of tables, an options file is used to specify all the storage areas and their parameter values. Unless this is done then, in the OpenVMS environment, the token limit will be exceeded.

10.2.3   **Moving an Rdb database**

Sometimes a database must be moved to another directory. The simplest way to achieve this is with RMU/MOVE_AREA or RMU/COPY_DATABASE. Alternatively, but using intermediate storage, the RMU/RESTORE command with the /DIRECTORY qualifier may be used. The RMU/MOVE_AREA command moves the storage area into the specified directory, whereas the RMU/COPY_DATABASE will copy a whole database to a specified destination.

10.3   RMU/UNLOAD AND LOAD

RMU/UNLOAD and LOAD may be used to load and unload data. Unlike SQL IMPORT and EXPORT, which can only manipulate a whole database, RMU/LOAD and UNLOAD work at the table level. Assuming they are working on different tables to avoid conflict, RMU/LOAD and UNLOAD jobs can be run in parallel.

Hint: Use RMU/EXTRACT to automatically generate RMU/LOAD and UNLOAD command files for each table in the database.

RMU/LOAD and UNLOAD are useful when the database has to be reorganized and the existing tools are inadequate. Suppose extra columns are needed in a table. The new columns easily could be added without affecting the existing data. In this instance, however, adding extra columns would force existing rows to fragment, compromising the database performance. The solution is to unload the individual table, reformat to include the new field, and reload the table. The process is a typical example of how RMU/UNLOAD and LOAD are used to manage an Rdb database.

It could be argued that ALTER with its reorganize options would perform the same task and eliminate the need for the intermediate file. But extracting all the data sometimes gives the database designer more control over the reload operation. The commit frequency can be specified and the task can be broken down into manageable portions.

10.3.1   RMU/UNLOAD

The RMU/UNLOAD command extracts data from a specific table or view. The following example is from the BANKING database. The BRANCH table is extracted into a file called branch_data, which has a file extension of .UNL One important point to remember with this utility is that the data is only copied from the Rdb database. Therefore, this command can be used to make copies of tables in the database.

```
$ RMU/UNLOAD eurobank:[uk.db]banking branch branch_data
%RMU-I-DATRECUNL, 14 data records unloaded
```

The command has an additional qualifier, /FIELDS, which is used to specify exactly which fields are to be written to the unload file. One problem with the RMU/UNLOAD command is that it provides very little opportunity to manipulate the data while extracting it from Rdb.

The output of RMU/UNLOAD can be a specially formatted file that contains the table metadata, in which case, the RMU/LOAD command can read this metadata later. Alternatively, the output file can be a file containing only data in which case it can be used by any software that can read file system files. A record-definition file can also be created in this case that describes the structure of the file. Note that only the specially formatted file can contain segmented strings.

To enable the output data to be read by a variety of software packages, it can be enhanced by the addition of a:

- Prefix

- Suffix

- Separator

- Row terminator

The following example shows the format of an RMU/UNLOAD command that unloads the BRANCH table, separates the fields with a comma and places double-quotes around those fields.

```
$ RMU/UNLOAD/RMS_RECORD_DEF=(FILE=branch.def,FORMAT=DELIMITED_TEXT)
    eurobank:[uk.db]banking branch branch.dat
```

The following example shows the format of an RMU/UNLOAD command that does the same as above but adds a prefix to each column.

```
$ RMU/UNLOAD/RMS_RECORD_DEF=(FILE=branch.def, FORMAT=DELIMITED_TEXT,
    PREFIX='$') eurobank:[uk.db]banking branch branch.dat
```

10.3.2   RMU/LOAD

When loading the data into the database, RMU/LOAD will accept either a sequential RMS file or the specially formatted file with the .UNL extension created by RMU/UNLOAD. Like the unload command, RMU/LOAD works on one table at a time and has a number of options to control the load. Using this command it is possible to specify:

- Commit after every *x* rows

- Load certain columns

- Pre-sort the data into dbkey order to speed up the load

- Skip over any rows

- Control how triggers are initiated

- Lock the database in a certain mode

- Load an OpenVMS security audit journal into an Rdb table

- Create an exceptions record of rows that failed to load

In the following example from the BANKING database, rows are loaded into the ACCOUNT table using RMU/LOAD.

```
$ RMU/LOAD eurobank:[uk.db]banking account account_data
%RMU-I-DATRECSTO, 978 data records stored
```

If the data requires modification before being loaded back into Rdb, this operation must be performed outside of the RMU/UNLOAD and LOAD commands. Any changes can be made provided the data is presented to RMU/LOAD in the expected format.

RMU/LOAD and UNLOAD should be all the load/unload capability a database administrator needs for most applications. For very large databases, however, it might be necessary to write an application program specifically to unload and load the database. The reason for this approach is that the application program would provide far more control over the process than RMU/LOAD and UNLOAD. Say, for example, that RMU/UNLOAD creates a fixed-length record, which might cause a problem if the database contains one million rows of fixed-length 600 bytes, but only 125 bytes were used. Writing an application program to perform the unload would save a vast amount of disk space because the application program could create variable-length record files.

10.3.3   RMU GUI MANAGEMENT UTILITY

An X/Windows GUI interface for building and executing RMU commands was introduced in V6.1. Invoked by specifying RMUwin, the first screen, Figure 10.3, determines the databases managed through the GUI. Clicking on the icon for the database displays Figure 10.4 from which the RMU commands are built.

Figure 10.3 The RMUwin Startup Screen

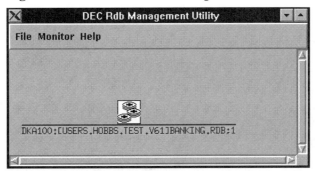

Figure 10.4 RMUwin Management Screen

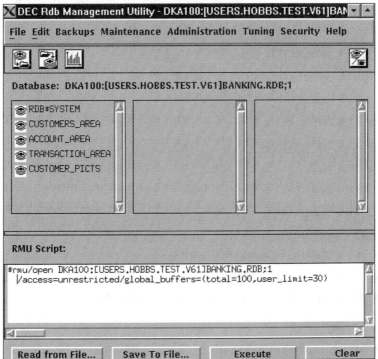

When Figure10.4 first appears, each storage area is displayed and information is provided about the tables and indexes in those areas. Some icons are provided to automatically invoke backup, restore, show statistics and dump header. Clicking on the far right icon changes the storage area display to the header information normally displayed by an RMU/DUMP HEADER command.

Figure 10.5 RMUwin Backup Options Screen

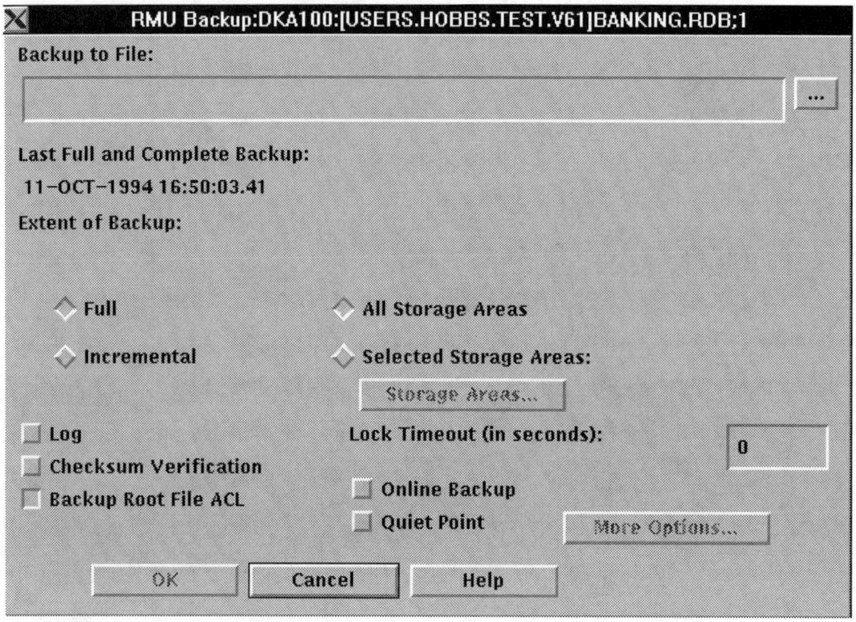

Building RMU commands with the complex array of options available is not a trivial task, especially to the newcomer to this utility. The GUI provides a friendly, easily used mechanism for defining them. Suppose it is required to create a backup command; then simply check the required boxes as illustrated in Figure 10.5, then watch the RMU command automatically appear in the lower box in Figure 10.4. This command should then be saved to a file. RMU commands saved in these files can be executed directly from within the GUI.

Whether you are a novice or an expert, once you get used to using the GUI, you will wonder how you ever managed without it.

10.4 EXPORT AND IMPORT

The last utility to mention is SQL EXPORT and IMPORT.

EXPORT creates a copy of the database in a special compressed form. No structural changes may be made when the database is being exported. All that this command does is to make an intermediate file with an extension of .RBR.

In the OpenVMS environment, it is worth changing the RMS default EX-
TEND value using $SET RMS_DEFAULT to a value more appropriate to
the export file size. For example, the default is 3 blocks. If the database is 500
Megabytes, the export file will extend many times. It would be more efficient
to set the extend quantity to perhaps 50,000 blocks.

**Hint: Compressed does not mean table compression, of course. All text
columns are stored in their full form, not in their compressed form as
inside Rdb. For this reason, the EXPORT file can occupy more space
than the original database and usually does.**

The IMPORT command takes as its input the file created by EXPORT and
loads the data into the Rdb database. At this stage, the format and structure of
the new database may be changed. Certain parameters, including buffer length,
can only be changed via an EXPORT and an IMPORT. A list of most amendments that can be made to the database when importing is given in Table 10.1.

EXPORT and IMPORT should be used to migrate to higher software versions
if an Rdb database may have to be restored later on a different version of Rdb
than it was created on. The IMPORT and EXPORT statement provide the
option of NODATA, which results in either exporting an empty database or
importing only the metadata definitions and structure from an exported database.

10.5   WHY REORGANIZE?

This chapter illustrated the wide range of tools that Rdb provides to restructure database design. Purists say that the relational model is so flexible that a
database reorganization utility is unnecessary. In theory this is true. Unfortunately, in the real world the model's flexibility sometimes is inadequate and
the database must be reorganized. Or, for performance reasons, an alternative
physical implementation may improve throughput. Rdb does, however, try to
ensure that changing database structure is a smooth and easy process.

11   Tuning and Optimization

Many relational databases are created with default parameters or parameters set by the database administrator, and never require amendment. However, since relational databases frequently play crucial roles in many organizations, the details of their performance characteristics are important. If fine-tuning relational databases were simple, experienced database designers would not be required. In reality, unfortunately, database tuning is something of a black art if the appropriate tools are not available. As this chapter will show, Rdb users have a number of tools available that enable them to completely optimize a database. These tools range from capabilities within Rdb through to RdbExpert, which is described in Chapter 16. RdbExpert is a new artificial-intelligence-based database design tool that can determine the optimum physical database design of a database for a given workload.

Describing in detail how to tune an Rdb database would fill a book. Instead, this chapter will discuss the techniques that should be used during database design to ensure that a database performs to its maximum potential. It also will review the tools available to the designer and will indicate some of the more obvious places to look if the database has a performance problem. For further information, consult the *Guide To Database Performance and Tuning* which is part of the Rdb documentation set.

Rdb databases do not require a lot of tuning. Rdb has been designed so that most databases created with the default parameters will perform adequately for most systems. However, if a system requires maximum performance, a wealth of tools is available to easily tune the database. Think of Rdb as a racing car. With a standard racing engine it runs very well, but in the hands of the trained mechanic it is transformed into a world-class winner. Most database designers will be able to tune their own databases. But maximum performance most likely can only be achieved at the hands of an Rdb tuning expert.

11.1 UNDERSTANDING THE PHYSICAL DESIGN

To achieve optimum performance, the database designer must understand how all the internal database structures, such as tables and indexes, are placed within each of the defined storage areas. Making assumptions about data positioning may lead to unexpected results because Rdb provides so many different placement options, such as clustered or random placement, or placement via a hashed index.

If the database is understood from this perspective, it is possible to determine whether extra I/O is being performed. For example, if a table is placed via a hashed index, reading a hashed index automatically brings the row into the buffer. Only a read from memory is required to read the table row because the row is already in the buffer. This procedure is considerably faster than reading from disk and results in improved performance.

Determining how data is placed inside the database requires searching through many pages of database definitions, referring to the table, index, and storage map definitions to see the whole picture. This is a tedious, time-consuming process that is prone to error. One way of understanding how the tables and indexes are placed within the database is to draw a picture of the physical implementation of the database. We will call such a picture a database placement map.

11.1.1 Database Placement Map

The database placement map is a simple picture of the physical database implementation that usually can be drawn on one or two sheets of paper. Once constructed, the database placement map is used to:

- Determine whether the tables and indexes are placed optimally inside the database

- Calculate database page size

- Describe the physical database design pictorially and concisely

- Display the overhead of internal database structures

- Assist during transaction analysis to determine I/O requirements

A database placement map can be constructed in approximately one hour by following a few simple steps. Ideally, it should be drawn on a computer because objects frequently are repositioned. If a computer is not available then one or two pieces of paper also will suffice, but make sure you draw using a pencil. And have an eraser – because you will certainly need it!

When constructing database placement maps, remember that they represent typical relationships and what a database page is expected to contain. Therefore, the following typical questions that must be answered:

- How are the BRANCH records accessed?

- How many TRANSACTION records typically are grouped together?

- Are the TRANSACTION rows clustered next to the ACCOUNT rows on a database page?

Once these questions are answered, work can begin on the database placement map.

Step 1

First, draw an open rectangle for each storage area that is specified in the database creation file. In the BANKING example, there are four storage areas. Figure 11.1 shows the first step completed.

If a storage area is partitioned into many physical storage areas and the contents of each partition are identical, only one storage area is drawn on the

INDEX_AREA

CUSTOMER

ACCOUNT

BRANCH

Figure 11.1 Database Placement Map – Step 1

database placement map for the sake of clarity. A note is inserted stating that this storage area actually is comprised of *x* partitions.

Step 2

Identify in which storage area each database table is positioned. To gather this information, first refer to the table definition and identify whether a storage map exists for a particular table. If it does, the storage map will specify in which area the table resides. Otherwise the table is stored in RDB$SYSTEM by default.

Hint: Each table should have a storage map. Do not store anything in RDB$SYSTEM except the system metadata.

In the storage area where the table resides, draw a small box to represent the table and write the table name inside the box. If all of the rows in a table are scattered throughout the storage area, only one box is drawn on the placement map. In Figure 11.2, the rows in the CUSTOMER table are scattered throughout the storage area; therefore only one box is drawn on the map in the CUS-TOMER storage area. Frequently, rows in a table are clustered together. This information is vitally important when trying to ascertain the number of I/Os required to access data.

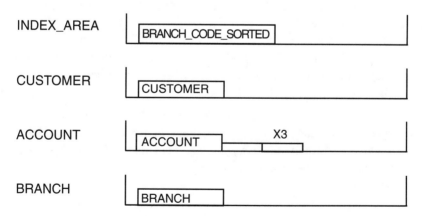

Figure 11.2 Database Placement Map – Step 2

To represent clustering on the database placement map, first determine from the storage map how the table is stored. If the table is stored via a hashed index, database clustering will occur. Clustering is represented on the database placement map by drawing several half-height boxes attached to the main table box. The typical number of entries clustered together is written above these half-height boxes.

In Figure 11.2 all the ACCOUNT records are clustered together. This is shown on the map as a full box and several half-height boxes. Because on the average there will be 3 accounts per customer, the number 3 is written above the boxes.

The BRANCH rows are placed in the Uniform page format storage area BRANCH_AREA, which means that the rows are placed together in the clump allocated to that table. The rows are stored together, but to differentiate from rows that are clustered via a hashed index, the table is drawn as two separate boxes, illustrating that the rows are together by default, rather than clustered.

Step 3

The next map structures are the two different types of index, the sorted b-tree and the hashed index. First include the sorted b-tree indexes. For each sorted b-tree index defined in the database, identify in which storage area the index is placed by referring to the index definition. If an index is in a specific storage area, a placement clause will be in the definition; if not, the index is stored in storage area RDB$SYSTEM. Next, draw a box on the map, write the index node name inside, and draw several half-height boxes to illustrate that many index nodes will be clustered together. In Figure 11.3, the branch index is shown as being in storage area INDEX_AREA. The next step is estimating roughly how many index nodes there will be. In our example, this index contains an estimated 1000 nodes; therefore, the number 1000 is written above the box to represent the index nodes.

Drawing the hashed index structure on the database placement map is a little more complicated because, as we have seen, a number of database structures make up a hashed index. As described in Chapter 5, a hashed index structure is made up of the following:

• A system record

- A hashed bucket

- A duplicate hashed bucket

Before drawing the hashed index onto the database placement map, first determine which parts of the hashed index structure are relevant. Every mixed format database page contains a system record. Its size varies according to the number of hashed indexes on the page. For each index defined, there is one hashed bucket which varies in size by the number of entries in the hash bucket. Although the hash bucket can overflow, we won't concern ourselves with that here because it is an unusual condition.

Duplicate hashed buckets will exist only when many rows have the same key. The buckets are of a fixed size of 92 bytes, which allows for 10 dbkeys. Therefore, there will be one duplicate hash bucket for every 10 duplicate keys.

Figure 11.3 shows a simple hash index on the CUSTOMER table made up of only a system record and a hash bucket. This situation is shown as a system record and a hashed bucket, therefore. In the case of the ACCOUNT_AREA storage area, the hashed index on ACCOUNT may be made up of up to 3 duplicates. The hashed index structure in this instance, therefore, is made up of:

- A system record

- A hash bucket

- Two duplicate hash buckets

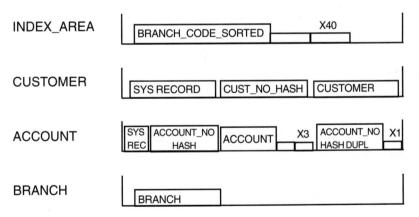

Figure 11.3 Database Placement Map – Step 3

Step 4

Our database placement map now is almost complete. The final step involves calculating the size of each of the structures in the storage areas. For each table and index node, write the expected size under the box representing the data structure. Hashed index structures are slightly more difficult to calculate because they vary in size according to the number of dbkeys inside the hashed index. If the hashed index structures are to be calculated reasonably accurately, the formulas in Table 11.1 should be used.

Table 11.1 Calculating the Size of a Hashed Index

Category	Bytes/Entry	Total
SYSTEM RECORDS		
No. of Hashed Indexes	a	a
Total System Record Size		
Overhead	4	4
Minimum	6	$(6*a)+4$
Maximum	10	$(10*a)+4$
HASH BUCKET		
Key Size	1	1
Key	k+1	k+1
Overhead/Entry	12	12
Total/Entry	12+1+k+1=b	b
No. of Entries	c	c
Overhead/Bucket	13	13
Total Bucket Size	$(b*c)+13$	$(b*c)+13$
DUPLICATE NODE RECORD		
No. of Duplicates	d	d
No. of Entries/Node	10	
No. of Duplicate Nodes	$(d+5)/10=e$	
Overhead/Node	92	92
Total	$e*92$	$e*92$

GRAND TOTAL $(((6*a)+4)$ or $((10*a)+4)) + ((b*c)+13) + (e*92)$

Figure 11.4 Database Placement Map – Step 4

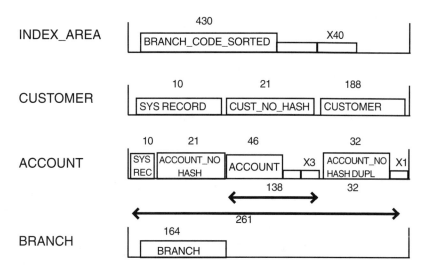

Consider the instances where a number of different data structures are grouped together, such as in the case of the ACCOUNT table and the hashed index to which the row is clustered. All the items are added together, and an arrow is drawn to illustrate which items in the storage areas are related and the total bytes required to store all of this data.

With this final piece of information it is possible to determine whether the database page sizes have been correctly calculated. The user can see exactly what should reside on a database page. The total space requirements can be compared with the specified page size.

Figure 11.4 is the completed database placement map. This map is now an essential component of the database design documentation. When tuning the database, it helps determine whether data is being efficiently retrieved from the database.

11.1.2   Physical Design Verification

After application programs are written, they usually go through a period of extensive testing before they are put into service. Database designs that do not go through the testing process may have design flaws that are not identified until the database is in use. This can result in expensive disruption to the company, with a loss in both time and potential business.

A simple technique that may be used to verify the database design is *transaction analysis*. It is a time-consuming manual process that frequently is overlooked. Transaction analysis involves taking a business transaction, such as Account Inquiry, and walking through the transaction to see how it accesses the database. Following this process involves checking the database to see that:

• Tables are present

• Indexes are available for fast access

• Whether rows are locked and the duration of locks

It is not uncommon to find databases performing badly because an index is missing. Transaction analysis could have avoided this situation. There is no right way to perform transaction analysis. The following approach involves completing the form shown in Figure 11.5 for each transaction that is being reviewed. This form is designed to take into consideration all the access that is likely to occur as the result of a database request:

• Read/write/delete a row

• Read/write/delete either to a sorted b-tree or a hashed index

• Write to the snapshot file

• Force a constraint check, which, in turn, can affect

  – Row/table

  – Index

  – Snapshot

• Activate a trigger

The example in Figure 11.5 illustrates a completed transaction analysis form for the deposit function for our BANKING example. The deposit function process involves finding the account using the account number, creating a transaction row that updates the balance in the account table by means of a Rdb trigger called *upd_bal*.

Figure 11.5 Transaction Analysis Form

Transaction Analysis

Function: Deposit								Date: AUG '94		
								Version: 1		
Description: Deposit an amount into an account								Page: 1		

Table	Action	Hashed B-tree Index	Constraint	Trigger	Snap Shot	Journal RUJ AIJ		Total I/O Man Opt
Account	Read 1	Acct_No						1
Transaction	Insert 1	Create 1		Upd_bal 1 -Account	2	2	2	9

Comments:	TOTAL I/O Mandatory	10
Assume 1 I/O to read both account row and hashed index	Optional	

Reading across each row on the transaction analysis form informs us that this transaction reads one row from the account table via the hashed index on account number. Since the account row is placed on the same database page as the hashed index, it is assumed that all the information is read in one I/O.

The next step is to insert one transaction record, which creates an entry in the hashed index. As a result, the trigger upd_bal is invoked, which updates the balance in the account table. All this writing to the database results in two I/Os to the snapshot file for updating the transaction and account table. The same I/O's also are included for writing out the changes to the journal file. On average, the deposit function requires approximately ten I/Os.

11.2   **A TUNING PLAN**

Before starting to tune the database, a plan should be formulated. Attempting to tune without a proper plan will require considerable extra effort. The plan should include:

- Tuning objectives

- A definitive starting position for all tests

- The conditions to be tested

- The expected results from the tests

The objectives of the tuning exercise must be clearly stated; for example, the Account Inquiry response must be improved from 1.5 seconds to 1 second. It also is imperative to create a database backup that contains the state of the database to be used for all tests. Then it will be possible to determine whether any improvements have been achieved through the tuning exercise.

Finally, all tuning activities should be logged and the results kept for examination later. Sometimes just writing down the elapsed and CPU time is not enough because the data may be required later for analysis, such as the Direct I/O count values, which were not recorded earlier.

11.3   **TUNING TOOLS**

A number of tools may be used to tune an Rdb database. Some belong to the native operating system, others are supplied with Rdb, and others are separate products. The main tools to use are:

- Certain operating system commands

- Rdb Debug Flags

- RMU/SHOW STATISTICS

- RMU/ANALYZE and /DUMP

- DECtrace and RdbExpert products

We will now consider each of these tools individually.

11.3.1 Operating System Commands

Before starting to tune the actual database, it is worth checking the general operating system parameters of the user account used to query the database. Frequently, queries to the database are slow because the user's own account is not granted enough resources.

Fragmented disks also must be considered. If the database files have been fragmented, extra I/O will be needed. On OpenVMS this is detected by checking whether there is more than one retrieval pointer on a storage area by using the $DUMP/HEADER command from the DCL prompt. OpenVMS is rich in useful performance monitoring commands, some of the more useful ones being:

- MONITOR DISK – shows disk I/O throughput
- MONITOR SYSTEM – shows system statistics
- MONITOR CLUSTER – shows VMScluster statistics
- MONITOR LOCK – shows the lock activity
- SHOW SYSTEM – shows the users on the system

11.3.2 Rdb Debug Flags

By setting the logical name RDMS$DEBUG_FLAGS, it is possible to see what action Rdb is taking to perform a query. The logical name is set to a number of different values, but the most useful one is 'S', because it advises which strategy the optimizer has chosen to resolve the query. This is especially useful when Rdb chooses an access path into the database that was unexpected, such as sequential access instead of index access, as shown below:

```
$ DEFINE RDMS$DEBUG_FLAGS 'S'

SQL> SELECT branch_code FROM branch;
Get Retrieval sequentially of relation BRANCH

BRANCH_CODE
SOT
POT
ROP
WICK
PLYM
```

It is good practice to test all major queries on the database to make sure that no unexpected paths are being taken. The most useful values that the debug flags may be set to are:

- O – Optimizer cost
- S – Optimizer strategy
- E – Dynamic optimization

11.3.3   RMU/SHOW STATISTICS

Without doubt, this RMU utility is one of the most powerful tools available to the database designer. It monitors all activity upon the database and collects a wealth of information, most of which may be replayed at a later date. The RMU utility displays the information either graphically or numerically on a standard VT terminal for a whole range of resource items. It collects information continually on all of the following items:

- Summary IO statistics
- Summary locking statistics
- PIO (physical IO) statistics - writes, data fetches & SPAMs
- Global buffer information
- Asynchronous PIO statistics
- IO stall time (seconds *100)
- Index statistics (retrieval, insertion & removal)
- Hash index statistics
- AIJ statistics
- AIJ information
- Checkpoint statistics
- Record statistics
- Snapshot statistics

- Virtual memory usage statistics

- Transaction duration

- IO statistics (by file)

- Per process information

- Stall messages

- Active user stall messages

- Process accounting

- Database recovery information

- Logical name information

- Lock timeout & deadlock history

- Locking (one lock type)

- Locking (one stat field)

- CPU

- Objects usage

- Summary objects

- Custom statistics

The data can be either displayed on the screen or collected into a data file for a specified period of time. It is collected at a specified interval, the default interval being three seconds.

From V6.1 the SHOW STATISTICS utility also has a GUI interface which is almost identical to its character cell version. Some sample screens will be shown at the end of this chapter.

The Rdb manual entitled *Guide to Database Maintenance and Performance* explains in detail the purpose of each individual data item on the screen. All of the screens are useful, but it depends upon the area being tuned as to which are the most relevant. This chapter will look at the most useful screens and will highlight some of the data items that should be observed.

The RMU utility is started at the DCL level by using the RMU/SHOW STATISTICS command. A number of different qualifiers may be specified. In the

Figure 11.6 RMU/SHOW STATISTICS – Summary IO Screen (Graph)

```
Node: ORION          DEC Rdb  6.0-0  Performance Monitor   14-MAR-1994 17:40:11
Rate: 3.00 Seconds            Summary IO Statistics        Elapsed: 00:02:28.49
Page: 1 of 1           EUROBANK:[UK.DB]BANKING.RDB;1                Mode: Online
------------------------------------------------------------------------------

statistic......... max. cur.       10        20        30        40        50
name.............. rate rate +---------+---------+---------+---------+---------+
                             |         |         |         |         |         |
transactions        0    0   |         |         |         |         |         |
verb successes      23   23  +---------+---------+--*      |         |         |
verb failures       0    0   |         |         |         |         |         |
                             |         |         |         |         |         |
synch data reads    10   10  +---------*         |         |         |         |
synch data writes   0    0   |         |         |         |         |         |
RUJ file reads      0    0   |         |         |         |         |         |
RUJ file writes     0    0   |         |         |         |         |         |
AIJ file reads      4    4   +---*     |         |         |         |         |
AIJ file writes     0    0   |         |         |         |         |         |
root file reads     12   1   |*        |         |         |         |         |
root file writes    1    0   |         |         |         |         |         |
                             +---------+---------+---------+---------+---------+
------------------------------------------------------------------------------

Display_menu Exit Help Numbers Options Reset Set_rate Time_plot Write_screen
```

following example, /TIME=1 advises Rdb to collect data once a second. If /OUTPUT was specified, Rdb would display the data and collect it into the named file, which would allow the statistics to be replayed later.

```
$ RMU/SHOW STATISTICS /TIME=1 banking
```

If the /INPUT qualifier is specified, a previously recorded statistics file can be replayed.

The collection of statistics for a database process can be disabled by the specification of a logical name or OSF/1 environment variable, RDMS$BIND_STATS_DISABLED. The following example disables the collection of statistics for a database process:

```
$ DEFINE RDMS$BIND_STATS_DISABLED 1
```

To disable the collection of statistics for the database as a whole, use the ALTER DATABASE statement:

```
SQL> ALTER DATABASE FILENAME banking
cont> STATISTICS COLLECTION IS DISABLED;
```

Figure 11.7 RMU/SHOW STATISTICS – Summary IO Screen (Numbers)

```
Node: RDB4ME         DEC Rdb  6.0-0  Performance Monitor    12-MAR-1994 12:04:13
Rate: 3.00 Seconds            Summary IO Statistics         Elapsed: 00:00:18.96
Page: 1 of 1         EUROBANK:[UK.DB]BANKING.RDB;1                   Mode: Online
--------------------------------------------------------------------------------

  statistic...........   rate.per.second............. total....... average......
  name................   max..... cur..... avg........ count....... per.trans....

  transactions                 0        0      0.0           0          0.0
  verb successes               0        0      0.0           0          0.0
  verb failures                0        0      0.0           0          0.0

  synch data reads             0        0      0.0           0          0.0
  synch data writes            0        0      0.0           0          0.0
  asynch data reads            0        0      0.0           0          0.0
  asynch data writes           0        0      0.0           0          0.0
  RUJ file reads               0        0      0.0           0          0.0
  RUJ file writes              0        0      0.0           0          0.0
  AIJ file reads               0        0      0.0           0          0.0
  AIJ file writes              0        0      0.0           0          0.0
  root file reads              1        0      0.2           4          0.1
  root file writes             0        0      0.0           0          0.0
--------------------------------------------------------------------------------
Display_menu Exit Graph Help Options Reset Set_rate Time_plot Write_screen Yank
```

The database administrator should only disable statistics for an operational database that is running at peak performance and is not likely to require that the database administrator has a look at it with RMU/SHOW STATISTICS.

Hint: The authors have never found one of these!

Once started, the RMU/SHOW STATISTICS utility begins with the default display shown in Figure 11.6.

This initial screen is the Summary IO Statistics which will be discussed shortly. The screen is displayed in Graph Display Mode which shows a histogram display. As visually striking as this is, the less spectacular Numbers Display Mode tends to be more useful. This is shown in Figure 11.7.

Hint: Use the /NOHISTOGRAM qualifier on RMU/SHOW STAT to make the intial display Numbers Display Mode .

There are a number of items displayed on the strip-menu at the bottom of the display which are activated by typing the first letter of the item. One of the items on the menu is *Options*. This enables the database administrator to dump all the screens into a file called STATISTICS.RPT. This captures a snapshot of all screens and is an extremely useful capability. If the database administrator observes an interesting phenomenon on one screen, the use of this item allows the contents of all the screens to be captured at that moment in time for later perusal.

In a similar fashion, the item *Write_screen* allows the database administrator to dump the screen that is being currently displayed into a file called RMU.SCR. This is useful in conjunction with the /OUTPUT qualifier on RMU/SHOW STAT. The background recording of statistics into a file specified by this /OUTPUT qualifier does not, for example, record *Stall Messages*. To capture an interesting stall message screen, therefore, can be done by typing 'W' and this can be later studied in conjunction with a statistics replay from the /OUTPUT file.

The *Time_plot* option enables a time plot of a selected item, such as root file reads. This may be very useful to confirm suspected peaks and troughs. Pressing R to Reset will reduce all the values in the display to zero, but not those collected in the data file.

Note that statistics are collected since the database was last opened; therefore, a database close will lose the statistics collected up to that point. Also note that in a VMScluster environment, the statistics are only collected for the machine on which the utility is running, not cluster wide.

The *Set_rate* item allow the statistics collection interval to be changed from its default value of three seconds. Entering a negative number allows a value to be specified in hundredths of a second.

By selecting the *Display_menu* item, a list of statistics options is displayed as shown in Figure 11.8. The desired statistics screen may be selected by moving the cursor to it and pressing Return or by entering its menu letter.

The *Yank* option will extract the Statistic and include it on the Custom Statistics screen.

Throughout this chapter, statements such as if the value is high will be made. You may be asking the question, what is high? Unfortunately, it is impossible to specify what is a high or low value because every system is different. For this reason, RMU/SHOW STATISTICS should be run regularly, not only when there is a performance problem. The typical values for your system

Figure 11.8 RMU/SHOW STATISTICS – Display Options Screen

```
A.  Summary IO Statistics          O.  Checkpoint Statistics
B.  Summary Locking Statistics     P.  Record Statistics
C.  Summary Object Statistics      Q.  Snapshot Statistics
D.  PIO Statistics--Writes         R.  VM Usage Statistics
E.  PIO Statistics--Data Fetches   S.  Custom Statistics
F.  PIO Statistics--SPAM Fetches   T.  Transaction Durations
G.  Asynchronous PIO Statistics    U.  IO Statistics (by file)    [->
H.  IO Stall Time (seconds x100)   V.  Per-Process Information    [->
I.  Index Statistics (Retrieval)   W.  Global Buffer Information[->
J.  Index Statistics (Insertion)   X.  Locking (one lock type)    [->
K.  Index Statistics (Removal)     Y.  Locking (one stat field)   [->
L.  Hash index statistics          Z.  Objects (one stat type)    [->
M.  AIJ Statistics                 0.  Objects (one stat field)   [->
N.  AIJ Information
```

should be noted so that they can be compared with the display when the system is exhibiting signs of poor performance. Then you will see that a value of 156890 is typical, for example, but 456832 would be higher than normal.

The various screens will now be discussed. The screens that are deemed to be most useful will vary depending on the reasons for looking at the statistics. However, the authors tend to look at Stall messages first quickly followed by the summary screens such as Summary Locking and Summary IO.

Summary IO Screen

The summary IO screen, shown in Figure 11.7, gives an overview of disk I/O activity occurring on the database. There are a number of interesting fields. The *transactions* entry shows the total number of transactions completed since the database was opened and the transactions per second rate. The *verb successes* entry shows the total number of successful verbs executed since the database was opened and the average number of verbs per transaction. The *verb failures* entry shows the total number of verbs executed since the database was opened and the average number of verbs per transaction where an error status was returned. This may be indicative of a problem. *Synch data reads* and *synch data writes* show the number of reads and writes issued to the storage area and snapshot files. These are synchronous disk I/Os as opposed to asynchronous disk I/Os issued by the asynchronous pre-fetch and asynchronous batch write features. The other entries refer to read and write operations to other files, that is, the root file, RUJ file and AIJ file. Look out for *RUJ file reads* which indicates a rollback operation has occurred.

Figure 11.9 RMU/SHOW STATISTICS – Stall Messages Screen

```
Node: RDB4ME          DEC Rdb  6.0-0  Performance Monitor   12-MAR-1994 12:04:13
Rate: 3.00 Seconds                  Stall Messages          Elapsed: 00:07:45.87
Page: 1 of 1          EUROBANK:[UK.DB]BANKING.RDB;1                   Mode: Online
--------------------------------------------------------------------------------
Process.ID Since......  Stall.reason...........................  Lock.ID.
00000063:1 12:02:54.38 - waiting for logical area 60 (PR)        01000707




--------------------------------------------------------------------------------
Alarm Display_menu Exit Help >next_page <prev_page Set_rate Write_screen
```

Stall Messages

The Stall Messages screen is one of the most useful because it advises which processes in the system are stalled and why. In the following example, process 63 is stalled because a user has area 60 locked in a lock mode not compatible with the lock requested by process 63 which is a protected read lock. Once the stall is clear, the message will disappear. Figure 11.9 shows the Stall Messages screen.

Hint: Use the L key to zoom in and see who is holding the lock blocking a user.

Active User Stall Messages

The Active User Stall Messages screen is similar in format to the Stall Messages screen described above. However, it differs in that a slot is reserved on the screen for every process that is accessing the database. The location of the process is fixed and thus can be easily found and hence this display is very

Figure 11.10 RMU/SHOW STATISTICS – Active User Stall Messages Screen

```
Node: RDB4ME          DEC Rdb  6.0-0  Performance Monitor   12-MAR-1994 12:04:13
Rate: 3.00 Seconds           Active User Stall Messages     Elapsed: 00:07:45.87
Page: 1 of 1          EUROBANK:[UK.DB]BANKING.RDB;1                  Mode: Online
--------------------------------------------------------------------------------
Process.ID Since......    Stall.reason............................ Lock.ID.
0000005F:1               reading pages 4:68 to 4:70




--------------------------------------------------------------------------------
Display_menu Exit Help >next_page <prev_page Set_rate Write_screen
```

useful for monitoring the stalls occurring for a particular process. Even when
the stall is finished, the stall message stays until it is overwritten. A finished
stall is recognized by having no timestamp in the *Since* entry. Because there
may be many users accessing the database and a slot is reserved in this display
for each user (to be accurate each user attach), the display may spread over a
number of pages. Figure 11.10 shows the Active User Stall Messages screen.

**Hint: In the OpenVMS environment, empty lines are not a peculiarity of
the display. They represent user attaches from another VMScluster node.**

Physical IO Statistics

The PIO screens, shown in Figures 11.11, 11.12, 11.13 and 11.14, are useful
for determining how the buffers are being searched and used. RMU/SHOW
STATISTICS can detect whether global buffers are enabled or not and will
display appropriate screens accordingly as shown in Figure 11.13.

Figure 11.11 RMU/SHOW STATISTICS – PIO (Writes) Screen

```
Node: RDB4ME          DEC Rdb  6.0-0  Performance Monitor   12-MAR-1994 12:04:13
Rate: 3.00 Seconds              PIO Statistics--Writes        Elapsed: 00:07:45.87
Page: 1 of 1          EUROBANK:[UK.DB]BANKING.RDB;1                    Mode: Online
-------------------------------------------------------------------------------
statistic...........   rate.per.second............. total....... average......
name................   max..... cur..... avg....... count....... per.trans....
unmark buffer              7        0       0.9        415           31.9
   transaction             7        0       0.1         25            1.9
   pool overflow           1        0       0.7        339           26.1
   blocking AST            0        0       0.0          0            0.0
   lock quota              0        0       0.0          0            0.0
   lock conflict           0        0       0.0          4            0.3
   user unbind             0        0       0.0          0            0.0
   batch rollback          0        0       0.0          0            0.0
   new area mode           0        0       0.0          0            0.0
   larea change            0        0       0.0          0            0.0
   incr backup             0        0       0.0          0            0.0
   no AIJ access           0        0       0.0          0            0.0
   truncate snaps          0        0       0.0          0            0.0
   checkpoint              0        0       0.1         47            3.6
   AIJ backup              0        0       0.0          0            0.0
 SPAM page                 1        0       0.0          9            0.7
-------------------------------------------------------------------------------
Display_menu Exit Graph Help Options Reset Set_rate Time_plot Write_screen
```

The **PIO Statistics – Writes** display shows statistics concerning writes to the database and the writing of buffers back to disk.

The *unmark buffer* entry represents a modified buffer being written back to disk. Beneath this entry are a list of entries giving a more accurate reason behind the buffer flushes. In Figure 11.11, a total of 415 buffers have been flushed, of which 25 flushes occurred because of a commit or rollback (*transaction*), 339 occurred because of a buffer pool overflow (*pool overflow*) and 47 due to a checkpoint (*checkpoint*) as fast commit processing is enabled. A total of 9 SPAM pages have been written back to disk.

A high *buffer pool overflow* figure implies that benefits may be derived from increasing the number of buffers in the local buffer pool. Buffer flushes caused by pool overflow are inefficient and should be minimized if possible. A high number of *lock conflict* entries might suggest that the buffers are too large, causing contention. To verify this, check the Stall Messages screen to see whether contention is occurring.

In the **PIO – Fetches** screen, the *fetch for read* and *fetch for write* entries represent the number of synchronous data page requests when a page is requested for read or write respectively. These requests can be satisfied in a number of ways as described in the other entries. *In LB: all OK* means that the

Figure 11.12 RMU/SHOW STATISTICS – PIO (Fetches) Screen

```
Node: RDB4ME          DEC Rdb  6.0-0  Performance Monitor    12-MAR-1994 12:04:13
Rate: 3.00 Seconds          PIO Statistics--Data Fetches     Elapsed: 00:07:45.87
Page: 1 of 1          EUROBANK:[UK.DB]BANKING.RDB;1                   Mode: Online
--------------------------------------------------------------------------------


statistic..........    rate.per.second............. total....... average......
name...............    max..... cur..... avg....... count....... per.trans....

fetch for read              190      190    140.2        65317         5024.4
fetch for write            1244     1244    250.3       116609         8969.9

in LB: all ok              1425     1425    394.0       183530        14117.7
   LB: need lock              2        2      0.3          151           11.6
   LB: old version            0        0      0.0           15            1.2

not found: read               6        6      3.3         1550          119.2
         : synth              0        0      0.0            0            0.0



--------------------------------------------------------------------------------
Display_menu Exit Graph Help Options Reset Set_rate Time_plot Write_screen
```

page was found in the buffer and no other work was necessary. *In LB: need lock* means that the page was found in the buffer but some page locking work was necessary. *In LB: old version* means that the page was found in the buffer but because its version number was not the current one the page had to be read again from disk. *Not found: read* means that the page was not found in the buffer and had to be read from disk. *Not found: synth* means that Rdb need not read the page as it can create it in memory.

If the *In LB: all OK* and *In LB: need lock* entries are high compared to the *Not found: read* and *In LB: old version*, this indicates that most entries are found in the buffer, so the buffer pool sizing probably is correct. If the buffer pool sizing was incorrect, there would be a high number in *Not found: read*.

Therefore a well sized buffer pool will have the sum of *In LB: all OK* and *In LB: need lock* entries nearly equal to the sum of the *fetch for read* and *fetch for write* entries.

Hint: In theory, the sum of *fetch for read* and *fetch for write* should equal the sum of the other entries but sometimes this is not the case when the statistics are dumped to a file.

Figure 11.13 RMU/SHOW STATISTICS – PIO (Fetches) Screen with Global Buffering Enabled

```
Node: ORION          DEC Rdb  6.0-0  Performance Monitor   14-MAR-1994 21:19:10
Rate: 3.00 Seconds         PIO Statistics--Data Fetches     Elapsed: 03:41:27.28
Page: 1 of 1         EUROBANK:[UK.DB]BANKING.RDB;1                   Mode: Online
-------------------------------------------------------------------------------

statistic..........   rate.per.second............. total....... average......
name...............   max..... cur..... avg....... count....... per.trans....

fetch for read            81       0       2.0       26219         1542.3
fetch for write           21       0       1.3       16862          991.9

in AS: all ok             64       0       3.2       43011         2530.1
   AS: lock for GB          0       0       0.0           1            0.1
   AS: need lock            8       0       0.0         216           12.7
   AS: old version          0       0       0.0           0            0.0

in GB: need lock           8       0       0.0         163            9.6
   GB: old version          0       0       0.0           0            0.0

not found: read            0       0       0.0         348           20.5
         : synth           0       0       0.0           0            0.0

-------------------------------------------------------------------------------
Display_menu Exit Graph Help Options Reset Set_rate Time_plot Write_screen
```

When global buffering is enabled for a database, the PIO screens reflect this fact. Figure 11.13 shows a screen that is essentially the same as for the local buffer case but with entries specific to global buffering. The entries differentiate between pages found in the process's allocate set and those found in the global buffer pool but not in the process's allocate set.

In Version 6.1, three new *Global Buffer* screens are available: GB Utilization, GB Hotpage Information and GB Frequency Information provide details as to which pages are being used.

Figure 11.14 shows PIO statistics for SPAM pages. The explanation of the entries is similar to that for Figure 11.12. This is not a very useful display but is included here for completeness with the other PIO screens.

The screen in Figure 11.15 provides statistics on the efficiency of the asynchronous pre-fetch and asynchronous batch write features. When a non-zero entry is seen for *data read request,* Rdb must be performing a sequential scan of the storage area as currently asynchronous pre-fetch is only enabled for sequential scans. The *data read IO* are the number of asynchronous read requests that actually become asynchronous reads to disk because they were not found in the buffer pool.

Figure 11.14 RMU/SHOW STATISTICS – PIO (SPAM) Screen

```
Node: RDB4ME           DEC Rdb  6.0-0  Performance Monitor   12-MAR-1994 12:04:13
Rate: 3.00 Seconds        PIO Statistics--SPAM Fetches       Elapsed: 00:07:45.87
Page: 1 of 1           EUROBANK:[UK.DB]BANKING.RDB;1                   Mode: Online
--------------------------------------------------------------------------------


statistic..........    rate.per.second.............. total....... average......
name...............    max..... cur..... avg....... count....... per.trans....

fetch for read             108      108      32.6      15205         1169.6
fetch for write            286        9       4.8       2223          171.0

in LB: all ok              286      116      37.4      17406         1338.9
   LB: need lock             1        1       0.0         15            1.2
   LB: old version           0        0       0.0          0            0.0

not found: read              0        0       0.0         17            1.3
         : synth             0        0       0.0          0            0.0



--------------------------------------------------------------------------------
Display_menu Exit Graph Help Options Reset Set_rate Time_plot Write_screen
```

Figure 11.15 RMU/SHOW STATISTICS – Asynchronous PIO Screen

```
Node: RDB4ME           DEC Rdb  6.0-0  Performance Monitor   12-MAR-1994 12:04:13
Rate: 3.00 Seconds        Asynchronous PIO Statistics        Elapsed: 00:07:45.87
Page: 1 of 1           EUROBANK:[UK.DB]BANKING.RDB;1                   Mode: Online
--------------------------------------------------------------------------------


statistic..........    rate.per.second.............. total....... average......
name...............    max..... cur..... avg....... count....... per.trans....

data read request            7        0       7.1       3320          255.4
data read IO                 2        0       2.3       1092           84.0

spam read request            0        0       0.0         10            0.8
spam read IO                 0        0       0.0         10            0.8

read stall count             0        0       0.0         15            1.2
read stall time              0        0       0.0         23            1.8

write IO                     0        0       0.4        185           14.2
write stall count            0        0       0.0          3            0.2
write stall time             0        0       0.0         11            0.8


--------------------------------------------------------------------------------
Display_menu Exit Graph Help Options Reset Set_rate Time_plot Write_screen
```

Figure 11.16 RMU/SHOW STATISTICS – Record Statistics Display

```
Node: RDB4ME        DEC Rdb  6.0-0  Performance Monitor   12-MAR-1994 12:04:13
Rate: 3.00 Seconds            Record Statistics           Elapsed: 00:07:45.87
Page: 1 of 1        EUROBANK:[UK.DB]BANKING.RDB;1                  Mode: Online
------------------------------------------------------------------------------


statistic...........    rate.per.second............. total....... average......
name.................    max..... cur..... avg....... count....... per.trans....

record marked             101      101      28.9       13443         1034.1

record fetched            297      297      69.8       32509         2500.7
    fragmented              0        0       0.0           0            0.0

   record stored          101      101       9.4        4372          336.3
      fragmented            0        0       0.0           0            0.0
   pages checked          101      101       9.4        4373          336.4

record erased               9        0       8.7        4070          313.1
    fragmented              0        0       0.0           0            0.0


------------------------------------------------------------------------------
Display_menu Exit Graph Help Options Reset Set_rate Time_plot Write_screen
```

The *read stall* count is the number of occasions that the process stalled while it waited for an asynchronous read request to complete. The idea behind the asynchronous pre-fetch is to minimize process stalls on I/O and therefore if this figure is high, the feature is not peforming well. Specifying that more buffers are pre-fetched may reduce these stalls.

Similarly, the *write stall* count is the number of occasions that the process stalled while it waited for an asynchronous write request to complete. Again, the idea behind the asynchronous batch write feature is to minimize process stalls on I/O and therefore if this figure is high, the feature is not peforming well. Specifying a larger clean buffer count may reduce these stalls.

Record Statistics

The Record Statistics screen is useful for determining how well rows are placed inside the database. *Records fetched* indicates the number of rows retrieved to execute a query, and *records fragmented* indicates how many of the rows retrieved have been fragmented. A row also can be a snapshot record. A high value in any of the fragmented rows will significantly affect performance because additional CPU time is required to join the fragmented records and extra I/O is necessary to collect the fragments.

Figure 11.17 RMU/SHOW STATISTICS – IO Stall Time Display

```
Node: RDB4ME          DEC Rdb  6.0-0  Performance Monitor   12-MAR-1994 12:04:13
Rate: 3.00 Seconds        IO Stall Time (seconds x100)      Elapsed: 00:07:45.87
Page: 1 of 1          EUROBANK:[UK.DB]BANKING.RDB;1                 Mode: Online
-------------------------------------------------------------------------------
statistic..........    rate.per.second.............. total....... average......
name...............    max..... cur..... avg....... count....... per.trans....

root read time              0        0       0.1         24            1.8
root write time             1        0       0.1         56            4.3

data read time             12       12       2.0        943           72.5
data write time             8        0       0.6        276           21.2
data extend time            0        0       0.0          0            0.0

RUJ read time              21        0       0.2         79            6.1
RUJ write time              0        0       0.3        135           10.4
RUJ extend time             1        0       0.6        290           22.3

AIJ read time               0        0       0.1         57            4.4
AIJ write time              1        0       0.2        114            8.8
AIJ extend time             0        0       0.5        214           16.5


-------------------------------------------------------------------------------
Display_menu Exit Graph Help Options Reset Set_rate Time_plot Write_screen
```

If pages checked is considerably higher than record stored, it is an indication that the first page selected to store a record is full and another suitable place has to be found. This can be caused by a number of factors including locked free space which is not reflected in SPAM entries, and SPAM thresholds.

IO Stall Time

The IO Stall Time screen indicates the amount of time spent reading and writing data to the database and journal files. Large numbers in the *extend* row would indicate time that was spent stalled while waiting for the file to extend. If users complain that the database suddenly stops for a brief period, the reason could be files extending. This screen should be checked in such a situation. Figure 11.17 shows an IO Stall Time screen.

Hint: The figures on this screen reflect the total time that all users have been stalled. Therefore, accumulating the stall time for all the users together will result in a figure that is larger than the actual stalled elapsed time for a user.

Figure 11.18 RMU/SHOW STATISTICS – Transaction Duration Display

```
Node: RDB4ME            DEC Rdb  6.0-0  Performance Monitor   12-MAR-1994 12:04:13
Rate: 3.00 Seconds               Transaction Durations        Elapsed: 00:07:45.87
Page: 1 of 1            EUROBANK:[UK.DB]BANKING.RDB;1                    Mode: Online
------------------------------------------------------------------------------------
Transaction rate (per second):   current = 0        average = 0.0
Transaction duration (seconds):  average = 39.3     95th pctile = ~82.8

           Scaled distribution of transaction lengths (in seconds)
 +----+----+----+----+----+----+----+----+----+----+----+----+----+----+----+---+
 |    |    |    |    |    |    |    |    |    |    |    |    |    |    |    |   |
 |    |    |    |    |    |    |    |    |    |    |    |    |    |    |    |   |
 |    |    |    |    |    |    |    |    |    |    |    |    |    |    |    |   |
 |    |    |    |    |    |    |    |    |    |    |    |    |    |    |    |   |
 |    |    |    |    |    |    |    |    |    |    |    |    |    |    |    |   |
 |    |    |    |    |    |    |    |    |    |    |    |    |    |    |    |   |
 |  **|    |    |    |    |    |    |    |    |    |    |    |    |    |  * |   |
 *  ***|    |    |    |    |    |    |    |  * |    |    |    |    |    |*****|
 +----+----+----+----+----+----+----+----+----+----+----+----+----+----+----+---+
 0....1....2....3....4....5....6....7....8....9....10...11...12...13...14...15+++
                  (Each "*" represents 1 transaction)
------------------------------------------------------------------------------------
Display_menu Exit Help Options Set_rate Write_screen
```

Transaction Duration

The Transaction Duration screen is used to determine how long the transactions exist. In Figure 11.18, the *95th pctile* value indicates the time period in which 95% of all transactions are completed. Once this value goes out beyond about 30 seconds, this value reverts to 99999.99. If it is suspected that an application is holding locks across terminal I/O, this screen should be monitored. An entry will appear in the *15+* column if a telltale delay occurs in responding to the screen. Version 6.1 also displays this information in a numeric format, providing comprehensive details as to how many transactions have completed and not completed.

IO Statistics by File

IO statistics are kept in the replay file, from Version 6.1. If they are required while monitoring, the *Write_screen* option should be used to write the screen frequently to a file called RMU.SCR for review later.

Once the IO Statistics option has been selected, another menu is presented that specifies all the physical files that make up the database:

Figure 11.19 RMU/SHOW STATISTICS – IO Statistics by File Display

```
Node: RDB4ME        DEC Rdb  6.0-0  Performance Monitor   12-MAR-1994 12:04:13
Rate: 3.00 Seconds           File IO Statistics           Elapsed: 00:07:45.87
Page: 1 of 1         EUROBANK:[UK.DB]BANKING.RDB;1                 Mode: Online
------------------------------------------------------------------------------
                       For File: All data files
statistic.......... rate.per.second............. total....... average......
name............... max..... cur..... avg....... count....... per.trans....
total I/Os                        6                2016             155.1
    (Synch. reads)      6         6       1.0       480              36.9
    (Synch. writes)     7         0       0.5       231              17.8
    (Extends)           0         0       0.0         0               0.0
    (Asynch. reads)     2         0       2.4      1117              85.9
    (Asynch. writes)    0         0       0.4       188              14.5

statistic.......... blocks.transferred........  stall.time.(x100)...........
name............... avg.per.I/O.. total........ avg.per.I/O... total........
total I/Os                 5.7      11522            0.6          1253
    (Synch. reads)         5.8       2776            2.0           943
    (Synch. writes)        4.9       1134            1.2           276
    (Extends)              0.0          0            0.0             0
    (Asynch. reads)        5.9       6572            0.0            23
    (Asynch. writes)       5.5       1040            0.1            11
------------------------------------------------------------------------------
Display_menu Exit Help Options Reset Set_rate Write_screen
```

- The AIJ file

- All data files

- The root file

- The RUJ file

- Individual data files

- Individual snapshot files

Watch the maximum I/O rate per second on a file. If it exceeds the value for the disk then it will be causing a performance problem. Remember the stall time will always contain a value because it records the time taken to execute an I/O action. The blocks transferred can help determine whether the buffer lengths are appropriately set. Figure 11.19 shows a File IO Statistics screen.

Figure 11.20 RMU/SHOW STATISTICS – Index Statistics (Retrieval) Display

```
Node: RDB4ME          DEC Rdb  6.0-0  Performance Monitor    12-MAR-1994 12:04:13
Rate: 3.00 Seconds          Index Statistics (Retrieval)     Elapsed: 00:07:45.87
Page: 1 of 1          EUROBANK:[UK.DB]BANKING.RDB;1                   Mode: Online
---------------------------------------------------------------------------------

statistic..........    rate.per.second.............  total.......  average......
name...............    max..... cur..... avg.......  count.......  per.trans....

transactions              0        0       0.0          13            1.0
verb successes          101      101       7.4        3451          265.5
verb failures             0        0       0.0           3            0.2

node fetches              6        4       5.4        2498          192.2
 leaf fetches             3        2       2.8        1291           99.3
 dup. fetches             0        0       0.1          47            3.6

index lookups             2        2       0.2          92            7.1
index scans               3        1       2.5        1152           88.6
 primary entries          3        2       2.5        1174           90.3
 dup. entries             1        0       0.7         327           25.2


---------------------------------------------------------------------------------
Display_menu Exit Graph Help Options Reset Set_rate Time_plot Write_screen
```

Index Statistics

Four screens are available for gathering data on index usage. Three of the screens are for sorted index nodes and collect data for retrieval, insertion, and removal options. The other screen collects data on hashed index usage. Figure 11.20 is a sample Index Statistics screen.

In this example, the *node fetches* entry indicates how many nodes have been read in order to execute the query. The *duplicate fetches* entry shows how many duplicate nodes have been read and the *leaf fetches* entry shows how many Level 1 (the level of nodes that point to the data or duplicate nodes) nodes have been read. This screen provides a quick way of determining whether duplicate nodes are being used in queries. Using duplicate nodes could cause a performance problem because of the time required to search them all.

The *index lookup* entry shows the number of times a direct single-key lookup is performed as opposed to the *index scans* entry that indicates range retrievals being performed. Figure 11.21 is a sample Hashed Index Statistics screen.

Figure 11.21 RMU/SHOW STATISTICS – Hashed Index Statistics Display

```
Node: RDB4ME          DEC Rdb  6.0-0  Performance Monitor    12-MAR-1994 12:04:13
Rate: 3.00 Seconds              Hash index statistics        Elapsed: 00:07:45.87
Page: 1 of 1          EUROBANK:[UK.DB]BANKING.RDB;1                   Mode: Online
--------------------------------------------------------------------------------


statistic..........    rate.per.second.............  total.......  average......
name...............    max..... cur..... avg.......  count.......  per.trans....

hash insertions              3        3      0.0           21           1.8
     duplicates              0        0      0.0            0           0.0

hash deletions               0        0      0.0            0           0.0
     duplicates              0        0      0.0            0           0.0

hash scans                   0        0      0.0            0           0.0

hash index fetches           0        0      0.0            0           0.0
   bucket fragments          0        0      0.0            0           0.0
   duplicate nodes           0        0      0.0            0           0.0


--------------------------------------------------------------------------------
Display_menu Exit Graph Help Options Reset Set_rate Time_plot Write_screen
```

In this example *hash insertions* indicates the number of hash key insertions made into the hash buckets and *hash deletions* the number of hash key deletions made from the hash buckets. The *hash index fetches* entry indicates the number of hash buckets fetched.

Hint: If you are using hashed indexes in your Rdb database but see no activity on this screen, it is a good indication that the programs are not using the hashed indexes for some reason.

AIJ Statistics

Most of what is seen on the AIJ screen, shown in Figure 11.22, is more informational than useful. The most useful entries are AIJ file writes, which advizes how frequently writes are occurring to a particular file.

Figure 11.22 RMU/SHOW STATISTICS – AIJ Statistics Display

```
Node: RDB4ME          DEC Rdb  6.0-0  Performance Monitor   12-MAR-1994 12:04:13
Rate: 3.00 Seconds              AIJ Statistics              Elapsed: 00:07:45.87
Page: 1 of 1          EUROBANK:[UK.DB]BANKING.RDB;1                  Mode: Online
--------------------------------------------------------------------------------
statistic...........   rate.per.second............. total....... average......
name................   max..... cur..... avg....... count....... per.trans....

AIJ file writes               0        0      0.0         22          1.7
     data                     0        0      0.0         22          1.7
     control                  0        0      0.0          0          0.0
     file extend              0        0      0.0          2          0.2
     switch over              0        0      0.0          0          0.0
records written              17        0     16.0       7445        572.7
blocks written                2        0      1.9        863         66.4
     filler bytes             3        0      2.5       1148         88.3
group commits                 0        0      0.0         22          1.7
cache overflows               0        0      0.0         12          0.9
quick flushes                 0        0      0.0          0          0.0
ARB pool searches             1        0      0.5        232         17.8
     pool empty               0        0      0.0          0          0.0
lock rebuilds                 0        0      0.0          1          0.1
     AIJ file reads           0        0      0.0         13          1.0
--------------------------------------------------------------------------------
Display_menu Exit Graph Help Options Reset Set_rate Time_plot Write_screen
```

The other useful entry is *file extend*, which advises that the AIJ file has extended. When this happens, all processing on the database is suspended while the file is extended, which, obviously, could have serious impact upon performance. If users complain that the system suddenly stops for a few moments, this screen should be checked for file extends. This situation should be avoided by pre-extending the after-image journal file.

Alternatively, the circular AIJ feature can be used and this approach is recommended by the authors. This feature is described in Chapter 9 as is the RMU/ SHOW STATISTICS AIJ Information screen.

Snapshot Statistics

The Snapshot screen indicates the amount of activity on all the snapshot files, providing mainly informational data. To see activity on a specific snapshot file, the IO Statistics by File screen is required. A Snapshot screen is shown in Figure 11.23.

Figure 11.23 RMU/SHOW STATISTICS – Snapshot Statistics Display

```
Node: RDB4ME       DEC Rdb  6.0-0  Performance Monitor   12-MAR-1994 12:04:13
Rate: 3.00 Seconds          Snapshot Statistics         Elapsed: 00:07:45.87
Page: 1 of 1       EUROBANK:[UK.DB]BANKING.RDB;1                  Mode: Online
------------------------------------------------------------------------------



statistic..........   rate.per.second............. total....... average......
name...............   max..... cur..... avg....... count....... per.trans....

retrieved record          1        0       0.9        441          33.9
  fetched line            1        0       0.9        441          33.9
    read snap page        0        0       0.0          4           0.3

stored snap record      102      102      13.9       6456         496.6
    page in use           2        2       0.3        123           9.5
    page too full         0        0       0.1         32           2.5
    page conflict         0        0       0.0          0           0.0
    extended file         0        0       0.0          0           0.0



------------------------------------------------------------------------------

Display_menu Exit Graph Help Options Reset Set_rate Time_plot Write_screen
```

Summary Locking

Chapter 7 described several of the situations that can result in lock conflicts in the system. When conflicts occur, three screens may be used to determine the type of locks being held:

- Summary locking statistics

- Locking (one lock type)

- Locking (one stat field)

The Summary Locking screen, seen in Figure 11.24, provides an overview of the locks held by Rdb. One of the most useful entries is *rqsts stalled*, which is a measure of the number of locks that could not be granted immediately. However, don't be fooled by the *stall time *100* entry. This value is the total time that all users have been stalled. Therefore, if one user stalls 100 other users for one second, the stall time would show a value of 100 seconds. This, of course, does not reflect the actual elapsed time lost.

Figure 11.24 RMU/SHOW STATISTICS – Summary Locking Statistics Display

```
Node: RDB4ME          DEC Rdb  6.0-0  Performance Monitor    12-MAR-1994 12:04:13
Rate: 3.00 Seconds          Summary Locking Statistics       Elapsed: 00:07:45.87
Page: 1 of 1          EUROBANK:[UK.DB]BANKING.RDB;1                   Mode: Online
--------------------------------------------------------------------------------
statistic..........  rate.per.second.............  total.......  average......
name...............  max..... cur..... avg.......  count.......  per.trans....

locks requested           29       11      5.8          2709         208.4
 rqsts not queued          0        0      0.1            36           2.8
 rqsts stalled             0        0      0.0             6           0.5
 rqst timeouts             0        0      0.0             0           0.0
 rqst deadlocks            0        0      0.0             0           0.0
locks promoted             5        5      1.0           458          35.2
 proms not queued          0        0      0.0             7           0.5
 proms stalled             0        0      0.0            16           1.2
 prom timeouts             0        0      0.0             0           0.0
 prom deadlocks            0        0      0.0             1           0.1
locks demoted             46        3      1.5           701          53.9
locks released            22       22      5.2          2404         184.9
blocking ASTs              0        0      0.1            28           2.2
stall time x100           15        0     14.0          6538         502.9


--------------------------------------------------------------------------------
Display_menu Exit Graph Help Options Reset Set_rate Time_plot Write_screen
```

Six lock requests have been stalled in Figure 11.24. To find out what types of locks they are, the *Locking (one stat field)* screen must be selected. The *rqst stalled* option must be selected from the menu list, as shown in Figure 11.25.

This screen shows that the six stalled locks occurred for page, record, and freeze locks.

Hint: A transaction-processing-style system will frequently have a high number of stalls on the RWROOT and TSNBLK locks, which is quite normal. These locks usually only stall for a very short period of time. If many of these lock requests have been stalled, the IO by File screen for the root file should be selected to determine whether the I/O requests to that disk are too high.

The locks that are of primary interest to us are the area, page, and record locks, which reflect locks held on the data retrieved and amended in the database. All the other locks specified on this screen are special locks, internal to Rdb.

Figure 11.25 RMU/SHOW STATISTICS – Locking (One Stat Field)
   Statistics Display

```
Node: RDB4ME          DEC Rdb  6.0-0  Performance Monitor   12-MAR-1994 12:04:13
Rate: 3.00 Seconds            Locking ( rqsts stalled)      Elapsed: 00:07:45.87
Page: 1 of 1          EUROBANK:[UK.DB]BANKING.RDB;1                  Mode: Online
-------------------------------------------------------------------------------
statistic..........   rate.per.second............. total....... average......
name...............   max..... cur..... avg....... count....... per.trans....

area locks                0        0       0.0           0            0.0
page locks                0        0       0.0           1            0.1
record locks              0        0       0.0           3            0.2
RWROOT lock               0        0       0.0           0            0.0
FILID locks               0        0       0.0           0            0.0
TSNBLK locks              0        0       0.0           0            0.0
RTUPB lock                0        0       0.0           0            0.0
ACTIVE lock               0        0       0.0           0            0.0
MEMBIT lock               0        0       0.0           0            0.0
AIJ locks                 0        0       0.0           0            0.0
snapshot locks            0        0       0.0           0            0.0
freeze lock               0        0       0.0           2            0.2
quiet point lock          0        0       0.0           0            0.0
logical area locks        0        0       0.0           0            0.0
GBPT slot locks           0        0       0.0           0            0.0
-------------------------------------------------------------------------------
Display_menu Exit Help Options Reset Set_rate Time_plot Write_screen
```

The *Locking (one lock type)* screen is selected to see the detail for a specific lock type. All the locks shown on the previous screen may be selected. In Figure 11.26 we can see that 377 record locks have been requested, another 19 record locks have been promoted, and 360 locks have been subsequently released. Check the *stalled* row on this screen. A high value could indicate lock conflicts occurring, and an entry in the *deadlock* row will indicate a fatal conflict.

Per-Process Information

Various statistics screens are grouped under the category of Per-Process Information.

- Stall Messages
- Active User Stall Messages
- Process Accounting
- Checkpoint Information

Figure 11.26 RMU/SHOW STATISTICS – Locking (One Lock Type)
Statistics Display

```
Node: RDB4ME          DEC Rdb  6.0-0  Performance Monitor    12-MAR-1994 12:04:13
Rate: 3.00 Seconds              Locking (record locks)        Elapsed: 00:07:45.87
Page: 1 of 1          EUROBANK:[UK.DB]BANKING.RDB;1                   Mode: Online
------------------------------------------------------------------------------
statistic...........    rate.per.second............. total....... average......
name................    max..... cur..... avg....... count....... per.trans....

locks requested           5       5       0.8          377          29.0
 rqsts not queued         0       0       0.0           13           1.0
 rqsts stalled            0       0       0.0            3           0.2
 rqst timeouts            0       0       0.0            0           0.0
 rqst deadlocks           0       0       0.0            0           0.0
locks promoted            0       0       0.0           19           1.5
 proms not queued         0       0       0.0            6           0.5
 proms stalled            0       0       0.0            5           0.4
 prom timeouts            0       0       0.0            0           0.0
 prom deadlocks           0       0       0.0            1           0.1
locks demoted             0       0       0.0           10           0.8
locks released            5       5       0.8          360          27.7
blocking ASTs             0       0       0.0            7           0.5
stall time x100          15       0      14.0         6517         501.3

------------------------------------------------------------------------------
Display_menu Exit Help Options Reset Set_rate Write_screen
```

- CPU Utilization

- DBR Activity

- Defined Logicals

- Lock Timeout History

- Lock Deadlock History

We have already met two of these - *Stall Messages* and *Active User Stall Messages*. Figure 11.27 shows a Process Accounting screen.

In the OpenVMS environment, as shown in Figure 11.27, this display shows OpenVMS process accounting information. The display can be viewed in brief or full modes by typing in B or F respectively. In brief mode the following information is displayed:

- Process ID

- Process name

- CPU time

Figure 11.27 RMU/SHOW STATISTICS – Process Accounting Display

```
Node: RDB4ME          DEC Rdb  6.0-0  Performance Monitor    12-MAR-1994 12:04:13
Rate: 3.00 Seconds                  Process Accounting         Elapsed: 00:07:45.87
Page: 1 of 1          EUROBANK:[UK.DB]BANKING.RDB;1                     Mode: Online
--------------------------------------------------------------------------------
Process.ID Process.name... CPUtime.... EnqCnt. PGflts. NumDio. WSsize. VMsize.
0000005F:1 _FTA4:          00:01:38.45   2807   18156    2825    3981   16305




--------------------------------------------------------------------------------
Display_menu Exit Full Help >next_page <prev_page Set_rate Write_screen
```

- Lock quota remaining

- Page fault count

- Direct I/O operations

- Working set size

- Virtual memory size

Figure 11.27 shows the brief mode. In full mode, another line of information is displayed. This contains:

- Username

- Image name

- Process state

- Page file quota count

- Direct I/O quota count

- Buffered I/O operations

- Buffered I/O quota count

Figure 11.28 RMU/SHOW STATISTICS – DBR Activity Display

```
Node: RDB4ME          DEC Rdb  6.0-0  Performance Monitor    12-MAR-1994 12:04:13
Rate: 3.00 Seconds                  DBR Activity              Elapsed: 00:07:45.87
Page: 1 of 1          EUROBANK:[UK.DB]BANKING.RDB;1                   Mode: Online
--------------------------------------------------------------------------------
Process.ID Activity... VBN.... Operation......................... Lock.ID.
00000067:1 TX undo           2 writing pages back to database



--------------------------------------------------------------------------------
Display_menu Exit Help >next_page <prev_page Set_rate Write_screen
```

The next statistics screen in the category of Per-Process Information is the DBR Activity screen which shows information for database recovery processes (Figure 11.28).

The next statistics screen in the category of Per-Process Information is the Defined Logicals screen which shows information on logical names or environment variables accessible to the process running RMU/SHOW STATISTICS.

This display also has a full and brief mode. Figure 11.29 shows the brief mode which is logicals actually defined and accessible to the RMU/SHOW STAT process. The full mode lists all the logicals known to Rdb whether they are defined or not. This is a useful means of checking spelling as logicals can start with RDM$, RDMS$ and SQL$ and it is easy to choose the wrong suffix.

The last two statistics screens in the category of Per-Process Information are similar. They are the Lock Timeout History screen which shows information on the database objects that caused lock timeouts to occur and the Lock Deadlock History screen which shows information on the database objects that caused deadlocks to occur. Figure 11.30 shows a lock deadlock history display. These history displays can be useful in spotting lock conflict problems.

Figure 11.29 RMU/SHOW STATISTICS – Defined Logicals Display

```
Node: RDB4ME           DEC Rdb  6.0-0  Performance Monitor    12-MAR-1994 12:04:13
Rate: 3.00 Seconds                Defined Logicals            Elapsed: 00:07:45.87
Page: 1 of 4           EUROBANK:[UK.DB]BANKING.RDB;1                    Mode: Online
--------------------------------------------------------------------------------
Logical.Name................ Table.Name......... Logical.Definition..........
RDM$BIND_BUFFERS                LNM$PROCESS_TABLE    200
RDM$BIND_LOCK_TIMEOUT_INTERVA LNM$PROCESS_TABLE    30




--------------------------------------------------------------------------------
Display_menu Exit Full Help >next_page <prev_page Set_rate Write_screen
```

Figure 11.30 RMU/SHOW STATISTICS – Deadlock History Display

```
Node: RDB4ME           DEC Rdb  6.0-0  Performance Monitor    12-MAR-1994 12:04:13
Page: 3.00 Seconds             Lock Deadlock History          Elapsed: 00:07:45.87
Page: 1 of 3           EUROBANK:[UK.DB]BANKING.RDB;1                    Mode: Online
--------------------------------------------------------------------------------
Process.ID Occurred...   Lock.deadlock.reason.................... #Deadlock
00000060:4                                                             0
00000065:1 15:05:10.12 - waiting for record 60:8:5 (EX)               1




--------------------------------------------------------------------------------
Display_menu Exit Help >next_page <prev_page Set_rate Write_screen
```

> **Hint: Version 6.1 introduced a Custom Statistics screen which allows the user to select specific items from all the screens and display them here. Make use of this facility, as it stops you having to move between screens.**

Figure 11.31 Initial RMU SHOW STATISTICS GUI Screen

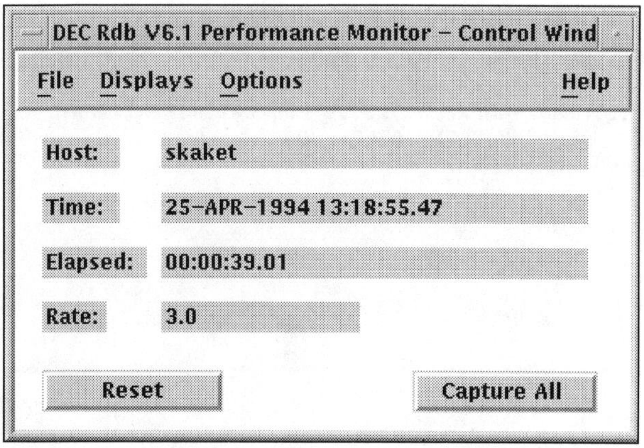

```
┌─ DEC Rdb V6.1 Performance Monitor - Control Wind ─┐
│  File  Displays  Options                    Help  │
├───────────────────────────────────────────────────┤
│  Host:     skaket                                 │
│  Time:     25-APR-1994 13:18:55.47                │
│  Elapsed:  00:00:39.01                            │
│  Rate:     3.0                                    │
│                                                   │
│  [    Reset    ]            [  Capture All  ]     │
└───────────────────────────────────────────────────┘
```

11.3.4   The RMU SHOW STATISTICS GUI

From V6.1 RMU has a GUI interface for managing Rdb databases. We have already seen the management part of the GUI in the previous chapter, but the SHOW STATISTICS GUI is the one most likely to be used.

When RMU/SHOW STATISTICS is invoked, Figure 11.30 is the first screen displayed. Don't hide this screen away because from here you invoke the screens to be displayed, change the display rate and capture all the screens.

The options available from the GUI version of SHOW STATISTICS are almost identical to the character cell version. The main advantage of using this version is the ability to display multiple screens for one database and the ability to select the columns to be displayed.

It's worth spending a few moments customizing the displays by removing columns not required such as the average value or the histogram. Once customized, the screens are smaller, allowing more of them to be displayed.

One of the problems with the GUI is that it's possible to display so many screens that the information can be lost!

Unique to the GUI version is a rolling histogram display, shown in Figure 11.32, which is useful to monitor resources used. The figure used to determine the rolling rate can be customized through the initial screen shown in Figure 11.31.

Figure 11.32 Sample RMU SHOW STATISTICS GUI Screen

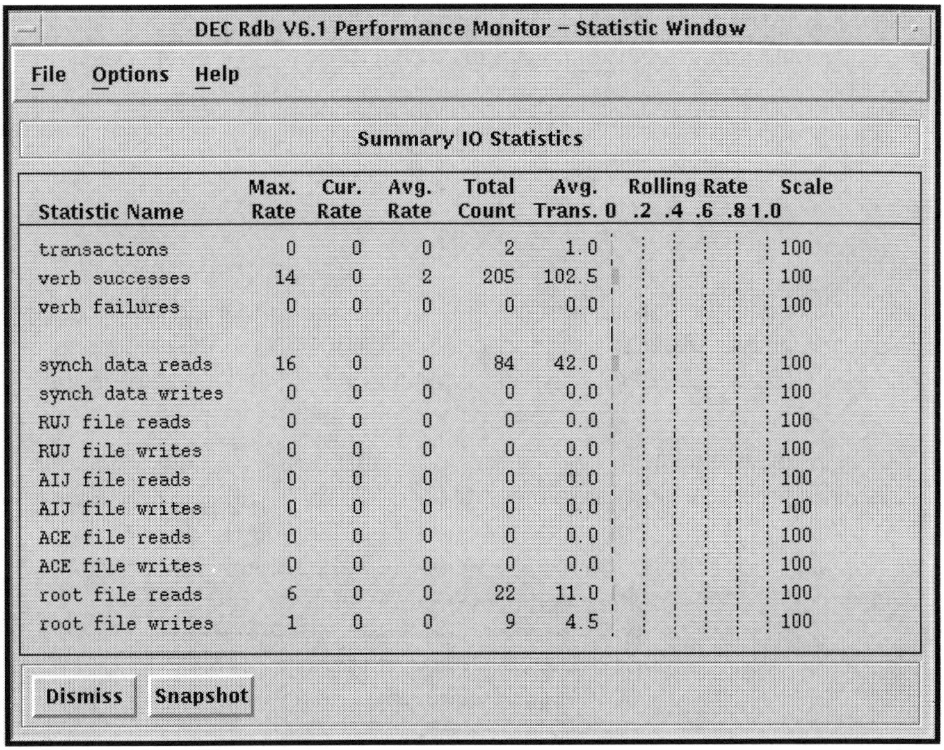

```
┌──────────────────────────────────────────────────────────────────────┐
│  —        DEC Rdb V6.1 Performance Monitor – Statistic Window        ◢ │
├────────────────────────────────────────────────────────────────────────┤
│  File   Options   Help                                                 │
├────────────────────────────────────────────────────────────────────────┤
│                        Summary IO Statistics                           │
│                                                                         │
│                   Max.  Cur.  Avg.  Total  Avg.   Rolling Rate   Scale  │
│  Statistic Name   Rate  Rate  Rate  Count  Trans. 0 .2 .4 .6 .8 1.0     │
│                                                                         │
│  transactions       0    0     0      2    1.0    :  :  :  :  :  100    │
│  verb successes    14    0     2    205   102.5   :  :  :  :  :  100    │
│  verb failures      0    0     0      0    0.0    :  :  :  :  :  100    │
│                                                                         │
│  synch data reads  16    0     0     84   42.0    :  :  :  :  :  100    │
│  synch data writes  0    0     0      0    0.0    :  :  :  :  :  100    │
│  RUJ file reads     0    0     0      0    0.0    :  :  :  :  :  100    │
│  RUJ file writes    0    0     0      0    0.0    :  :  :  :  :  100    │
│  AIJ file reads     0    0     0      0    0.0    :  :  :  :  :  100    │
│  AIJ file writes    0    0     0      0    0.0    :  :  :  :  :  100    │
│  ACE file reads     0    0     0      0    0.0    :  :  :  :  :  100    │
│  ACE file writes    0    0     0      0    0.0    :  :  :  :  :  100    │
│  root file reads    6    0     0     22   11.0    :  :  :  :  :  100    │
│  root file writes   1    0     0      9    4.5    :  :  :  :  :  100    │
├────────────────────────────────────────────────────────────────────────┤
│  Dismiss   Snapshot                                                    │
└────────────────────────────────────────────────────────────────────────┘
```

Single screens can be captured by pressing the *snapshot* button on any screen, which creates an *rmu.scr* file in the current directory.

The File IO Summary screen can be extensively customized in the GUI version. More than a dozen statistics can be displayed, as opposed to the four given in the character cell version.

From Figure 11.32 we can see that the contents of the GUI screens are virtually identical to its character cell counterpart. Therefore, once you have invoked the GUI and customized a few screens, you will then feel at home.

11.3.5   RMU/ANALYZE

The output from RMU/ANALYZE is used to see how efficiently the index structures and data have been placed inside the database. Three options are available:

- NORMAL

- FULL

- DEBUG

The recommended approach is to use the FULL option, although NORMAL also is acceptable. DEBUG will produce a file that fills a disk and uses reams of paper. However, DEBUG is useful for looking at a small range of pages to check how many records of a given type are being stored on a page.

This is useful when checking your sizing calculations, especially for hash indexes and row clustering. Note that RMU/ANALYZE will also produce a binary output file whose format is documented in the *Rdb Guide to Performance and Tuning*. Programs may be written or various tools can be used to read and process this data in a company specific way.

```
$RMU/ANALYZE/OPTION=FULL/OUTPUT=analysis.txt
    eurobank:[uk.db]banking
```

Data Placement

Some care is required to analyze the RMU/ANALYZE output because so much information is provided. Nevertheless, useful information is provided that may point out to a performance problem.

The following example shows that for the BRANCH table, there are 999 data records, each with an average length of 13 bytes. The records have been placed in less than 1% of the space allocated to this table. Since the table is compressed, the second histogram tells us that all rows are using 0 to 10% of the full row space.

```
Logical area: BRANCH for storage area : BRANCH_AREA
Larea id: 60, Record type: 25, Record length: 172, Compressed

   Data records: 999, bytes used: 12978 (1%)
      average length: 13, compression ratio: .08
```

```
                    used/used+free  vs  # pages

        >90%    | (0)
      80-90%    | (0)
      70-80%    |== (32)
      60-70%    | (0)
      50-60%    | (0)
      40-50%    | (0)
      30-40%    | (0)
      20-30%    | (0)
      10-20%    | (0)
       0-10%    |======================================= (622)


                  % of max length  vs  # records

        >90%    | (0)
      80-90%    | (0)
      70-80%    | (0)
      60-70%    | (0)
      50-60%    | (0)
      40-50%    | (0)
      30-40%    | (0)
      20-30%    | (0)
      10-20%    | (0)
       0-10%    |======================================= (999)
```

Information also is provided on each storage area. In the following example, 42 data records are in the CUSTOMER_AREA, 21 of which are hash index records.

```
Storage analysis for storage area: CUSTOMER_AREA - file:
EUROBANK:[UK.DB]CUST Area_id: 2,Page length: 1024,Last page: 504

Bytes free: 484164 (94%), bytes overhead: 30845 (6%)
Spam count: 3, AIP count: 0, ABM count: 0
Data records: 42, bytes used: 1087 (0%)
    average length: 26, compression ratio: .22
    index records: 21, bytes used: 735 (0%)
    B-Tree: 0, Hash: 735, Duplicate: 0, Overflow: 0
```

Index Path Lengths

RMU/ANALYZE/PLACEMENT can be used to report the path lengths for any type of index. This display is useful because it lets the database administrator determine the number of I/Os required to retrieve a row via an index. A sample output follows.

```
Indexes for database - EUROBANK:[UK.DB]BANKING.RDB

Hashed Index CUST_NO_HASH for relation CUSTOMER duplicates not allowed
Levels: 1, Nodes: 21, Keys: 21, Records: 21
Maximum path length — DBkeys: 3, IO range: 1 to 1
Average path length — DBkeys: 3.00, IO range: 1.00 to 1.00

Index BRANCH_CODE_SORTED for relation BRANCH duplicates allowed
Levels: 2, Nodes: 37, Keys: 1035, Records: 999
    Dup nodes: 0, Dup keys: 0, Dup records: 0
Maximum path length — DBkeys: 3, IO range: 3 to 3
Average path length — DBkeys: 3.00, IO range: 3.00 to 3.00
```

In this example, we can see that the hashed index CUST_NO_HASH is made up of 21 hash buckets for 21 storage segments, requiring, on the average, 3 dbkey accesses to retrieve a row using 1 physical I/O. For BRANCH_CODE_SORTED, there are 999 storage segments, all of which need 37 index nodes on two levels. Therefore, three dbkeys have to be fetched to retrieve a row using three physical I/Os.

11.3.6   RMU/DUMP

The RMU/DUMP command is an often under-used tool that dumps the internal database format into a user-readable display. When tuning databases, it is useful to dump a random selection of pages to see which tables are being stored on a database page and how much space is being used.

11.3.7   DECtrace and RdbExpert

Two Digital products can be optionally purchased to assist in physical database tuning:

- DECtrace – an event-based performance monitoring and collecting tool

- RdbExpert – an expert system-based physical database design tool

DECtrace automatically collects workload information on the current system. While the system is running, DECtrace collects data into one of its own special files. These files are formatted into a special DECtrace database, which may be queried for event-related data. This formatted database is fed into RdbExpert, which generates a revised database design. Refer to Chapter 16 for a more detailed explanation on how to use these tools to tune the database and third-party tools such as ISG's DBTune.

11.4   THE NEED TO TUNE

Database tuning is somewhat of a black art. Many databases perform well without any tuning, while some may require a little help along the way to enable them to perform better. There always will be high-performing databases that regularly need tuning by people or by database tools. If the database structure must be changed and it cannot be be amended online as discussed in Chapter 10, the database must be restructured using the SQL IMPORT and EXPORT, ALTER, or RMU/UNLOAD and /LOAD commands. It is important to note that performance problems become worse if left alone. The multifile capability and choice of index types in Rdb are just two facilities that allow the database designer to create extremely high-performance databases. Since database tables and indexes can be spread over any available disk drives and Rdb fully supports Digital VMScluster and symmetric multiprocessing architectures, a CPU or disk I/O bottleneck can almost always be overcome.

12   Distributing Rdb Databases

The distributed capabilities in Rdb have greatly increased during the product's lifetime. It is now possible to create and access physically separate Rdb databases or database management systems, distributed around a network to support a company's business. This chapter discusses remote database access, remote data extraction and replication, and DEC Database Integrator for accessing distributed databases as well as distributed transaction management.

A great deal of discussion today centers on distributed database technology. This is still an emerging technology that has made some advances in recent years. Creating a truly distributed heterogeneous database system has not proved as easy as first imagined. A lack of agreed standards has resulted in vendor specific implementations to solve many of the distributed database issues. Despite the work of the SQL Access Group we are still some years away from database vendors creating an environment where integrating and maintaining integrity is easy.

In a distributed database environment, one has the ability to partition fragments of tables over a network, yet keeping the end-user unaware that a table is composed of several physically separate parts. We are beginning to see these features come alive along with distributed query optimizers which ensure that a query is not just optimized for access to a local database, but also for access to distributed tables. However, when one compares the features expected in a fully distributed database system and those available in Rdb, for most companies, the capabilities of today's Rdb products are more than sufficient for their distributed processing needs.

12.1   REMOTE DATABASE ACCESS

Every Rdb version since 1.0 has provided remote database access. This allows a program or 4GL or tool on a PC to access a Rdb database on another machine in the network as if it were accessing a local database. The only difference is that the database filename, as specified in the ATTACH statement, includes a node name. A program or 4GL on the node TAURUS can access to a database on the node ORION by specifying a database name, such as:

```
SQL> ATTACH 'FILENAME orion::eurobank:[uk.db]banking';
```

Alternatively an OpenVMS user could define a logical name. For example:

```
$DEFINE BANKING orion::eurobank:[uk.db]banking
        :
SQL> ATTACH  ' FILENAME banking';
```

The advantage of this method is that a program or 4GL can refer to the database as BANKING. The physical location of the database on the network could be changed, in which case the logical name could easily be modified. The program or 4GL would not need changing. So, in the previous example, we could decide to move the database to the node AQUILA. The logical name definition and database declaration now would be:

```
$ DEFINE BANKING aquila::eurobank:[uk.db]banking
        :

        :
SQL> ATTACH ' FILENAME banking';
```

Only the definition of the logical name is changed; the attach declaration remains unchanged.

When an attempt is made to attach to a remote database, a process is created on the remote node. This database server process then attaches locally to the database. In Figure 12.1 for example, if a TAURUS program tried to attach to a database on ORION, a database server process would be created on ORION that would attach to the ORION database. Requests for data and the data itself would pass across the network between the database server process on ORION and the user process on TAURUS. The security Access Control List on the ORION database would see the database server process try to attach to the database. If this process had a valid UIC, it would be allowed to attach; if not, access would be denied. In other words, the database server process is treated like any other process that attempts to attach to a database.

Figure 12.1 Accessing a Remote Rdb Database

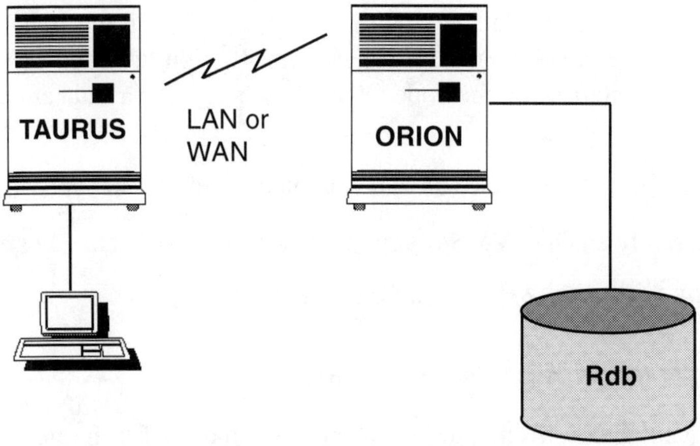

The database server process must execute under a username just as any other process. So, to gain remote access, the user must have the privilege to create a remote process under the remote account. Various methods can specify which usernames are acceptable for the database server process. One method is to specify a username and password on the ATTACH statement. This may compromise the security of the system, however, and is not recommended. For OpenVMS users the use of *proxy accounts* is recommended. More detail concerning proxy accounts may be found in the *OpenVMS Authorize Utility Manual*.

With authorization identifiers, there is no reason why a program or 4GL should not be attached to more than one remote database. Special considerations apply where more than one remote database is to be updated. This process is discussed further in the distributed transaction management section later in this chapter.

12.2   **DEC DATA DISTRIBUTOR**

DEC Data Distributor is a product designed to distribute subsets of the data in tables in an Rdb database to one or more satellite Rdb databases, usually residing on other nodes in the network. In Figure 12.2, subsets of a source database on the node TAURUS can be sent to target databases on the nodes ORION and AQUILA. DEC Data Distributor also can distribute subsets of the databases on ORION and AQUILA to one database on TAURUS.

Figure 12.2 Extraction and Replication Transfers

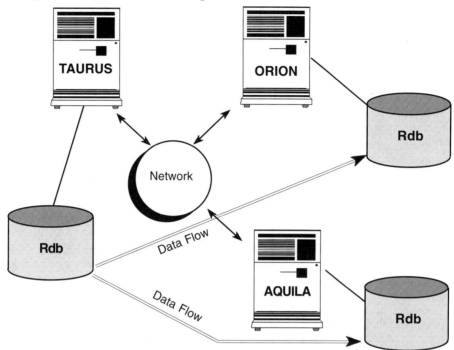

Why would a company want to distribute subsets of Rdb databases over the network? Performance, availability and cost are the main reasons. If subsets of the database on TAURUS are distributed to ORION and AQUILA, users can be moved to these nodes, offloading processing to ORION and AQUILA and freeing up system resources on TAURUS. If TAURUS holds production databases that support critical transaction-processing systems such as order entry, being able to move ad-hoc users onto another node and their unpredictable workload to another database is very useful.

If departments on the network need information from the TAURUS database but they are geographically distant or located with ORION, normally they would have to perform network accesses to get the data they require. If the data is distributed to ORION, they can perform local access to a local database and see improved response time. They also can now continue to work if the network fails. The network only needs to be available for these users when DEC Data Distributor transfers the data from the source database on TAURUS to the target database on ORION. The company may save money by bringing up the network only for the duration of the transfer. In DEC Data Distributor, command procedures may be executed before and after a transfer. These command procedures could dial up a network or send electronic MAIL to a network manager informing that a transfer has completed.

DEC Data Distributor can distribute data using one of three methods:

- Extraction

- Extraction rollup

- Replication

Whether a company uses extraction or replication methods to distribute data depends on the application requirements.

12.2.1   Extraction

Every time DEC Data Distributor executes an extraction transfer, a new version of the source database is created. In Figure 12.2, a new database is created on ORION every time an extraction transfer sends data from TAURUS to ORION. Once the transfer completes, users on ORION may manipulate the data in the target database in any way they like. They may retrieve, update, insert, or delete the data because no changes are ever transferred back to the source database. Users on ORION could, for example, create indexes on the target database that were not present on the source database. They also could modify the data in the target database to do what-if-style calculations.

12.2.2   Extraction Rollup

Extraction rollup is similar to extraction, but it can extract data from multiple-source databases into a new target database.

Figure 12.3 shows DEC Data Distributor performing an extraction rollup from multiple-source databases on ORION and AQUILA and creating a new target database on TAURUS.

12.2.3   Replication

This is probably the most popular method for distributing data. A new target database is only created the first time that a particular replication transfer

Figure 12.3 Extraction Rollup Transfers

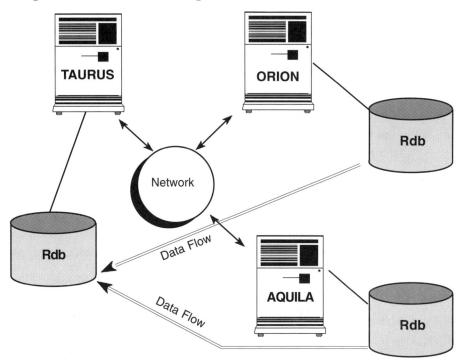

executes. Subsequent transfers contain only the changes that have been made in the source database. Users are only permitted to query the replicated tables in the target database; they are not allowed to update them, but they may update other tables in the database. The reason for this restriction is because of the relationship between the source and the target databases. Should a failure occur during a transfer, DEC Data Distributor will ensure that consistency between the source and target database is maintained.

12.2.4   Defining Transfers

The CREATE TRANSFER statement creates a transfer definition and stores it in the transfer database. A transfer definition defines the subset of data to be transferred, the type of transfer and where the target database resides. The following example shows a transfer being defined, assuming that the ATTACH statement has already been issued:

```
SQL> CREATE TRANSFER marketing_dept TYPE IS EXTRACTION
cont> MOVE TABLES
cont> SELECT customer_no,
cont>     surname,
cont>     first_name,
cont>     address_line1,
cont>     address_line2,
cont>     address_line3,
cont>     address_line4,
cont>     postcode
cont> FROM customer WHERE credit_limit > 10000
cont> TO orion::mkt$db:good_customers_db
cont> LOG FILE IS extract.log
cont> COMMENT IS 'Extraction of customers with large credit limits';
```

In the previous example, an extraction transfer named MARKETING_DEPT was defined, specifying that the rows from the CUSTOMER table with the CREDIT_LIMIT column containing a value greater than $10,000 are to be transferred to the node ORION. A new version of the database, with a full file specification of MKT$DB:GOOD_CUSTOMERS_DB, will be created each time the transfer executes. Only the columns specified will be transferred. When the transfer executes, a log file named EXTRACT.LOG will be created with details about the success or failure of the transfer. It will be created, by default, in the login directory of the definer of the transfer. To check the details of a transfer, the SHOW TRANSFER statement can be issued:

```
SQL> SHOW TRANSFER marketing_dept;

Definition for transfer MARKETING_DEPT:
Definer      THE_DBA
Type         EXTRACTION
Comment      Extraction of customers with large credit limits
From         EUROBANK:[UK.DB]BANKING.RDB
To           ORION::MKT$DB:GOOD_CUSTOMERS_DB
Log file     EUROBANK:[THE_DBA]EXTRACT.LOG
No prologue file
No epilogue file
```

```
Move table
  Select All
      CUSTOMER_NO,
      SURNAME,
      FIRST_NAME,
      ADDRESS_LINE1,
      ADDRESS_LINE2,
      ADDRESS_LINE3,
      ADDRESS_LINE4,
      POSTCODE
    From CUSTOMER
    Where
      credit_limit > 10000
```

```
Schedule for transfer MARKETING_DEPT:
No schedule found
```

```
Status for transfer MARKETING_DEPT:
State    UNSCHEDULED since 16-MAY-1994 16:07:48.88
Last completion status Transfer has never executed successfully
```

Note that a schedule has not yet been defined; thus the status must be that a transfer has never successfully executed.

12.2.5   Defining Schedules

The CREATE SCHEDULE statement specifies when and how often a transfer should execute. A schedule definition is stored in the transfer database. The following example defines a schedule for the transfer MARKETING_DEPT. The schedule specifies that the initial transfer is to execute on June 10, 1994 at 4 p.m. and, after that, every Monday at 4 p.m., every Wednesday at 2 p.m., and every Friday at 2 p.m. No attempt will be made to retry a failed transfer because the RETRY clause has not been specified.

```
SQL> CREATE SCHEDULE FOR marketing_dept
 cont> START 10-JUN-1994 16:00
 cont> EVERY MONDAY,
 cont> WEDNESDAY AT 14:00, FRIDAY;
```

A SHOW TRANSFER statement can be issued to check the schedule. For example:

```
SQL> SHOW TRANSFER marketing_dept;

Definition for transfer MARKETING_DEPT:
Definer      THE_DBA
Type         EXTRACTION
Comment      Extraction of customers with large credit limits
From         EUROBANK:[UK.DB]BANKING.RDB
To           ORION::MKT$DB:GOOD_CUSTOMERS_DB
Log file     EUROBANK:[THE_DBA]EXTRACT.LOG
No prologue file
No epilogue file
Move table
   Select All
        CUSTOMER_NO,
        SURNAME,
        FIRST_NAME,
        ADDRESS_LINE1,
        ADDRESS_LINE2,
        ADDRESS_LINE3,
        ADDRESS_LINE4,
        POSTCODE
     From CUSTOMER
     Where
        credit_limit > 10000

Schedule for transfer MARKETING_DEPT:
Start          10-JUN-1994 16:00:00.00
Frequency      Every Monday at 16:00:00.00
               Every Wednesday at 14:00:00.00
               Every Friday at 14:00:00.00
Number of retries    0 times

Status for transfer MARKETING_DEPT:
State            SCHEDULED since 16-MAY-1990 16:11:38.47
Next transfer    10-JUN-1994  16:00:00.00
Last completion status Transfer has never executed successfully
```

If desired, a transfer can be executed on demand with the START TRANSFER statement. If a transfer already has a schedule defined, subsequent transfers execute according to the schedule. The following example starts the MARKETING_DEPT transfer executing:

```
SQL> START TRANSFER marketing_dept NOW;
```

Transfers may be suspended with a STOP TRANSFER statement, in which case they will not execute again until a START TRANSFER statement is issued. While a transfer is in a suspended state, a schedule definition or transfer definition can be deleted with the DROP SCHEDULE or DROP TRANSFER statements.

12.3   DEC DATABASE INTEGRATOR

In 1994 Digital released a product called DEC Database Integrator which is commonly known as DBI. It provides distributed database functionality, allowing users to integrate data in a wide variety of database systems, not just Rdb, such that they seamlessly appear as one database. DBI does not have its own user interface; instead it uses SQL, or it can be used from a wide variety of tools such as PC products like Microsoft Access or Forest & Trees or from within a program or 4GL tool. The key to using this product lies in the initial setup of the metadata information; once completed the remote databases appear as if they are local databases, thus providing the user with location transparency.

To use DBI to access multiple Rdb databases or data in other database systems such as Oracle one must first create a database in which the metadata that describes the databases to be accessed is stored. All applications that use DBI then refer to this database rather than the actual remote databases.

In all the examples so far the BANKING database has been a single Rdb multifile database located on a single node. Let us now assume that the BANKING database is split into two databases, as shown in Figure 12.4, EUROBANK_ACCT and EUROBANK_CUST, where each database contains two of the four tables in the BANKING database.

To use DBI to access these two databases the first step is to create an ordinary Rdb database, although it could be an Oracle or Sybase database, using the SQL CREATE DATABASE statement. Next the DBI logical database is

Figure 12.4 Using DBI against Remote Databases

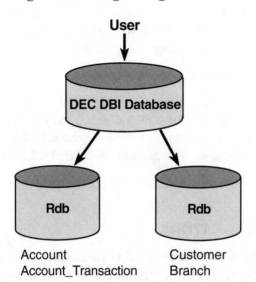

created by using the SQL CREATE DATABASE statement with the additional qualifier of /TYPE=DBI. This step probably confuses most people because one wonders why it is necessary to do this in two steps, but this is the way it is to be. The second step has the effect of importing the DBI metadata into the database that is required before DBI can be used. The example below illustrates this first step.

```
SQL>CREATE DATABASE FILENAME eurobank_dbi_db PROTECTION IS ANSI;

SQL> ATTACH 'ALIAS eurobank_dbi FILENAME eurobank_dbi_db';
SQL> GRANT DISTRIBTRAN ON DATABASE ALIAS eurobank_dbi TO PUBLIC;
SQL> COMMIT;

SQL> CREATE DATABASE FILENAME '/TYPE=DBI/DBNAME=eurobank_dbi'
cont>     PROTECTION IS ANSI;
```

Hint: Don't forget to grant the DISTRIBTRAN privilege to the DBI databases, otherwise, you won't be able to use DECdtm to guarantee the integrity of the transactions.

Once the DBI database is created, the next step is to create the links to the actual databases as shown below. Each link is given a name and then all subsequent references to the database are via this link name, so it's a good idea to specify sensible names.

```
SQL> CREATE LINK eurobank_acct TO
cont>   'london::dka0:[eurobank]eurobank_acct';
SQL> CREATE LINK eurobank_cust TO
cont>   'bristol::dka100:[eurobank]eurobank_cust';
SQL> COMMIT;
```

Hint: When specifying links make sure that you specify the full location of the database.

Additional commands are available to monitor the status of the link.

```
SQL> SHOW LINKS
User links in database with filename /TYPE=DBI/DBNAME=eurobank_dbi_db
Link EUROBANK_ACCT
   Connection information: EUROBANK_ACCT
   To database type: Rdb
   State: Inactive

Link EUROBANK_CUST
   Connection information: EUROBANK_CUST
   To database type: Rdb
   State: Inactive
```

Now that the links to the database have been established, the next step is to define the tables. The tables don't have to keep the same names and one can see from the example below that the TRANSACTIONS table has been re-named to TRANS. Note that to specify in which database the table is located, the link name is used.

```
SQL> CREATE TABLE account LINK TO account USING eurobank_acct;
SQL> CREATE TABLE branch  LINK TO branch  USING eurobank_cust;
SQL> CREATE TABLE trans   LINK TO account_transaction
cont>   USING eurobank_acct;
```

```
SQL> CREATE TABLE customer LINK TO customer USING eurobank_cust;
SQL> COMMIT;

SQL> SHOW TABLES
User tables in database with filename /TYPE=DBI/DBNAME=eurobank_dbi_db
    ACCOUNT
    BRANCH
    CUSTOMER
    TRANS
```

This could be the final stage in the setup of the DBI database and we would now be ready to start retrieving and updating data. However, it is highly likely that incompatibilities will exist between the databases that have to be integrated, such as the columns are named differently, have different formats, i.e., CHAR(4) and INT, or they require some conversion because codes are not the same.

To resolve these problems VIEWS are created and DBI provides a wide range of methods to resolve all these issues. The view BRANCH_DETAILS below illustrates how two columns can be merged into one column; in this instance a new column BRANCH_ADDR is created from the two columns BRANCH_NAME and BRANCH_ADDRESS.

```
SQL>CREATE VIEW branch_details
cont> ( branch_cd, branch_addr) AS
cont> (
cont>   SELECT branch_code, (branch_name || ' ' ||
cont>   branch_address) FROM  BRANCH
cont>   );
```

In the next example the VIEW ACCT_TRANS joins together data from the two databases, from the tables ACCOUNT, CUSTOMER and TRANSACTIONS.

```
SQL> CREATE VIEW acct_trans
cont> (account_no, customer_no, tran_date, tran_amt) AS
cont> SELECT a.account_no, a.customer_no, t.tran_date, t.tran_amt
cont>   FROM account a, trans t WHERE a.account_no = t.account_no;
SQL> COMMIT;
```

The possibilities with DBI are very comprehensive indeed and the examples shown here are but a few of the many possibilities. For more detailed information the reader should consult the *DEC Db Integrator Handbook*.

Once the environment has been established, DBI can be used to retrieve and update data. When using DBI, the SQL specified is exactly the same as for a single Rdb database except for the ATTACH statement containing a /TYPE=DBI.

For instance, take the example below which is joining data from two tables in two different databases. The SQL to achieve this is:

```
SQL>ATTACH 'FILENAME /TYPE=DBI/DBNAME= eurobank_dbi_db;

SQL> SELECT a.account_no, c.customer_no FROM
cont> account a, customer c WHERE c.customer_no = a.customer_no;
```

A.ACCOUNT_NO	C.CUSTOMER_NO
1551290	100201
9167890	100201
1567890	100201
9551490	100201
9561490	100205
1561290	100205

```
6 rows selected
```

Since all access to the distributed databases is achieved by referencing the DBI database, this makes it very easy to use DBI with PC products using the ODBC driver. In this instance the database is specified as per normal, but the ATTACH includes the /TYPE and /DBNAME qualifiers.

Hint: Many PC products do not always access distributed databases efficiently, but due to DBI's distributed cost query optimizer and database buffering techniques it is usually much more efficient to use this tool.

The one area that may cause some concern and extra work is defining security. The only security that can be defined on the DBI database is at the table level. Therefore once a user has access to the database they can see all the tables. However, they will only be allowed access to the actual tables if access has been granted in the distributed database.

12.4   **DISTRIBUTED TRANSACTION MANAGEMENT**

The fact that a program or 4GL can access more than one remote Rdb database was mentioned in section 12.1. In such a situation, guaranteeing the integrity of these distributed databases is important. A problem can arise when changes are made to one of the remote databases but a failure prevents the changes from being made to the other remote database.

This situation can create serious problems. Suppose in Figure 12.5 that a program running on TAURUS attaches to a BANKING database on ORION and a BANKING database on AQUILA. Imagine that a transaction debits an account on ORION and credits an account on AQUILA; that is, money is transferred between the two accounts. If the credit to the account on AQUILA is committed to the database but a failure aborts the debit of the account on ORION, the bank has potentially lost money. Indeed, the integrity of the distributed database domain was compromised even though the integrity of the individual databases was not.

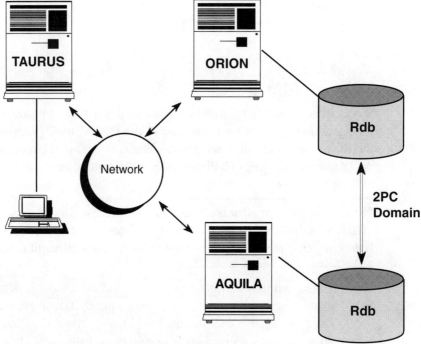

Figure 12. 5 Distributed Transactions

This is a classic distributed integrity problem. Rdb uses a transaction processing service known as DECdtm, which is an OpenVMS component.

DECdtm uses a two-phase commit protocol to ensure that distributed integrity is maintained. The two-phase commit protocol, or 2PC, is well-known for dealing with this problem. Briefly, it involves defining a global transaction composed of a number of local database transactions. The global transaction either commits or aborts.

In our example, both the databases on ORION and AQUILA either commit or abort; the situation should not arise where one commits and the other aborts. A coordinator is responsible for asking all the participants in the global transaction whether they are ready to commit or not (in DECdtm terminology, they are asked to *vote*). If they are not ready, the transaction is aborted and all the databases involved are rolled back. If they all agree to commit, they cannot change their minds later – they lose their unilateral abort capability. The coordinator then decides whether to commit or abort the transaction and communicates the decision to the participants. All the participants at some point must follow that instruction.

Failure can occur in many ways, and the protocol can deal with all of them. The worst-case scenario is if the participants lose contact with the coordinator after they have voted but before they have received the coordinator's decision to commit or abort. In this situation, the participants cannot make a decision on their own and must wait for communication to be re-established with the coordinator.

If the node on which the coordinator resides is located in a computer room that was destroyed in an earthquake, re-establishing communication clearly may take some time. Because of the possibility that this scenario could occur, as remote as it is, DECdtm and Rdb allow the database administrator to manually decide whether to commit or abort local transactions.

12.4.1   Programming Distributed Transactions with SQL

Section 12.1 showed that accessing a remote Rdb database was a simple matter. The only difference between accessing a local database and a remote database is the addition of a node name in the database file specification. Section 12.1 also showed that it was possible to make life even simpler for the developer by the use of OpenVMS logical names. We can take this idea a step further by showing that it is just as easy to attach to two remote databases as it is to attach to one. The developer must merely specify an alias to uniquely identify each database that the program has attached to. For example:

```
SQL> DECLARE london ALIAS FILENAME 'orion::eurobank:[uk.db]banking';

SQL> DECLARE leeds ALIAS FILENAME 'aquila::eurobank:[uk.db]banking';
```

A developer must use the alias to qualify table names in the program so it becomes clear which table in which database is being used. For example:

```
SQL> SELECT * FROM london.branch;
```

In this example, the branch table is present in the database in London residing on the node known as ORION and in the database in Leeds residing on the node known as AQUILA. The SELECT statement, therefore, must be qualified with the alias – in this case *london* – to resolve the ambiguity.

So far we have seen how it is possible to easily retrieve data from more than one database by using an alias. But can data be updated in more than one database? It can as long as the aliases are used. Suppose we wanted to move a customer's details from the Leeds branch to the London branch. We could achieve this as follows:

```
SQL> DECLARE london ALIAS FILENAME 'orion::eurobank:[uk.db]banking';

SQL> DECLARE leeds ALIAS FILENAME 'aquila::eurobank:[uk.db]banking';

SQL> SET TRANSACTION ON london USING (READ WRITE RESERVING
cont>       london.CUSTOMER FOR SHARED WRITE)
cont>   AND ON leeds USING (READ WRITE RESERVING
cont>       leeds.CUSTOMER FOR SHARED WRITE);

SQL> INSERT INTO london.customer
cont> SELECT * FROM leeds.customer WHERE customer_no = '4545332211';
1 row(s) inserted
SQL> DELETE FROM leeds.customer WHERE customer_no = '4545332211';
1 row(s) deleted

SQL> COMMIT;
```

We added a row to the CUSTOMER table in the London database and deleted a row from the CUSTOMER table in the Leeds database. We assume that the COMMIT statement made both the INSERT and DELETE permanent. However, as has been said, there is no guarantee that a network or node failure at a critical moment did not result in the customer being removed from the Leeds branch but not added to the London branch. To guarantee distributed transaction integrity, we need the two-phase commit support of DECdtm.

How can a developer of SQL-based applications code in distributed transaction integrity? A developer may use either embedded SQL or SQL Module Language to create applications that execute distributed transactions. It is simple to program distributed transactions with Rdb. All programs that use either embedded SQL or SQL Module Language to access more than one Rdb database will automatically benefit from the distributed transaction integrity provided by Rdb. In this case, DECdtm is said to be called implicitly, and virtually no application code or SQL needs to be changed.

An application program may call DECdtm implicitly or explicitly. In most cases, a developer should not bother with explicit calls. Explicit calls must only be made to DECdtm when more than one database management system participates in a transaction. For example, if a transaction updates an Rdb database and an RMS sequential file, an explicit call must be made to DECdtm to start a global transaction. If a transaction updates two Rdb databases, explicit calls to DECdtm would not have to be made. Whether DECdtm is called implicitly or explicitly, a distributed transaction is started by DECdtm and associated with a *transaction identifier*, or TID. All subsequent Rdb transactions (or DBMS or RMS) that form part of the distributed transaction are passed this transaction identifier and thus join the distributed transaction. If implicit calls are made to DECdtm, for example in the case of multiple Rdb databases, the developer should not be concerned about transaction identifiers. If explicit calls are made to DECdtm, such as when Rdb and DBMS multiple database systems are used, the developer must handle the passing of the unique transaction identifier to the local transactions in the program. The distributed transaction as a whole either commits or aborts and, consequently, the local transactions must all commit or abort.

When a program explicitly calls DECdtm, the SYS$START_TRANS and SYS$END_TRANS system service calls must be made to start and end the distributed transaction. The SYS$START_TRANS call returns a transaction identifier, which is passed within the program using methods that depend on whether embedded SQL or SQL Module Language is used. The following is an example of the DECdtm call used to start a distributed transaction in COBOL:

```
CALL "SYS$START_TRANSW" USING OMITTED,
        BY VALUE ddtm$m_sync
        BY REFERENCE io-sb,
        OMITTED,
        OMITTED,
        BY REFERENCE dist-tid
        GIVING status.
```

The format of the call, which is familiar to anyone who has used OpenVMS system services, is independent of the method used to implement the SQL statements. The OpenVMS documentation set details all the parameters of the call, but it is worth mentioning the parameter DIST-TID here. DIST-TID is a variable used to hold the unique distributed transaction identifier returned by the call. It is defined as a 16-byte field. Typically, if the application was being written in COBOL, the developer would define the transaction identifier in the WORKING-STORAGE section as:

```
01 transaction-ident.
     05 low_date     PIC 9(9) COMP.
     05 high_date    PIC 9(9) COMP.
     05 date_incarn  PIC 9(4) COMP.
     05 node_id      PIC 9(4) COMP.
     05 node_idh     PIC 9(9) COMP.
```

The reader may deduce that the transaction identifier contains dates and times and also the Ethernet address of the coordinating node. The data item IO-SB is the I/O status block, which is familiar to anyone who has used OpenVMS system services.

Once the transaction identifier has been obtained, it must be associated with the SQL statements in the program. It should be noted here that a program may start more than one distributed transaction, so SQL statements may be associated with different transaction identifiers. The transaction identifier and SQL statement association is made using a context structure. In SQL Module Language, a context structure is declared in the host language program and passed to the called module. This context structure contains the transaction identifier, amongst other things. When the SQL Module is compiled, the /CONTEXT qualifier also must be used to specify that the compiler must allow for this additional context parameter.

In embedded SQL programs, a context structure is again declared. Each executable SQL statement, however, must now include a USING CONTEXT clause. The USING CONTEXT clause informs SQL that the SQL statement is part of a particular distributed transaction.

The *Rdb Guide to Distributed Transactions* manual contains detailed examples of program code to demonstrate these two methods. An example of the declaration of a context structure in COBOL follows:

```
01  WS-CONTEXT.
      05 CTX-VERSION  PIC 9(9) COMP.
      05 CTX-TYPE     PIC 9(9) COMP.
      05 CTX-LENGTH   PIC 9(9) COMP.
      05 CTX-TID.
         10 LOW_DATE   PIC 9(9) COMP.
         10 HIGH_DATE  PIC 9(9) COMP.
         10 DATE_INCARN   PIC 9(4) COMP.
         10 NODE_ID    PIC 9(4) COMP.
         10 NODE_IDH   PIC 9(9) COMP.
      05 CTX-END PIC 9(9) COMP.
```

The embedded SQL will now have the additional USING CONTEXT construct. For example:

```
EXEC SQL USING CONTEXT :ws-context
    INSERT INTO london.customer
    SELECT * FROM leeds.customer WHERE customer_no = :cust_no
END-EXEC.

EXEC SQL USING CONTEXT :ws-context
    DELETE FROM leeds.customer WHERE customer_no = :cust_no
END-EXEC.
```

In the previous example, the transaction identifier contained in the context structure WS-CONTEXT will be associated with the INSERT and DELETE operations. In other words, the INSERT and DELETE operations will be part of the same distributed transaction. *Both* the INSERT and DELETE will happen or neither will.

There may be occasions when the developer does not want a program to use DECdtm implicitly. In this case, the OpenVMS logical name SQL$DISABLE_CONTEXT can be used. For example:

```
$ DEFINE SQL$DISABLE_CONTEXT TRUE
```

Hint: The definition of this logical name is checked at compile time, not at run time. If the logical is found and set as true, distributed transaction management is disabled for that application.

12.4.2   Distributed Deadlocks

We have already learned about deadlocks in single databases. A deadlock also may occur in a distributed scenario. In this case, processes on more than one node in a network are waiting for one another in a deadly embrace. Rdb cannot detect such distributed deadlocks because the lock manager can only detect deadlocks on a local network. Instead, timeouts are used. After a transaction has been waiting for a lock for a specified time, the transaction aborts and breaks the deadlock. The length of time the transaction waits can be specified in two ways. A OpenVMS logical name RDM$BIND_LOCK_ TIMEOUT_INTERVAL can be specified. For example:

```
$ DEFINE RDM$BIND_LOCK_TIMEOUT_INTERVAL 20
```

The WAIT clause also can be used in the SET TRANSACTION or DECLARE TRANSACTION statements. For example:

```
SQL> SET TRANSACTION READ WRITE WAIT 20;
```

In both the previous examples, a transaction will wait 20 seconds.

The *Rdb Guide to Distributed Transactions* manual explains distributed transactions and should be studied by anyone requiring further information.

13 Interoperability

More and more organizations today have a wide range of different hardware and software systems, and they rarely depend on only one hardware or software vendor. They may also have legacy systems from which they require information or which they need to integrate into their existing systems. As different groups within an organization begin to see the benefits of sharing each other's data, there is a growing need for interoperability or gateway products to access data on other platforms and in other database management systems.

Digital provides a number of products including gateways which provide transparent access to relational and non-relational data such as RMS and the CODASYL product DBMS. These products are:

- SQL/Services

- ODBC Driver

- DEC DB Integrator Gateways for

    - Custom Drivers

    - DB2

    - DBMS

    - DSM

    - EDA/SQL

    - Oracle

    - RMS

    - Sybase

13.1   SQL/SERVICES

Access to the corporate Rdb database from personal-computer-based applications is almost mandatory for many organizations today. Simply placing a database on a personal computer is unacceptable, because personal computers lack the processing power or storage capabilities required to hold large volumes of data. SQL/Services makes holding data on a personal computer unnecessary.

SQL/Services is a standard component of Rdb. Based on the client/server architecture, it provides access to Rdb and other databases from clients on MS-Windows, MS-DOS, Macintosh, OpenVMS and OSF/1 systems. By embedding standard SQL statements in a program using the Application Programming Interface (API), a program is constructed to access the Rdb database from a number of different platforms. The API itself is made up of only a dozen statements, so it is easy to learn and use. In OpenVMS systems the API calls may be embedded in any language; from other systems, only the C language may be used. All SQL statements written in the application code are converted to dynamic SQL to provide access to Rdb.

However, most users of SQL/Services are unaware of the previously described process because the tool they are using already has the calls embedded. For example, a user in MS-Windows requires data from a DB2 database on an IBM and an Rdb database on an Alpha AXP system. The query is specified and SQL/Services passes it to the Alpha and the IBM system. Each system identifies the data and then returns it to the PC user. Once it has been returned to the personal computer, the data can be manipulated with various PC tools.

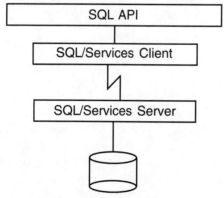

Figure 13.1 SQL/Services

The entire SQL/Services environment is changing from Version 6.1 to handle the client/server environment more efficiently. For Version 6.1 it will be implemented on OSF/1 only. The changes are described in Chapter 19.

13.1.1 Multi-versioning

SQL/Services supports multiple versions of Rdb via use of the class server. In a configuration file one can specify which servers are to be started such as V60 for Version 6 and V51 for Version 5.1. A tool or application calling SQL/Services will specify which class server it requires, otherwise it will use the generic server which will belong to the default version of Rdb running at the time SQL/Services was started.

Hint: Not all applications support SQL/Service class servers. If this is the case use the ODBC driver instead, if this is possible.

13.2 DEC DB GATEWAYS

There are eight different gateway products that may be used to access data in other data managers or on other hardware platforms, as shown in Figure 13.2. They have been developed such that they can be used without Rdb present; however, the software can be written as if were accessing an Rdb database. Purchasing the gateway software provides all the necessary components including SQL/Services. Each gateway varies slightly in the functionality offered; for instance, some are read-write while others are read-only. The supported networks are DECnet, TCP/IP, Novell and Appletalk.

One of the main benefits of gateways is that they provide an almost transparent interface to the end-user, enabling them to use a number of tools, including:

- SQL, interactive, pre-compiled, dynamic or Module Language
- ODBC compliant tools
- Apple's DAL
- DEC DATATRIEVE
- DEC Data Distributor
- RALLY

Figure 13.2 Digital Gateways

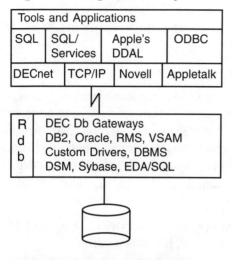

Hint: When accessing multiple databases, it is recommended that DB
Integrator, described in Chapter 12, is used to join the data because it
can perform the task very efficiently.

13.2.1   DEC Db Integrator Gateway for DB2

DEC Db Integrator Gateway for DB2 provides read-write access to DB2,
which is the primary relational database on IBM mainframe computers. This
is a true interoperability product because it provides either interactive access
to or bulk data transfer from an IBM DB2 database, using the LU6.2 communication protocol to ensure efficient data transfer. Based on the client/server
architecture, DB Gateway software is installed on the OpenVMS and IBM
system. With the client and servers installed on each hardware platform, all
the work is done by the software. Hence, the gateway decides on which platform it is most efficient to execute a query and which data conversions are
necessary. (IBM uses EBCDIC and the VAX uses ASCII.) The software tries
to make all operations as transparent as possible to the user.

Users requiring access to the data on the IBM DB2 database need not worry
if they are unfamiliar with the IBM software. The same knowledge and skills
used to access an Rdb database are used to access the IBM DB2 database.

There is no need to learn a new query language – simply use your favorite Rdb query tool.

CDD/Repository may be effectively used to manage and control the data within an organization. One useful feature in the DEC Db Gateway for DB2, is that it allows definitions to be extracted from the DB2 catalog and placed into CDD/Repository. This is a very simple mechanism for extracting and copying data definitions from one system to the other. CDD/Repository is described in more detail in Chapter 14.

Using the DEC Db Gateway for DB2 software is a relatively simple task. Consider the BANKING database where a subsidiary of the EUROBANK uses DB2. To query the IBM DB2 database using interactive SQL on the Digital platform, SQL would be invoked in the normal fashion. When the attach to the database is made, an additional qualifier, /TYPE=VIDA2, is specified to tell Rdb that it must access a DB2 database instead of Rdb.

Once the ATTACH has been specified, statements are issued as if an Rdb database were being queried. The software does the rest. The next example shows just how little extra data is required to access the IBM DB2 database.

```
SQL> ATTACH 'FILENAME /TYPE=DB2/DATABASE=eurobond';

SQL> SET TRANSACTION READ ONLY;

SQL> SELECT * FROM bonds WHERE bond_code = 'WST1';
```

This example shows how transparent it is to the user that the database being accessed is DB2. The SQL statements are identical to those issued to access an Rdb database.

13.2.2   DEC Db Gateway for Oracle

DEC Db Gateway for ORACLE provides read-write access to ORACLE databases the same way as the DB Gateway for DB2 provides read-write access to DB2 databases. The ORACLE database must be running on an OpenVMS system somewhere on a DECnet or TCP/IP network. A program written using embedded SQL, SQL Module Language or dynamic SQL can access ORACLE tables and views. In fact, an end-user can use interactive SQL, DATATRIEVE or RALLY to access ORACLE data and can use SQL/Services to access ORACLE through applications running on MS-DOS,

OS/2, Macintosh, ULTRIX, or OpenVMS operating systems. The SQL ATTACH statement would use /TYPE=ORACLE.

The ORACLE metadata can be integrated into CDD/Repository through the SQL INTEGRATE command. Once this has been done, the metadata definitions can be shared by other software, such as application programs or forms.

DEC Data Distributor can also be used to extract data from ORACLE databases into Rdb databases, and data from multiple ORACLE databases can be rolled up in a single Rdb database. DEC Data Distributor was described in Chapter 12.

13.2.3   DEC Db Gateway for RMS

DEC Db Gateway for RMS provides read/write access to non-relational data in the form of DEC RMS files and read-only access to remote RMS files and IBM MVS and VM/CMS data sets. A program written using embedded SQL, SQL Module Language, or dynamic SQL can access RMS files and IBM VSAM files transparently. In fact, an end-user can use interactive SQL, DATATRIEVE, or RALLY to access the non-relational data. The user also can use SQL/Services to access it through applications running on MS-DOS, OS/2, Macintosh, ULTRIX, or OpenVMS operating systems.

DEC Db Gateway for RMS retrieves the data definitions from CDD/Repository and combines the definitions with the source data to allow relational operations to be performed. Of course, the metadata definitions also can be shared by other software, such as application programs or forms.

DEC Data Distributor can be used to extract data from the files into Rdb databases on the network. Data from multiple files also can be rolled up into a single Rdb database.

13.2.4   DEC Db Gateway for Custom Drivers

DEC DB Gateway for Custom Drivers is the software that allows the creation of gateways to provide relational access to data sources without a driver. Using the gateway's interactive SQL or dynamic SQL interface, applications and tools have read/write access to the data. Client/server access is supported through SQL/Services and the ODBC driver.

13.2.5   **DEC Db Gateway for DBMS**

There are still many users of the CODASYL database DBMS who would like
to use the SQL interface to access their data. This is now possible with this
gateway which allows read-only access to the data. The DBMS schema is
mapped onto the relational schema by translating records and sets into SQL
tables. A sample attach statement is shown below:

```
SQL> ATTACH 'FILENAME /TYPE=NSDS
cont>   /PATH=dbms_schema:[schema]parts.parts1
cont>   /DICTIONARY_DRIVER = DBMSQL$SHR';
```

13.2.6   **DEC Db Gateway for DSM**

The DEC DB Integrator Gateway for DSM allows transparent access to Digital
Standard Mumps (DSM) data, via interactive SQL, dynamic SQL, pre-compiled
SQL, and the SQL Module Language. Support for client/server access is pro-
vided by SQL/Services and the ODBC driver.

The gateway for DSM retrieves data definitions for DSM data sources from a
variety of data and metadata sources. Support is for Digital Application Software Library (DASL) tables, FileMan files, and user-defined data and metadata
sources, by providing an M routine call interface definition.

13.2.7   **DEC Db Gateway for Sybase**

DEC DB Integrator Gateway for Sybase provides read/write access to
SYBASE SQL Server databases. Access is via SQL using the interactive or
dynamic interfaces. Support for client/server access is provided by SQL/Ser-
vices or the ODBC driver. Using DEC Db Integrator which is described in
Chapter 12, it is possible to perform cross-database joins.

13.3   **ODBC DRIVER**

Microsoft defined an interface for accessing data in heterogeneous data systems which they called ODBC which stands for Open Database Connectivity.
Although ODBC has now become a de facto industry standard, it is based upon
the work of the SQL Access Group. The SQL Access Group is a consortium

Figure 13.3 ODBC Data Source Definition

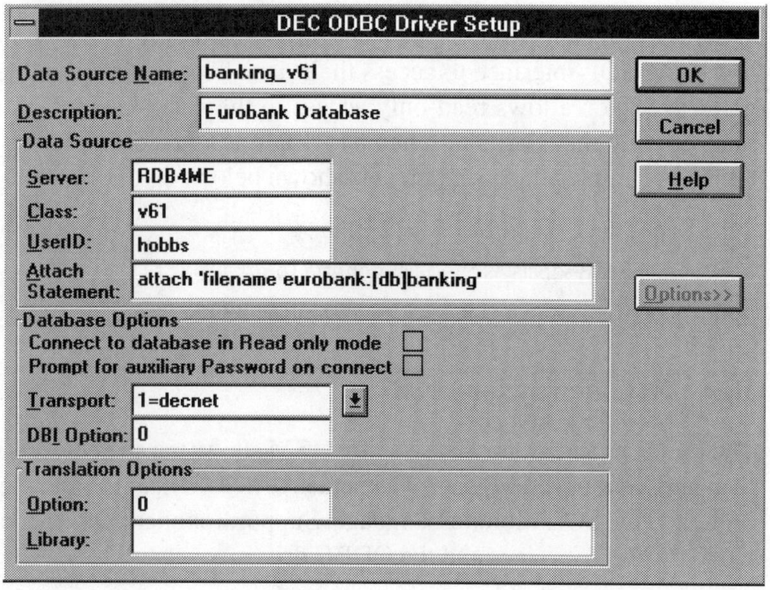

```
┌─────────────────────────────────────────────────────────┐
│ ─ │            DEC ODBC Driver Setup                     │
├─────────────────────────────────────────────────────────┤
│ Data Source Name:  │banking_v61              │   ┌──────┐ │
│                                                  │  OK  │ │
│ Description:        │Eurobank Database        │   └──────┘ │
│ ─Data Source──────────────────────────────────┐ ┌──────┐ │
│   Server:    │RDB4ME            │              │ │Cancel│ │
│                                                │ └──────┘ │
│   Class:     │v61               │              │          │
│   UserID:    │hobbs             │              │ ┌──────┐ │
│   Attach     │attach 'filename eurobank:[db]banking'│ │Help│ │
│   Statement:                                   │ └──────┘ │
│ ─Database Options─────────────────────────────┐ ┌───────┐│
│   Connect to database in Read only mode   □    │ │Options>>││
│   Prompt for auxiliary Password on connect □   │ └───────┘│
│   Transport: │1=decnet          │ │▼│          │          │
│   DBI Option:│0                                │          │
│ ─Translation Options──────────────────────────┐          │
│   Option:    │0                 │              │          │
│   Library:   │                  │              │          │
└─────────────────────────────────────────────────────────┘
```

of both vendors and software users who defined a standard for accessing heterogeneous remote databases. An ODBC driver is defined by the software vendor using the ODBC API. Therefore to use ODBC, the tool on the client must be ODBC compliant and then the database server must be able to accept calls from the ODBC tool.

Using ODBC compliant tools to access Rdb or other data sources is proving very popular and Rdb's ODBC driver uses SQL/Services to access remote data, though the user need not be concerned by this fact. This is probably one of the easiest methods for accessing remote data because once the data source has been defined, it is then used by any ODBC compliant tool. Figure 13.3 shows the screen for defining an ODBC data source.

Each data source is given a name; in the example it is *banking_v61*. It is important to choose a sensible name because this is what the user will see in their tool when it is asked to display a list of ODBC compliant data sources. Each source can be given a description, but that information will only be displayed in the ODBC Administrator.

The server where the database resides is specified; in this case it's *RDB4ME*. The class server corresponds to the version of Rdb required. If the default version is required then use the generic class. Other information that must be specified is the user ID, transport mechanism and database attach statement. At the time of attach the user will be prompted for the password. The tool or application will determine whether the password will be required each time or can be stored.

Hint: Do not include a semicolon (;) at the end of the ATTACH statement. The ODBC driver does not like it and will fail.

The full SQL attach statement must be specified which includes the location and name of the database. Figure 13.3 shows how to access the banking database but if you were accessing a DBI database then the ATTACH statement would include the /TYPE=DBI/DBNAME= and if were using a DB Gateway product then the type would correspond to the database or driver name such as DB2 or NSDS.

There are now many ODBC client tools available in the marketplace, offering the user a wide variety of client applications. Although this route is usually slower, the performance degradation is overlooked due to the flexibility and ease of access provided by the client tools.

14   CDD/Repository

CDD/Repository has become a core component in computer-aided software engineering (CASE). Rdb is integrated with Digital's Data Repository product, CDD/Repository, which is an open, distributed repository system that integrates with many Digital products and other companies' products.

Please note that CDD/Repository is not available to Rdb OSF/1 users.

Digital's Data Repository product was known as CDD, Common Data Repository, through Version 3.4. In 1988, the product was radically changed to use Rdb for data storage. In this version the product was changed to hold many different types of objects and to provide messaging and pieces tracking. This new product, which still supported past CDD versions, was renamed CDD/Plus in Version 4.0. Digital announced Version 5.0 of the Data Repository in 1990 and changed the name to CDD/Repository. At the time of writing, it is about to be sold to the Oracle Corporation.

CDD/Repository is at the core of the CASE environment, sharing information with all the surrounding application-building tools. Many of these tools have read-write access to the repository, which means that they can extract information from the repository as well as write it back. The list of tools that only have read access to the repository is decreasing. CDD/Plus, which is based on the entity/relationship model, is able to define records and fields. Once defined in the repository, these definitions can be used by:

- Compilers, copying record definitions into a program

- Rdb

- RALLY

- DEC ACMS TP Monitor

- DEC Db Gateway products

- Any program using the Callable Interface

Figure 14.1 CDD/Repository Integration with Digital Products

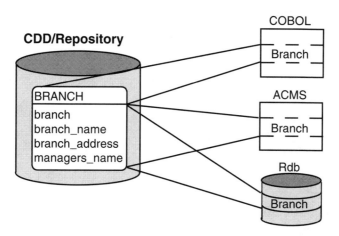

Figure 14.1 illustrates how the BRANCH record definition is defined in CDD/Repository and then is used by Rdb to build the database, by a COBOL program, and by an ACMS task.

Many different types of objects may be stored in the repository directory structure that the data administrator has specified. CDD/Repository's directory structure is a completely flexible hierarchical structure, which means it may be defined differently for each repository. A typical structure is shown in Figure 14.2. The format for specifying exactly where an object resides in the repository is:

```
repository anchor    directory path    object name
```

To locate the record definition for the BRANCH record, the repository anchor used is the OpenVMS file directory where the repository resides, which in this case is EUROBANK:[UK.DICT]. The directory path to the BRANCH record is BANKING.RECORDS. Therefore, the full specification to retrieve the BRANCH record definition is:

```
eurobank:[uk.dict]banking.records.branch
```

```
<----Anchor---> <----Path---> <-Object->
```

The repository is made up of one logical repository that is physically implemented as one or more repository files, which may be located anywhere on the network. These distributed repository files can then be seen as one repository

Figure 14.2 Typical CDD/Repository Structure

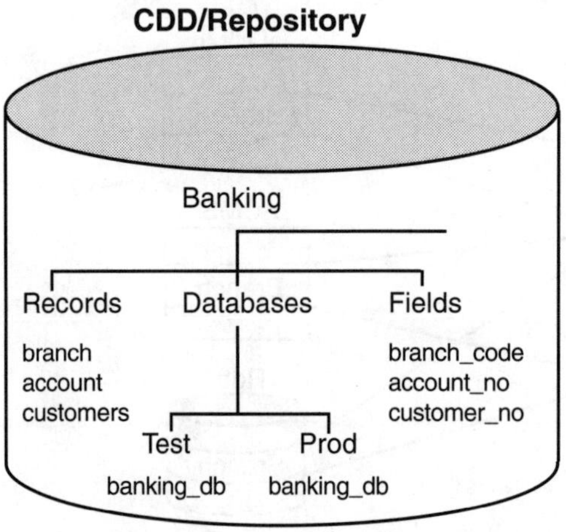

CDD/Repository

joined together using a OpenVMS search list logical. The rest of this chapter will concentrate on the structure inside one repository.

14.1   RDB AND CDD/REPOSITORY

An Rdb database may be defined separately from the repository. This is done when the database is created by specifying the REPOSITORY IS NOT REQUIRED clause on the CREATE DATABASE statement.

When the clause REPOSITORY IS REQUIRED and the PATHNAME are specified on the CREATE DATABASE statement, a link is established between the database and the repository. Once this relationship has been defined, metadata changes can only take place if the pathname option is specified on the ATTACH statement.

Therefore, creating the BANKING database requires the following:

```
SQL> CREATE DATABASE PATHNAME
cont>    eurobank:[uk.cdd]database.banking FILENAME banking
cont>    REPOSITORY IS REQUIRED;
```

This creates a single-file database and establishes a permanent link between the Rdb database and the CDD/Repository. The CREATE DATABASE statement creates an object in the CDD/Repository called *banking* of type CDD$DATABASE. This object serves as the link between the repository and the Rdb database and is known as a *proxy entity*. Once the relationship between the repository and the database is formalized, no changes can be made to the data definitions without the repository being present. If a change is made to the data definition in the repository from which the Rdb database has been built, a message is sent to the proxy entity, BANKING, advising of the change because CDD/Repository cannot talk to Rdb directly. Messages will be discussed later in this chapter.

14.1.1   Using Table and Field Definitions

One of the important roles of the repository is to hold the definitions of all the records and fields used in the system. Once it is defined in this central place, all application-building tools can extract the definition, thus ensuring consistency. Rdb can extract from the repository both record and field definitions, which equate to table and domains in SQL terminology. To use this approach, the record and fields must be defined in CDD/Repository using the CDD/ Repository command language CDO. The following example from the BANKING database illustrates the fields and records that make up the BRANCH record.

```
CDO> DEFINE FIELD branch_code      DATATYPE TEXT SIZE IS 4 CHARACTERS.
CDO> DEFINE FIELD branch_name      DATATYPE TEXT SIZE IS 20 CHARACTERS.
CDO> DEFINE FIELD branch_address   DATATYPE TEXT SIZE IS 120 CHARACTERS.
CDO> DEFINE FIELD managers_name    DATATYPE TEXT SIZE IS 20 CHARACTERS.

CDO> DEFINE RECORD branch.
cont> branch_code.
cont> branch_name.
cont> branch_address.
cont> managers_name.
cont> END branch RECORD.

CDO> DIRECTORY

Directory  EUROBANK:[UK.DICT]DATABASE
  BRANCH;1            RECORD
  BRANCH_ADDRESS;1    FIELD
  BRANCH_CODE;1       FIELD
  BRANCH_NAME;1       FIELD
  MANAGERS_NAME;1     FIELD
```

To define a table in the Rdb database using these repository definitions, the Rdb database first must be attached and the link with the repository must be opened. This is achieved using the PATHNAME qualifier on the ATTACH statement. Without this option, Rdb will only open the database, which is the normal procedure for production applications. When a formal link has been defined between the Rdb database and the repository, metadata changes are not allowed in SQL unless the PATHNAME qualifier is specified on the ATTACH statement.

Hint: The Rdb database should not be accessed by PATHNAME in a production system. Start-up of the application will be slower because a transaction is started against the Rdb database and the repository.

In the following example, the domain STANDARD_NAME and the table BRANCH have been created using the repository definitions.

```
SQL> ATTACH 'PATHNAME eurobank:[uk.dict]database.banking';

SQL> CREATE DOMAIN FROM eurobank:[uk.dict]database.standard_name;

SQL> CREATE TABLE FROM eurobank:[uk.dict]database.branch;
```

If we show the table definition in SQL, it looks identical to the one created without the repository. The only additional information is the inclusion of the CDD pathname.

```
SQL> SHOW TABLE branch;

  CDD Pathname:    eurobank:[uk.dict]DATABASE.BRANCH;1

Columns for table BRANCH:
Column Name             Data Type        Domain
------------            ---------        -------

BRANCH_CODE             CHAR(4)          BRANCH_CODE
BRANCH_NAME             CHAR(20)         BRANCH_NAME
BRANCH_ADDRESS          CHAR(120)        BRANCH_ADDRESS
MANAGERS_NAME           CHAR(20)         MANAGERS_NAME
```

There are two advantages in demanding that only data definitions defined in the repository be used in the database:

- Everyone uses the same definition, ensuring consistency

- CDO pieces tracking identifies which applications are using various records and fields

One important point to remember is that not all the components of a database definition, such as storage areas, maps, and triggers, are held in the repository. Hence, when a database is defined, the SQL command file should contain all the information required to build the database. Only the table and domain definitions should be extracted from the repository.

Hint: It is important to ensure that the repository object name and the Rdb domain or table name are identical. If they differ, problems will occur later when integrating the database into the repository.

14.1.2   Pieces Tracking

The pieces tracking capability in CDD/Repository is used to report what is using an object. CDO has two pieces tracking commands, SHOW USES and SHOW USED_BY. In the following example, CDO states that the BRANCH record and an Rdb database called BANKING are using the object BRANCH_NAME in the repository.

```
CDO> SHOW USES branch_name
Owners of EUROBANK:[UK.DICT]DATABASE.BRANCH_NAME;1
 |  EUROBANK:[UK.DICT]DATABASE.BRANCH;1  (Type : RECORD)
 |  |  via CDD$DATA_AGGREGATE_CONTAINS
 |  BANKING           (Type : CDD$RDB_DATABASE)
 |  |  via CDD$RDB_DATA_ELEMENT
```

14.1.3   Managing Change

Once a database has been created using the objects in the repository, the proxy entity creates a permanent link between the database and repository.

Attaching a message to the database object in the repository automatically alerts the database to changes in the repository definition. When the next attach to the database is made using the PATHNAME, which also creates a link to the repository, a warning message is displayed advising of the change to the repository definition. Since this is only a warning message, the database designer is not forced to include the repository change into the repository immediately.

The following example illustrates changing the length of the field MANAGERS_NAME to 30 characters and shows the message that is sent to Rdb and the data administrator.

• In CDO change the field manager's name to 30 characters

```
CDO> CHANGE FIELD managers_name DATATYPE TEXT SIZE 30.
%CDO-I-DBMBR, database EUROBANK:[UK.DICT]BANKING;1 may need to
    be INTEGRATED
```

• In SQL, invoke the database by pathname. This displays the informational message that a data definition has changed

```
SQL> ATTACH 'PATHNAME eurobank:[uk.dict]database.banking';
%SQL-I-DIC_DB_CHG1, A repository definition used by schema
  EUROBANK:[UK.DICT]DATABASE.BANKING;1 has changed
  -SQL-I-DIC_DB_CHG2, Use the INTEGRATE statement to resolve
    any differences between the repository and the database
%CDD-I-MESS, entity has messages
```

• Return to CDO, and display the messages for the banking database object

```
CDO> SHOW MESSAGES banking
  EUROBANK:[UK.DICT]DATABASE.BANKING;1 is possibly invalid,
    triggered by
  CDD$DATA_ELEMENT  EUROBANK:[UK.DICT]DATABASE.MANAGERS_NAME;1
```

The tight integration between the repository and the database illustrated here is not limited to Rdb. It applies to any product that has read/write access to the repository, including RALLY and ACMS.

Figure 14.3 Repository and Database Integration

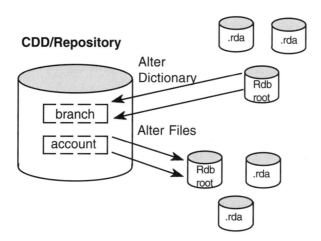

14.1.4   Maintaining Repository and Database Integration

Since no system is perfect, there may be times when the repository and database will contain differences. In the previous example, the data definition in
the repository changed but the database still contained the old definition. SQL
provides an INTEGRATE command in the interactive query language that
transfers the metadata definitions from the repository to the Rdb database, or
from the database to the repository.

Figure 14.3 illustrates using the repository to reconcile definitions in an Rdb
database (ALTER FILES) or reconciling definitions in the repository using
the database definitions (ALTER DICTIONARY).

Integrating Repository and Database

The repository and database must be integrated when repository definitions
change and the Rdb database has to be updated. Integration is a straightforward procedure, but it does illustrate the reason why the naming conven-
tions used in the database must match those in the repository. If they do not
match, the Rdb definition will be overwritten when the data definition is read
from the repository.

In the following example from the BANKING application, a new definition in the
repository for the field MANAGERS_NAME is loaded into the Rdb database.

- Display the columns in table BRANCH; the MANAGERS_NAME is 20 characters

```
SQL> SHOW TABLE branch

Columns for table BRANCH:
Column Name        Data Type        Domain
-----------        ---------        ------

BRANCH_CODE        CHAR(4)
BRANCH_NAME        CHAR(20)
BRANCH_ADDRESS     CHAR(120)
MANAGERS_NAME      CHAR(20)         STANDARD_NAME
```

- Reconcile the definitions in the Rdb database from the

```
SQL> INTEGRATE DATABASE PATHNAME
cont>      eurobank:[uk.dict]database.banking ALTER FILES;
```

- Display the columns in table BRANCH; the MANAGERS_NAME is now 30 characters

```
SQL> SHOW TABLE branch

  CDD Pathname:  EUROBANK:[UK.DICT]DATABASE.BRANCH;1

Columns for table BRANCH:
Column Name        Data Type        Domain
-----------        ---------        ------

BRANCH_CODE        CHAR(4)
BRANCH_NAME        CHAR(20)
BRANCH_ADDRESS     CHAR(120)
MANAGERS_NAME      CHAR(30)         MANAGERS_NAME
```

14.1.5 Integrating Database to Repository

Many Rdb users find themselves having to integrate the Rdb database into the repository. In our example, no links were established with the repository when the database was created. Later, it was decided to formalize links with the repository, which is done using a different form of the INTEGRATE command. One of the problems with INTEGRATE is that all it appears to create in the repository is a database object name for the database. All the database tables and columns in the repository are created as well. They simply are not immediately visible. To make the tables and columns visible, the CDO ENTER command must be used on each. Once the ENTER command has been used, each object is visible and can be used by all tools that read the repository.

In the following example, the BANKING database is integrated into the repository. Then the ACCOUNT table and ACCOUNT_NO column are made visible in the repository.

```
SQL> INTEGRATE DATABASE FILENAME eurobank:[uk.db]banking
 cont> CREATE PATHNAME eurobank:[uk.dict]database.banking;

CDO> DIRECTORY

 Directory EUROBANK:[UK.DICT]DATABASE

 BANKING;1           CDD$DATABASE

CDO> ENTER RECORD account FROM DATABASE banking
CDO> ENTER FIELD account_no FROM RECORD account

CDO> DIRECTORY

 Directory EUROBANK:[UK.DICT]DATABASE

 ACCOUNT;1          RECORD
 ACCOUNT_NO;1       FIELD
 BANKING;1          CDD$DATABASE
```

If the database contains hundreds of fields and many tables, the process of using ENTER is tedious indeed. It is helpful to build from the repository whenever possible.

14.1.6   Integrating Domains and Tables

Using CDD V5.4 and from Rdb V6.1, one no longer has to integrate the entire database whenever a change is made to a domain or table. Now it is possible to specifically identify the domains or tables that have changed and integrate only these, thus saving a considerable amount of time and system resources.

Integration is possible in both directions, that is from Rdb to the repository or from the repository to Rdb. The syntax is the same as that for integrating the database except the words DOMAIN or TABLE are substituted as appropriate. Therefore in the following example where the definition of the BRANCH table changed, to include this in the Rdb database the required command would be:

```
SQL> INTEGRATE TABLE  branch  ALTER FILES;
```

where the definition for the BRANCH table has been obtained from the DATABASE.RECORDS.BRANCH path in the repository.

14.1.7   Database Objects Supported by CDD/Repository

So far the objects we have seen in CDD/Repository for Rdb are:

- CDD$DATABASE

- RECORD

- FIELD

The list does not end here. When the database is integrated into the repository, other objects also are created in the repository, such as:

- CDD$INDEX

- CDD$CONSTRAINT

These objects are made visible using the ENTER GENERIC command. Once available, however, there is nothing that can be done with them. They are best left hidden.

14.1.8   Field Definitions and Validation

Ideally, the repository should contain all the information about the data definitions, including display formats and validation rules. Rdb is able to take advantage of the column validation rules and to include them in the database definitions.

In the BANKING example, a new column that contains the number of accounts in each branch is added to the BRANCH table. The field definition for

BRANCH_ACCOUNTS in the repository has a VALID IF clause, which is part of the database definition. The Rdb database or the new field is integrated into the repository to include the new definition. Any attempt to insert a value of BRANCH_ACCOUNTS less than 1000 will generate an error, as shown in the following example.

```
CDO> DEFINE FIELD branch_accounts DATATYPE signed longword
cont> VALID IF branch_accounts > 1000.

CDO> SHOW FIELD branch_accounts
 Definition of field BRANCH_ACCOUNTS
 |  Datatype          signed longword
 |  Valid if          (BRANCH_ACCOUNTS GT 1000)
```

The record definition for BRANCH is amended in CDO to include the new column:

```
SQL> INTEGRATE DATABASE PATHNAME
cont> 'eurobank:[uk.dict]database.banking' ALTER FILES;
```

Or you could just integrate table:

```
SQL> ATTACH 'PATHNAME eurobank:[uk.dict]database.banking';
SQL> INTEGRATE TABLE branch ALTER FILES;

SQL> SHOW TABLE branch

 CDD Pathname:   EUROBANK:[UK.DICT]DATABASE.BRANCH;2

 Columns for table BRANCH:
```

Column Name	Data Type	Domain
BRANCH_CODE	CHAR(4)	BRANCH_CODE
BRANCH_NAME	CHAR(20)	BRANCH_NAME
BRANCH_ADDRESS	CHAR(120)	BRANCH_ADDRESS
MANAGERS_NAME	CHAR(30)	MANAGERS_NAME
BRANCH_ACCOUNTS	INTEGER	BRANCH_ACCOUNTS

```
SQL> INSERT INTO branch VALUES
  cont> ('345','Westhampton','12 High St','Miss West','789');
%RDB-E-NOT_VALID, validation on field BRANCH_ACCOUNTS caused
      operation to fail
```

14.1.9   **Defining Primary and Foreign Key Constraints**

It is now possible to define the constraints in the repository and then build the database using those definitions. Previously this was not possible and the SQL ALTER command had to be used to include the constraints in the database. Within CDD one can define the following types of constraints:

- Primary key

- Foreign key

- Unique

- Check

- Not Null

In CDO the constraint definition is defined before the columns in the record definition with the exception of the NOT NULL constraint, which is defined on the column. For example, to define the primary key on BRANCH_CODE the record definition would now be:

```
CDO> DEFINE RECORD branch
 cont>  CONSTRAINT branch_code_primary key PRIMARY KEY branch_code.
  cont> branch_code.
  cont> branch_name.
  cont> branch_address.
  cont> managers_name.
  cont> END branch RECORD.
```

If we were defining the foreign key from the table ACCOUNT for BRANCH_CODE then the record definition in the CDD would be:

```
CDO> DEFINE RECORD ACCOUNT
 cont>  CONSTRAINT invalid_branch_code FOREIGN KEY branch_code
 cont>      REFERENCES branch branch_code.
 cont> account_no
 cont> customer_no.
 cont> branch_code.
 cont> balance NOT NULL.
 ................rest of definition
 cont> END account RECORD.
```

14.2   CDD/ADMINISTRATOR

CDD/Administrator is a GUI Motif-based tool for managing the repository. CDD/Administrator is of interest to database designers because it provides the ability to view repository information in a graphic format and also to generate customized reports.

There are a number of presentation styles or *navigators*, as they are known within CDD/Administrator. A number of default navigators are supplied, but if these are unsuitable they can be customized, or you can create your own navigators. The Hierarchy Navigator shows the directory for the BANKING example and some of the records and fields that make up the data definitions. Each element in the repository has its own icon to represent its object type.

Another problem for the database designer is knowing how many databases are in use throughout the system. This is one area where CDD/Administrator and the repository can help the database team. By selecting an object type in the type hierarchy navigator, CDD/Administrator shows all the objects of that type. For example, if the object type database is selected, it shows that only two databases are in this repository, the BANKING and the ASTRONOMY databases.

Other useful navigators include the version graph which describes the versions that are in use by the various objects.

CDD/Repository provides fairly tight integration with Rdb to permit efficient management and control of the data definitions. This enables a central data definition to be managed by the repository, which is responsible for advising the users that the data definition has changed. This fulfills an essential role in the maintenance of today's complex, integrated systems.

15   Transaction Processing

We have already mentioned that Rdb can be used for ad-hoc or predefined work. This chapter discusses predefined work and how Rdb and Digital Equipment's transaction processing architecture and products can help corporations build high-performance, resilient transaction processing (TP) systems.

In the past, relational database technology was not fast enough to support high-performance TP systems, but this is not the case now. Today, Rdb is frequently found at the heart of such systems.

15.1   WHAT IS A TRANSACTION PROCESSING SYSTEM?

A widely accepted picture of a TP system shows many users doing predefined work against a shared resource, such as a database. Compare this with the profile of an ad-hoc system, in which, typically, a few users issue ad-hoc queries against a shared resource, probably a database. Unlike the TP system, the ad-hoc system's database designer cannot easily tune the database to efficiently process a class of known transactions. The transactions are not known when the database is physically designed in the ad-hoc system. In the TP system, the database's physical design is only one of a number of system components that can be tuned to efficiently execute predetermined transactions. The TP system also can be compared with a classic timesharing system. Such a system may support many users, but usually they do not share a resource such as a database.

In practice, most organizations have applications that fit the three systems just described. Some organizations allow TP and ad-hoc work to execute against the same database. Many organizations, however, do not allow ad-hoc work to be executed against the production databases. Since production databases reflect second-by-second changes in business, they help keep the business running smoothly. Order input is one example of a production application. It is so crucial that these databases perform efficiently that an organization must not risk allowing unplanned work to be submitted against them. One answer is to take periodic copies of subsets of the production databases and to permit ad-hoc queries against these reference databases. DEC Data Distributor, discussed in Chapter 12, is an ideal product with which to create these subsets.

Now let us turn to some examples of TP systems in everyday use. Many TP systems involve high performance and high availability. Typical TP systems include:

- Airline reservation systems

- Vacation booking systems

- Financial transaction systems

- Customer information systems

- Sales-order entry systems

Ad-hoc systems are often used in marketing and statistical systems to search for groups of subjects within a class, such as all the customers who live in Paris, are married, and have brown hair. Office systems or application-development systems are typical timesharing systems. Although sharing some resources, the users typically manipulate their own documents and files.

Many applications that run in a timesharing environment would run more efficiently under a Digital TP monitor. Digital TP monitors can be used to develop Rdb applications if they are form based, with the end-user filling in predefined screens of information. Such systems will perform more efficiently and need less hardware power.

15.2 WHAT ARE DECTP AND DECDTA?

DECtp is a transaction processing system environment composed of:

- A distributed transaction processing architecture (DECdta)

- Software and hardware products

The architecture and software products, such as ACMS (Application Control and Management System), will be discussed in this chapter. Originally developed for OpenVMS, ACMS is now also available on other Digital platforms.

15.3   DECDTA

DECtp is built around a distributed transaction processing architecture. An architecture is a framework in which all the components have strictly defined interfaces and clearly understood relationships. DECdta has well-defined interfaces that allow the components of a TP system to be physically separated without having to modify any application code. This is important for the TP system to grow smoothly and to add users onto the database. Figure 15.1 shows some of the architected TP services.

Since DECdtm's distributed transaction management services reside in the OpenVMS operating system, they are available for use by timesharing and batch systems, as well as the TP monitor.

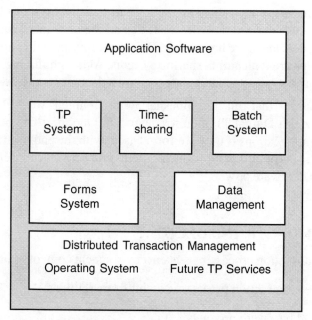

Figure 15.1 Architected TP Services

DECdta is designed to allow unbounded, flexible growth in a TP system because of the following features in its architecture:

- Separation of function

- Replication of components

- Distribution of processing power

- Data partitioning

Combined, these features allow Rdb databases to service transactions that were requested anywhere in the network and span databases on remote machines, while ensuring database and data integrity. These features are described in the following sections.

15.3.1   Separation of Function

A DECdta TP system is conceptually grouped into two parts:

- TP Client

- TP Server

The two parts are shown in Figure 15.2. This is a conceptual separation; the physical separation of these parts may occur in a number of ways, as we shall see shortly. The TP Client is the part of the TP system that initiates requests; for example, to execute a transaction. The requests are typically put into action by the TP Server. The TP Client often interfaces with the end-users, executing a forms management system such as Digital's DECforms. In this case, the TP Client is responsible for the presentation of the forms interface, the character I/O processing, and the local validation of form fields.

The TP Client can communicate with a device other than a video terminal, such as a badge reader, and can interact with an interface other than a human, such as an external data feed.

The TP Server is made up of the application and the database management system, which in our case is Rdb. This conceptual separation gives the designer the flexibility to define the client-server topology. The TP Client and TP Server can reside in a single machine, in which case they are not physically separated. Because of DECdta, however, they are logically separated.

Figure 15.2 Separation of Function

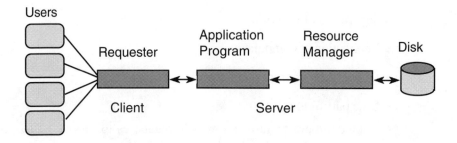

The designer can physically separate the TP Client and TP Server, placing the TP Client in one machine and the TP Server in another. These nodes may be separated in a local-area network (LAN), a wide-area network (WAN), or different VMScluster nodes. Because these components have architected interfaces, no application code has to be changed. By placing the TP Client on one machine and the TP Server on another, the designer can offload the CPU demand of forms processing from the application server to a client machine in the appropriate department.

In this example, the total CPU power of the system has been smoothly increased without any extra space being taken up in the computer room. This may seem trivial, but computer rooms have a finite size and their floors can take only a certain amount of weight. Increasing a growing business's computing power without having to create a new computer room saves money. DECdta allows both distributed and centralized TP systems to be built. A company can start off with a small centralized system and move to a distributed system consisting of many machines in a network without changing a line of application code.

Another interesting point is that the client machine on which the TP Client resides handles the screen I/O processing of the forms interface. It efficiently sends requests and records containing data over the network to the TP Server over another architected interface.

Separate client and server machines often are referred to as *front-end* and *back-end* machines. So far it has been assumed that a TP Client exists in only one front-end machine and a TP Server exists in only one back-end machine. In fact, DECdta allows the replication of these components.

Figure 15.3 Replication of Components

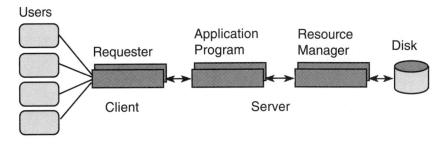

15.3.2   Replication of Components

The ability to replicate components lets the designer increase the CPU power available to the TP system and also its availability. Figure 15.3 shows the components that may be replicated.

The TP Client may be replicated so each department within an organization has its own front-ends to do local forms processing, for example. These departments could be in the same building or geographically distant. In this way, new departments could start to use the application without too much extra CPU power being needed on the back-end system. The TP Server also can be replicated, if necessary. A common approach would be to have a VMScluster back-end with shared disks holding an Rdb database. A TP Server would reside on each node in the VMScluster, running the same application code and attached to the same database. The request workload coming into the TP Servers from the TP Clients could be shared. This would allow the back-end VMScluster to deal with many requests. If more power were needed at the back-end, another machine could be easily added to the VMScluster without having to modify the application.

The ability to replicate the TP Client and TP Server means that highly available distributed TP systems can be built. With more than one front-end machine in a department, the TP system can be designed so that end-users can easily connect to the TP service on another front-end machine if the one they are connected to fails. For added protection, fault-tolerant machines could be used as front-end processors.

Using VMSclusters as back-end application servers also provides failover protection in case of node failure. If a TP Server is lost because its VMScluster node has failed, the users' transactions active on that node are aborted.

The VMScluster support in Rdb ensures that the aborted transactions are rolled back by a surviving VMScluster node. Because the TP Servers are replicated on the VMScluster nodes, another TP Server will be used if a user reselects the business function from the menu. The users can continue their work with only minimal disruption.

15.3.3   Data Partitioning

One way to increase database performance would be to split up the database into separate physical databases that are attached to separate processors. In this situation, partitions have dedicated processors and disks. These separate processors can be connected by a LAN or a WAN, although for performance reasons a LAN may be more suitable.

Because of the DECdtm component, DECdta allows systems to be practically designed with such partitioning. Without this component, updates that span more than one database could not be guaranteed to perform the same action. They would either commit the transaction or abort it. The DECdtm component of DECdta allows TP systems to maintain the integrity of distributed databases. Involving more than one database in a transaction was discussed in detail in Chapter 12.

15.3.4   Distribution of Processing Power

With the features of DECdta that have been mentioned so far, a distributed TP system such as the one in Figure 15.4 can be built.

In this system, client front-end machines can be geographically dispersed around the network so they are physically close to the end-users. Local forms processing and field validation can be performed quickly and efficiently at the local processor in this way. When interaction with the back-end TP Servers is necessary, the communication is as efficient as possible. Transactions can span Rdb databases on each of these back-end TP Servers under the control of DECdta's DECdtm component.

Users working at the front-end machines do not need to know where the various back-end TP Servers are. A user typically would be presented with a series of menus containing the business functions that he or she is allowed to select. The user would have no idea that the CUSTOMER INFORMATION

Figure 15.4 Distribution of Processing Power

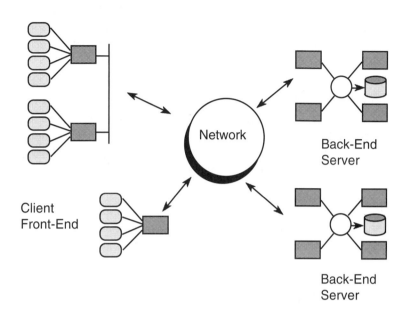

menu item caused transactions to execute on systems in London and the ANALYZE ACCOUNT HISTORY menu item to manipulate the BANKING database in Boston.

Failures in the front-end TP Client systems and the back-end TP Server systems can be overcome, as explained earlier in this chapter, but what happens if the network fails? In this scenario, the front-end TP Client systems and the back-end TP Server systems could not communicate. Business, however, would grind to a halt until the network was re-established. A TP service, although possibly degraded, may still be offered because of two DECdta features. One is failover, which was introduced earlier; the other is transaction queuing often known as *store and forward replication* in the database marketplace. Let us use a network failure to explain queuing.

If the network fails, the front-end TP Clients will detect this and attempt to fail over to an alternative service on another back-end TP Server. The sequence of back-end TP Servers in this procedure can be specified to the front-end TP Client by the logical name searchlists. The front-end TP Client will try to fail over to each specified back-end TP Server, but will fail because no connection is possible when the network is down. Suppose, however, the last entry specified in the searchlist was for a local TP service. No network communication is necessary to connect to this service, so the fact that the network is down is of no concern. The user has now connected to a TP Server on the departmental client.

What can this local TP service do for the end-user? Take the case of retrieval. Suppose that a business application is primarily concerned with looking up data in a database. Imagine that a credit card must be validated. Given a card number, the application must return a credit limit and also check whether the card was stolen. All this data, held on a large, central Rdb database, would be inaccessible across the network if the system were down.

However, suppose that once a day the stolen credit card information is sent to a small Rdb database held locally on the departmental processors. This could be done in the OpenVMS environment by using the DEC Data Distributor product described in Chapter 12. This local database would be available to the local TP Server. Consequently, the salesclerks in the departments could determine whether a card was stolen. They could not, however, find the exact credit limit of an individual cardholder. A blanket credit limit as decided by the credit card company would have to be applied. In this case, business continued as usual, although in a somewhat limited fashion. The credit card company continued to provide a service to its customers, who were told whether a credit card could be used.

What about update operations? In this situation a transaction queue can be used. Take the credit card company example again. Suppose that a store has telephoned in a query about a purchase, giving the credit card number. The local TP Server has supplied information to the salesclerk about whether the card is stolen. Suppose the card is good and the purchase is given the go ahead. How can a record of this purchase be sent to the central database when the network is still down?

The solution is to use a transaction queue. The details of the credit card purchase are written to a local queue. A component of DECdta tries to take this information from the queue and send it across to the back-end TP Server for processing. Because the network is down, it cannot, so it merely waits awhile and tries again. Eventually, the network comes back up, the transaction queue gets emptied, and the central database is updated. Even if the business operation involves updating or storing information on a central database, business does not have to stop if the network fails. An example of the queuing mechanism used by ACMS will be given shortly.

15.4   ACMS

ACMS was created to support transaction-processing-style workloads against Rdb and other database systems. It can work in conjunction with Digital's forms product, DECforms, or with client software running on, for example, an IBM PC, via ACMS Desktop. In fact, ACMS can be used with any front-end device, since Digital publishes the definition of the ACMS System Interface to allow developers to interface any device with the product.

15.4.1   ACMS Architecture

ACMS is built on the DECdta architecture, so it is client-server in nature. An ACMS system, therefore, can reside in one machine or the front-end and back-end components can run on separate machines in the network. In this case, the front-end components deal with the client presentation, and the back-end components run the application and interface to Rdb.

Far fewer operating system processes are present in a typical ACMS system than in a typical timesharing system. When a user logs onto, for example, the OpenVMS operating system in a timesharing system, a process is created for each user. A hundred users would have a hundred processes, all taking up memory and requiring a significant amount of CPU resource to create. An ACMS system uses far fewer processes. Some specialized multi-threaded processes handle terminal interaction and forms presentation. A special process called an *application execution controller* executes tasks and manages the server pool. Figure 15.5 shows the main ACMS component processes in an ACMS application. Additional processes concerned with housekeeping duties have been omitted for clarity.

Tasks are the high-level definitions of business transactions and will be discussed in the next section. The *server process pool* is a pool of dedicated processes that ACMS uses to execute third-generation-language code to access the database. Usually, the server pool contains few processes. When these server processes are created, user-written server initialization code can be executed to automatically attach to the Rdb database (and stay attached).

Figure 15.5 Simplified ACMS Architecture

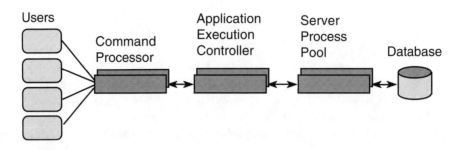

15.4.2   ACMS Tasks

A developer typically writes an ACMS application in one of the following:

- Task-definition language

- 3GL code

- SQL or SQL Module Language

If a program must be written to store orders in a database, for example, a programmer usually would structure the code so that some mainline code called code modules to perform database access and to handle forms processing. In an ACMS task definition, the mainline 3GL code is replaced by high-level task statements. These statements control the logic flow within the task. Instead of calling code modules to handle forms processing, an ACMS task can make calls directly to DECforms. These calls are called exchange steps. An ACMS task accesses a database by executing processing steps, which call 3GL procedures written by the developer. In Rdb, these procedures usually would include embedded SQL or calls to SQL Module Language routines. Chapter 17 has more information on embedded SQL and SQL Module Language.

Figure 15.6 shows a simplified ACMS task structure, with terminal I/O handled by exchange steps and database access by processing steps.

Figure 15.6 ACMS Task Structure

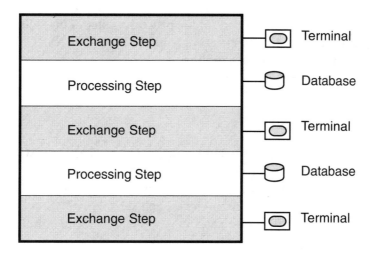

It is interesting to note the processes within which these steps execute. In the case of DECforms, a multi-threaded process known as a command process executes the DECforms component. A number of command processes may be in an ACMS system. In distributed systems, these command processes execute on the front-end machine. The task language is interpreted by another application execution controller, which passes the DECforms requests to the command process. It also manages the server pool, which contains the servers that will attach to the Rdb database and will execute the 3GL code and SQL. When the application execution controller must execute a processing step, it looks to see if the correct type of server is free. If it is, the server is asked to execute the necessary code procedure; if not, ACMS will suspend the task until the correct server is available. Extra server processes also can be dynamically created, depending on the settings of various control parameters. When the processing step has completed, the server usually is returned to the server pool for use by other processing steps. Within the task, data is passed between exchange and processing steps in workspaces. Workspaces are similar to record definitions and are defined in CDD/Repository. In fact, a CDD/Repository record definition can be used to define a workspace and an Rdb table.

Hint: Rdb transactions may be started and ended at the ACMS task-definition level, although it is not recommended. Transactions should be started and ended in the code of the processing step. This facilitates error handling, such as trapping errors from the SET TRANSACTION statement and deadlock error handling.

15.4.3   ACMS Queuing

A set of queue management routines helps create and manage ACMS queues, queue services allowing developers to deposit (enqueue) items and remove (dequeue) items from a queue, and a queued task initiator (QTI), which automatically removes items from queues and submits ACMS tasks locally or remotely. Figure 15.7 shows a queuing configuration, with a local queue holding tasks ready for remote submission.

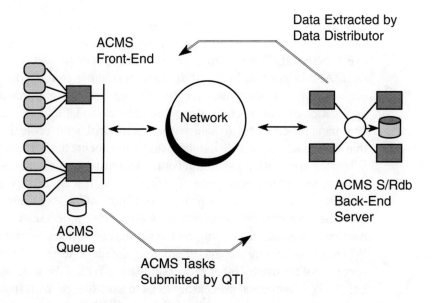

Figure 15.7 ACMS Queuing

Usually, a developer uses the enqueue service from an ACMS task-processing step or a free-standing program to place an item on a queue for subsequent processing. The queued item typically would contain:

- The name of an ACMS task

- The name of an ACMS application

- A number of workspaces

- Control information

The QTI automatically dequeues the item and submits the task to the local or remote ACMS application, passing the task and the workspaces containing the user data. The task then is executed in the specified ACMS application. If the application was remote and the network was down, the QTI would continue to retry the task submission until the network was functioning.

15.4.4   ACMS and Rdb

The ACMS architecture benefits Rdb in many ways, including:

- Performance

- Distribution

- Availability

Performance

ACMS can boost the performance or reduce the drain on system resources of Rdb in a number of ways. Where there are many users, ACMS uses far fewer processes to support them than a traditional timesharing system would use. This reduction can save a company a considerable amount of memory. Indeed, some of this saved memory can be given to the server processes. Since there are few server processes, they can be given large numbers of buffers, which will use up some of the memory that was saved.

We also can go a step further. Chapter 4 described how a table can be partitioned over a number of disk drives based on values in a table column or columns. Based on the same columns and range of values, we can execute a processing step in an ACMS server process that is dedicated to processing

Figure 15.8 ACMS Server Partitioning

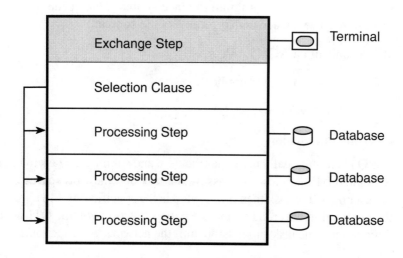

that table partition only. Figure 15.8 shows a SELECT clause in an ACMS task diverting the processing of database information to the appropriate ACMS server.

Any access to the partition is through the dedicated process and the dedicated buffer pool. This can result in efficient buffering and low resource contention, allowing very high transaction rates to be achieved.

We saw in Chapter 7 that when many users update a table, lock contention can result. Dedicated servers can drastically reduce or even remove this lock contention. If only one dedicated server with a large number of buffers accesses one table partition, for example, no other process could be in contention for locks.

As was mentioned, when a server process is created (usually at the start of day), initialization code may be executed. At this point a server usually can be attached to a database. Once the server has initialized, it waits in the pool, ready to work with the database attached. When a request to start a transaction occurs, the server is ready to execute.

Distribution

Chapter 12 described the remote access capabilities of Rdb, particularly a program's ability to attach to a remote database. In this situation, a remote server process is created on the machine that performs the local access to the database. If many remote attaches are being performed from across the network to a database, many server processes will be created on the local machine, with the possibility of many process creations and deletions as the remote attaches and deattaches occur. Server-process creation and database attachment is expensive in terms of CPU and memory resources. In this case, it is much better to use the inherent distributed capabilities of ACMS if the application is a transaction-processing application. A small number of server processes will be on the machine local to the database. These servers will be created only once and will attach to the database only once, which is much less costly in terms of CPU and memory.

Availability

Chapter 9 explained how Rdb data integrity is preserved when a VMScluster node fails. The database users on the surviving nodes experience no disruption except for a small delay as the VMScluster state transition occurs. However, the users who were logged onto the failed node will be returned to the terminal server prompt on their terminal, where they can reconnect to the service and log in to OpenVMS.

In a distributed ACMS application, the failover to a surviving node is smoother and requires less intervention on the part of the end-user than with Rdb alone. If a user is executing a transaction on a VMScluster node that fails, the transaction will be aborted and the user will be returned to the ACMS menu with an error message displayed. The user can reselect the menu item and be automatically failed over to a surviving node. If the user was not executing a transaction at the time of the failure but was examining a menu, he or she will not even know a VMScluster node has failed.

16   Database Tools

16.1   DECTRACE

DECtrace is an application event-based collector, which collects data for subsequent analysis and report generation. This section briefly describes how to use DECtrace to help tune an Rdb database or to provide workload information for the artificial intelligence database-design tool, RdbExpert.

DECtrace collects information for *facility definitions*. By default, DECtrace provides facility definitions for Rdb, DBMS, ACMS, and ALL-IN-1, plus some third-party tools like Smartstar, but the examples in this section will refer only to the Rdb facility definition. In practice, a facility definition would be defined for the business system that makes up the application programs and the database.

There are two ways that DECtrace can be used:

- Online monitoring of activity using the DECtrace monitor

- Analysis of data after monitoring is complete

Using DECtrace to analyze the performance of an Rdb database is not complex but a number of steps must be followed, as shown in Figure 16.1.

The first step in collecting data is to create a selection. In the following example, a selection for the BANKING example has been defined, that collects information for the facility RDBVMS. This means that DECtrace will collect information for any Rdb database. For this reason, it is important to specify a new facility definition that includes the application to restrict the data that is returned to DECtrace.

```
DECtrace> CREATE SELECTION collect_banking -
_DECtrace> /COMMENT= 'banking_example' -
_DECtrace> /OPTIONS
```

Figure 16.1 Steps in Using DECtrace to Analyze an Rdb Database

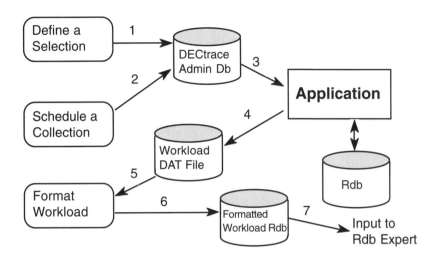

```
Option> FACILITY RDBVMS /CLASS= ALL
Option> Exit
```

This example shows that when defining a selection, the classes of data to be collected can be specified. Classes can be either user-defined or, in the case of Rdb, specified so that the data collected can be input into RdbExpert.

Once a selection has been made, the next step is to ask DECtrace to collect some data. This is done through the SCHEDULE COLLECTION command, which specifies which selections to collect data for and when this should occur. Typically, many collections for a given selection will be specified. Once a collection starts to gather the data, the information is written to a special file with an extension of .DAT.

```
DECtrace> SHOW COLLECTION
5-APR-1994 16:58            Scheduled Collections              Page 1
Brief Report                                              DECtrace V2.1-0

Collections scheduled for the entire cluster

    Collection Name    Selection Name    Start                End
    ---------------    ---------------    ------------------   ------------------
->  BANKING_DATA       COLLECT_BANKING    5-APR-1994 16:58     5-APR-1994 17:18
```

Figure 16.2 Sample Schedule Collection Display

Figure 16.3 Sample Output from SHOW REGISTER

```
DECtrace> SHOW REGISTER
5-APR-1994 16:59     Register Information for node RDB4ME           Page 1
                                                          DECtrace V2.1-0

Registrations actively collecting

  Node: RDB4ME  Collection: BANKING_DATA       Selection: COLLECT_BANKING

   Process   Process Name    Facility  Version   Registration Id
   --------  -------------   --------  --------   ----------------------
-> 000004C4  HOBBS           RDBVMS    V6.0-0
   DBSUK1$DKA300:[SYS0.SYSCOMMON.][SYSEXE]SQL$60.EXE;6
   EUROBANK:[UK.DB]BANK_DATA.DAT;1
```

In the BANKING example, a collection is scheduled to start at 16:58 and to run for 20 minutes for the selection COLLECT_BANKING. The data it gathers is to be written to the collection file BANK_DATA.DAT.

```
DECtrace> SCHEDULE COLLECTION banking_data bank_data -
_DECtrace> /BEGIN='16:58:00' /DURATION='00:20'-
_DECtrace> /SELECTION =collect_banking
%EPC-S-SCHED, Data collection BANKING_DATA is scheduled
```

Several commands can be issued while a collection is executing. The most useful ones are SHOW COLLECTION and SHOW REGISTER. The arrow -> against the collection name advises that the collection is active; ** indicates it is aborting. The SHOW REGISTER command details the actual active images from which DECtrace is collecting data.

The event data that is written to the data collection file (.DAT) now must be formatted to permit the analysis. The event data is not directly written to the formatted structure because this would affect the performance of the running application and defeat the object. The data files from the collection stage should be formatted into an Rdb database, using the DECtrace FORMAT command in the following example:

```
DECtrace> FORMAT eurobank:[uk.db]bank_data.dat banking_dectrace_data
```

Once an existing, formatted database has been created, additional collections can be formatted into the database using the /MERGE qualifier.

The next stage is very important because once the data has been formatted into an Rdb database the information can be analyzed. (It can be passed into an RMS file, but then the Report Writer and RdbExpert cannot read it.) DECtrace has its own report writer, but it will never be a sophisticated one.

Inside the DECtrace formatted database a number of tables are defined as a result of the formatting process. The one of primary interest to the database tuner is EPC$1_221_REQUEST_ACTUAL. Each column has a start and end value; to determine the actual resources used for an individual request, the start value must be subtracted from the end value. This is achieved by creating a new column in the table which is computed from the end and start value. The resource information available is listed here:

AIJ_WRITES	AS_BATCH_WRITE	AS_READ_STALL
AS_WRITE_STALL	BIO	BUFFER_READS
CLIENT_PC	COLLECTION_RECORD_ID	COMP_STATUS
CONTEXT_NUMBER	CPU	CURRENT_PRIO
D_ASYNC_FETCH	D_ASYNC_READIO	D_FETCH_RET
D_FETCH_UPD	D_GB_NEEDLOCK	D_GB_OLDVER
D_LB_ALLOK_START	D_LB_GBNEEDLOCK	D_LB_NEEDLOCK
D_LB_OLDVER	D_NOTFOUND_IO	D_NOTFOUND_SYN
DBS_READS	DBS_WRITES	DIO
FREE_VM_BYTES	GET_VM_BYTES	IMAGE_RECORD_ID
LOCK_RELS	LOCK_REQS	LOCK_STALL_TIME
PAGEFAULT_IO	PAGEFAULTS	PROM_DEADLOCKS
REQ_DEADLOCKS	REQ_ID	REQ_NOT_QUEUED
REQ_STALLS	REQUEST_OPER	ROOT_READS
ROOT_WRITES	RUJ_READS	RUJ_WRITES
S_ASYNC_FETCH	S_ASYNC_READIO	S_FETCH_RET
S_FETCH_UPD	S_GB_NEEDLOCK	S_GB_OLDVER
S_LB_ALLOK	S_LB_GBNEEDLOCK	S_LB_NEEDLOCK
S_LB_OLDVER	S_NOTFOUND_IO	S_NOTFOUND_SYN
STREAM_ID	TIMESTAMP_END	TIMESTAMP_START
TRANS_ID	VIRTUAL_SIZE	WS_GLOBAL
WS_PRIVATE	WS_SIZE	

The authors' recommendation for analysis of the data is to use SQL or PC tools like Forest & Trees and Business Objects. The reason for this approach is that viewing the information graphically means that it is easier to spot anomalies.

From the columns one can see that by using DECtrace it is possible to identify queries that use an excessive amount of resource, such as too many direct I/Os or buffer reads. This information is very useful, but when it is joined with table EPC$SQL_QUERIES on column SQL_ID the actual SQL used for the query is reported. A typical query is shown below which displays the SQL for all queries where the number of buffer reads used exceeds 100.

```
SQL> SELECT BUFFER_READS, SQL_STRING FROM
cont> DB_ACTUALS D, EPC$SQL_QUERIES Q  WHERE
cont> D.SQL_ID = Q.SQL_ID AND BUFFER_READS > 100;
```

Hint: When creating new columns, some PC tools do not like certain datatypes such as BIGINT. Therefore check with your tool before amending the DECtrace formatted database.

16.1.1   DECtrace Monitor

One of the problems with using the previous method of analyzing DECtrace data is that it cannot be done while the application is running. The solution to the problem is to invoke the DECtrace monitor which reads the specially formatted file and does not require the formatted Rdb database.

```
$ COLLECT MONITOR BANK_DATA
%EPC-S-MONITOR, Monitor spawned successfully
```

The monitor is spawned up as a separate process and must be displayed on an X/Windows device. It runs well on a PC using software like Digital's eXcursions.

When a collection is scheduled for use by the monitor, the /FLUSH qualifier should be specified to ensure that information is regularly written to the data collection file.

```
 DECtrace> SCHEDULE COLLECTION banking_data bank_data -
_DECtrace> /BEGIN='17:11:00' /DURATION='00:20' -
_DECtrace> /FLUSH='00:00:01' /SELECTION=collect_banking
%EPC-S-SCHED, Data collection BANKING_DATA is scheduled
```

The monitor has three screens. The first one, shown in Figure 16.4, displays all the processes that it is monitoring. By default it displays the direct I/O being used, but it can be changed to a number of different resources.

We can see in this example that only one user, HOBBS on node DBSUK1, is using the application and is currently using about 24 DIOs. By double clicking on user HOBBS the next screen shown in Figure 16.5 is displayed.

Figure 16.4 Initial DECtrace Monitor Screen

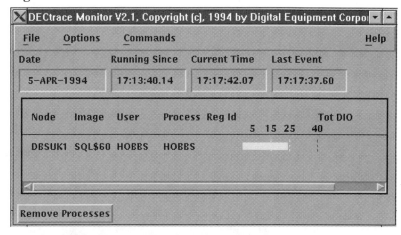

Figure 16.5 Resource Used by User HOBBS

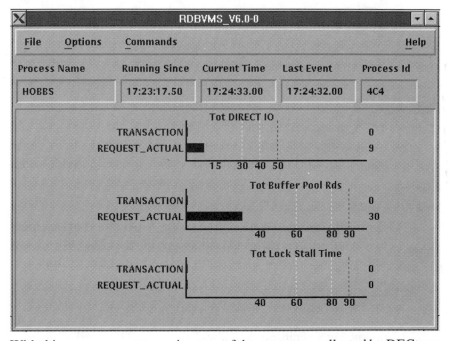

With this screen one can monitor any of the resources collected by DECtrace that were listed in the table earlier. In this example we have decided to collect *Direct IO*, *Buffer Reads* and *Lock Stall Time*. The threshold values for each of the resources can be customized and saved for subsequent use.

Figure 16.6 Resources Grouped by Client PC

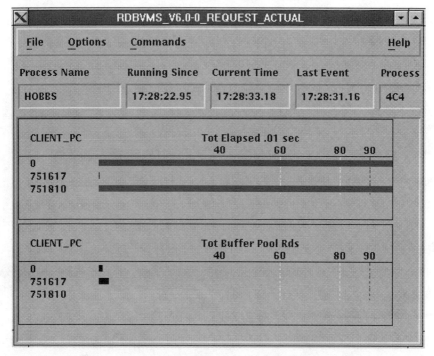

The final screen available, Figure 16.6, permits a further level of analysis. A resource selected from this screen, such as buffer reads, can be grouped by another item such as *client_pc*. The *client_pc* can be used sometimes to refer back to a specific location in the application code.

Hint: When observing DECtrace data, remember that information is only displayed when a request has been completed. Therefore, a long sequential read will appear as one entry with high values,;blink and you may miss it!

The monitor also supports a replay facility, and has a very useful screen pause option, but you must be quick with the mouse! It is ideal to use in an interactive environment, but there is still no substitute for the detailed analysis possible afterwards using the formatted database.

16.2 RDBEXPERT

RdbExpert is an artificial-intelligence-based physical database design tool that can generate physical designs for an Rdb database. To generate a design, RdbExpert requires the following information:

- Logical database design

- Workloads

- Volumes

- Environment

RdbExpert does not replace the database designer. It complements the designer's work the same way that CASE tools assist the analyst and modeler.

We will briefly describe how to generate a revised Rdb database design using the BANKING example. All the examples shown use the Motif interface. However, a workstation is not mandatory because RdbExpert has a command line interface that can be used from a standard VT terminal or can be displayed on a PC using software that supports X/Windows displays such as eXcursions from Digital.

The first step in using RdbExpert is to define the name of the design and create the design directories. A typical directory screen is shown in Figure 16.7.

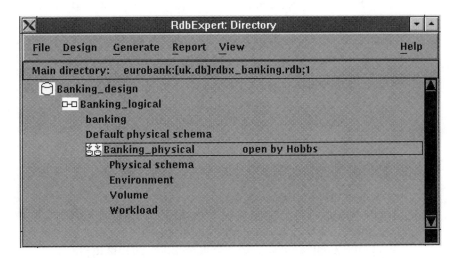

Figure 16.7 RdbExpert Directory

16.2.1   Logical Database Design

The logical database design is extracted from the metadata definitions of an existing Rdb database root file or an SQL text file. Hence, the database must first exist, even in some very basic form, to use this tool. Once this step has been completed, the volume, workload, and environment information can be specified.

16.2.2   Workload

It is impossible to design a database successfully without information about how it will be used. RdbExpert needs accurate workload information, such as database access paths, types of access, and frequency. The workload data is defined in terms of applications, the programs that make up the application, and the transactions and requests upon the database within each program.

Since specifying the workload information manually is a very time-consuming task, it should be derived from DECtrace. In this case, RdbExpert will accept as input the formatted Rdb database generated by DECtrace. Otherwise it would be necessary to manually specify each individual SQL request to RdbExpert.

The main advantage of using DECtrace to collect the workload information is that DECtrace will automatically identify all requests and pass them across to RdbExpert. Manually specifying all the program access paths and database request statements would be a very time-consuming exercise otherwise.

Hint: If the user decides to specify the workload manually, it may take days, weeks, or even months to accurately enter all the data.

16.2.3   Volume

Volume information can be extracted from an existing Rdb database or specified manually. Once the basic information has been gathered, the data can be amended to reflect the minimum, average, and maximum volume of rows in the table, along with a factor advising how volatile the table is.

16.2.4   Environment

The environment information, such as number of disks, memory available, space available on each disk, is the only data that must be specified manually.

16.2.5   Database-Design Generation

Once all the information has been specified, RdbExpert generates a proposed database design that includes all the database creation parameters, including allocation size, page size, buffers, storage area placement, clustering, hashing, and index node sizes. Various reports are generated which include:

- Analysis report
- Audit report
- Export SQL to create the database
- Redesign procedure
- Schema report
- Workload report

Analysis Report

The analysis report explains the proposed new design. The section headings are:

- Overview
- User tables
- Storage areas
- Disk requirements
- Implementation

It is presented in the form of an English report with section headings and page numbers.

Audit Report

The audit report explains the actions taken during the analysis. This report, which can be quite large, is useful to read when a question arises over the approach taken by RdbExpert.

Export SQL

Once the design has been created the schema required to create the new database can be generated by RdbExpert.

Redesign Procedure

For an existing database the commands to unload and load the database can be generated. RdbExpert provides various options to customize the resulting file, such as whether to include the postload index creation commands or include the constraint creation commands. If you are not familiar with DCL the command file is worth browsing for an education in writing DCL!

Schema Report

The schema report comprises a number of reports and provides useful information about the schema. It should not be confused with the actual SQL database file used to create the database. It begins with general information about the database such as buffer sizes, number of tables, indexes and views, then it details:

- Collating Sequences Summary

- Domain Summary – Each domain and its type

- Table Summary – Each table, its size, columns and keys

- Constraint Summary – Each by name

- Trigger Summary – By Name

- Grant Summary – Object and privileges granted

- Index Summary – Index by type, size and columns

- Area Summary – Includes type, page size, and allocation extents

- Disk Summary – Each disk, its size and files placed on it

- Area Mappings – Indicate indexes and tables in each area

- Cross Reference Summary – For each domain and table where it is used

Workload Report

The workload report is invaluable to the database designer because it lists for each table which requests are using it and for each table how it has been accessed. The later report can be compared to the actual indexes defined in the database for comparison. It usually makes interesting reading, spotting the differences.

16.2.6   Command Line Interface

If a workstation is not available, all the required information can be specified using the command line interface supplied with RdbExpert. The one disadvantage of working with this interface is that it is impossible to edit the design. To make any changes, the current values must be deleted before the new values can be created.

16.3   GRAPHICAL SCHEMA EDITOR

Defining an Rdb database using SQL can be a daunting task, especially if one is not familiar with SQL syntax or a design comprising many tables and columns has to be built. The Graphical Schema Editor tool is a GUI tool for designing and maintaining databases. It graphically displays each table and its columns as shown in Figure 16.8. A column with a primary key has the symbol of a key alongside it, such as ACCOUNT_NO in Figure 16.8. Likewise column BRANCH_CODE in table ACCOUNT has the symbol of a lock alongside, denoting a foreign key and the line between BRANCH and ACCOUNT shows the primary and foreign key relationship.

Hint: Using the Graphical Schema Editor to check for constraints is a fast way of checking if any are missing.

Figure 16.8 Graphical Schema Editor

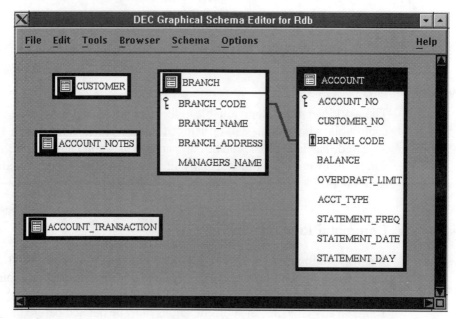

The Graphical Schema Editor can be used to define all the components in an SQL database definition. A validation process checks that the definition is consistent. Therefore, errors, such as a storage map referencing a storage area that does not exist, are highlighted immediately, rather than during the execution of the SQL statements. Using GSE to create the SQL to define the database means that it will complete in one pass, rather than the many that are normally required.

16.4   INSTANTSQL

There are still many application programmers who are not familiar with SQL or unable to write complex SQL queries. This is when tools like InstantSQL are invaluable. Using a GUI, the application programmer simply draws lines between boxes to define the joins, and clicks on columns to specify the predicates and a host of other options. At the touch of a button the SQL for the query is generated.

Figure 16.9 InstantSQL

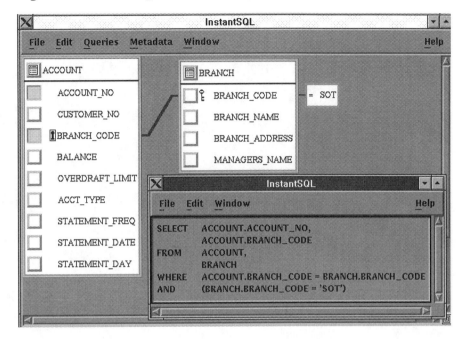

In Figure 16.9 the columns to be displayed are filled, that is ACCOUNT_NO and BRANCH_CODE. A line is joined between the tables BRANCH and ACCOUNT between column BRANCH_CODE. A predicate is defined on column BRANCH_CODE.

Another window is generated where the SQL for the query is displayed.

16.5 THE FREND FAMILY

The FrEnd family of tools are produced by the Information Systems Group Inc. of 605 North Courthouse Road, Richmond, Virginia 23236, USA, telephone: (804) 794-0354. There are a number of tools in the family but we have singled out three that should be of major interest to Rdb sites. These are:

- DBAnalyzer

- DBTune

- DBXact

Figure 16.10 A DBAnalyzer Display

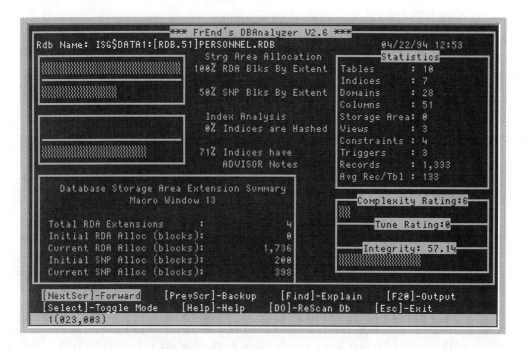

The tools are aimed at database administrators and designers, and although initially aimed at Rdb, they are also now available for other databases such as Oracle.

16.5.1   DBAnalyzer

The DBAnalyzer tool is designed such that a busy database administrator can spot trouble occurring in the database quickly. DBAnalyzer scans through a database and inspects various physical design attributes. The findings are synthesized and displayed in a graphical, easy to read format. A workstation is not necessary as DBAnalyzer can display its information graphically on a character cell VT terminal. Some of the useful information that is summarized includes storage area mappings, the indexes with the most duplicates and storage area extensions. Figure 16.10 shows a typical DBAnalyzer display.

Figure 16.11 A DBTune Display

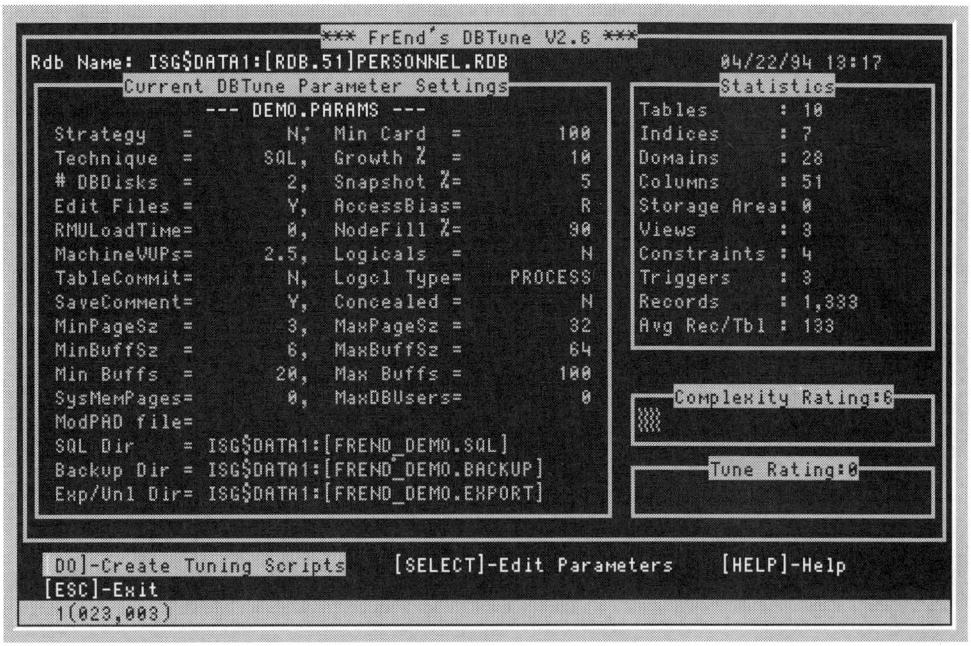

```
                    *** FrEnd's DBTune V2.6 ***
Rdb Name: ISG$DATA1:[RDB.51]PERSONNEL.RDB            04/22/94 13:17
           Current DBTune Parameter Settings            Statistics
                  --- DEMO.PARAMS ---           Tables     : 10
      Strategy    =       N,  Min Card  =     100 Indices    : 7
      Technique   =     SQL,  Growth %  =      10 Domains    : 28
      # DBDisks   =       2,  Snapshot %=       5 Columns    : 51
      Edit Files  =       Y,  AccessBias=       R Storage Area: 0
      RMULoadTime =       0,  NodeFill %=      90 Views      : 3
      MachineVUPs =     2.5,  Logicals  =       N Constraints: 4
      TableCommit =       N,  Logcl Type= PROCESS Triggers   : 3
      SaveComment =       Y,  Concealed =       N Records    : 1,333
      MinPageSz   =       3,  MaxPageSz =      32 Avg Rec/Tbl: 133
      MinBuffSz   =       6,  MaxBuffSz =      64
      Min Buffs   =      20,  Max Buffs =     100
      SysMemPages =       0,  MaxDBUsers=       0
      ModPAD file=                                 Complexity Rating:6
      SQL Dir     = ISG$DATA1:[FREND_DEMO.SQL]
      Backup Dir  = ISG$DATA1:[FREND_DEMO.BACKUP]      Tune Rating:0
      Exp/Unl Dir= ISG$DATA1:[FREND_DEMO.EXPORT]


  [DO]-Create Tuning Scripts    [SELECT]-Edit Parameters    [HELP]-Help
  [ESC]-Exit
  1(023,003)
```

16.5.2   DBTune

The DBTune tool is designed such that an existing Rdb physical design can be optimized. This often means changing a single-file Rdb database into a multifile one, although an existing multifile database will often benefit from DBTune. After scanning the database, an SQL procedure is automatically generated that uses either RMU/LOAD and RMU/UNLOAD or SQL IMPORT and EXPORT, depending on whether the source database is single file or not. Workload information can be collected via another member of the FrEnd family, described next, and this can be fed into DBTune to further enhance its tuning capabilities. Figure 16.11 shows a typical DBTune display.

Figure 16.12 A DBXact Display

```
FrEnd's DBXact Display    Database Trend Analysis           22-APR-1994
$1$DIA2:[GIS]GIS.RDB;1                                       09:40:42

           Item          Total       Trend     Cur.
RUJ Read IOs                  2        0.0         0
RUJ Write IOs                44        1.0         0
RUJ Extend IOs               13        1.0         0
AIJ File Read                30        1.0         0
AIJ File Write              286        2.0         0
AIJ Extend IOs                1        0.0         0
Root File Read IOs          228        0.0         0
Root File Write IOs        1440       10.0         3   ▒▒▒▒
Root File Extend IOs          0        0.0         0
All Files Read IOs         3025       44.0        33   ▒▒▒▒▒▒▒▒▒▒
All Files Write IOs        1608       22.0         0
All Files Extend IOs          2        0.0         0
Transactions                554        5.0         1   ▒▒▒
Pages Checked               540        5.0         0
Verb Successes            53203     1129.0▌       93

[Changes per Scan]

    Statistic    Display_Units    Change_Rate    Alarms_On    Modify_Basis
        Trend_Basis      Change_Rdb    Prev_Scr     Help            Exit
    1(019,046)
```

16.5.3   DBXact

The DBXact tool is designed to monitor all the active Rdb databases on a
system. A view of all the databases can be chosen or individual databases can
be observed. While holding trend information, DBXact inspects current activity information and can trigger alarms if anything out of the ordinary is
spotted. Specific resources can be selected and observed, such as root file
read I/Os, and as the data can be stored into a Rdb database, PC tools can
access and display the information via Microsoft ODBC if required. Figure
16.12 shows a typical DBXact display.

16.6   FOREST & TREES

The Trinzic Corporation's Forest & Trees is a multi-platform tool for accessing data and reporting against it. It uses an intuitive user interface running
under Microsoft Windows to access spreadsheets through to mainframe

Figure 16.13 A Forest & Trees View

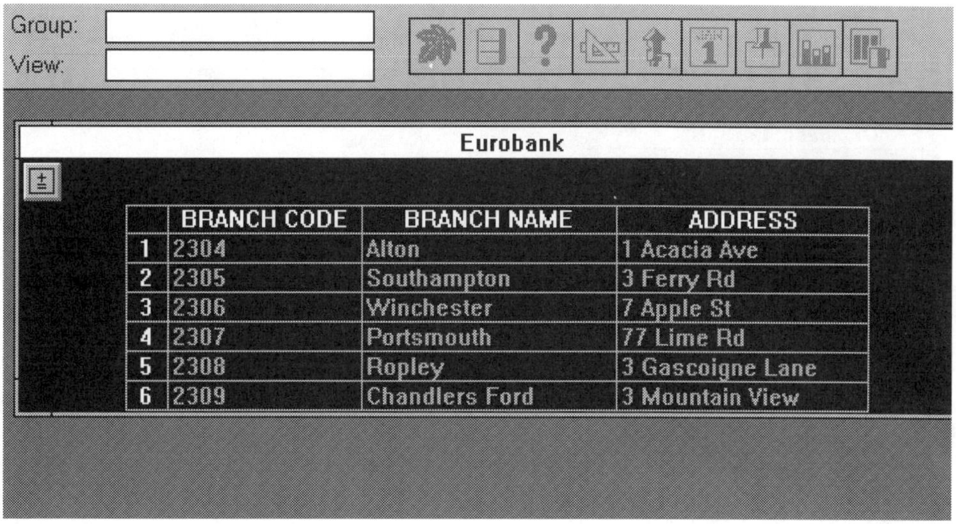

databases and combine the information where necessary. Its data sources can include Rdb where it can quickly and easily analyze Rdb data, graph it, report on it and integrate it with other information. A scheduler refreshes the data at user-defined intervals and any exceptions to predefined value ranges can trigger actions and alarms. Figure 16.13 shows a typical Forest & Trees view displaying some data from the BANKING database.

16.7   MICROSOFT ACCESS

Microsoft Access is an easy to use but powerful desktop database product. It can be used in a stand-alone mode, in which case a user can easily create tables, queries (similar to Rdb views in many respects), forms and reports. However, tables in external databases can be accessed via the Microsoft Access attach table option. The attach to external databases is achieved via Microsoft ODBC as described in Chapter 13. To access an Rdb database table, an ODBC data source is first created using the ODBC Administrator. This data source contains information such as the server name, the database location, the network protocol and the username. Once the data source has been created, it need not be created again. It can then be used as input to the attach table process which prompts for a data source name.

Figure 16.14 Creating a Microsoft Access Query

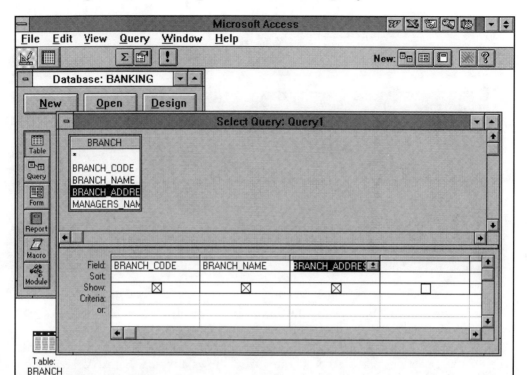

Assuming the server is accessible, the user will be prompted for a password and the Rdb database will be accessed. A list of tables and views will be displayed and the user can then select one to attach to Microsoft Access. This operation need not be performed again; a user merely has to treat the table as a local table, supplying their password as appropriate. This Rdb table can be joined with other tables or updated if the relevant permission has been granted. It can also be used in Microsoft Access queries, forms and reports. Figure 16.14 shows Microsoft Access windows that are being displayed while a user creates a query by choosing columns from the BRANCH table.

17 Application Programming

This chapter provides brief guidelines on how to write application programs to access an Rdb database. Application programs must be written in either RDO or SQL, and SQL was described in the Data Manipulation chapter. Now everyone writes programs in SQL, unless they have some legacy systems written in a proprietary language like RDO; therefore the only decision to make is whether to use:

- SQL precompilers
- SQL Module Language
- Dynamic SQL

The advantage of writing applications in SQL is that theoretically it makes applications more portable and easier to program. But it should be borne in mind that unless the application is written strictly to the SQL standard, it will not be portable if vendor specific extensions are included. Another consideration is that database engines do not all behave in the same fashion. Perhaps an application may run on one database engine, but when it is taken to another engine it fails due to, say, differences in the locking mechanism.

Including SQL statements in a programming language is a straightforward process; simply begin each statement with an EXEC SQL clause. Although writing application programs is not very difficult, there are a number of issues that must be considered, which include:

- Transactions
- Error handling
- Lock conflicts
- Manipulating streams of data
- Trapping end-of-stream conditions

A read/write transaction is automatically initiated if a transaction is not explicitly started. However, it is good programming practice to specify the start of the transaction with a SET TRANSACTION statement because then one can control when objects are locked and released.

Managing some of these conditions, such as error handling, requires writing a considerable amount of extra code. The amount depends on the sophistication of the error-trapping routines. In lock conflicts, for example, you should keep trying to solve the problem until the lock is released, or try x times, waiting y seconds between successive tries. A WHENEVER clause can be used to control actions when errors occur and from Version 5.1 three error-handling routines are available:

```
SQL_REGISTER_ERROR_HANDLER
SQL_GET_ERROR_HANDLER
SQL_DEREGISTER_ERROR_HANDLER
```

The name of the error-handling routine is registered using SQL_REGISTER _ERROR_HANDLER, but if a program needs to use more than one error-handling routine, then call the routine using SQL_GET_ERROR_HANDLER.

The following sections will include some COBOL program examples of how to use the data manipulation languages.

All programs also must include the SQL Communications Area (SQLCA), which contains various special parameters required by SQL. The programs also must always be linked with the library image SQL$USER.

Hint: Remember that if working in a multi-version environment, then the library to be included must include the version number, e.g., SQL$USER60 or SQL$USER51.

17.1   SQL PRECOMPILERS

The following is an example of a COBOL program that includes precompiled SQL. Note that each statement begins with EXEC SQL and ends with END_EXEC. The example shows how to specify the database statements SET TRANSACTION, INSERT and COMMIT. To transfer data from the program variables into the database, a working storage area is created with a structure that matches the database table. In the INSERT statement, a colon prefixing the working storage name is enough to transfer data from the application to the database.

Hint: On OpenVMS systems, using CDD/Repository to build the data definitions enables the same data definition to be used to build both the database table and the working storage record within the program. With this approach, everyone uses the same data definition.

On OpenVMS systems the procedure for precompiling is:

```
$ SQLPRE :== $SYS$SYSTEM:SQL$PRE   !Set up an OpenVMS symbol

$ SQLPRE/COBOL bank_enquiry

$ LINK bank_enquiry, SYS$LIBRARY:SQL$USER/LIB

$ RUN bank_enquiry

IDENTIFICATION DIVISION.
PROGRAM-ID. SQLPRE_example.
ENVIRONMENT DIVISION.
DATA DIVISION.
WORKING-STORAGE SECTION.

01 COLL-CODE-IND        PIC S9(4) USAGE IS COMP.

*      Define the SQLCA.
       EXEC SQL INCLUDE SQLCA END-EXEC.

*      Declare the database.
       EXEC SQL DECLARE ALIAS FILENAME 'BANKING' END-EXEC.
01 Branch_details.
   02 Branch_code          PIC X(4).
   02 Branch_name          PIC X(20).
   02 Branch_address       PIC X(120).
   02 Managers_name        PIC X(20).
```

```
01  data_base_key               PIC X(8).
01  dbhandle                    PIC S9(9)      COMP.
01  accept_data                 PIC X.
01  success_flag                PIC X.
    88 successful               VALUE 'Y'.
01  transaction_started_flag    PIC X.
    88 transaction_started      VALUE 'Y'.
01  retry_count                 PIC S9(4)      COMP VALUE 5.
01  lock_error_flag             PIC X.
    88 lock_error               VALUE 'Y'.
01  Continue_key                PIC X.

PROCEDURE DIVISION.

Add_branch.
* This procedure adds a new BRANCH record to the BRANCH relation

    DISPLAY SPACE LINE 1 COLUMN 1 ERASE TO END OF SCREEN
    DISPLAY "Add Branch " LINE 1 COLUMN 20
    DISPLAY "" LINE 2 COLUMN 1

* Prompt user for input.

    DISPLAY "Branch Code: "      NO ADVANCING
    ACCEPT Branch_code           PROTECTED  REVERSED
    DISPLAY "Branch Name: "      NO ADVANCING
    ACCEPT Branch_name
    DISPLAY "Branch Address: "   NO ADVANCING
    ACCEPT Branch_address
    DISPLAY "Managers name: "    NO ADVANCING
    ACCEPT Managers_name.
    DISPLAY " "
    DISPLAY "Accept Branch Code Y or N: "  NO ADVANCING
    ACCEPT accept_data.
    IF accept_data = "Y" THEN GO TO Store_branch ELSE
        GO TO Add_branch.
```

```
Store_branch.

EXEC SQL SET TRANSACTION READ WRITE RESERVING branch FOR
    SHARED WRITE
END_EXEC.

EXEC SQL   INSERT INTO branch   VALUES (:branch_details)
END_EXEC.

EXEC SQL   COMMIT

END_EXEC.

END PROGRAM SQLPRE_example.
```

17.2　SQL MODULE LANGUAGE

The SQL Module Language provides a modular approach to writing SQL statements. Instead of embedding the SQL statements in the application program, calls are made to the module language code, which is made up of a separately written, compiled, and linked module.

The major benefits of this approach are that standard modules, such as 'read branch record' or 'find all the transactions for an account', can be written and tested. These modules are used by all application programs, saving application development and testing time. This approach is especially beneficial if only a few application programmers are familiar with writing database access code. These knowledgeable people can write the database access modules, leaving the other programmers the easy task of calling these modules from their application programs. A sample SQL module to retrieve the balance on an account is shown in the following example:

```
—
— SQL Module to retrieve account balance
—

MODULE          find_balance_module
LANGUAGE        cobol
AUTHORIZATION   rdb$handle
PARAMETER       colons
```

```
— DECLARE statements
DECLARE ALIAS FILENAME BANKING

— Procedure section
PROCEDURE find_the_balance
  ( sqlcode
     :acct_no bigint,
    :bal bigint(2) );

SELECT balance INTO :bal FROM account WHERE account_no = :acct_no ;

PROCEDURE start_trans
  sqlcode;

  SET TRANSACTION READ ONLY;

PROCEDURE commit
  sqlcode;


  COMMIT;
```

The following example compiles the module:

```
SQLMOD:== $SYS$SYSTEM:SQL$MOD      !set up an OpenVMS symbol

SQLMOD find_bal.sqlmod
```

Once a module is compiled, it is called from the application program using the standard system calls. The program is compiled normally for that source language. When it is linked, the SQL Module Language object is included in the LINK statement. Shown below is the COBOL program which calls the SQL module.

```
IDENTIFICATION DIVISION.
PROGRAM-ID.                 balance_enquiry.
ENVIRONMENT DIVISION.
DATA DIVISION.
```

```
WORKING-STORAGE SECTION.
01 SQLCODE                    PIC S9(9) COMP.

01 dbhandle                   PIC S9(9) COMP.

01 account_details.
 02    account_number         PIC S9(9) COMP.
 02    current_balance        PIC S9(9)v99 COMP.

PROCEDURE DIVISION.

Input_data.

     DISPLAY "Account Number: " WITH NO ADVANCING
     ACCEPT account_number WITH CONVERSION.

account_enquiry.

     CALL "start_trans" USING SQLCODE.

     CALL "find_the_balance" USING SQLCODE, account_number,
         current_balance.

     CALL "commit" using sqlcode.
     DISPLAY "Current Balance is: ", current_balance
         WITH CONVERSION.


END PROGRAM BALANCE_ENQUIRY.
```

● Now compile the COBOL program and link the SQL module.

```
$ COBOL BALANCE_ENQUIRY.COB
$ LINK BALANCE_ENQUIRY, FIND_BAL, SYS$LIBRARY:SQL$USER/LIB

$ RUN BALANCE_ENQUIRY
Account Number:     9561490
Current Balance is:    56.76
```

17.3   DYNAMIC SQL

Dynamic SQL is an API that allows a program to access an Rdb database
without first precompiling the statements. This API is appropriate when the
statements used to access the database are unknown until query-execution
time. For this reason, the Dynamic SQL interface is used in products such as
SQL/Services, where the calls are unknown at the outset. Since there is no
precompilation, the execution time of statements using the Dynamic SQL interface will be slightly longer.

Dynamic SQL statements are embedded in a program using some special statements that tell the precompiler that this is dynamic SQL. The non-dynamic
statements are PREPARE, DESCRIBE, EXECUTE, EXECUTE IMMEDIATE,
DECLARE CURSOR, OPEN, FETCH, and RELEASE. The SELECT statement cannot be specified directly; it must be issued from within a cursor.

In the following example, the EXECUTE IMMEDIATE statement is used to
take and immediately execute a command. A small sample of error handling
code also is included.

```
IDENTIFICATION DIVISION.
PROGRAM-ID.               Dynamic_SQL.
ENVIRONMENT DIVISION.
DATA DIVISION.
WORKING-STORAGE SECTION.

01 COLL-CODE-IND          PIC S9(4) USAGE IS COMP.
01 COMMAND_STRING         PIC X(240).
01 BUFFER                 PIC X(300).
01 LEN                    PIC S9(4) USAGE IS COMP.

*    Define the SQLCA
     EXEC SQL INCLUDE SQLCA END-EXEC.

*    Declare the database
     EXEC SQL DECLARE ALIAS FILENAME 'BANKING' END-EXEC.

01 data_base_key          PIC X(8).
01 dbhandle               PIC S9(9)    COMP.
```

```
PROCEDURE DIVISION.
Enter_statement.

    DISPLAY "Enter an SQL statement".
    ACCEPT COMMAND_STRING.

EXEC SQL       EXECUTE IMMEDIATE :COMMAND_STRING
END-EXEC.

    PERFORM CHECK_FOR_ERROR.

EXEC SQL       EXECUTE IMMEDIATE 'ROLLBACK'
END_EXEC.

END_OF_PROGRAM.
    STOP RUN.

CHECK_FOR_ERROR.

    IF SQLCODE NOT = 100 AND SQLCODE NOT = 0
      DISPLAY "SQL Code Error: "SQLCODE WITH CONVERSION
      CALL "SQL$GET_ERROR_TEXT" USING
        BY DESCRIPTOR BUFFER,
        BY REFERENCE LEN
      DISPLAY BUFFER(1:LEN)
    END-IF.

END PROGRAM Dynamic_sql.
```

Once the statements have been included, the program is compiled and linked as if it were any other SQL application program, as the following example shows:

```
$ SQLPRE :== $SYS$SYSTEM:SQL$PRE    !Set up a OpenVMS symbol

$ SQLPRE/COBOL Dynamic_sql.RCO

$ LINK Dynamic_sql,SYS$LIBRARY:SQL$USER/LIB

$ RUN Dynamic_sql
```

17.4   2-PHASE COMMIT PROTOCOLS

On OpenVMS systems, DECdtm system service calls may be embedded in a program to coordinate and guarantee updates to multiple databases or resource managers using 2-Phase Commit Protocols. It is not necessary to embed any of the DECdtm system service calls unless the program has to manage different resource managers together, namely Rdb and RMS.

If it is necessary to embed the DECdtm system calls, changes must be made to the application program. The programmer must do the following:

• Declare variables required by DECdtm system services

• Declare the context structure for SQL

• Include the DECdtm system service calls

• Add a USING CONTEXT clause to all SQL statements

• Remove the COMMIT and ROLLBACK statements and replace them with the DECdtm system service calls

A sample SQL program that includes the DECdtm system service calls follows. The underlined words indicate the changes required to use DECdtm.

```
IDENTIFICATION DIVISION.
PROGRAM-ID. SQLPRE_DIST_EXAMPLE.
ENVIRONMENT DIVISION.
DATA DIVISION.
WORKING-STORAGE SECTION.
*
* Declare the variables needed for the DECdtm system services.
*
    01 SS$_NORMAL     PIC S9(9) COMP VALUE EXTERNAL SS$_NORMAL.
    01 SS$_SYNCH      PIC S9(9) COMP VALUE EXTERNAL SS$_SYNCH.
    01 DDTM$M_SYNC    PIC 9(9) COMP VALUE 1.
    01 IOSB.
      05 COND-VAL     PIC 9(4) COMP.
      05 BYTE-CNT     PIC 9(4) COMP.
      05 DEV-INFO     PIC 9(9) COMP.
    01 RET-STATUS     PIC S9(9) COMP.
```

```
*
* Declare the context structure for passing to SQL.
*
  01 CONTEXT.
     05 CONTEXT-VERSION    PIC 9(9) COMP.
     05 CONTEXT-TYPE       PIC 9(9) COMP.
     05 CONTEXT-LENGTH     PIC 9(9) COMP.
     05 CONTEXT-TID.
        10 LOW_DATE        PIC 9(9) COMP.
        10 HIGH_DATE       PIC 9(9) COMP.
        10 DATE_INCARN     PIC 9(4) COMP.
        10 NODE_ID         PIC 9(4) COMP.
        10 NODE_IDH        PIC 9(9) COMP.
     05 CONTEXT-END        PIC 9(9) COMP.

  01 COLL-CODE-IND         PIC S9(4) USAGE IS COMP.

*    Define the SQLCA

     EXEC SQL INCLUDE SQLCA END-EXEC.

*    Declare the database
     EXEC SQL DECLARE DB1 ALIAS FILENAME 'bank1' END-EXEC.
     EXEC SQL DECLARE DB2 ALIAS FILENAME 'bank2' END-EXEC.


  01 branch_details.
     02 branch_code        PIC X(4).
     02 branch_name        PIC X(20).
     02 branch_address     PIC X(120).
     02 managers_name      PIC X(20).

  01 data_base_key         PIC X(8).
  01 dbhandle              PIC S9(9)    COMP.
  01 accept_data           PIC X.
  01 success_flag          PIC X.
     88 successful         VALUE "Y".
```

```
01   transaction_started_flag   PIC X.
     88 transaction_started      VALUE 'Y'.
01   retry_count                PIC S9(4)     COMP VALUE 5.
01   lock_error_flag            PIC X.
     88 lock_error              VALUE 'Y'.
01   Continue_key               PIC X.

PROCEDURE DIVISION.

Setup_variables.
* Initialize the context structure.

     MOVE 1 TO CONTEXT-VERSION.
     MOVE 1 TO CONTEXT-TYPE.
     MOVE 16 TO CONTEXT-LENGTH.
     MOVE ZERO TO CONTEXT-END.
*
* Invoke the SYS$START_TRANSW system service and check the
status.
*
     DISPLAY "Starting distributed transaction".
     CALL "SYS$START_TRANSW" USING OMITTED, BY VALUE DDTM$M_SYNC,
                BY REFERENCE IOSB, OMITTED, OMITTED,
                BY REFERENCE CONTEXT-TID
            GIVING RET-STATUS.

     IF RET-STATUS NOT EQUAL SS$_SYNCH THEN
        CALL "LIB$STOP" USING BY VALUE RET-STATUS.

Add_branch.

* This procedure adds a new BRANCH record to the BRANCH relation
     DISPLAY SPACE LINE 1 COLUMN 1 ERASE TO END OF SCREEN
     DISPLAY "Add Branch " LINE 1 COLUMN 20
     DISPLAY "" LINE 2 COLUMN 1
```

```
*  Prompt user for input.

   DISPLAY "Branch Code: " NO ADVANCING
   ACCEPT branch_code PROTECTED REVERSED
   DISPLAY "Branch Name: " NO ADVANCING
   ACCEPT branch_name
   DISPLAY "Branch Address: " NO ADVANCING
   ACCEPT branch_address
   DISPLAY "Managers name: "NO ADVANCING
   ACCEPT managers_name.
   DISPLAY " "
   DISPLAY "Accept Branch Code Y or N: " NO ADVANCING
   ACCEPT accept_data.

   IF accept_data = "Y" THEN GO TO Store_branch ELSE
      GO TO Add_branch.

Store_branch.


EXEC SQL USING CONTEXT :context
         SET TRANSACTION
            read write RESERVING db1.branch FOR SHARED WRITE ,
                     db2.branch FOR SHARED WRITE
END_EXEC.

EXEC SQL USING CONTEXT :CONTEXT
         INSERT INTO DB1.Branch
         VALUES (:branch_details)

END_EXEC.

      IF SQLCODE NOT = 1 THEN
       CALL "SQL$SIGNAL"
      END-IF.
```

```
EXEC SQL USING CONTEXT :CONTEXT
        INSERT INTO DB2.Branch
        VALUES (:branch_details)

END_EXEC.

    IF SQLCODE NOT = 1 THEN
     CALL "SQL$SIGNAL"
    END-IF.
* Invoke the SYS$END_TRANSW system service to end
*   the distributed transaction.

DISPLAY "Ending distributed transaction".
CALL "SYS$END_TRANSW" USING OMITTED, OMITTED, BY REFERENCE IOSB,
         OMITTED, OMITTED, BY REFERENCE CONTEXT-TID
           GIVING RET-STATUS.

* Check the return status of the call.

   IF RET-STATUS EQUAL SS$_NORMAL THEN
     IF COND-VAL OF IOSB NOT EQUAL SS$_NORMAL THEN
        DISPLAY "Error......."
        CALL "LIB$STOP" USING BY VALUE COND-VAL OF IOSB
     END-IF
   ELSE
     CALL "LIB$STOP" USING BY VALUE RET-STATUS.
   EXIT PROGRAM.

END PROGRAM SQLPRE_DIST_EXAMPLE.
```

The examples shown here just skim the surface of what can be done within an SQL application. One could easily devote a whole book to writing programs, in fact the Rdb documentation bears testament to that.

18   Multimedia Databases

There was a time when the only thing that people wanted to store in a database was textual or numerical data but that is now changing. Increasing today people are demanding information that contains pictures, sounds and full-motion video. PC users at home already have the capability to retrieve all this data, now they are beginning to see the potential for exploiting this technology in the workplace. Everyone is talking about gaining access to the Information Superhighway, the place where all types of information is exchanged and obtained, irrespective of its source and datatype. New technology makes it feasible but what role does the relational database play in turning this dream into a reality?

In the beginning, if a database contained pictures then they were usually stored in a file system outside of the database. This method, while satisfactory, caused a number of problems. For instance, it was difficult to guarantee data integrity between the picture and the text. The text could be deleted, but the picture would still exist. Suppose changes were made to the pictures; then since this was done outside of the database it was unlikely that any auditing or security control occurred. When backups of the data were taken, one had to remember to backup picture files and the database.

To overcome these and many other issues, the requirement is to store objects like pictures in the database. During this chapter we will concentrate on the picture object, but remember that multimedia is more than pictures. The techniques discussed here apply equally to sounds, motion video or any other form of unstructured data.

To qualify as a multimedia database then it must support not only magnetic disks, but also tertiary storage, such as optical and tape. When we talk about the types of data likely to be seen inside a multimedia database then we mean:

- Audio

- Characters

- Fax

- Graphics

- Image

- Telephone

- Text

- Video

The old addage a picture can say a thousand words is literally true. Slowly over the last few years Rdb has been evolving to support the multimedia explosion. Today it offers basic functionality but this is one area where we will be seeing definite expansion in the future.

18.1   BLOBS

Multimedia evolves around storing and manipulating unstructured datatypes, usually called BLOBS (binary large object). Since V1.0 Rdb has been able to read and write BLOBS and these are known as the datatype list of byte varying. Using our BANKING example, suppose the bank wanted to keep a photograph of each of its customers for the purpose of security and inclusion on credit cards. Two solutions to this problem are:

- Include the new column as part of the CUSTOMER table.

- Create a new table which includes the photographs for each CUSTOMER.

Both of these solutions are perfectly valid. We will include the new column CUSTOMER_PHOTO as part of the CUSTOMER table.

```
SQL> ALTER TABLE customer
cont>  ADD COLUMN customer_photo LIST OF BYTE VARYING (32000);
```

```
SQL> SHOW TABLE (col) customer
Information for table CUSTOMER

Columns for table CUSTOMER:
Column Name          Data Type          Domain
-----------          ---------          ------

CUSTOMER_NO          CHAR(10)
SURNAME              CHAR(20)           STANDARD_NAME
FIRST_NAME           CHAR(20)           STANDARD_NAME
ADDRESS_LINE1        CHAR(30)
ADDRESS_LINE2        CHAR(30)
ADDRESS_LINE3        CHAR(30)
ADDRESS_LINE4        CHAR(30)
POSTCODE             CHAR(10)
CREDIT_LIMIT         BIGINT(2)
STATUS               INTEGER
CUSTOMER_PHOTO       VARBYTE LIST
                     Segment Length: 32000
```

Although the BLOB column is defined as part of the table definition, when the information is stored, it is placed separate from the row. The row contains only a pointer to the actual BLOB. Using this approach, although extra I/O is required to retrieve the BLOB, this disadvantage is out weighed by the adverse affect it would have if it was stored with the data. It would generate huge row sizes which would cause the row to fragment. By taking so much space, rows would not hash to their target pages.

The placement of the BLOBS is achieved through the LISTS STORAGE MAP. Unlike tables which have their own storage map, there is one storage map for all BLOBS where you specify in which area they are to be stored. The options available are:

- All BLOBS in these areas

- All BLOBS for this table in these areas

- All BLOBS for this column in a table in these areas

A typical list storage map would be as follows:

```
SQL> CREATE STORAGE MAP blob_map
cont> STORE LISTS IN  photo_area
cont> FOR (customer.customer_photo) ;
```

Traditional magnetic media is often unsuitable for storing large amounts of unstructured data. A popular alternative is to use WORM (write once read many) optical disks and Rdb supports some third-party optical disks. Denoting a WORM device is achieved by using the WRITE ONCE clause in the storage area definition.

```
ADD STORAGE AREA photo_area
    FILENAME eurobank:[pictures]photo_area
    ALLOCATION IS 25000 PAGES
    PAGE SIZE IS 8
    WRITE ONCE;
```

When the storage area is created, it is defined as a WRITE ONCE device, which tells Rdb to not create SPAM pages in this storage area. Then on the storage map definition, specifying the FILL SEQUENTIAL option causes the device to fill up sequentially rather than randomly as per normal magnetic media.

Manipulating BLOBS is not an easy task; in SQL they are managed through list cursors. There are two types of list cursors:

- Read-only (default)

- Insert

A BLOB may only be inserted or deleted. Modification is achieved by deleting and then reinserting. Below is an example of how to insert a BLOB into an Rdb database using SQL. The steps involved are to set up two cursors, one for the rows in the table and the other for the BLOB. Create a link between the table cursor which inserts the row, and the list cursor which inserts the BLOB. Then insert the row and the BLOB. Note that in the example here we have just inserted some text, but in an application this would have been our photo. Finally commit the data and close the cursors.

```
SQL> DECLARE insert_cust INSERT ONLY TABLE CURSOR FOR
cont> SELECT customer_no, surname, first_name, customer_photo
cont>  FROM customer;
SQL> DECLARE insert_pict INSERT ONLY LIST CURSOR FOR
cont> SELECT customer_photo WHERE CURRENT OF insert_cust;

SQL> OPEN insert_cust;
SQL> INSERT INTO CURSOR insert_cust
cont> (customer_no, surname, first_name) VALUES
cont>  ( '15645789','Hagan','Steve');
1 row inserted

SQL> OPEN insert_pict;
SQL> INSERT INTO CURSOR insert_pict VALUES ('Picture to go here' );
SQL>
SQL> COMMIT
SQL>
SQL> CLOSE insert_pict;
SQL> CLOSE insert_cust;
```

As can be seen from the example, including all this code in an application is not a trivial task. A simpler mechanism is required to manage BLOBS. This is provided by SQL Multimedia which is a 3GL library supplied with Rdb. There are only a few calls in the API, but it takes all the hard work out of using them. Using the API, only two steps are required, one to insert the row data and the other the BLOB.

```
EXEC SQL ATTACH 'FILENAME banking';

EXEC SQL INSERT INTO customer
 (CUSTOMER_NO, SURNAME, FIRST_NAME, ADDRESS_LINE1, ADDRESS_LINE2,
   ADDRESS_LINE3 , ADDRESS_LINE4 , POSTCODE ,
   CREDIT_LIMIT , STATUS )
   VALUES ('156235', 'Hobbs', 'Lilian', '10 New Farm Lane',
          'Alton', 'Hampshire', ' ', '', 5000, 1);
```

```
status = SQLMM$SQL_INSERT (     src_object_desc,
                          'IMAGE' , /* Object class */
                          'DDIF',    /* Object format */
                          [transaction_context] ,
                          'CUSTOMER', /* Table */
                          [object_key_column_names] ,
                          [object_key_values],
                          'CUSTOMER_PHOTO', /*Object Column Name */
                          [object_processing_options],
                          [addr_buffer_put_in],
                          [buffer_put_param],
                          [first_buffer_address],
                          [first_buffer_length] ) ;
```

If neither of these approaches are desirable then an alternative and increasingly popular method for building multimedia applications is to use a PC tool such as Microsoft Access to load and read BLOB data from an Rdb database. The complete environment can be built on the PC and normally an application can be written without the need for the user to specifically call any SQL or SQL Multimedia, because this already been included in the API used by the tools to communicate with Rdb.

For example, an Rdb database is created in SQL which includes a definition for a BLOB. Within Microsoft Access an attachment is made to this database and an environment created that includes a form to display and insert data. Via this form, pictures can be inserted and retrieved from the database without any code being written. For many users this will undoubtedly be the preferred method to develop applications.

Figure 18.1 shows one of the authors in an Rdb Multimedia application built around Microsoft Access.

This chapter is short because using Rdb to create a multimedia database is very straightforward. If you are concerned about using SQL list cursors or SQLMultimedia API then use a PC to read and insert the data. This is the authors' favorite method.

Figure 18.1 Microsoft Access Retrieving Rdb Multimedia Pictures

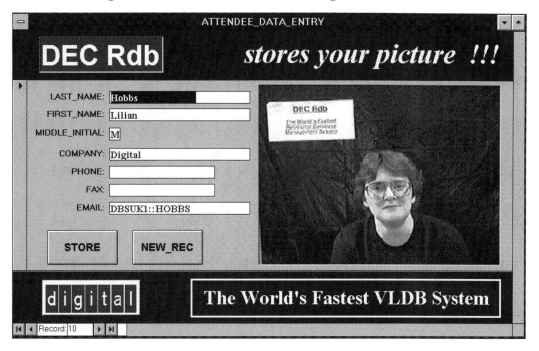

19 Rdb on OSF/1

1994 was a momentous year for Rdb, 10 years old and now released onto an operating system other than OpenVMS. This heralds a new beginning for Rdb, because it was always perceived as a product that could run on OpenVMS only. Now it is being launched onto other platforms, the first, OSF/1 and the Windows NT for Alpha.

The purpose of this chapter is to highlight the differences when Rdb is run on a platform other than OpenVMS. These differences occur due to the operation system environment, such as file specifications and functionality that may not be available.

19.1   OSF/1 DIFFERENCES

Rdb OpenVMS users should not be concerned about using the OSF/1 version. It's like coming home to a house you almost know. The hardest aspect is learning the OSF/1 commands!

As one can see from the list below, there are only a few features that are not available in this version.

19.1.1   Functionality not Available on OSF/1 V6.1

- Bound volume set
- CDD/Repository integration
- Cluster support
- Collating sequences for internationalization
- RMU commands, ALTER, AUDIT, CONVERT and tape libraries

- 2PC support
- Partitioned lock trees

19.1.2   Key Differences with OpenVMS

The reader familiar with Rdb on OpenVMS will notice the primary differences are in the following areas:

- Configuration files
- Different naming convention for databases
- Logical names now called environment variables
- Operation system specific file specifications
- Syntax differences
- SQL/Services architecture
- The dbsmgr account

19.1.3   Client/Server

Rdb on OSF/1 runs as a typical client/server application which is a major difference from the OpenVMS version. In the OpenVMS version the user's applications connects directly to the database, as illustrated in Figure 19.1.

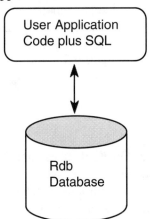

Figure 19.1   A Typical OpenVMS Application

Figure 19.2   The OSF/1 Architecture

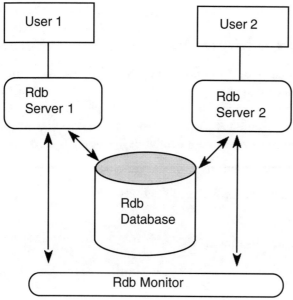

On an OSF/1 system the environment is different as illustrated in Figure 19.2. A client application contains the SQL code which then attaches to a database server process. In V6.1 the server is single threaded; that is, one client is serviced by one server. However, this is very likely to change in a future version. This server is a separate process on the machine and runs under the username *dbsmgr*. Only these servers are allowed to attach to a database and it is their responsibility to communicate with the Rdb monitor and to coordinate all shared database access and recovery in the event of a failure.

19.1.4   Processes

There are more processes involved in an OSF/1 database application. The Rdb monitor and AIJ processes still exist, but now because of the client/server architecture, for each user process there is an additional database server process. All of these processes runs under the *dbsmgr* user ID.

19.1.5 dbsmgr Account

All OSF/1 systems must have a dbsmgr account, which is from where the monitor must be started and stopped. When a database is created then it is owned by the dbsmgr account, but it is still acessible by users granted access rights. The server process is run under dbsmgr, which is the reason behind the files being owned by it.

Hint: Don't forget the password for dbsmgr because you will use it frequently and do remember to tell everyone if you change it.

19.1.6 Logicals Are Now Environment Variables

One of the powerful features in the OpenVMS version of Rdb is the ability to tune the database and enable/disable feature using logicals. This feature is still available on OSF/1 by using environment variables which are held in configuration files. The values specified are identical to those in OpenVMS but the names have changed to RDB, as described in Appendix B.

Hint: Environment variables cannot be defined manually.

19.1.7 Configuration Files

Defining a configuration file is a new concept for Rdb users. Its purpose is to describe the environment. There are two types of configuration files, system and users. The system configuration files are:

```
dbengine.conf     (Rdb client)
rdb.conf          (Rdb servers)
rdblck.conf       (Lock Manager)
sql.conf          (Client and SQL Applications)
```

For the majority of Rdb systems it is unlikely that these will require modification.

The user configuration file is called *.dbsrc* and a typical one is shown below where the buffers are set to 100, the debug flags are set to S and E and the default database is BANKING. Only environment variables defined here will be used by Rdb.

```
RDB_BIND_BUFFERS     100
RDB_DEBUG_FLAGS      SE
SQL_DATABASE         /eurobank/uk/db/banking.rdb
```

19.1.8   Database Files

On an OSF/1 system any number of Rdb databases can be created, which is different from some other OSF/1 database systems. Anyone can create the database, provided they have the appropriate file system privileges to create the files.

An OSF/1 Rdb database comprises .RDB, .RDA and .SNP files like its OpenVMS counterpart but the structure is slightly different. In OSF/1, if you wanted to create the database at */eurobank/uk/db* and the storage areas, the SQL to achieve this would be:

```
SQL> CREATE DATABASE FILENAME
cont>    /eurobank/uk/db/banking.rdb
cont> CREATE STORAGE AREA  customer_area
cont>     FILENAME /eurobank/uk/dbfiles/customer_area
cont>  ......
cont> ;
```

The syntax shown in the Data Manipulation chapter can be used on OSF/1. In the example above the database is formed by creating a directory called *banking.rdb* and in this directory is located the root file which is called *rdb_system*. The .RDA and .SNP files will be located in this directory unless you specify otherwise, which in this example is in the *eurobank/uk/dbfiles/* directory.

When a database is created, all the files are owned by the dbsmgr account, as shown below. It is very important that the file protections are not changed because otherwise the database servers will be unable to access the database.

```
# ls -l /eurobank/uk/db

/eurobank.rdb
total 57
-rwxr-r-  1 dbsmgr  system         0  Oct 12 16:57 rdb.protect
-rwxr-r-  1 dbsmgr  system     58368  Oct 22 00:42 rdb_system.rdb

#ls -l  /eurobank/uk/dbfiles/*.rda
-rwxr-r-  1 dbsmgr  system    417792  Oct 12 16:57 bank_acct.rda
-rwxr-r-  1 dbsmgr  system   2900992  Oct 12 16:57 bank_cust.rda
-rwxr-r-  1 dbsmgr  system   3193856  Oct 18 14:21 bank_system.rda
-rwxr-r-  1 dbsmgr  system    515072  Oct 12 16:57 bank_trans.rda
-rwxr-r-  1 dbsmgr  system    411648  Oct 12 16:57 customer_pics.rda
```

To delete a database, the same rules applies as for OpenVMS systems; use the SQL statement DELETE DATABASE and not the rm command in OSF/1.

The only place where databases cannot be created is on NFS mounted devices.

19.1.9   RMU Utility

The RMU utility is a little different on OSF/1. Like OpenVMS the GUI version is available, but in addition there is a command line prompt facility. By specifying the RMU command an RMU prompt is obtained. At this prompt you can execute RMU commands and overflow onto continuation lines. It is invoked using lowercase *rmu*.

Using the standard command interface, all RMU commands are prefixed with a minus sign (-), e.g.,

```
rmu -dump -header  -output=
rmu -backup -log /eurobank/uk/db/banking.rdb /eurobank/
    backups/bank_0111
```

If you use the RMU prompt, you would not have to enter the minus sign (-) for the first command, e.g.,

```
rmu> dump -header   -output=
rmu> backup -log /eurobank/uk/db/banking.rdb /eurobank/
     backups/bank_0111
```

All the RMU commands except ALTER, AUDIT and CONVERT are available and they function as described in previous chapters and the output is identical. Therefore, will quickly feel at home with RMU if you used it on OpenVMS.

The RMU GUI is invoked by specifying *RMUwin*. It then behaves exactly as per the OpenVMS version and RMU SHOW STATISTICS is only available on the GUI version.

19.1.10   SQL

Using SQL on OSF/1 is almost identical to SQL on OpenVMS. The syntax is the same, so the only differences are due to the operating system. Therefore all the examples shown in Chapter 3 can be tried on an OSF/1 system.

Let's look at the example below where we attach to a database:

To invoke SQL enter *sql* in lowercase and obtain an SQL> prompt. If SQL_DATABASE has been defined in the .dbsrc configuration file, then the user will automatically be attached, otherwise:

```
SQL> ATTACH 'FILENAME   /eurobank/uk/db/banking' ;
```

Once attached all commands are the same as for OpenVMS:

```
SQL>SHOW TABLES
User tables in database with filename   /eurobank/uk/db/banking
      ACCOUNT
      BRANCH
      CUSTOMER
      TRANSACTIONS
SQL> SHOW DATABASE
Default alias:
      Rdb database in file   /eurobank/uk/db/banking
```

Therefore all the features in SQL that you are used to using on OpenVMS are available, such as functions, invoking external command files and command line recall. The only feature not implemented is the ability to edit previous commands. Therefore the authors recommend that commands are placed in files and invoked from within SQL.

19.1.11   Naming Conventions

OSF/1 is a case sensitive language; therefore objects must be referenced exactly as they are described. Therefore if a storage area is named using lowercase letters, it is physically created as described. However SQL parses all names to uppercase.

Hint: The SQL parser always converts to uppercase; therefore in utilities like rmu -load, the table name must be specified in uppercase.

The example below illustrates a sample RMU command:

```
rmu -load banking BRANCH branch.dat
```

19.1.12   File Versions

Often it is necessary to create multiple versions of a file, such as a bugcheck dump, but this is not standard on OSF/1. To achieve multiple versions, the version number is appended to the filename. Therefore a bugcheck dump would be named as

```
rdmbugchk.dmp.1
```

Therefore when searching for files, don't forget the version number, otherwise OSF/1 will state that none of these files exist.

19.1.13   Lock Manager

The lock manager is different under OSF/1, but this is transparent to the Rdb user. The monitor creates lock tables which are held in shared memory. There is only one set of these tables and they contain lock information for all the OSF/1 Rdb databases on the system. The locking mechanisms employed by Rdb are unchanged in the OSF/1 version. Therefore users will still encounter area, page and record locks, which can be monitored through the screens in RMU SHOW STATISTICS.

19.1.14   **Security**

Working in this client/server environment, authentication of the user is different. The first time the client attaches to the server, the server identifies who the user is, or the client explicitly states who they are when they attach to the database, by specifying the username and password in the dbsrc configuration file or as part of the ATTACH statement as illustrated below.

```
SQL> attach 'filename /eurobank/uk/db/banking.rdb -
cont> USER ''lmhobbs'' USING ''Itsasecret'' ';
```

In the above example a valid username and password was specified. If it is invalid then the user is denied access to the database as shown below.

```
SQL> attach 'filename /eurobank/uk/db/banking.rdb -
cont> USER ''larry'' USING ''ResistanceisFutile'' ';


%SQL-F-ERRATTDEC, Error attaching to database
    /eurobank/uk/db/banking.rdb
-RDB-E-NO_PRIV, privilege denied by database facility
-COSI-F-NOPRIV, no privilege for attempted operation
```

Below is an example of specifying in the .dbsrc file:

```
SQL_USERNAME   lmhobbs
SQL_PASSWD     itsasecret
```

If you do not wish to comprise security by writing the password in a configuration file, you can request it be input on the SQL attach by declaring the variable *:passwrd*.

```
 SQL> ATTACH 'FILENAME banking USER ''hobbs'' USING :passwrd ;
```

The X/Open standard defines that the username and password can be specified as part of the CONNECT statement.

Alternatively, if the user does not state who they are, the server finds out the user ID of the client.

In Chapter 8 we discussed securing the database on OpenVMS and the techniques described there apply to OSF/1 systems. Identifiers are specified on OSF/1 systems using the group and username.

In the example below we can see that user *larry* has all access rights except ALTER and DROP:

```
SQL> SHOW PROTECTION ON DATABASE   rdb$dbhandle
Protection on Alias RDB$DBHANDLE
   (IDENTIFIER=[users,larry],ACCESS=SELECT+INSERT+UPDATE+DELETE+SHOW+CREATE+
      DBCTRL+OPERATOR+DBADM+SECURITY+DISTRIBTRAN)
   (IDENTIFIER=[system,lmhobbs],ACCESS=SELECT+INSERT+UPDATE+DELETE+SHOW+CREATE+
      ALTER+DROP+DBCTRL+OPERATOR+DBADM+SECURITY+DISTRIBTRAN)
   (IDENTIFIER=[*,*],ACCESS=NONE)
```

The following grants user *hagan* access to this system. Note that entries are always added at the beginning, but just as with OpenVMS, they can be positioned anywhere in the list using the POSITION clause.

```
SQL> GRANT all ON DATABASE ALIAS rdb$dbhandle TO [hagan];

SQL> SHOW PROTECTION ON DATABASE   rdb$dbhandle
Protection on Alias RDB$DBHANDLE
   (IDENTIFIER=[users,hagan],ACCESS=SELECT+INSERT+UPDATE+DELETE+SHOW+CREATE+
      ALTER+DROP+DBCTRL+OPERATOR+DBADM+SECURITY+DISTRIBTRAN)
   (IDENTIFIER=[users,larry],ACCESS=SELECT+INSERT+UPDATE+DELETE+SHOW+CREATE+
      DBCTRL+OPERATOR+DBADM+SECURITY+DISTRIBTRAN)
   (IDENTIFIER=[system,lmhobbs],ACCESS=SELECT+INSERT+UPDATE+DELETE+SHOW+CREATE+
      ALTER+DROP+DBCTRL+OPERATOR+DBADM+SECURITY+DISTRIBTRAN)
   (IDENTIFIER=[*,*],ACCESS=NONE)
```

19.1.15 SQL/SERVICES

The SQL/Services component of Rdb has been completely changed for the OSF/1 version and will be released into future versions of Rdb on OpenVMS. This change has occured because with the ever increasing number of client/ server applications being developed, an efficient, fast access mechanism is required.

The new SQL/Services architecture is illustrated in Figure 19.3.

Figure 19.3 OSF/1 SQL/Services Architecture

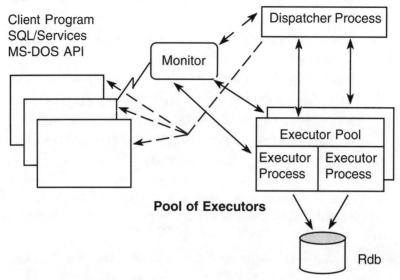

SQL/Services has a *monitor* process which is responsible for starting and stopping servers, managing the configuration database and various other system management functions.

The *dispatcher* is responsible for routing and scheduling the client requests to the executors.

The *executor* receives the client requests from the dispatcher, accesses the database and returns the results of these requests to the dispatcher.

To create this environment there is a configuration file called SQS_CREATE.SQS. Here is where we describe which server to connect to, how to create the dispatcher, which services are to be provided and the executors to provide for each service.

Services (defined using CREATE SERVICE) can be described as generic or for a particular database. A generic service is described as being *session re-usable* which means that every associate call from a client will create a new process. Database class services may be either session or transaction re-usable. The advantage of a using a transaction re-usable service is that multiple clients can share the same executor, but the executor can only execute one transaction at a time. Therefore if the executor receives too many requests, other users will be stalled in a queue waiting to be served. Therefore to reduce the queue, you will have to create more executors for this service.

Once a configuration has been defined, its details are permanently recorded. Therefore every time the monitor and the server is started, the same environment is created. A sample startup procedure is held in the file SQL_STARTUP.SQS.

Hint: The default server creates a shared memory file of 2 Mb. If many users are attaching through SQL/Services, this will not be adequate. Therefore specify a large memory size on the CREATE SERVER command.

SQL/Services now has its own management utility in the form of SQL_MANAGE. From its own command line interface, the commands shown below are available.

Table 19.1   SQS_MANAGE Commands

ALTER EXECUTORS FOR SERVICE	Change executors for a service
ALTER SERVER	Change server parameters
CONNECT TO SERVER	Connect to a specific server
CREATE DISPATCHER	Create dispatcher for current server
CREATE EXECUTORS FOR SERVICE	Create an executor for a service
CREATE SERVER	Create a server
CREATE SERVICE	Create a service
DISCONNECT SERVER	Disconnect a server
DROP	Drop an executor, dispatcher, server or service
GRANT USE ON SERVICE	Grant a user access to a service
REVOKE USE ON SERVICE	Revoke a user's right to use a service
SET CONFIG_FILE	Specify a different configuration file
SET SERVER	Set to a server to be the current one
SHOW CLIENTS FOR SERVICE	Display the active users of a service
SHOW CONNECTS	Information about the current server
SHOW DISPATCHER	Status of dispatcher objects
SHOW EXECUTORS FOR SERVICE	Status of executors of a service
SHOW PRIVILEGES FOR SERVICE	Show privileges for a service
SHOW SERVER	Display status of servers
SHOW SERVICE	Show service status
SHOW SETTINGS	Details on SQS_MANAGER settings
SHUTDOWN SERVER	Shut down the current server
START DISPATCHER	Start dispatchers
START EXECUTORS FOR SERVICE	Start executors for a service
START MONITOR	Start the monitor
START SERVER	Start dispatcher and executors for current server

This is an impressive list of commands available to manage the SQL/Services environment. The reader should not feel daunted by all these commands. They are extremely well described in the SQL/Services documentation which also explains in considerable detail all the issues to be checked, reviewed and planned when creating this environment. After a short period of time using this product, you will wonder how you ever managed before.

Hopefully this chapter has convinced the reader that the differences between the OSF/1 and OpenVMS versions are few and far between. It's easy to use, so enjoy!

20 The Future of Rdb

At the time of writing this chapter, Rdb has been in existence for ten years. The product is almost unrecognizable from when it first came into being. Many early users will remember the delight when it was possible to achieve double figure TPS numbers. In April 1994, Rdb delivered 3692 TPS at a cost of $4866 running the TPC-A benchmark on a 766 gigabyte database. This is a far cry from those days when double figure TPS numbers seemed a dream.

It is estimated that there are in excess of a million users of Rdb world-wide and over 80,000 licenses. Every day we use systems that we take for granted, not realizing that behind the systems, there is an Rdb database providing the information.

Over the years Rdb has grown into a product that is rich in functionality. In the beginning all information was held in a single-file database which restricted Rdb to databases the size of the disk or volume set. With the introduction of multifile databases and partitioning, today databases occupying tens or hundreds of gigabytes are possible, and in the future we will no doubt see Rdb databases using many terabytes of space. At first glance one wonders how anyone could accumulate a terabyte of data, but with the growing interest in multimedia applications, even a terabyte may seem small. Now that Rdb supports WORM devices, it's quite easy to build a database using that much space. As new types of storage devices are developed, Rdb will be modified to support them.

20.1 NEW ENHANCEMENTS

Today the highest performance is expected from a relational database. Since many are used in 'bet your business' applications, a long response time often means keeping a client waiting. Have you ever noticed how waiting for only 2 or 3 seconds on the telephone seems like an eternity? Every release sees new enhancements to improve performance. For example, global buffers in V4.1 increased the throughput on many systems and asynchronous batch writes and the new AIJ features in V6.0 helped considerably. V6.1 gave us the ability to create huge in-memory structures, resulting in an almost memory resident database for small databases in the single-figure gigabyte arena. At the time of writing Rdb 6.1 is the only 64 bit native database in the industry.

Reducing the time to read and write I/O is another area to watch. Asynchronous pre-fetch introduced in V6.0 currently only works for sequential scans, but is a technique that could equally be applied to other types of searches and structures in the database. One wonders what other new ideas the Rdb engineers will develop to increase the performance of Rdb.

There is a wealth of tools out there that support Rdb, across the broad spectrum of 3rd and 4GL tools, to TP monitors and of course the PC tools. The adoption by many vendors of the de facto standard ODBC means that any ODBC compliant software can access an Rdb database.

So many organizations are adopting client/server technology in the 90s that we will undoubtedly see improvements in Rdb to support this environment more efficiently. The revised SQL/Services code, first released on OSF/1 and later on OpenVMS, is an indication of the direction being taken.

1994 is a significant year for Rdb because it heralds the move away from being a database that runs on only OpenVMS to one that runs on OSF/1 and Windows NT. Perhaps now it will be acknowledged as being a portable database product. In the future we will undoubtedly see Rdb appearing on other operating systems.

Distributed databases were once a very key aspect of relational database systems. Today there seems to be more emphasis on accessing legacy systems and integrating heterogeneous data. The release of DEC DB Integrator in 1994 has shown that it is possible to easily access remote data. This product is in its infancy as to product functionality. Therefore in the coming years, we will no doubt see enhancements that will benefit anyone wishing to create a distributed Rdb environment.

The multimedia business is proving to be a growth area in the 90s. There is a growing need to store complex data, such as voice, graphics, image, and video. Rdb already contains the basic building blocks to support this type of data storage, the BLOB and the SQL Multimedia API to manage the objects. The functionality provided in this area is very limited, but by V7.0 content based retrieval will be available. The proposed SQL3 standard contains many changes to support multimedia and object-oriented extensions. Since Rdb is following the standard very closely, in the future we are likely to see many of these appearing in Rdb.

From V7.0 Rdb will become an object-oriented database, providing capabilities such as attribute level encapsulation, virtual attributes, polymorphism. Abstract datatypes like document, image and video and collection types of lists, set, multi-set and arrays will exist.

Many users may be surprised to learn that Rdb V6.0 contains the work from 14 successful patent applications. Therefore watch out in the future for more innovative work from the Rdb engineering team.

We already have the ability to create indexes in parallel and enhancements were introduced in V6.1 to support DBI. Therefore more parallelism is another feature that we are likely to see in the future.

Finally, at the time of writing, Digital is selling Rdb to the Oracle Corporation, which will ensure that Rdb has a very bright future. As part of the deal, the entire engineering team is transferring to Oracle, who plan to continue enhancing Rdb for at least three years and supporting it for seven. Sometime in the future, the Rdb and Oracle database engines will converge into one. Through a standard product upgrade, users will be able to take advantage of the new database engine without disruption to existing applications.

Despite being ten years old, there is still much that can, and will, be done to improve Rdb. So don't think that you can give up looking at the release notes. There is still plenty of reading ahead and much to learn.

A   Banking Database Definition

```
!————————————————
! set default environment
!————————————————

set language ENGLISH;
set default date format 'SQL92';
set quoting rules 'SQL92';
set date format DATE 001, TIME 001;


!————————————————
! create database files
!————————————————

create database
    filename 'EUROBANK:BANKING.RDB'
    dictionary is not required
    protection is acl
    buffer size is 6 blocks
    number of buffers 50
    number of recovery buffers 50
    global buffers are enabled (number is 400, user limit 20)
    statistics collection is enabled
    system index compression is enabled
    reserve 10 storage areas
    reserve 1 journals
    snapshot is enabled immediate
        segmented string storage area is LIST_AREA
```

```
create storage area RDB$SYSTEM
   filename 'eurobank:BANK_SYSTEM.RDA'
   locking is row level
   page format is uniform
   page size is 2 blocks
   allocation is 5000 pages
   snapshot filename 'eurobank:BANK_SYSTEM.SNP'
   snapshot allocation is 100 pages

create storage area CUSTOMER_AREA
   filename 'eurobank:CUSTOMER_AREA.RDA'
   locking is row level
   page format is mixed
   page size is 2 blocks
   allocation is 500 pages
   snapshot filename 'eurobank:CUSTOMER_AREA.SNP'
   snapshot allocation is 100 pages
   snapshot extent is (minimum 99, maximum 9999, percent growth 20)

create storage area ACCOUNT_AREA
   filename 'eurobank:ACCOUNT_AREA.RDA'
   locking is row level
   page format is mixed
   page size is 2 blocks
   allocation is 1000 pages
   snapshot filename 'eurobank:ACCOUNT_AREA.SNP'

create storage area BRANCH_AREA
   filename 'eurobank:BRANCH_AREA.RDA'
   locking is row level
   page format is uniform
   page size is 2 blocks
   allocation is 1000 pages
   snapshot filename 'eurobank:BRANCH_AREA.SNP'
```

```
create storage area TXN_AREA_93
    filename 'eurobank:TXN_AREA_93.RDA'
    locking is row level
    page format is uniform
    page size is 2 blocks
    allocation is 2000 pages
    snapshot filename 'eurobank:TXN_AREA_93.SNP'
    snapshot allocation is 100 pages

create storage area TXN_AREA_94
    filename 'eurobank:TXN_AREA_94.RDA'
    locking is row level
    page format is uniform
    page size is 2 blocks
    allocation is 2000 pages
    snapshot filename 'eurobank:TXN_AREA_94.SNP'
    snapshot allocation is 100 pages

create storage area TXN_AREA_95
    filename 'eurobank:TXN_AREA_95.RDA'
    locking is row level
    page format is uniform
    page size is 2 blocks
    allocation is 2000 pages
    snapshot filename 'eurobank:TXN_AREA_95.SNP'
    snapshot allocation is 100 pages

create storage area INDEX_AREA
    filename 'eurobank:INDEX_AREA.RDA'
    locking is row level
    page format is uniform
    page size is 2 blocks
    allocation is 2000 pages
    snapshot filename 'eurobank:INDEX_AREA.SNP'
    snapshot allocation is 100 pages
```

```
create storage area LIST_AREA
   filename 'eurobank:LIST_AREA.RDA'
   locking is row level
   page format is uniform
   page size is 2 blocks
   allocation is 2000 pages
   snapshot filename 'eurobank:LIST_AREA.SNP'
   snapshot allocation is 100 pages;

!————————————————————————
! create domains
!————————————————————————

create domain SPECIAL_TEXT          list of byte varying (1);

create domain STANDARD_DATE    date;

create domain STANDARD_NAME    char (20);

!————————————————————————
! create tables
!————————————————————————

create table CUSTOMER
   (
   CUSTOMER_NO        char(10)
      constraint  CUSTOMER_CUSTOMER_NO_PK
      primary key
      deferrable,
   SURNAME            STANDARD_NAME,
   FIRST_NAME         STANDARD_NAME,
   ADDRESS_LINE1         char (30),
   ADDRESS_LINE2         char (30),
   ADDRESS_LINE3         char (30),
   ADDRESS_LINE4         char (30),
   POSTCODE              char (10),
   CREDIT_LIMIT       char (10),
   STATUS             integer
   );
```

```
create table BRANCH
    (
    BRANCH_CODE             char (4)
        constraint BRANCH_BRANCH_CODE_PK
        primary key
        deferrable,
    BRANCH_NAME             char (20),
    BRANCH_ADDRESS          char (120),
    MANAGERS_NAME           char (20)
    );

create table ACCOUNT
    (
    ACCOUNT_NO              char (10)
        constraint ACCOUNT_ACCOUNT_NO_PK
        primary key
        deferrable,
    CUSTOMER_NO             char (10),
    BRANCH_CODE             char (4)
        constraint ACCOUNT_FK01
        references BRANCH (BRANCH_CODE)
        deferrable,
    BALANCE                 bigint,
    OVERDRAFT_LIMIT         bigint,
    ACCT_TYPE               integer,
    STATEMENT_FREQ          integer,
    STATEMENT_DATE          STANDARD_DATE,
    STATEMENT_DAY           integer,
        constraint ACCOUNT_FK_02
        foreign key (CUSTOMER_NO)
        references CUSTOMER (CUSTOMER_NO)
        deferrable
    );

create table ACCOUNT_NOTES
    (
    ACCOUNT_NO              char (10),
    ACCOUNT_TEXT            SPECIAL_TEXT
    );
```

```
create table ACCOUNT_TRANSACTION
   (
   ACCOUNT_NO              char(10),
   TRAN_DATE              char(4),
   TRAN_AMT               bigint,
   DC_IND                 integer,
   TRANS_CD               char(4),
        constraint ACCOUNT_TRANSACTION_FK_01
        foreign key (ACCOUNT_NO)
        references ACCOUNT (ACCOUNT_NO)
        deferrable
   );

!————————————————————————
! create views
!————————————————————————


create view CUSTOMER_MAILING
   (
   CUSTOMER_NO,
   SURNAME,
   FIRST_NAME,
   ADDRESS_LINE1,
   ADDRESS_LINE2,
   ADDRESS_LINE3,
   ADDRESS_LINE4,
   POSTCODE
   )
   as select    CUSTOMER_NO,
                SURNAME,
                FIRST_NAME,
                ADDRESS_LINE1,
                ADDRESS_LINE2,
                ADDRESS_LINE3,
                ADDRESS_LINE4,
                POSTCODE
   from CUSTOMER;
```

```
create view CUSTOMER_ACCOUNT_INFO
  (
  CUSTOMER_NO,
  SURNAME,
  FIRST_NAME,
  CREDIT_LIMIT,
  ACCOUNT_NO,
  BALANCE
  )
  as select    C.CUSTOMER_NO,
               C.SURNAME,
               C.FIRST_NAME,
               C.CREDIT_LIMIT,
               A.ACCOUNT_NO,
               A.BALANCE
    from CUSTOMER C, ACCOUNT A
    where  C.CUSTOMER_NO = A.CUSTOMER_NO;

create view  BIG_TRANSACTIONS
   as select * from ACCOUNT_TRANSACTION
   where TRAN_AMT > 10000
   with check option constraint   CHECK_VIEW;


!————————————————————————
! create triggers
!————————————————————————


create trigger CHANGE_BRANCH_CODE
   before update of BRANCH_CODE   on BRANCH
   referencing OLD as OLD_BRANCH_CODE
   NEW as NEW_BRANCH_CODE
     (update ACCOUNT A
        set A.BRANCH_CODE = NEW_BRANCH_CODE.BRANCH_CODE
        where  A.BRANCH_CODE = OLD_BRANCH_CODE.BRANCH_CODE)
   for each row;
```

```
!————————————————————————————
! create indexes
!————————————————————————————

create unique index CUST_NO_HASH on CUSTOMER
   (CUSTOMER_NO)
   type is hashed scattered
   store in CUSTOMER_AREA;

create index ACCOUNT_NO_HASH on ACCOUNT
   (CUSTOMER_NO)
   type is hashed scattered
   store in CUSTOMER_AREA;

create index CUST_SURNAME_SORTED on CUSTOMER
   (SURNAME)
   type is sorted
   enable compression
   (minimum run length 2)
   store in INDEX_AREA;

create index BRANCH_CODE_SORTED on BRANCH
   (BRANCH_CODE)
   type is sorted
   node size 400
   usage query
   store in INDEX_AREA;

create index ACCT_TXN_SORTED on ACCOUNT_TRANSACTION
   (ACCOUNT_NO,
    TRAN_DATE)
   type is sorted
   store in INDEX_AREA;
```

```
!————————————————————
! create storage maps
!————————————————————

create storage map CUSTOMER_MAP
    for CUSTOMER
    store in CUSTOMER_AREA
    placement via index CUST_NO_HASH;

create storage map ACCOUNT_MAP
    for ACCOUNT
    disable compression
    store in ACCOUNT_AREA
    placement via index ACCOUNT_NO_HASH;

create storage map BRANCH_MAP
    for BRANCH
    store in BRANCH_AREA;

create storage map ACCOUNT_TXN_MAP
    for ACCOUNT_TRANSACTION
    store using (TRAN_DATE)
    in TXN_AREA_93 with limit of ('1993')
    in TXN_AREA_94 with limit of ('1994')
    in TXN_AREA_95 with limit of ('1995');
```

B   Rdb Logical Names/ Environment Variables

Rdb OpenVMS	Rdb OSF/1
RDB$CHARACTER_SET	SQL_CHARACTER_SET

defines an alternate character set

RDB$RDBSHR_EVENT_FLAGS	SQL_RDBSHR_EVENT_FLAGS

used to override the event flag numbers

RDB$REMOTE_BUFFER_SIZE	SQL_REMOTE_BUFFER_SIZE

defines the default buffer size of network transfers

RDB$REMOTE_MULTIPLEX_OFF	SQL_REMOTE_MULTIPLEX_OFF

disallows a single local process to access multiple remote databases on the same node through a single remote RDB_SERVER process

RDBVMS$CREATE_DB

restricts the creation of databases

RDM$BIND_ABW_DISABLED	RDB_BIND_ABW_DISABLED

disables asynchronous batch-write operations

RDM$BIND_AIJ_STALL	RDB_BIND_AIJ_STALL

processes wait time after AIJ commit records submission

RDM$BIND_APF_DEPTH	RDB_BIND_APF_DEPTH

defines number of buffers to asynchronously pre-fetch for a process

RDM$BIND_APF_DISABLED	RDB_BIND_APF_DISABLED

disables asynchronous pre-fetch

RDM$BIND_BATCH_MAX	RDB_BIND_BATCH_MAX

defines the number of buffers that are written to the database as part of a batch-write operation

RDM$BIND_BUFFERS	RDB_BIND_BUFFERS

defines the number of buffers used by an attach

Rdb OpenVMS   ## Rdb OSF/1

RDM$BIND_CKPT_TRANS_INTERVAL   RDB_BIND_CKPT_TRANS_INTERVAL
    defines a process-specific checkpoint interval

RDM$BIND_CLEAN_BUF_CNT   RDB_BIND_CLEAN_BUF_CNT
    specifies the number of clean buffers to be maintained at the end of a process's least recently
    used queue of buffers for replacement

RDM$BIND_COMMIT_STALL   RDB_BIND_COMMIT_STALL
    defines the amount of time a transaction waits after attempting to become the group commit
    process

RDM$BIND_LOCK_TIMEOUT_INTERVAL   RDB_BIND_LOCK_TIMEOUT_INTERVAL
    defines a default lock wait interval

RDM$BIND_READY_AREA_SERIALLY   RDB_BIND_READY_AREA_SERIALLY
    causes lock requests for logical and physical areas to be granted in the order that the lock
    requests were made

RDM$BIND_RUJ_EXTEND_BLKCNT   RDB_BIND_RUJ_EXTEND_BLKCNT
    extends value for .RUJ files

RDM$BIND_STATS_DISABLED   RDB_BIND_STATS_DISABLED
    disables the writing of database statistics for a process

RDM$BIND_VM_SEGMENT   RDB_BIND_VM_SEGMENT
    prevents memory fragmentation

RDM$BUGCHECK_DIR   RDB_BUGCHECK_DIR
    specifies the location of bugcheck files

RDM$MAILBOX_CHANNEL
    contains the node-specific address of the database monitor

RDM$MONITOR   RDB_MONITOR
    specifies the location of bugcheck files

RDM$MON_USERNAME
    specifies the username whose quotas the monitor process will inherit

RDMS$AUTO_READY   RDB_AUTO_READY
    allows a process to obtain an area lock in CU mode when requesting CR

RDMS$BIND_OUTLINE_FLAGS   RDB_BIND_OUTLINE_FLAGS
    causes Rdb to ignore query outlines

Rdb OpenVMS   Rdb OSF/1

RDMS$BIND_OUTLINE_MODE   RDB_BIND_OUTLINE_MODE
    specifies which class of outlines are used by the optimizer

RDMS$BIND_QG_CPU_TIMEOUT   RDB_BIND_QG_CPU_TIMEOUT
    restricts the amount of CPU time used to optimize a query for execution

RDMS$BIND_QG_REC_LIMIT   RDB_BIND_QG_REC_LIMIT
    limits the number of rows a query returns

RDMS$BIND_QG_TIMEOUT   RDB_BIND_QG_TIMEOUT
    limits the amount of time the optimizer spends compiling a query

RDMS$BIND_SEGMENTED_STRING_BUFFER   RDB_BIND_SEGMENTED_STRING_BUFFER
    reduces the overhead of I/O operations when using segmented strings

RDMS$BIND_SEGMENTED_STRING_COUNT   RDB_BIND_SEGMENTED_STRING_COUNT
    defines the number of entries in the segmented string ID list

RDMS$BIND_SEGMENTED_STRING_DBKEY_SCOPE   RDB_BIND_SEGMENTED_STRING_DBKEY_SCOPE
    specifies whether the dbkey of a modified segmented string may be re-used by the process

RDMS$BIND_SORT_WORKFILES   RDB_BIND_SORT_WORKFILES
    specifies how many work files the Sort utility is to use if work files are needed

RDMS$BIND_VALIDATE_CHANGE_FIELD   RDB_BIND_VALIDATE_CHANGE_FIELD
    validates records changed by CHANGE FIELD statement

RDMS$BIND_WORK_FILE   RDB_BIND_WORK_FILE
    redirects the location of temporary files

RDMS$BIND_WORK_VM   RDB_BIND_WORK_VM
    specifies the amount of virtual memory to be allocated to the process

RDMS$DEBUG_FLAGS   RDB_DEBUG_FLAGS
    allows the examination of optimizer access strategies and their estimated cost

RDMS$DEBUG_FLAGS_OUTPUT   RDB_DEBUG_FLAGS_OUTPUT
    specifies an output file in which to collect the output from RDB_DEBUG_FLAGS

RDMS$DIAG_FLAGS   RDB_DIAG_FLAGS
    assists in locating erroneous queries

RDMS$KEEP_PREP_FILES   RDB_KEEP_PREP_FILES
    causes the RDBPRE preprocessor to retain the intermediate .MAR and language files

RDMS$RUJ   RDB_RUJ
    specifies the location of the .RUJ file

Rdb OpenVMS   **Rdb OSF/1**

RDMS$USE_OLD_CONCURRENCY   RDB_USE_OLD_CONCURRENCY
        specifies the use of isolation level behavior in earlier versions

RDMS$USE_OLD_SEGMENTED_STRING   RDB_USE_OLD_SEGMENTED_STRING
        retains the old format of segmented strings

RDMS$USE_OLD_UPDATE_RULES   RDB_USE_OLD_UPDATE_RULES
        specifies Rdb to continue to use the old update rules

RDO$EDIT
        specifies the system editor selected to edit interactive RDO queries

RDOINI
        specifies the name of the file that contains the RDO initialization information

SQL$DATABASE   SQL_DATABASE
        specifies the database that SQL declares if a database is not explicitly defined

SQL$DISABLE_CONTEXT   SQL_DISABLE_CONTEXT
        disables the two-phase commit protocol

SQL$EDIT
        specifies the system editor selected to edit interactive SQL queries

SQLINI   SQLINIT
        specifies the name of the file that contains the SQL initialization information

SQL$KEEP_PREP_FILES   SQL_KEEP_PREP_FILES
        causes the SQL precompiler and SQL Module Language compiler to retain the intermediate .MAR and
        language files

                                                    SQL_USERNAME
        Username for SQL attach

                                                    SQL_PASSWD
        Password for SQL attach

Glossary

ABM	See *Area Bit Map*
ABW	See *Asynchronous Batch Writes*
Access Control List ACL	A table that lists the users allowed to access an object and how it may be accessed
Access Mode	See *Reserving*
ACMS and **ACMSxp**	A Digital transaction processing monitor. It is used to define, run, and control transaction processing applications. Acronym for Application Control and Management System
Adjustable Locking Granularity	A process that allows Rdb to minimize the number of locks used to enforce consistency. Resources are locked according to a hierarchy, commencing with the database, then a storage area, and several levels of groups of pages, before the page itself
After-Image Journal	One or more files which contain copies of the rows in the databases after they have been updated. The after-image journal files are used to roll the database forward to a given point
Aggregate Functions	Functions in SQL which return a single value as a result of grouping together many rows, such as SUM or COUNT.
AIJ	See *After-Image Journal*
AIJ Log Server	A process which manages the writing of data to the AIJ file. Not enabled by default.
AIP	See *Area Inventory Page*
ALG	See *Adjustable Locking Granularity*
Alias	A name given to an Rdb database to distinguish it from other active databases in an application program
Anchor	An OpenVMS file directory which contains all the files making up the CDD/Repository
ANSI	American National Standards Institute and a leading force in the SQL standard
APF	See *Asynchronous Pre-Fetch*
Application Control and Management System ACMS	See *ACMS*
Area	See *Storage Area*

Area Bit Map Page   Maps tables on database pages to logical areas. An ABM page is specific to a logical area. ABM pages are pointed to by AIP pages

Area Inventory Page   A database page that contains information on logical areas. A logical area entry includes a pointer to the area's first ABM page

Ascending Order   A sorting order that starts with the lowest key value and proceeds to the highest value

Asynchronous Batch Writes   When pages are written back to the database they are batched and written in parallel asynchronously. Processes do not have to wait for the writes to complete to continue processing

Asynchronous Pre-Fetch   The process of predicting the next pages required and then pre-reading the information into the buffer. Works only for sequential scans to improve performance.

ASCII   A computer character set and collating sequence. Acronym for American Standard Code for Information Interchange

Attribute   Another name for a column in a table

Authorization ID   Identifier of who issued an SQL statement. For example user HOBBS

Backup Server for AIJ   A process which automatically backups the contents of the AIJ files when they become full

Batch Update   A transaction mode that takes exclusive access to the database or table and executes without the overhead of a run-unit journal. If an error occurs during the processing of a batch update transaction, the entire database is marked as corrupt

Before Image Journal   A file that contains copies of the row before the table is updated. Rdb uses these before images to roll back a database transaction

B-tree   A balanced tree or sorted index structure for a specified table

BLOB   Binary Large Object. A datatype used for storing unstructured data such as pictures, sound or video. The actual datatype in Rdb is list of byte varying. Also known as a segmented string

Boolean Expression   A string that specifies a condition that is either true or false

Boolean Operator   A symbol or word that facilitates joining two or more Boolean expressions. Typical Boolean operators are AND, OR, NOT

Buffers   Can be of type local or global and is where all the pages read from the database are held in memory

Call Interface   A mechanism for a program to access components of a software product

Callable RDO   An interpretative call interface consisting of a single external routine that accepts an Rdb data manipulation language DML or data definition language DDL statement as a parameter

Cardinality   The number of rows in a table

Catalog   Defined in the SQL92 standard as a group of schemas which are treated as an object

CDD   Original Data Dictionary product. Managed via the command language DMU

CDD/Plus   See *CDD/Repository*

CDD/Repository A data dictionary system that supports the creation, analysis and administration of metadata. Support for CDD/Repository by Rdb lets the user define global field and record definitions; copy field or record definitions from the dictionary into an Rdb database; receive informational messages about the shared use of CDD/Repository field and record definitions; and integrate shareable dictionary definitions into an Rdb database

CDO CDD/Repository Common Dictionary Operator CDO utility

Cluster See *VMScluster*

CODASYL Acronym for Conference on Data Systems Languages. A network model database management system. VAX DBMS is CODASYL-compliant

Collating Sequence The sequence in which characters are ordered for merging, sorting, and comparisons

Column A relational model term that equates to a field. Also called an attribute.

Commit A statement that finishes a transaction and makes all changes upon the database permanent

Common Data Dictionary See *CDD/Repository*

Common Dictionary Operator CDO Utility The command line interface to CDD/Repository

Composite Key Any type of key that comprises one or more columns

Computed By Column A virtual field that appears in a table or view definition, but not physically in the table; therefore, it occupies no space in the database

Concurrency The simultaneous use of a database by a number of users

Consistency The level to which a database system guarantees that tables being read by a user cannot be changed by another user at the same time

Constraint The rules that define the permitted values a column make take

Context Variable A temporary name that is used in an RDO statement to identify a record stream

Correlation Names A temporary name for an object defined in a SELECT clause which exists for the duration of the query only

Cross Operation See *Join*

Cursor An object that is used to store the output of a query for subsequent row by row processing

Data Compression Optimizes data storage for a table

Data Definition Language The statements that describe the metadata definitions

Data Distributor An optional layer for Rdb that provides the ability to make copies of a database that are either a subset or a complete copy. See also *Extraction* and *Replication*

Data Manipulation Language The statements that allow data in the Rdb database to be stored, retrieved, modified, or deleted

Data Table See *Table* or *Relation*

Database	A collection of data in which usually more than one user can access the data at the same time. The database maintains its own data integrity and security
Database Integrator	Database Integrator is a tool from Digital which allows the end-user or application programmer to link multiple local or remote databases and work with them as if a single database
Database Key dbkey	A unique value that identifies precisely where a storage segment is located in a database
Database Page	The structure used to store data within an Rdb database. The minimum database page size is 512 bytes or one disk block. Pages increase in increments of 512 bytes or one block
DATATRIEVE	A Digital query language for manipulating, storing, and modifying tables or records in an RMS, DBMS, or Rdb database
Datatype	The type of data assigned to a column or field such as Text or Integer
Dbkey	See *Database Key*
Db Gateways	Database gateways provide transparent access to relational, non-relational and custom data sources from a wide variety of tools.
DBI	See *Database Integrator*
DBMS	Acronym for *Database Management System*
DCL	See *Digital Command Language*
DDL	See *Data Definition Language*
Deadlock	The situation where two or more transactions request the same resources and nothing can be done to resolve the conflict, except aborting one of the transactions
DECnet	The Digital networking software
DECtrace	A tool that works with Rdb applications to collect event and point based data on resources used to complete a task, e.g., the direct I/O and buffer reads to perform an SQL statement are just some of the information collected by this tool
Deferred Snapshots	Update transactions only written to the snapshot file when a read-only transaction is in progress
Denormalization	The reverse process of normalization
Descending Order	A sorting order that commences with the highest value of a key and goes down to the lowest value
Dictionary Object	A data definition stored in CDD/Repository, such as ACMS definitions; CDD/Repository field and record definitions; DATATRIEVE domains, records, procedures, plots; DBMS schemas; and Rdb database entry
Digital Command Language DCL	A command interpreter for the OpenVMS system
Digital Standard Relational Interface DSRI	An architecture and calling standard for relational database systems developed by Digital Equipment Corp.
DMU	The command line interface to CDD

Domain	An object that is used to define a column. Based on an existing datatype, new columns can be defined based on this object
Dynamic SQL	SQL from an application that is executed at runtime
EBCDIC	Acronym for Extended Binary Coded Decimal Interchange Code, the computer set and collating sequence for IBM systems
Equi-join	A join operation that matches a column from one table with a corresponding column in another table
Embedded SQL	SQL code that is embedded in an application and precompiled before execution
Extraction	A Data Distributor facility that transfers either a complete database or a subset of a database to a new database
Field	A single division in a record where data is stored. See *Column*
File Type	The part of a file specification that describes the type of file. In Rdb databases the file types are: RDB, a database root file; RDA, storage area files; SNP, snapshot files; RUJ, run-unit journal file; AIJ, after-image journal file; RBF, backup file created by RMU/BACKUP; RBR, backup file created by SQL EXPORT; UNL, RMU/UNLOAD; and RRD, a file created by using the /RMS=FILE= option with RMU/UNLOAD
Foreign Key	A field in one table that is a primary key in another table
Free Space	The space on a database page that is available for new data
Function Callouts	The ability to define a user-function which calls 3GL code
Gateway	See *DB Gateways*
Global Buffer	A memory resident structure that allows all users on that machine to share the pages retrieved from the database
Graphical Schema Editor	A GUI tool used to define and alter the metadata definitions. Using graphical objects the user defines what is required in the schema. The SQL to create the database is then output by the tool
Hashed Index	An index structure that is created when a row is stored in a hashed index. There are two types of hashed index, scattered and ordered
Hashing	The conversion of a key field into a database page number using a special algorithm
Index	A structure within the database that locates a row based on a key value
Index Fill Factor	A parameter that controls the initial fullness of a sorted index
Index Key	A column in an index that determines the retrieval criteria
Index Node	A sorted index data structure that contains the key values and pointers to tables in the database and other index nodes in the structure
InstantSQL	A graphical based tool for defining SQL queries. Creates the SQL or SQL module which can then be incorporated into a program or compiled as appropriate.
Integrity	The correctness of the information in an Rdb database. There are three types of integrity control: integrity constraints, concurrency control, and recovery during or after a system failure

Interval   The period of time between two dates

Isolation Level   Specifies how a transaction is affected by other transactions accessing the same data

Join Operation   A relational operation that selects a row from a table, associates it with a row from another table, and presents them as though they were one table

Journal File   A file that contains all the data structures modified during a transaction. The journal file is used to reconstruct the database and maintain integrity during a system or application failure

Journaling   The process of recording all operations applied to the database. The type of information recorded depends on the whether an after-image or a before-image journal file is created

Key   A column in a table that is used to locate one or more tables

Line Index   A portion of a database page that acts as a directory to data on the page by indexing the page offsets of individual storage data segments

Local Buffers   All the pages retrieved from the database are held in the user's own private memory which cannot be shared with any other user

Locking   A mechanism for protecting transactions against interference from concurrently executing transactions

Logical Area   Another name for a table or index

Logical Name   A user-specified name for any portion of or all of a file specification

Mapping Values   An option available on an index to restrict the range of values that an index can take

Metadata   Data that is used to describe other data

Module   One or more procedures grouped together and stored as system metadata

Multifile Database A database made up of a root file .RDB and a number of storage areas .RDA

Multistatement Procedures A group of SQL statements defined as a procedure which is stored as system metadata

Multi-threaded Backup/Restore The ability to backup and restore a database using multiple databases

No-Quiet Point   The reverse of a quiet point. That is, do not wait for all transactions to complete.

Normalization   The process of reducing a database to its simplest form and eliminating data redundancy

Null   An indicator in SQL used to indicate that a value has not been supplied

Object   There are many objects in the database such as catalog, schema, tables, columns and indexes

ODBC   Microsoft's de facto standard for PC client access to database servers. Acronym for Open Database Connectivity

Online Transaction Processing OLTP An environment that supports many users performing the same critical business functions. Typically, an OLTP system is made up of many simultaneous users, all performing the same function

OpenVMS   The major operating system for VAX computers and one of the operating systems that can be used on the Alpha chip computers. Acronym for Virtual Memory System

Optimized Page Transfers   A mechanism that prevents shared pages being flushed to disk everytime they are changed and required by another user. Instead the page remains in the buffer, thus eliminating the need for any disk I/O

Page Header   A fixed-length section at the beginning of a database page

Page Locking   The ability to specify for a storage area that all information retrieved is locked at the page level rather than the default row level

Page Number   The number of a page in a storage area

Partitioned Lock Trees   All the locks in Rdb are held in a tree structure. Partitioned lock trees split the storage area locks by storage area and will be located on any machine

Precompiler   A utility that reads data manipulation language statements in a high-level language and translates them into low-level database routines

Primary Key   A column or group of columns that uniquely identifies a row. A primary key cannot be null or contain duplicates

Privileges   To execute RMU commands or access information within the database privileges must be granted which specify what can be accessed

Query Outline   An outline is stored as part of the metadata and it tells the optimizer how a query should be executed. Such as in which order to join the tables and which indexes to use

Quiet Point   A time when no run unit is accessing the database. Quiet points can occur between transactions

Rdb   Digital's relational database management system

Rdb Management Utility RMU   A DCL-level Rdb utility that allows the database administrator to manage the database

RdbExpert   A tool for designing new Rdb databases or tuning existing ones. Given the environment such as number of disks, table cardinalities and the application workload, RdbExpert generates a new database design and the unload/load script

RDML   See *Relational Data Manipulation Language*

RDO   Acronym for *Relational Database Operator*

Read-Only   Refers to a database transaction that allows data only to be read

Read-Write   Refers to a database transaction that allows data to be read and changed, inserted or deleted. According to the SQL standard this is the default transaction mode when a transaction is not specifically started

Record   A table

Record Locking   Reserving a table or rows in a table for a specific user

Record Selection Expression (rse)   Defines a selection of rows that satisfy a specified condition

Record Stream   A group of records formed by an rse

Recoverable Latches A new mechanism that replaced the GBPT slot locks for controlling access to pages in the global buffer

Recovery   The process of restoring a database to a known state after a system or program failure

Recovery Unit Journal   See *Before-Image Journal*

Reflexive Join   An operation that joins a table upon itself

Relation   A method of presenting a collection of data made up of rows and columns

Relational Data Manipulation Language RDML A data manipulation language for the C and PASCAL languages

Relational Data Operator RDO   An interactive utility for maintaining databases, creating and modifying definitions of database elements, and storing and manipulating data

Relational Database A database model that describes data as a set of independent tables. Within each table, the data is organized into rows and columns

Remote Server   The part of Rdb that provides access to data on another database using the DECnet, TCP/IP or other networking protocol

Replication   The process in DEC Data Distributor of transferring to a remote database, only those rows in the database that have changed since the last replication transfer

Request   A set of instructions to the Rdb database

Request Handle   A variable that uniquely identifies a request

Reserving Option   Defines the locking and sharing modes for tables and rows accessed

Restore   The process of rebuilding a database from a backup or copy of the database

Rollback   A statement that restores the database to the state at the beginning of the transaction, as opposed to COMMIT, which makes the changes to the Rdb database permanent

Rollforward   The process of using an after-image journal file to restore a database to a specific point in time

RMU   See *Rdb Management Utility*

Root File   Part of the database that contains all the database control information, such as when last backed up, which users are bound to the database, and where the run-unit journal files are located

Row   The relational-model term for a record

RSE   See *Record Selection Expression*

RUJ   See *Before-Image Journal*

Schedule Definition In DEC Data Distributor, a definition that specifies when a transfer is to take place

Security   The protection of the data held in the database against unauthorized access

Segmented String   See *BLOB*

Select Operation   The SQL statement for specifying which rows should be retrieved from the database

Share Mode	The degree of sharing of data that Rdb permits when other users require access to the data. Possible share modes are EXCLUSIVE, PROTECTED, and SHARED
Snapshot	A consistent view of the database as at a specific time
Sort Key	A column used for sorting a table
Sorted Index	An index structure where the key values are maintained in sorted order in a b-tree
Space Area Management Page	A database page that specifies the percentage fullness of each database page in a range of pages
SPAM	See *Space Area Management Page*
SQL	Structured SQL Language. The standard query language for accessing relational databases. It is an official standard. Comprises of both a data definition and a data manipulation language
SQL2	The name for SQL-92 while it was a working standard
SQL3	The next revision to the SQL standard that is under discussion and review
SQL 86	The original SQL standard
SQL 89	Further enhancements to the original SQL standard
SQL 92	Is a major enhancement to the SQL standard which defines many new features and incorporated into the standard a number of features that had already been introduced into relational database systems. There are three levels to this standard: entry level, intermediate and full
SQL/Services	A component of Rdb that enables remote database access from a number of platforms
Storage Area	A physical OpenVMS file that is separate from the root file, but that is the component of the database where the actual data is stored
Storage Segment	Any structure that is stored in an Rdb database
Stored Procedures	A group of SQL statements defined as a procedure and stored in the system metadata
System Relation	A table that contains information required for the operation of the database management system
Table	See *Relation*
Thresholds	Thresholds are defined for an entire mixed storage area or for a uniform area by a logical area stored within that area. The threshold can take one of four values, 0, 1, 2 and 3 and it advises the percentage of space used on the page. Using this value the database designer can control how much information is stored on a database page
Transaction	The grouping of a number of statements together such that all are applied or none of them
Transaction Handle	A variable that uniquely identifies a transaction
Transaction Processing	A style of computing supporting multiple users performing predefined tasks against a shared database
Transfer Database	In DEC Data Distributor, the location of all transfer and schedule definitions

Transfer Monitor	The process on behalf of DEC Data Distributor that controls the execution of all data transfers
Tuple	Relational database terminology for a row or record
UIC	See *User Identification Code*
User Identification Code	A code identifying a OpenVMS user
View	A logical definition of a table that includes rows and columns from one or more tables
VMScluster	A highly integrated organization of OpenVMS systems that communicate over a high-speed communications path. In a VMScluster, CPUs share resources, queues, and disks
WORM	Write once read many device
X/Open	An independent, world-wide, open systems organization that is supported by most of the leading information system suppliers, software companies and user organizations
X/Open XPG3	An X/Open product branded as XPG3 would adhere to the SQL 89 standard
X/Open XPG4	An X/Open product branded as XPG4 would adhere to the SQL 89, SQL 92 entry level and some SQL 92 intermediate and full features

Index